Jesus Christ as Logos Incarnate and
Resurrected Nana (Ancestor)

african christian studies series (africs)

This series will make available significant works in the field of African Christian studies, taking into account the many forms of Christianity across the whole continent of Africa. African Christian studies is defined here as any scholarship that relates to themes and issues on the history, nature, identity, character, and place of African Christianity in world Christianity. It also refers to topics that address the continuing search for abundant life for Africans through multiple appeals to African religions and African Christianity in a challenging social context. The books in this series are expected to make significant contributions in historicizing trends in African Christian studies, while shifting the contemporary discourse in these areas from narrow theological concerns to a broader inter-disciplinary engagement with African religio-cultural traditions and Africa's challenging social context.

The series will cater to scholarly and educational texts in the areas of religious studies, theology, mission studies, biblical studies, philosophy, social justice, and other diverse issues current in African Christianity. We define these studies broadly and specifically as primarily focused on new voices, fresh perspectives, new approaches, and historical and cultural analyses that are emerging because of the significant place of African Christianity and African religio-cultural traditions in world Christianity. The series intends to continually fill a gap in African scholarship, especially in the areas of social analysis in African Christian studies, African philosophies, new biblical and narrative hermeneutical approaches to African theologies, and the challenges facing African women in today's Africa and within African Christianity. Other diverse themes in African Traditional Religions; African ecology; African ecclesiology; inter-cultural, inter-ethnic, and inter-religious dialogue; ecumenism; creative inculturation; African theologies of development, reconciliation, globalization, and poverty reduction will also be covered in this series.

SERIES EDITORS

Dr. Stan Chu Ilo (DePaul University, Chicago, USA)
Dr. Esther Acolatse (University of Toronto, Toronto, CA)
Dr. Mwenda Ntarangwi (Calvin College, Grand Rapids, MI, USA)

Jesus Christ as Logos Incarnate and Resurrected Nana (Ancestor)

An African Perspective on Conversion and Christology

RUDOLF K. GAISIE

FOREWORD BY
ANTHONY OSWALD BALCOMB

◈PICKWICK *Publications* • Eugene, Oregon

JESUS CHRIST AS LOGOS INCARNATE AND RESURRECTED
NANA (ANCESTOR)
An African Perspective on Conversion and Christology

African Christian Studies Series 19

Copyright © 2020 Rudolf K. Gaisie. All rights reserved. Except for brief quotations in critical publications or reviews, no part of this book may be reproduced in any manner without prior written permission from the publisher. Write: Permissions, Wipf and Stock Publishers, 199 W. 8th Ave., Suite 3, Eugene, OR 97401.

Pickwick Publications
An Imprint of Wipf and Stock Publishers
199 W. 8th Ave., Suite 3
Eugene, OR 97401

www.wipfandstock.com

PAPERBACK ISBN: 978-1-7252-5285-1
HARDCOVER ISBN: 978-1-7252-5286-8
EBOOK ISBN: 978-1-7252-5287-5

Cataloguing-in-Publication data:

Names: Gaisie, Rudolf K., author. | Balcomb, Anthony Oswald, foreword.

Title: Jesus Christ as Logos incarnate and resurrected nana (ancestor) : an African perspective on conversion and Christology / by Rudolf K. Gaisie ; foreword by Anthony Oswald Balcomb.

Description: Eugene, OR: Pickwick Publications, 2020 | African Christian Studies Series 19 | Includes bibliographical references and index.

Identifiers: ISBN 978-1-7252-5285-1 (paperback) | ISBN 978-1-7252-5286-8 (hardcover) | ISBN 978-1-7252-5287-5 (ebook)

Subjects: LCSH: Jesus Christ—Person and offices | Christianity—Africa, Sub-Saharan | Africa, Sub-Saharan—Religion | Ancestor worship—Africa | Akan (African people) | Religion and culture—Africa

Classification: BT205 G357 2020 (print) | BT205 (ebook)

Manufactured in the U.S.A. 10/14/20

To my ancestors, family, and teachers

Contents

Foreword by Anthony Oswald Balcomb | ix
Preface | xiii
Acknowledgements | xv
Abbreviations | xvii
Introduction | xix

Chapter 1
Christology and the Process of Conversion | 1

Chapter 2
Jesus Christ as Logos (Incarnate): A Story of Conversion in Early Graeco-Roman Christianity | 12

Chapter 3
The African Experience of Jesus | 71

Chapter 4
The Idea of Nana (Ancestor) in Akan Traditional Life and Thought | 84

Chapter 5
Ancestor Christology and the Process
of Conversion in African Christianity | 127

Chapter 6
The Logos as Nana (Ancestor): Towards
a Logos-Ancestor Christology | 174

Conclusion | 196

Bibliography | 201
Author Index | 223
Subject Index | 225

Foreword

THIS BOOK RECOUNTS THE story of how a peripatetic Jewish rabbi from Nazareth with a background in carpentry and fishing, a penchant for healing and teaching, and a radical message, becomes on the one hand the Reason that is behind all existence and on the other the Original Ancestor that is the source of all human identity. It is a fascinating story the Graeco-Roman side of which has been told many times. The African side of the story not so often, and the comparison between the two only once, by Kwame Bediako. The astonishing thing about both Greeks and Africans, so powerfully portrayed in this book, is that the Greeks were able to establish the coherence of all reality through one idea—the idea of the *logos*, and Africans are able to establish coherence within all human relationships through one notion—the notion of ancestor. The extrapolation is waiting to be made that the essence of western thinking is to do with ideas and the essence of African thinking is to do with relationships. But this book demonstrates that ideas are powerless if they are not believed by people, Greek or African, and the people behind the ideas are as equally fascinating as the ideas themselves. In any case, as Gaisie demonstrates, ideas and ancestors are not that far apart. The idea of the *logos* in Greek thought becomes the person of the Logos for Greeks who convert to Christianity, and the person of the ancestor in African thought becomes the person of Christ for Africans who convert to Christianity. So, ideas are like relationships. The Greeks have for ever had a relationship with the idea of the *logos*, and Africans have for ever had a relationship with the idea of ancestor. And when the gospel intervenes, Christ becomes the Logos for Greeks, and Original Ancestor for Africans.

The transition from *logos* to Logos, and from ancestor to Ancestor, is predicated, according to Gaisie, using Walls, on the notion of conversion as the project of turning what is already there in a new direction. Conversion, unlike proselytism which is simply the exchange of one set of customs and beliefs for another, involves risk, tension, and controversy. At the heart of the process is how to understand, for Greeks, the Logos, and for Africans, the Original Ancestor. So, Christology becomes the dogmatic equivalent of conversion, and translation of the living Christ into the receiving culture the project that unfolds as a direct consequence of the incarnation, which is itself the supreme act of divine translation, of God becoming flesh. The work of theology is to take up God's project of conversion, which is nothing less than the incarnation of God into the world in Christ and the subsequent incarnation of Christ into the ways of being in the world of countless particular cultures who are recipients of the good news of the gospel.

But outlining the agenda for God's project in broad strokes is one thing, giving substance to it is another. Walls makes the point that this is, and will be until the Parousia, an unfinished project. The call is made to the African community of scholars to do the work of translating the gospel into the lives, images, thought forms, structures, traditions, practices, dreams, hopes and imaginations of African people. On the one hand this requires utmost intellectual rigor, indeed the rigor of no less a figure than that of Origen of Alexandria, and on the other the simple gift of discerning how it is that Christ has already been inscribed into the receiving cultures, thus making these cultures hospitable to the gospel. Indeed, one of the hallmarks of this project are the efforts of ordinary people of faith throughout Christian history in making their own judgements, doing their own translations, formulating their own values, and constructing their own rituals and teachings, in the light of their own conversions in the context of their own cultures. And because of the endless translatability of the gospel and the rich diversity of the cultures in which it makes its appearances, the resultant manifestations of the faith are equally as diverse and, at times, utterly incomprehensible for some cultures as they are utterly obvious to others.

It is the call for rigorous intellectual enquiry that Bediako responded to in his *Theology and Identity: The Impact upon Culture of Christian Thought in the Second Century and Modern Africa* and that Gaisie responds to in this book. The terrain they enter is truly full of the risk, tension, and controversy that Walls identified as hallmarks of true conversion. These have emerged in the responses of well known African critics on both sides of the ideological spectrum and which Bediako treats with typical African deference. On the one hand there is Okot p'Bitek who rejected Christianity as untrue to Africa and on the other Byang Kato who saw all attempts to integrate Christianity with African culture (including those of John Mbiti) as untrue to the Christian gospel. There are intellectual giants such as Wole Soyinka who reject both Christianity and Islam as being fundamentally foreign to African soil and who famously mocked Senghor's doctrine of negritude by suggesting that a tiger does not shout about its tigritude, it simply pounces. There are also fervent critics of the attempt to interpret African Religion as *praeparatio evangelica* (another phrase coined by a patristic scholar) for Christianity. Why should indigenous religion not be seen as having integrity in its own right without being reduced to the status of a handmaiden of Christianity? Indeed, there is controversy even around the use of the word "primal" when describing indigenous religion because it has largely been associated with the *praeparatio* thesis. With the revived interest in indigenous religions and world-views what was originally seen as a distinctly progressive move in the discourse around indigenous religion as "primal", as opposed to "primitive", has turned out not to be progressive enough for some scholars. On the other hand the critics of inculturation theology have to reckon with the massive presence of Christianity on the African continent and its multifarious manifestations—indisputable signs that the faith has found a home in Africa that demands, at the least, some kind of explanation.

Gaisie appears not to be intimidated by these risks and controversies. Instead he picks up the cudgels offered to him by his forebears and mentors and applies his considerable talents to the task before him. This means understanding the theologies involved, the cultures involved, and the languages involved which, in this case, are Greek, Latin, and some Aramaic, as well as African vernaculars. Gaisie demonstrates competency in all of these departments. To each side of the story, Greek and African, he applies Walls' threefold stages of conversion—missionary, convert, and refiguration, of the concepts of *logos* and ancestor. But the first question to ask is how the concepts of *logos* and ancestor were originally understood in their respective cultures. So Gaisie introduces us to the *logos* in Heraclitus, Plato, Aristotle, the Stoics, the Septuagint and Philo on the Greek side and the Akan concept of ancestor on the African side with J. B. Danquah and Harry Sawyerr as its chief protagonists. He then takes us on an historical journey through the three stages of conversion on each side of the story. The first stage is how the first exponents translated Christ into their cultures as Christian missionaries. So we are introduced to Paul and John on the Greek side and John Pobee and Kwesi Dickson on the African side. The second stage is how the converts themselves understood Christ in terms of their culture so we are introduced, among others, to the Logos Christologies of Tatian, Irenaeus, Tertullian, and Justin Martyr on the Greek side and, among others, the Ancestor Christologies of Francois Kabasele and

Abraham Akrong on the African side. Finally, we are introduced to those who embark on the work of refiguring Christ into the thought forms of the cultures into which he has been introduced. So, we are introduced to Origen of Alexandria on the Greek side and Kwame Bediako and Charles Nyamiti on the African side, as well as Oseadeeyo Nana Addo Dankwa as a grassroots representative of the African project.

This is an extraordinary piece of work accomplished by an extraordinary young man—one of the rising stars, in my opinion, of African theological scholarship.

Prof. Anthony Oswald Balcomb
Senior Research Associate
School of Religion, Philosophy, and Classics
University of Kwazulu-Natal
February 2020

Preface

THIS BOOK IS LARGELY the substance of a doctoral thesis submitted to the Akrofi-Christaller Institute of Theology, Mission and Culture in March 2015. It explores the development of Ancestor Christology in African Christianity against the backdrop of the development and application of Logos Christology within early Graeco-Roman Christianity. The journey of Logos Christology is assessed within the three stages of the conversion process (identified by Andrew F. Walls) that occurs as traditional thought engages Christian teachings, namely, the *missionary*, *convert*, and *refiguration*. The development of Logos Christology seen within this framework, from the foundation of the Gospel of John to Origen, reveals three respective stages of the *mode* of Logos Christology, viz., *suggestive*, *clarificatory*, or *elucidative* and *innovative*.

Similarly, the exploration of Ancestor Christology in Africa within the process of conversion shows a corresponding three stages, with the *refiguration* or *innovative* stage yet to be exhausted. At the *refiguration* stage, with the explicit foundation of the significance of the Resurrection, Ancestor Christology should take more cognizance of indigenous "ancestor" terminology in tradition and the translated Scriptures. In line with this, an Akan reading of the Prologue of the Gospel of John, the foundation of Logos Christology, with the Logos (*Asεm*) as subject matter is engaged in dialogue with the Akan conception of *nana* (ancestor), especially as conceptually delineated by J. B. Danquah. The Logos-Ancestor (Nanasεm) discourse invites reflections from "academic" and "grassroots" levels, as well as addressing some of the expressed limitations of Ancestor Christology that have usually stemmed from the employment of non-indigenous terminology.

The structure of the study is as follows: The first chapter examines the relation between Christology and the process of conversion highlighting the experience of the first disciples of Jesus. In chapter 2, the journey of Logos Christology in Graeco-Roman Christianity is explored from the perspective of the three stages of conversion. This is followed by a survey of the Christological efforts in African Christianity in chapter 3 in such a way to locate Ancestor Christology in the wider context of Christology in Africa. The religio-cultural and social significance of the Akan concept of *nana* (ancestor) is the focus of chapter 4. In chapter 5 Ancestor Christology is assessed within the three stages of conversion. The case is made for a Logos-Ancestor Christology in chapter 6 where an Akan reading of the prologue of John's Gospel, taken as the foundational text of Logos Christology, is dialogued with the conceptual view of the Akan *nana*.

Acknowledgements

IN THE GRACIOUS PROVIDENCE of almighty God, I have received much help and encouragements from relations, friends, students, and colleagues at the Akrofi-Christaller Institute (ACI) where I now serve. I acknowledge the positive influence of the late Rev. Prof. Kwame Bediako not only as my eventual first academic teacher in the discipline of theology but also for his encouragement to me to continue in this vocational path. Prof. Mary G. Bediako (Aunty Mary) has guided me as a mother on this journey of Christian scholarship. Rev. Prof. Benhardt Y. Quarshie and Rev. Prof. Philip T. Laryea were patient guides through the doctoral period and have continued to inspire me as mentors.

It was a delight to both meet and share fellowship with Prof. Andrew Walls in the lecture room, and at communal devotions and mealtimes. Prof. Walls gave his encouragement through my doctoral studies and even offered some introductory (reading) lessons in the Greek and Latin languages at various times. Together with Dr Ingrid, Prof Walls has continued to encourage and inspire me as a student of early Graeco-Roman and African Christianity. Prof. Allison Howell spurred me on ("go for it Rudolf!") to pursue a semester essay on Justin Martyr's Logos conception and little did I know that the essay would eventually inform the subject area of my doctoral thesis. A deep appreciation also goes to Very Rev. Dr. James Walton and the late Very Rev. J. Yedu Bannerman for their assistance in thinking through the subject in Mfantse as well as rendering of some of the Mfantse sentences.

My gratitude to members of the ACI community and to the management for securing the scholarship funds for the doctoral studies and particularly also to Mr. Ben Asiedu for his assistance in managing allocated funds. A special thanks to my extended family (Michael, Ruby, Sharon, Ben and especially uncles Max and Noel) and friends (especially Nnamdi and Rachel Okolie, Kwabena Anane-Agyekum, David Adamptey, and Samuel Ayenu-Prah) for their concern, support, and words of encouragement along this journey.

Finally, my love and appreciation to my wife Millicent Ewuraesi and to our children Zerach Abayie, Eliezrah Efriyie and Netanel Nyameye for love and commitment shared in this journey of faith.

Abbreviations

ANF	Ante-Nicene Fathers (Series)
CCP	The Cambridge Companion to Philo
GBT	Ghana Bulletin of Theology
HE	Historia Ecclesiastica
IBMR	International Bulletin of Missionary Research
JACT	Journal of African Christian Thought
JBL	Journal of Biblical Literature
JETS	Journal of The Evangelical Theological Society
JTS	Journal of Theological Studies
Lit.	Literal
Pl.	Plural
Sing.	Singular
SVF	Stoicorvm Vetervm Fragmenta
SWC	Studies in World Christianity
TDNT	Theological Dictionary of the New Testament
WHO	The Westminster Handbook to Origen

Introduction

CHRISTOLOGY IS A CULTURAL construct. It is as dynamic as culture itself. In its pristine sense, Christology is a response to the experience of Jesus Christ and the impact of his living reality on persons within a cultural context.[1] Christology invariably makes use of pre-Christ or pre-Christian ideas and yet this cultural exercise cannot lose sight of "biblical and historical developments."[2] It is therefore not the case that Christology is just about giving (cultural) names to Jesus Christ. The names eventually given should serve as avenues aiding in the continuous process of the cultural response to the reality of Jesus Christ. Christology thus becomes a product of the process of conversion.

The organic nature of Christian history and mission implies that the interaction between various cultural responses to Jesus Christ is possible for clarification and renewal. In other words, present responses can benefit from the insight of previous responses and previous responses can also be illuminated from present happenings. Kwame Bediako's recognition of the relevance of the nature of theological activities in early Graeco-Roman Christianity for the theological concerns in modern African Christianity,[3] can therefore be applied further in the area of African Christology. The concrete expression of early Christian theology (and Christology) took place at a time following a "massive presence" of non-Jewish Christians in the

---

1. Fuller, *The Foundations of New Testament Christology*, 15; Marshall, *The Origins of New Testament Christology*, 13.
2. Kärkkäinen, *Christology*, 9.
3. Bediako, *Theology and Identity*.

Graeco-Roman world. The recognized significance of African Christianity in world Christianity makes the Christological efforts coming from particularly Africa an unavoidable voice.[4]

Traditional Thought and Christian Conversion: Some Ideas from A. F. Walls

Andrew F. Walls observes that the present fact of massive Christian presence in Africa, Asia, Latin America, and the Pacific and the role of translation in Christian evangelization and outlook could address Richard Baxter's seventeenth-century concern over "the geographical restriction" and hindrance of the "diversity of [indigenous] language" to evangelization.[5] The nature of Christian conversion with respect to cultural traditions has contributed to Christian survival and growth and this is evidenced in the various geographical models of Christianity in the course of history. In the first model of Christianity, Jesus was a "Jewish saviour, whose work could not be fully understood without reference to the destiny of the [Jewish] nation."[6] The accounts in the book of Acts do not show any systematic plan employed by the early Jewish Christians to reach out to non-Jews.[7]

The significant encounter between the Jewish understanding of Jesus and the religious understanding of a non-Jewish world was what happened at the Greek city of Antioch (on the Orontes) where unnamed individuals instructively proclaimed or preached "the Lord Jesus" to Greeks (Acts 11:20). The use of Kyrios rather than Christ, for Walls, was a "daring piece of cross-cultural translation" which was "transformative for Christian history" and it also "opened the way to a truly Hellenistic understanding of Jesus."[8] Jesus as Lord and not only as Christ in Antioch meant that he was more than the destined Jewish national savior and has also become Lord among the lords of the Antiochene cult of divinities. Walls notes further that the title "[Lord] Jesus Christ" is an indication of the fact that Jesus as Lord did not supersede the understanding of Jesus as Messiah.[9]

The cross-cultural translation of Christ (Messiah) to Lord was a symbolic or conceptual one rather than the "narrow sense of word equivalence."

---

4. Walls, "Old Athens and New Jerusalem," 153.
5. Walls, "Old Athens and New Jerusalem," 146.
6. Walls, "Old Athens and New Jerusalem," 146.
7. Bosch, *Transforming Mission*, 42.
8. Walls, "Old Athens and New Jerusalem," 146.
9. Walls, "Old Athens and New Jerusalem," 146. There are instances in Acts where the phrase "The Lord Jesus Christ" is also used (Acts 11:17; 15:26; 28:31).

Symbolic or conceptual forms of translation, the use of indigenous cultural symbols, are deeper than the limits of word equivalence. The recognition of Jesus as Lord in a predominantly Greek context "took the understanding of Jesus into new realms of thought."[10] The coming together of Jews and non-Jewish people under the lordship of Jesus Christ also meant an inevitable review of aspects of their respective traditions. The level and depth of review may have varied, but both groups unavoidably shared the challenge. The issue of circumcision in relation to salvation in Jesus Christ eventually sprung up from the missionary activities in Antioch. Circumcision was not an issue for Jewish and Jewish proselyte believers for whom it would have been natural to see Gentile believers as proselytes who needed circumcision as a mark of the covenant with God and who also needed instructions from the Torah (Law).[11] This was not the same for the Greek believers who had no Jewish association prior to faith in Jesus Christ.

The decision taken by the Council in Jerusalem over the issue of circumcision is a "pivot on which Christian history turns."[12] That Gentile believers did not need to be circumcised meant that they were not to become *like* Jews in becoming believers. The Gentile believers thus became converts and not proselytes.[13] Walls identifies three "new departures" following the Council's decision which made clear the distinction between a convert and a proselyte. First is the guarantee of the "cultural diversity of Christianity" which has contributed to the distinct forms and expression of Christianity over the centuries.[14] The second highlighted the nature of Christian conversion as the turning of "*what is already there in a new direction*", in contrast to proselytization which, unlike conversion, does not involve "risks, tension and controversy."[15] The third departure following the above nature of Christian conversion is the "expanded process of Christian understanding" which meant that Jesus was going to be understood outside Palestine in terms that the Jewish language and vocabulary took for granted or for which it was limited to communicate.[16]

---

10. Walls, "Old Athens and New Jerusalem," 146.
11. Walls, "Old Athens and New Jerusalem," 147.
12. Walls, "Old Athens and New Jerusalem," 148.
13. Walls, "Old Athens and New Jerusalem," 148.
14. Walls, "Old Athens and New Jerusalem," 148.
15. Walls, "Old Athens and New Jerusalem," 148, (emphasis in the original). On Walls' thoughts on Christian conversion in general, see *The Cross-Cultural Process in Christian History*, 67–68 & 79; *The Missionary Movement in Christian History*, 51–53. And especially as opposed to proselytization, "Converts or Proselytes?," 2–6.
16. Walls, "Old Athens and New Jerusalem," 148.

The application of the concept of Kyrios to Jesus as parallel to Kyrios Serapis implied that such a concept "needed explanation, qualification, supplementation and definition as the identity of Jesus was explored in terms of Hellenistic language and thought."[17] Employing "Hellenistic language and thought" in responding to Jesus meant that "conversion had to enter the whole realm of Hellenistic intellectual discourse, opening that discourse to Christ."[18] Hence, until the language and thought of a culture is employed in responding to Jesus, conversion will invariably strive at the periphery and the opening up of the culture's "intellectual discourse" to the conversion process will remained closed. It is a helpful question to raised, then, of how African Christology is making use of African languages and thought patterns and how these are helping to open the African intellectual experience and discourse to Jesus?

The opening of the Hellenistic intellectual discourse to Christ took place in three stages, namely, the *missionary*, *convert* and *refiguration* stages, with Apostle Paul, Justin Martyr, and Origen as respective representatives.[19] These three stages are not unique to the conversion of Hellenistic thought.[20] In this book they serve as the framework within which the understanding and application of Jesus as Logos in early Graeco-Roman Christianity is compared with Jesus as Ancestor in African Christianity. A way of assessing the depth of the penetration of Christian thought in a cultural context is to be mindful of any discerned stage of penetration. Christian history gives us an analogue in Logos Christology and African Christianity can benefit from it.

Since Christology invariably makes use of pre-Christ(ian) indigenous ideas within the matrix of the process of the conversion it serves as an indicator of Christian penetration. The level of the penetration of Christian understanding into the traditional world of thought can be measured by the amount of pre-Christian ideas or concepts incorporated into Christian reflections and expressions (Christology). In the same token the amount of

17. Walls, "Old Athens and New Jerusalem," 148.
18. Walls, "Old Athens and New Jerusalem," 148.
19. Walls, "Old Athens and New Jerusalem," 148–49. Walls also regards the stages as "levels of translation" (p. 149). The term "missionary" in Walls' discussion is used in a limited sense to refer to a convert from one cultural milieu working in a different context. All the various personalities in the identified respective stages are missionaries, although, in Walls' scheme, they are at different stages or levels with respect to a context. In this way the term "missionary" is descriptive of a stage. The word "convert" is applied to those who had shared in a pre-Christian traditional context before turning to Jesus Christ and is not strictly applied here in the sense of those who grew up in Christian families but come to the point of "turning to Jesus Christ."
20. Walls, "Old Athens and New Jerusalem," 150.

pre-Christian ideas transformed into Christian reflection makes it possible to discern the stage of the conversion process. This is the central concern of this book and the arguments presented point to the fact that pre-Christian concepts employed in Christology have discernible stages in their lifespan. In the specific case of Logos Christology, there are the *suggestive, explicative,* and *innovative* modes in the use of the *logos* concept in Christological reflections. Ancestor Christology has followed a similar trajectory in African Christianity (which is at the threshold of the *refiguration* stage).[21]

The Potential of Ancestor Christology in African Christianity

Uchenna Ezeh's *Jesus Christ the Ancestor* situates Ancestor Christology within the Christological formulae of the early councils in the first five centuries AD.[22] Ezeh takes the decisions of the Councils of Nicaea, Ephesus, and Chalcedon in resolving the challenges in communicating the person of Jesus as both divine and human, and connects their respective implications to Ancestor Christology in Africa.[23] Though he essentially affirms the efforts of Benezet Bujo and Charles Nyamiti, Ezeh's distinctiveness is in his systematic exploration in the light of the early Church Councils. However before the councils there is much that can be learnt from the Christological efforts, particularly that of Logos Christology, when examined within the stages of conversion.[24]

---

21. Walls has again made a clarion call for "Origens" in Africa: "the task that absorbed Origen's whole life is precisely the exercise before those who are now engaged in thinking the Christian faith into the fabric of thought of Africa and Asia and Pacific societies. . . . The theological task has passed the stage where missionaries can be very significant; . . . In many areas, perhaps most, it is not the task of the convert generation, relentlessly turning their ways of thinking toward Christ. . . . The weight of responsibility lies on a new generation of Origen's people brought up in the Christian faith, confident in the Scriptures, and yet at home in the old cultural tradition—people who are heirs to both the Christian and that other tradition. . . . On such people depends, not only the future of African, Asian, and Pacific theology, but the future of Christian theology and of theological scholarship as a whole." Walls, "In Quest of the Father of Mission Studies," 104.

22. Uchenna A. Ezeh, *Jesus Christ the ancestor*.

23. Chapter five of the work; Ezeh, *Jesus Christ the ancestor*, 139–256.

24. Paul Bruderer has assessed the proponents of Ancestor Christology in Africa under Stephen Bevans' models of contextual theology; Synthetic and Anthropological models (Bénézet Bujo and Abraham Akrong), Translation and Synthetic (John Pobee and François Kabasélé) Synthetic (Charles Nyamiti and Kwame Bediako. Paul Bruderer, "African Ancestor-Christologies". See Bevans, "Models of Contextual Theology," 185–201; Bevans, *Models of Contextual Theology*. While Bruderer's effort may well be a way to assess the efforts of the proponents of Ancestor Christology it is inadequate to

Similarly, Cletus C. Nwaogwugwu's evaluation of Ancestor Christology under the two-dimensional approaches of *ascending* (from below) and *descending* (from above) to Christology tends to limit it to helping in "understanding" the existence of the Church in Africa.[25] However, the efforts in Ancestor Christology should be understood also in relation to the Church's proclamation of the Gospel message in Africa.

Ancestor Christology has the potential of an enduring missiological impact in African Christianity and beyond. I define Ancestor Christology (in African Christianity) as the attempt to articulate the reality and impact of Jesus Christ through the medium of the concept of ancestor in Africa in such a way that the concept of ancestors is opened up for the desired Christian transformation. The various proponents of Ancestor Christology have sought to be both faithful to historical Christian teaching and the African experience of reality. Ancestor Christology is not merely a "Christian Evaluation of the [African] Ancestral Cult" but articulates the engagement between the reality and impact of Jesus Christ and the discerned value and underlying philosophy of the place of ancestors in traditional thought.[26] Ancestor Christology, however, does eventually provide the resources to re-evaluate and incorporate the "cult of ancestors" in Christian liturgy as F. Kabaselé and Charles Nyamiti have suggested, both of whom had earlier explored Ancestor Christology.[27]

There have been a few critical responses to Ancestor Christology expressing its limitations despite some prospects at both the grassroots and academic levels.[28] I propose that an indigenous mother tongue formulation of Ancestor Christology can help address these expressed limitations. The mother tongue formulation should be in close connection with the translated Bibles which have not only contributed to the growth of African Christianity

---

show the extent of the missiological endeavour of Ancestor Christology.

25. Nwaogwugwu, *Ancestor Christology*.

26. Nwaogwugwu's description of Ancestor Christology as "an enquiry into the various ways of understanding the ancestor, his role and symbol in the worldview of the sub-Saharan Africans, in order to support or reject the designation of Jesus Christ as ancestor" (Nwaogwugwu, *Ancestor Christology*, xxii) is rather limited when one considers the efforts of proponents such as Nyamiti. Ancestor Christology cannot concern itself with "rejecting the designation of Jesus Christ as Ancestor". The following may be cited as examples of studies primarily concerned with the Christian response to the cult of ancestors: Daneel, "The Christian Gospel and the Ancestor Cult"; Fasholé-Luke, "Ancestor Veneration and the Communion of Saints".

27. See Kabaselé Lumbala, *Celebrating Jesus Christ in Africa*. Nyamiti, *Jesus Christ, the Ancestor of Humankind*.

28. Küster, *The Many Faces of Jesus Christ: Intercultural Christology*; Ezigbo, *Re-Imagining African Christologies*.

but serve as veritable sources for African theology and Christology at both the grassroots and academic levels. As a case study I have dialogued an Akan reading of the prologue of the Gospel of John with an Akan Nana (Ancestor) Christology to demonstrate how mother tongue reflections can avoid traps set by contextual reflections done in a foreign language.

Grassroots theological reflections are quite obviously interspersed with biblical imagery. Such reflections in the indigenous languages are aided by mother tongue Bibles. For example, the Christological reflections of Madam Afua Kuma were originally in her mother tongue (Twi) and her knowledge of biblical verses and imagery is significant. Two instances may suffice here. Madam Kuma notes,

> *Yesu na ɔwɔ ɔman kɛse a ɛrehyerɛn*
> *Kontonkurowi na abɔ ho ban,*
> *Na anyinam rebɔ ho nsra hyia*
>
> . . . .
>
> *Obi mma hɔ mfa ahwehwɛ nhwɛ n'anim*
> *ɔman no hann no ne w'ahwehwɛ*
> *Otumifo Nyankopɔn ne ɔhenkɛse*
> *Wo na wowɔ kurow kronkron,*
> *Ampa ara,*
> *eyɛ anuonyam kurow!*²⁹
>
> A great and shining nation belongs to Jesus;
> The rainbow protects its rampart
> while lightning marches round.
>
> . . .
>
> One does not have to take a mirror there
> To see one's face:
> The brilliance of the city is his [or her] mirror!
> Almighty God, you are a great Chief.
> To you belongs the holy city.
> Truly, it is a glorious city.³⁰

The Asante Twi (UBS 1964) of the text in Revelation 21:22-23 reads;

> *Na manhunu asɔredan biara wɔ (kuro no) mu; na Awurade Nyankopɔn, ade nyinaa so tumfoɔ, ne adwammaa no ne n'asɔredan. Na ɛnhia sɛ owia anaa ɔsrane bɛpae wɔ kuro no mu, ɛfiri sɛ Nyankopɔn animuonyam hyerɛn wɔ mu, na ne kanea ne adwammaa no.*

---

29. Kuma, *Kwaeberentwu Ase Yesu—Ayeyi Ne Mpaebɔ*, 12.
30. Translation by Jon Kirby.

One can take note of the words *Otumifo* and *tumfoɔ* both of which translate "Almighty." The preceding verses talk of a "holy city" (21:10), which is "pure gold, clear as glass" (21:18).[31] The Pauline description of "death" being "swallowed up in victory", *wɔamene owuo nkonim mu*, in 1 Corinthians 15:54 is also hinted at in Afua Kuma when she declares,

> *Yesu a*
> *Woamene owu ne ɔyaredɔm*
> *Ama yɛn ho atɔ yɛn*

> O Jesus
> You have swallowed death and every kind of disease,
> And have made us whole again.[32]

The legitimacy of Bible translation carries with it the occasional difficulty of conveying concepts crafted in a language from one cultural context to another. While a literal rendering of words may invoke unintended meanings, a conceptual equivalent also leads to unforeseen vistas. Although the risks involved in biblical translations may be high there is no other enduring viable way than to enter the world of the Bible in one's mother tongue. Thus, the effort to appropriate a New Testament Christological imagery in the mother tongue is also an attempt to "indigenize" such an image. While the pre-Christian concept informing the New Testament Christological image may be foreign to the receiving culture, its Christian mode will necessarily demand familiar indigenous associations. In other words, mother tongue New Testament images of Jesus are received through the lens of associated pre-Christian indigenous terminologies.

Some of the New Testament Christological images are familiar in African cultures such as *king, priest,* and even *prophet* and African Christians have readily embraced these. There are others such *word* or the *firstborn from the dead*, however, that may require further comments. In a similar way some African images of Christ such as *master of initiation* and as *ancestor* may not readily fit in the New Testament Christological gallery. That does not suggest their illegitimacy or inferiority. At any rate, such African imageries of Jesus Christ take their root also in the New Testament precedents. However, since mother tongue Bibles afford "indigenous" reading of New Testament images of Jesus Christ such readings can be placed alongside African images. Here lies a functional distinction between grassroots and written Christology. While written Christology may have the benefit of the traditions informing

---

31. Cf. Laryea, "Mother Tongue Theology: Reflections on Images of Jesus in the Poetry of Afua Kuma," 50–60 (51) and n.21.

32. Kuma, *Jesus of the Deep Forest*, 11.

the New Testament Christological images, grassroots Christology, relying quite heavily on the translated New Testament documents, operates with "indigenized" New Testament images of Jesus Christ. Thus, a comparative exercise between New Testament images of Jesus explored in the mother tongue and the images of Jesus arising from the socio-political environment in contemporary sub-Saharan Africa.

In the following pages, I have endeavored to demonstrate the significance of the development of Logos Christology for the ongoing project of Ancestor Christology in Africa. I argue that Christology strives in the process of conversion, itself as part of the missionary mandate and the cultural witness of Jesus. The functional task of Christology is that it aids in the continuous process of giving Christian answers to traditional and contemporary cultural questions. Jesus as the Logos helped Graeco-Roman Christians to find answers to cultural questions posed by the presentation and penetration of the gospel. Jesus as Ancestor is helping in the further appropriating of the gospel in especially sub-Saharan Africa and remains a potential force in the gospel's engagement with social, economic, and political challenges in Africa. In the latter sense I emphasize that Ancestor Christology ideally should be pursued in the language of the relevant cultural context.

Chapter 1

Christology and the Process of Conversion

THE ENCOUNTER BETWEEN THE life of Jesus and contemporary first-century Jewish culture is a paradigm for assessing gospel and culture issues.[1] The early Jewish disciples of Jesus responded to him by employing Jewish cultural elements. The disciples turned Jewish inheritance towards "a new direction" in Jesus resulting in a transformed inheritance and a Jewish "model of thought and life that was 'Christian' because Christ was at its centre."[2] Thus the growth in the disciples' view of Jesus Christ and his impact on their lives reveal a link between Christology and the process of conversion.

The Experience of the Early Disciples in the New Testament

The primary concern for the early Jewish followers or disciples of Jesus Christ was not so much with the nature of his being as to the significance of his words and works.[3] Though his life primarily evoked religious or spiritual sentiments, Jesus' words and actions also resonated with the political expectations of his followers. Jesus' close associates were not devoid of this tendency towards political liberation even after his death and resurrection (Acts 1:6). Following Jesus for these individuals involved a cultural reworking of seeing their life and the destiny of their nation in view of the events prior

---

1. Bediako, "Gospel and Culture," 10.
2. Walls, "Old Athens and New Jerusalem," 148.
3. Peter's remark to follow Jesus because he has the words of life (John 6:68).

to and after the resurrection. What remains instructive for all subsequent followers of Jesus is his desire for the opinion of what his close associates thought of him. It is hard to guess whether the disciples anticipated Jesus's identity question (known as the "Christological question")[4] in the time and manner it came. Though apparently unanticipated it was a "momentous question" that "marked a turning point" in the education of the disciples.[5] The same question was asked twice. The first question for the opinion of others is rendered differently in the Synoptics,[6] while that for the disciples' view is the same in all the three accounts ("Who do you say I am?").[7] The time and place where the question was asked and the immediate events prior to that are presented differently. However, the immediate events following Peter's declaration are the same in all three accounts.[8]

Following Peter's confession that he is the "Christ [Messiah], Son of the living God" or "the Christ of God," Jesus employed the title "Son of Man" in his discourse as is typical in the Synoptics. If the "Son of Man" title explicitly suggested Messiahship then the identity question would have been quite unnecessary. An implicit Messianic connotation, however, may have served at least two purposes. It could have been an exercise for the disciples to voice out what they may have assumed all along as well as an opportunity for Jesus to ascertain and correct his disciples' opinion of him before his last days in Jerusalem. The lesson following Peter's confession was about Jesus' imminent suffering, death and resurrection as part of the destiny of the Christ of God. The identity question provided the opportunity for Jesus to review the disciples' perception and expectation of him. The disciples were to have a clearer perspective of Jesus by virtue of their proximity. The opinion of the others did not connect Jesus as Messiah.[9] Peter's recognition of Jesus as the Messiah points to a personal encounter and experience of Jesus that precedes any (cultural) Christological affirmation.

---

4. See, for example, Cummings "Who do you say that I am? A North American Minority Answer to the Christological Question," 217–36. Asamoah-Gyadu, "Who do You Say That I Am? Revisiting Kwame Bediako's Responses to an Eternal Christological Question". Grey, "Who Do You Say That I Am?—Images of Christ in Feminist Liberation Theology," 189.

5. Bernard, *A Critical and Exegetical Commentary on the Gospel according to St. John Volume One*, cxxxi.

6. In Matthew, the phrase "the Son of Man is" (16:13) replaces, or perhaps otherwise, the "I am" in Mark (8:27) and Luke (9:18). In Luke it is the opinion of the "crowd" or "people" and in Matthew and Mark it is that of the "humans" or "men" or "people."

7. Matthew 16:15; Mark 8:29; Luke 9:20.

8. Matthew 16:1–13, 16, 21f; Mark 8:13–21; 8:22–29; Luke 9:10–27.

9. Dickson, *The Gospel according to Luke*, 110.

Christology in Cultural Context

Jesus as the Messiah was itself a cultural insight. The God of Israel is the living God who in Jewish conception is the God of all flesh.[10] Peter's declaration of the Messiah as the Son of the Living God suggests (at least at this stage) a universal significance of Jesus. Whether this was so, and how that affected Peter's view of Jesus, is beyond the present discussion. However, Peter's choice of words in responding to who he had come to see Jesus to be were within the spectrum of Jewish religious vocabulary. Peter had a "Christological journey" as his view or understanding of Jesus and his significance was a learning process for him. The verbal declaration was not the endpoint of his view since that needed some clarification and maturing in his experience with Jesus the Messiah. Yet prior to that declaration he held some form of Messianic views of Jesus of Nazareth.[11]

Quite a lot had happened between Jesus and the disciples before the identity question episode as found in the Synoptics.[12] The disciples' recognition of Jesus as Christ (Messiah) in the Synoptics appears as a "gradual development," unlike the Fourth Gospel where Andrew and Philip recognized that early in their discipleship.[13] Peter, like his colleague disciples, shared in the general traditional Jewish conception of the image of the Messiah. It was in the medium of this cultural world, with the foundation of the Jewish Scriptures intertwined with human traditions, that the revelation of God's Son was enacted. Peter's idea of a Messiah in connection to Jesus, though valid, was incomplete in scope and significance and was eventually transformed in the process of time. Thus, like the title Messiah, the scope and significance of cultural elements are transformed in their use in Christology.

The cultural element employed in people's response to Jesus Christ serves as an avenue for a deepening impact of Jesus on the respective culture. It is inadequate to see Christology primarily as a systematic reflection

---

10. Numbers 27:16; Jeremiah 32:27.

11. In the Fourth Gospel, it was his brother Andrew (then a disciple of John the Baptist) who first told him about having found the Messiah (1:35–42). There is no indication that Peter had an initial doubt about the Messiah that Andrew and his friend had found. The Fourth Gospel does not reference the identity question incident. Peter's remark in 6:68–69 is close to his response to the identity question. It is obvious this episode of the first meeting with Jesus took place long before the identity question was posed. Andrew and his brother Peter from this narration had a view of, and were expectant of, the Jewish Messiah even before both met Jesus in person.

12. In Matthew's twenty-eight chapters it is found in chapter sixteen; in Mark chapter eight of the sixteen chapters and in chapter nine of Luke's twenty-four chapters.

13. Bernard, *A Critical and Exegetical Commentary on the Gospel according to St. John*, cxxxiv.

"on the person, being and activity of Jesus of Nazareth,"[14] or as the "doctrine of the person of Jesus Christ."[15] Jesus of Nazareth lived as a person and functioned within the cultural world of first-century Palestine. The spread of the teachings about Jesus Christ has been a cross-cultural exercise and thus it is helpful keep in mind the cultural dimension of the "descriptions and understanding of Jesus which emerge in the course of Christian history."[16] Christology is not only what people with one language and way of thinking say but also what others of different languages and thought patterns say of Jesus. Even when Christology is connected to revelation and salvation, it is still a cultural endeavor because revelation and salvation connect with a people's use of language and way of responding to reality.[17] Divine revelation disentangles the intricacies of a culture via its language and the transformations of such elements constitute salvation. The cultural element may limit the significance of an earlier Christology for later generations but not necessarily its truth and validity. The language and concept employed by a culture as it responds to Jesus could turn out to be inadequate or foreign to a later generation of that culture or another.

The task of contemporary Christology is not only to be limited to understanding the significance of Jesus in contemporary societies.[18] Walter Kasper's three fundamental tasks of (Western) Christology; "historically determined," "universally responsive" and "soteriologically determined" remain helpful.[19] His insistence that "Christology is not concerned solely with the nature of Jesus Christ, but with the Christian understanding of reality in general" underscores the need for the Christian influence upon the cultural view of reality in Christology.[20] Christology should explore ways in which the response to Jesus leads to the conversion of cultures, that is, the turning of cultural thought forms in the direction of Jesus.

The question of the starting point of, or emphasis in, Christology is apparently culturally addressed. The Incarnation presents a meeting place of

14. O'Collins, *Christology*, 1.

15. Fuller, *The Foundations of New Testament Christology*, 15.

16. Moule, *The Origin of Christology*, 1. Raymond Brown may have taken for granted the cultural dimension in his view of Christology. Brown, *An Introduction to New Testament Christology*, 3.

17. Hengel, *Studies in Early Christology*, vii.

18. Kärkkäinen, *Christology: A Global Introduction*, 9.

19. Kasper, *Jesus the Christ*, 20–23. These identified three approaches are examples of the Western cultural responses to Jesus Christ in the matrix of Enlightenment thinking. For a discussion on the Enlightenment and Christology in Europe, see Greene, *Christology in Cultural Perspective*, 74–95.

20. Kasper, *Jesus the Christ*, 38.

the fullness of God and of the fullness of humanity. The resurrection of Jesus brought with it the significance of his origin as demonstrated in the Gospel narratives, all of which are post-resurrection documents.[21] In terms of Christological developments two tendencies are identified and given various terms in either looking more at the divinity or humanity of Jesus, namely, "Christology from below" (humanity) and "Christology from above" (divinity).[22] These two tendencies cannot be mutually exclusive but must "complement each other" since, to an extent, the cultural image given or assumed by Jesus determines an apparent stress on his divinity or humanity.[23]

Each cultural milieu presents various images, titles, symbols, or concepts in the responses to the impact of Jesus. Jesus was given a name and a title at the angel Gabriel's visit to Mary. In his life and work there were various images and symbols applied to him and these served as avenues to convey the essence of his person and work. The name, titles, images, and symbols concerning Jesus in the Gospels are primarily Jewish cultural expressions. They had pre-Incarnation usages. As they were applied to Jesus the traditional or usual understanding and scope of these titles and images were enlarged and, in some sense, transformed. That is, people came to see what those titles or images communicated in a new light.

Jesus as the Messiah enlarged the traditional and contemporary understanding and scope of the idea of "Messiah." Under the jurisdiction of the Romans the Jewish nation wished for nothing less than a political liberation in the Messiah of God. Instead of a political emancipation Jesus "the Messiah" emphasized spiritual freedom. As the idea of Messiah was reconfigured in the light of Jesus, the national salvation anticipated was raised to an inter-national or universal one. The discovery of the expected Messiah in the person of Jesus for the disciples was undoubtedly in the context of the interplay between the image of the Messiah in the Jewish Scriptures (tradition) and the life, works, and words of Jesus the Nazarene (the gospel).

---

21. John 1:14, 17; Matthew 1:18, 35; Jesus of Nazareth was "a man attested by God with deeds of power, wonders, and signs that God did through him," as Peter recalls in his speech on the Day of Pentecost (Acts 2:22).

22. Associated terms describing the idea behind the "from below" approach include "ascending," Antiochene, "cosmological" and "low" with the Synoptics also being linked with this view. Terms such as "descending," Alexandrine, "anthropological," "high" and the Fourth Gospel are associated with "Christology from above." See Kasper, *Jesus the Christ*, 48–49. Also associated quite loosely with "from above" and "from below" are "ontological" and "functional." The former "is concerned with who and what Jesus is in himself" and the latter "focuses on his saving work or redemptive activity for human beings in their world." See O'Collins, *Christology*, 16–9 and Kärkkäinen, *Christology*, 12–15.

23. O'Collins, *Christology*, 17.

While the desire for national salvation lingered even after the resurrection for the disciples they undoubtedly grew in their sense of identity as the "true" or "real" Jews with the conviction that they had obeyed God by recognizing and receiving his Messiah.[24]

Jesus the Messiah meant for the Jewish disciples a new sense of identity. This self-awareness involved a reconfiguration of a traditional concept or idea of the Messiah. Though it took some time, the recognition of the universal significance of the Messiah in the life and ministry of Jesus was instrumental in how the disciples came to see themselves in the economy of God and their relation to other non-Jewish peoples. Jesus the Christ also implied that they should go to the other nations and make them his disciples. It is instructive that Jesus did not "invent" a concept through which his Jewish disciples were to recognize him as God-sent. He assumed a traditional concept and transformed it in communicating his life and ministry as coming from God and the consequences thereof.

Michael Amaladoss rightly observes the "double roots" informing the images of Jesus across cultural contexts.[25] According to him, it is in "the context of the dialectic" between the "person and life" of Jesus and the life of his disciples that all the (cultural) images of Jesus arise. The Gospels furnish us with the life of Jesus on the one hand and the "culture and history" of his disciples on the other hand inform the images of Jesus. One of these roots may be "stronger in a particular image" as in the case of the "crucified Jesus" and the "Sacred Heart" where the former is more rooted in the life of Jesus and the latter more cultural.[26] The life of Jesus presented in the Gospels is itself in a "culture and history" of its own. The Gospel accounts are cultural responses to the Jewish life of Jesus the Messiah. While it is helpful to be mindful of the "double roots" of the images of Jesus, the cultural interaction between the world of the Gospel accounts and that of the disciples in subsequent cultural contexts is crucial.

Every culture has its ways of expressing conceived or unseen realties. Images, symbols, and titles in most cases express incidents that happened in the life of a people and serve as a memory invoking past sentiments for present stimulation or reflection. The Akan title *ɔsáagyefo*, for example, may indicate a period of war when someone skillfully mobilized and led a group or community to victory.[27] The title *ɔsáagyefo* may therefore in

---

24. Acts 1:6–8; 4:18–20.

25. Amaladoss, *The Asian Jesus*, 2.

26. Amaladoss, *The Asian Jesus*, 2.

27. It is rendered as a "byname of a king" and is derived from *ɔságyefo* which Christaller's Akan dictionary etymologically expresses as *ɔhene anasɛ obiara a ogye sa*, that is "a king or anyone who takes (or receives) war." The word *sa* is a derivative of *ɔsa*

addition to expressing the bravery of the holder, remind the present generation of past periods of war(s). Applied to Jesus Christ, the image or title may rather invoke a spiritual reality. Jesus Christ neither took arms nor fought any physical war. His weaponless and violent sacrificial death won a spiritual victory in the understanding of his followers. When the followers of Jesus choose to see him and what he did in the light of an ɔsáagyefo by according him that title, they, by so doing, give a new meaning to the title. Jesus the Ɔsáagyefo or rather Ɔsáagyefo Jesus adds the significance of Jesus to the original meaning of the title.

The universal significance of Jesus as the Savior of the world gives a universal value to a local image applied to him. The enlarged scope of the image in turn opens and enlarges the local context that produced the image. Without losing its local meaning or value, the image, since it is culturally rooted or connected, opens its culture both to the influence of Christ and to a reworking of its thought form regarding the image. This is what happened to the Messiah image and title when the followers of Jesus saw him in that light and applied it to him.[28]

No single image can claim to say or reveal everything there is about Jesus and so images of Jesus are necessarily complementary and "neither monopolistic nor exclusive."[29] The penetrative depth of the application of an image to Jesus can be realistic to an indigene more than an outsider. As there may be other historical indigenous claimants of an image it is an "insider" who would be at home to pursue any deeper comparison between Jesus and other claimants. The "foreigner" may only attempt to perceive Jesus in the light of a traditional image, but the "insider" has the advantage for any superlative comparison. In other words, Christology is not the work for one generation but for successive generations.

Christology has cultural risks and the associated difficulties in reducing realities into concepts. There is the risk of faithfully portraying Jesus or eventually "betraying" him.[30] Yet different cultural contexts will continue to respond to Jesus Christ who is not bound to any specific context.[31] Thus one cannot presume in Christology to already have the "fullness," or a prior

---

"war" and may stand alone as in such expressions as *yɛ / nõa sa* "to prepare for war" and *kɔ / tu sa* "to go to war or make war." It therefore can be rendered as "one who hires an army to join his own [for war]" and can also mean "deliverer." Christaller, *Dictionary of the Asante and Fante Language*, 416 and 421.

28. The Jewish Saviour turned out to be the Saviour of the world and his significance was not only for the Jewish nation but also for the rest of the world.

29. Amaladoss, *The Asian Jesus*, 2.

30. Wessels, *Images of Jesus*.

31. Wessels, *Images of Jesus*, 192.

complete knowledge, of Jesus's identity.[32] Jesus's "definite character" and the unity of his teachings, actions, and paschal fate are to be appropriated through different cultural lenses.[33] As cultures are transformed in their experience and appropriation of the reality of Jesus, they provide the opportunity for others to review their cultural assumptions of Jesus. In this way the full stature of Jesus is revealed as people of different cultural worlds express their experience of him.[34]

Christology as an Intricate Product of the Process of Conversion

Peoples' experience of Jesus is a story of conversion. Christology is thus intimately connected to the process of conversion. There is a correlation between a mature cultural reflection of the person and impact of Jesus and the level at which that culture has been opened for his influence. Christian conversion is about redirection of content in the direction of Jesus. In this process of redirection cultural concepts are invariably employed in varying degrees. The early community of Jewish believers went through the process of redirecting traditional concepts or ideas towards Jesus:

> They [the earliest Jewish Christians] had not abandoned animal sacrifice but saw it in a new context—the self-offering of the Servant of God. Above all, they saw Jesus as the Messiah, the Agent of God. In doing so, they transformed the traditional concept of messiahship by stressing his crucifixion and resurrection; but this did not destroy the traditional concept. Rather, it enlarged it by tying it to the symbols of Son of Man and Suffering Servant.[35]

Since the disciples' earlier view of Jesus as the Messiah did not anticipate the crucifixion and resurrection, the transformation of messiahship is linked to the impact of the resurrection.[36] Peter himself rebuked the idea of suffering and death for the Messiah of God and these sentiments could still

---

32. Wessels, *Images of Jesus*, 163.

33. Niebuhr, *Christ and Culture*, 12.

34. Walls highlights how the penetration of Christ into the "Hellenistic universe of thought" brought the realization "that he is greater, grander, more active, and his relations with God and humanity more complex than the earliest [Jewish] concepts could convey" and that "[t]he full stature of Christ is revealed only as a fresh cultural entity is incorporated into the church, which is his body." Walls, *Old Athens and New Jerusalem*, 149.

35. Walls, "Old Athens and New Jerusalem," 146.

36. Dahl, *Jesus the Christ*, 37–40.

be felt from his speech on the day of Pentecost.[37] The transformed view of Messiah enabled the earliest Jewish believers to see themselves as the ones truly obeying God by receiving Jesus Christ as Messiah.[38] Apostle Paul, as a representative of those who did not see Jesus in the flesh before the resurrection, became convinced of this act of obedience in proclaiming the Messiah Jesus.[39] After "several days" following his visionary encounter with the risen Lord Jesus, Paul immediately began to proclaim that Jesus is "the Son of God" and proving that he was the Messiah.[40] Paul continued in the process of conversion in turning an ancestral understanding in the direction of the life and ministry of Jesus even in his strict education in the "ancestral law" and his zeal in it.[41] The Christologies from the New Testament are the result of the attempt by the early followers of Jesus in turning their culture towards him. The various cultural imageries and concepts gained an enlarged scope and significance. This was true for both traditional Jewish concepts and those that had currency in the larger Graeco-Roman world.

The process of Christology reaches its concrete stage over a considerable period of Christian presence. So, the initial, and perhaps apparent neglect of the centrality of Christology in African theology may be understandable. John Parratt's view of the discontinuity between African Traditional Religion (ATR) and Christianity "in their view of history" as a possible reason for the initial neglect of Christology in Africa is inadequate.[42] Christian presence in sub-Sahara Africa needed an inevitable clarification of the continuity of God with respect to the African religious past. This fundamental step in working out an authentic Christian identity by way of clarifying the issue of continuity was not only found in Africa but could also be seen in the beginning of Graeco-Roman Christianity. Christological issues invariably ensue after a fair attempt at resolving the

---

37. The man Jesus of Nazareth "attested to you by God with mighty works and wonders and signs which God did through him in your midst," Peter addressed his listeners, " you crucified and killed by the hands of lawless men" (Acts 2:23, RSV). Yet God raised Jesus up from the dead, Peter continued, "because it was not possible for him to be held by it" (2:24). In his final words as if to highlight the significance of Jesus' crucifixion, Peter emphasized "[l]et all the house of Israel therefore know assuredly that God has made him both Lord and Christ (Messiah), this Jesus whom you crucified" (2:36).

38. Even before Stephen's speech in which he indicated how the believers of Jesus were the ones responding to God in faith (Acts 7:1–53), Peter and John had earlier on expressed their proclamation of Jesus as the Messiah as an act of obedience to God before the Jewish leadership in Jerusalem (Acts 4:19–20).

39. 1 Corinthians 15:1–8.

40. Acts 9:1–20.

41. Acts 22:3; Galatians 1:14; Philippians 3:4–6; 1 Corinthians 15:9.

42. Parratt, *Reinventing Christianity*, 78–80.

view of the God and Father of the Lord Jesus Christ as being the Sovereign God who has not left "himself without witness" and whom humans have sought in hope to "feel after him and find him."[43] For the early Jewish Christians this was a given.

When the process of conversion is not leading to creative Christology the transformation of cultures via their images, concepts or symbols is inhibited. In other words, the process of conversion should lead to an ongoing Christological exploration and exploitation of cultural images. It is instructive that the titular phrase "the Lord Jesus Christ" is a Christological product of the conversion process within the early Jewish and Hellenistic cultural matrix. The title "Christ" in most mother-tongue Bibles is given an indigenous transliterated rendering (ex. *Kristo* in Akan) and may not have the weight of meaning as it does in the Jewish cultural world. While "Christ" has assumed various meanings over the centuries, the testimony of Jesus in other cultural contexts has relied on cultural resources for its elucidation. The working of a Christology with indigenous cultural resources such as language is a creative step in the process of conversion. This is a natural development since Jesus cannot be forced into the center of a people's thinking. He rather occupies the center stage gradually, as people respond to him in recognizing the significance of his life and work in the will of God for humanity, including their sense of reality. The deeper Jesus gets to the heart of a people and hence to the heart of a culture the more cultural elements are employed in articulating his impact.

The early Church creeds have left their unquestionable stamp of Graeco-Roman cultural elements as they were expressed in the principal languages of Greek and Latin.[44] They serve as evidence of the fact that over the early centuries Jesus penetrated deeper into the heart of Graeco-Roman culture. While from the outside, Graeco-Roman Christology may owe much to pre-Christian ideas or concepts, the rescue and renewal of much in these ideas may also be indebted to Christianity (Christology).[45] As early Graeco-Roman Christian authors critiqued and affirmed traditional ideas or concepts in the light of their Christian convictions, the Hellenistic view of Jesus Christ continuously took form and shape. The nexus of responding to critics and those with unorthodox or heterodox views also had its place in the eventual outlook of Graeco-Roman Christology. For indigenous

---

43. Acts 14:17; 17:26–27. Satyavrata, *God Has Not Left Himself Without Witness*.

44. Pelikan and Hotchkiss, *Creeds and Confessions of Faith in the Christian Tradition—Volume I*, 5.

45. Walls, "Scholarship under the Cross," 18.

Christian critics and heretics as cultural challenges contribute to the Christological development in the process of conversion.

Conclusion

There is much to discern from the use of cultural images in Christology and its associated missiological import through the perspective conversion. The process of conversion is open-ended and not limited to one cultural generation. The Christian conviction of the universal significance of Jesus Christ implies that no cultural response to him is inferior to any other. All cultures (nations) are called to respond to Jesus. Christians from various cultural traditions share a common belief of who Jesus is and yet this shared reality is diverse in manifestation and expression. Since Jesus does not come to cultureless communities, a task of Christology is to unpack the dynamism of receiving him with cultural spectacles and yet appreciating his cultural transcendence. Jesus as Logos enabled Graeco-Roman Christians to appropriate the significance of Jesus in relation to their inherited cultural world of thought and practice and those of others in the (known) world. In the next chapter I examine the journey of Logos Christology in relation to the process of conversion in early Graeco-Roman Christology.

Chapter 2

Jesus Christ as Logos (Incarnate)

A Story of Conversion in Early Graeco-Roman Christianity

EARLY GRAECO-ROMAN CHRISTIAN WRITERS exploited the ambiguity of the Greek word λόγος (*logos*)[1] in their missionary literary outputs. The verbal noun of the word λέγω (*legō*) with the root word λέγ- indicating "count" or "speak," the meaning of λόγος includes the senses of "word," "thought," "reason" and "account."[2] The pre-Christian (conceptual) exploration of *logos* provided a background for Christian understanding and application of Jesus Christ as Logos (incarnate), following the implicit declaration in the Gospel of John.

---

1. The Greek as well as the English transliteration are used interchangeably in the present work. Sometimes the Greek is maintained to emphasize a point from a respective text. The lowercase *logos*, unless it is from a author, is used for references other than Jesus Christ in which case the capital Logos is employed.

2. Liddell and Scott, *A Lexicon*, 416–17. Debrunner, "The Words λέγω, λόγος, ῥῆμα, λαλέω in the Greek World," 71–77; Mounce, *The Analytical Lexicon to the Greek New Testament*, 303.

Pre-Christian Logos Doctrine[3]

An Idea

The technical use of *logos* is usually traced to Heraclitus (Heracleitus) of Ephesus.[4] There is no evidence from the fragments of Heraclitus to suggest he personified the *logos* or saw it as a material or corporeal substance. Freeman is helpful in suggesting that when Heraclitus describes the *logos*, "it is as something knowable" and not as material.[5] Modern commentators of Heraclitus are not unanimous on the exact sense of his *logos* concept.[6] Heraclitus did not see his *logos* as a personal entity but as rational and impersonal, which is in all things such that it is possible to recognize it. Heraclitus does not suggest any reverence for the *logos* to take the place of any deity, though he calls his contemporaries to listen to it to realize the unity in all things. That an idea of a *logos* is explicated right at the beginning of Heraclitus' book (extant in fragments) may indicate its central or pivotal place in his thought process.[7] The longest surviving reference or fragment (fr.1), which, among others, forms a basis for understanding Heraclitus' *logos* doctrine, is curiously not found in Diogenes' account:

> Of the *Logos* which is as I describe it men always prove to be uncomprehending, both before they have heard it and when once they have heard it. For although all things happen according to this *Logos*, they [men] are like people of no experience, even when they experience such words and deeds as I explain, when I distinguish each thing according to its constitution (φύσιν) and

---

3. What is presented below is a summary. There is an extended treatment on this subject in my doctoral thesis, Gaisie, "The Logos as Nana (Ancestor)."

4. The primarily biographical source of Heraclitus is given by Diogenes Laertius in his *Lives and Knowledge of Eminent Philosophers*. Though the exact dating of Heraclitus is not unanimously fixed, he is thought to have been "at his prime" in the sixty-ninth Olympiad, around 500 BC. He is considered a pioneer in a few ways; Werner Jaeger saw Heraclitus with his *logos* concept as "the first man to approach the problem of philosophical thought with an eye to its social function." Jaeger, *The Theology of the Early Greek Philosophers*, 115. Also, Geoffrey Kirk, Heraclitus as "the first [Greek] thinker" to have indicated explicitly "a connexion between the apparent plurality of the phenomenal world and an underlying unity." Kirk, *Heraclitus*, 61 & 70.

5. Freeman, *Pre-Socratic Philosophers*, 116–17.

6. As "truth" (Jaeger, *The Theology of the Early Greek Philosophers*, 113), "reason" or "rationality" (Kahn, *The Art and Thought of Heraclitus*, 102), "measure" (Freeman, *The Pre- Socratic Philosophers*, 116).

7. It is likely the book by Heraclitus was still in existence by second century AD judging from the extensive references by Plutarch and later by Clement of Alexandria. Kahn, *The Art and Thought of Heraclitus*, 5 & 6.

declare how it is; but the rest of men fail to notice what they do after they wake up just as they forget what they do when asleep.[8]

Here Heraclitus apparently uses *logos* to represent an active entity that determines the cause of all things. Humans prove to be ignorant even before and after they have heard the *logos*. Elsewhere Heraclitus notes that the *logos* is not his own words ("listening not to me but to the Logos it is wise to agree [*homo-log-ein*] that all things are one")[9] and that it is common ("therefore it is necessary to follow the common . . . but although the Logos is common the many live as though they had a private understanding").[10]

If the view of modern scholars of the *logos* is that it is not just Heraclitus' discourse but something beyond is sustained, it remains a puzzle that the closest notable sources were apparently silent on such a concept from him. Aristotle, one of the closest notable sources for Heraclitus' teachings, in indicating that many connecting words or clauses and difficult punctuation affect the easy reading and delivery of a written composition, cites part of the opening sentence in fr.1 as an example.[11] Socrates applied some of Heraclitus's ideas as hinted by Plato.[12] About four decades separate the death of Heraclitus of Ephesus and the birth of Plato in Athens and at least this period had produced active followers of Heraclitus "vigorous" in supporting his teachings.[13] Almost all the references to Heraclitus and his teachings found in Plato are to the idea of things being in motion and none is to a *logos* idea.[14] Plato's idea of a *logos*, aside the general sense of "account," is partly in the sense of "reason" and in connection to the "forms"

---

8. Sextus Empiricus *Adv. Math.* VII, 132 with Kirk's translation quoted in Kirk, *Heraclitus*, 33. Emphasis added.

9. Hippolytus, *Refutatio* IX, 9, I quoted in Kirk, *Heraclitus*, 65, with Kirk's translation.

10. Sextus Empiricus *Adv. Math.* VII, 133 quoted in Kirk, *Heraclitus*, 57, with Kirk's translation. Kirk takes διὸ δεῖ ἕπεσθαι τῷ ξυνῷ as Heraclitus' words, but Kahn sees them as a comment by Sextus; Kahn, *The art and thought of Heraclitus*, 28 & 29.

11. Aristotle, *Rhetorica*, 1407b 11ff Book III.5 English translation by W. Rhys Roberts in Ross (ed.), *The Works of Aristotle*.

12. Plato, *Cratylus*, 401c in Burnet (ed.), *Platonis Opera*.

13. Heraclitus' demise is set between 480 B.C and 475 B.C at age sixty. The exact date of Plato's birth is unknown, but it is traditionally held to be the first year of the 88th Olympiad, 428–427 BC, and that of his death to the first year of the 108th, 348–347 BC at about eighty or eighty-one years. Taylor, *Plato*, 1. Plato, *Theaetetus*, 179d in Burnet, *Platonis Opera*.

14. Among others, in relation to something being "beautiful" (καλόν) Plato, *Greater Hippias*, 289a in Burnet, *Platonis Opera* and in relation to opposites and harmony *Symposium*, 187a. There is also a reference to Heraclitus' "sun," *Republic*, 6.498b. Plato, *Theaetetus*, 160d.

more as a "formula."[15] Apart from the senses of "speech" and "rational principle," in Aristotle's biological theories, *logos* appears in the several names or descriptions for the "soul."[16]

A Religio-Philosophical Construct

While neither Plato nor Aristotle explicitly commented on a *logos* idea of Heraclitus, if such an idea was important to Heraclitus the two notable figures might have been taken it for granted. It is in the ideas of the significant school of thought originating with Zeno of Citium, after both Plato and Aristotle and taking root in Athens, that a technical use of *logos* showed affinities to Heraclitus. Interestingly though, their technical conception of *logos* was not devoid of some of the earlier ideas of Plato and Aristotle. Stoicism developed into an influential philosophical system between third century BC and second century AD.[17] It became popular among politicians and leaders during the Graeco-Roman period.[18]

Beyond the rendering as "reason" or "word," *logos* among the early Stoics represented a concept in their exploration of the birth or origin and the development of the cosmos (universe).[19] The cosmogony and cosmology of the early Stoics were laid out analogous to the origin of animal life in their discourses on nature or physics (φυσικόν), one of the three parts of their philosophy.[20] Though in the area of physics, Heraclitus was an early influ-

---

15. Fine, "Knowledge and Logos in the Theaetetus," 366–97. Shields, "The Logos of 'Logos': "Theaetetus' 206c–210b," 107–24. Cross, "Logos and Forms in Plato," 433–50. Bluck, "Logos and Forms in Plato: A Reply to Professor Cross," 522–29. There is an instance of a link between *logos* and mind (νόος). Plato, *Republic*, 7.534b-c.

16. Aristotle, *Politics*, I.1 1253a and VII.XII 1332a. Aristotle, *Nicomachean Ethics*, I.XIII 1102a-b.

17. Zeno started his public teaching close to the end of the third century BC, possibly around 300 BC or earlier and though his followers were initially known as "Zenonians" they soon got their name from the place Zeno held his lectures, the Stoa. Those who attended Zeno's lectures at the open painted colonnade, according to Diogenes (*Lives*, VII, 5), were eventually called Στωικοὶ "those (men) of the Stoa or the Stoics" and that that the designation had initially been given to a group of poets who also frequented the same spot, which further popularized the title. Sellars, *Stoicism*, 5. Hahm, *The Origins of Stoic Cosmology*, xiii.

18. Notable among these were Lucius Annaeus Seneca (ca. 4 BC–AD 65) and emperor Marcus Aurelius (ca. AD 121–180). Asmis, "Seneca and His World," vii–xxvi (vii).

19. The "early Stoics" here refers primarily to the three successive personalities: Zeno, Cleanthes and Chrysippus.

20. The Stoics beginning, with Zeno, in most cases divided philosophy into three parts, physics, ethics, and logic. Diogenes, *Lives*, VII, 39.

ence possibly via Cleanthes' work on Heraclitus, in their cosmology the Stoics made use of prevailing ideas of particularly Plato and Aristotle.[21]

The Stoics held that there are two "principles" of the "whole (cosmos)," namely, active (ποιοῦν) and passive (πάσχον).[22] The principles are in contrast to the (four) elements (of fire, water, air, and earth) and are neither generated nor destructed and are incorporeal and formless.[23] While the passive principle ("matter"), is an "unqualified substance"[24] or one "without quality," the active principle is the *logos* in matter and is God (θεόν).[25] There is reference to a life of virtue which is one lived in accordance to nature, an individual's nature being part of the whole of nature.[26] Living such a life is to avoid any activity that the "common law" forbids and this "common law" is the right (ὀρθὸς) *logos* which "pervades all things" and is Zeus (Διί), the leader or guide of "all that is."[27]

The association of "common law" and *logos* is reminiscent of Heraclitus though he does not speak of a "common law" but a "common *logos*" (fr. 2). Heraclitus appealed for the common *logos* to be followed just as the common laws of a city, which is nourished by one divine law, should be followed (frr. 1, 2, 114). The Stoics may have built their understanding of a "common law and *logos*" from Heraclitus' idea of "one divine law" nourishing individual city laws.

Heraclitus did not connect the *logos* to Zeus but held the view that the "wise" is only one (ἕν) willing and unwilling to be named Zeus.[28] For the Stoics, Zeus is one of the many names addressed to *God* by virtue of him being "the cause of life."[29] Thus the name Zeus has to do with the life-giving

21. Sellars, *Stoicism*, 7. Hahm, *The Origins of Stoic Cosmology*, 200.

22. Diogenes, *Lives*, VII, 134.

23. An element, according to Diogenes, is "that from which particular things first come to be at their birth and into which they are finally resolved." Diogenes, *Lives*, VII, 136 and 134. The elements on the other hand are destroyed when things "resolve into fire" and are with form. Heraclitus held that "all things are composed of fire, and into fire they are again resolved." Diogenes, *Lives*, IX, 7.

24. Hahm, *The Origins of Stoic Cosmology*, 29.

25. Diogenes, *Lives*, VII, 134. In the above instance, *logos* as "reason" is inadequate, and it rather suggests a technical sense and hence its designation *God*. Hence the transliteration *logos* may suffice in such contexts when a technical sense is implied. Hahm, *The Origins of Stoic Cosmology*, 29.

26. Diogenes, *Lives*, VII, 87–88.

27. Diogenes, *Lives*, VII, 88.

28. Fr. 32. Cf. Clement, *Strom.*, V, 14; 115, 1. Diels, *Die Fragmente der Vorsokratiker*, 72.

29. These are given "according to its various powers". Diogenes, *Lives*, VII, 147. Hicks translates θεὸν as "the deity" here.

power of *God* who is as a "living being, immortal, rational" is, among others, the craftsman of the universe and the "father of all."[30] Cleanthes' well-known *Hymn to Zeus* gives a relational function between Zeus and the *logos*, which is twice referred to in this piece. The hymn combines the traditional belief of Zeus and Cleanthes' philosophical appropriation of him.[31] Zeus is hailed as the "most honored among immortals," "ever all-powerful," having many names, and as the "originator of nature" governing all things with law.[32] With his thunderbolt, Zeus directs the common (κοινὸν) *logos* "which moves through all things." Zeus has "joined all things into one (ἓν), the good with the bad that they have all become one everlasting" *logos*.[33] Thus *logos* in this hymn then, as Runia infers, "represents the cosmic activity of the all-pervading deity identified with Zeus."[34]

The work of *God* on "matter" (fire, water, air, and earth) is likened the process of generation or biological reproduction.[35] Just as the seed (σπέρμα) is surrounded (by fluid) so also *God*, as the "seminal [*spermatikos*] *logos*" of the things of the universe, "remains behind the moisture" to work on matter in creation.[36] The biological exploration was also explained to mean "matter" receiving the *spermatikos logoi* from Zeus as *God* for the ordering of the universe.[37] The "seminal *logos*" was responsible for the operation of nature as a self-moving "force."[38] The references to the plural *spermatikos logoi* suggests the strands of a single unit since the Stoics spoke of a (single) "seminal *logos*" as *God*.

The importance of the idea of *logos* in the system of the (early) Stoics may, arguably, be akin to Heraclitus, even though they differed in their applications. What is significant, however, is that though the Stoics' conceptual use of *logos* in their cosmology is possibly an (ingenious) appropriation of Aristotle and, as Halm has helpfully indicated, it was still distinct from the latter and not totally discontinuous with Heraclitus.

---

30. Diogenes, *Lives*, VII, 147; VII, 137.
31. Asmis, "Myth and Philosophy in Cleanthes' Hymn to Zeus," 413–29.
32. *SVF* 1.537.
33. *SVF* 1.537.
34. Runia, "Logos," 526.
35. Diogenes, *Lives*, VII, 136–37.
36. Diogenes, *Lives*, VII, 136.
37. Arnim, *SVF* 2.1074. Origen, *Contra Celsum* IV, 48. Origen adds that, "it is because of these myths and thousands of others like them that we are unwilling to call the supreme God Zeus, or even to use the name, or to call the sun Apollo and the moon Artemis." H. Chadwick's translation.
38. Diogenes, *Lives*, VII, 148 & 156.

Logos in Hellenistic Judaism: A Critical Synthesis

The Greek translation of the Hebrew Scriptures, the Septuagint (LXX), did open the Jewish world of thought and belief to that of the Greek.[39] In the first five books of the Hebrew Scriptures (Pentateuch), *logos* and *rhema* synonymously translate the Hebrew דָּבָר (*dabar*).[40] Outside the Pentateuch, *logos* dominates as a rendering for *dabar* except Joshua, Judges, and Ruth.[41] In Zechariah 1:13 both *logos* and *rhema* translate *dᵉbārîm* ("words") separately in the same verse. Both words also translate *'ēmer* and *millâh*.[42] God's word or message to his people, frequently captioned in the Hebrew דְּבַר־יְהוָה (*Dabar Yahweh*, "the Word of the LORD") is translated with both *rhema* and *logos*.[43] God's *dabar* brought the awareness of his immediacy and the demand for obedience in realizing his will in the lives of his covenant community.[44] The "word of the LORD" is occasionally

---

39. The term "Septuagint" (LXX) is used here primarily to denote the Greek translation(s) of the Hebrew Scriptures beginning with the Pentateuch and the eventual translation of the other texts and those originally composed in Greek. Jobes and Silva, *Invitation to the Septuagint*, 30–33. The legendary story by (pseudo-) Aristeas of the origin of the LXX (in Egypt) gives a mid-third century BC dating. Shutt, "Letter of Ariteas—A New Translation and Introduction," 7–34.

40. Apart from its basic meaning as "word(s)" (Genesis 44:18; Exodus 19:6, 8; and Deuteronomy 10:4) and frequently "the word of the LORD" (Genesis 15:1; Exodus 9:20; Numbers 15:31), *dabar* can also, among others, be rendered as "message" (Numbers 23:5; Deuteronomy 18:22), "thing" (Genesis 18:25; Deuteronomy 19:20), "matter" (Genesis 24:9; Deuteronomy 19:15), "plan" (Genesis 41:37), "thought" (Deuteronomy 15:9) and "commandment(s)" (Exodus 34:28). In Exodus 34:27, the two words *logos* and *rhema* are used to translate different instances of *debārîm*. The Hebrew *'ēmer* is rendered by *logos* and *rhema* in the sense of "word(s)" or "oracle" (Exodus 24:4 & 16, Deuteronomy 32:1). Brown, Driver, Briggs, *The B-D-B Hebrew and Greek Lexicon*; Muraoka, *A Greek-English lexicon of the Septuagint*.

41. Procksch, "The Word of God in the Old Testament," 91–100. Procksch notes the following statistics: Pentateuch (L=56x, R=147x); Joshua, Judges, and Ruth (L=26x, R=30x); Samuel, Kings, Ezra, Nehemiah, Esther (L=365x, R=200x); Job, Psalms, Proverbs, Ecclesiastes, Song of Solomon (L=159x, R=72x) but specifically in Job (L=19x, R=50x); the Prophets and Daniel (L=320x, R=40x); Wisdom, Judith, Sirach, Tobit, Baruch, and 1–4 Maccabees (L=221x, R=40x) [L=*logos*, R=*rhema*, x=times].

42. As "thing" (Daniel 2:5), "word(s)" (Psalms 19:14 [18:15]; 107:11 [106:11]; Proverbs 22:21; Isaiah 41:26); *Rhema* translates *'ēmer* as "answer" (Judges 5:29), "word(s)" (Job 6:10 & 25; Psalms 5:2; Hosea 6:5); *logos* and *rhema* respectively translate *millâh* in the senses of "word" in 2 Samuel 23:2 and "say" in Job 23:5.

43. Genesis 15:1; 2 Samuel 7:4; Deuteronomy 5:5; 2 Kings 7:1; 1 Kings 18:1; Jeremiah 1:2; Ezekiel 1:3; Hosea 1:1; Jonah 1:1.

44. Gerleman notes a comparison between *dabar* and *shêm* ["name"] (שֵׁם), that while the former is "an expression of the thoughts and will of God ['voluntary manifestation']" the latter "indicates God's presence in the world ['representative manifestation']." Gerleman, 331, דָּבָר.

personified in its creative nature,[45] and its personification akin to that of "wisdom" (חָכְמָה, *chokmâh*).[46]

The LXX opened the Jewish religious and thought world to the Hellenistic way of thinking, and in its application also opened the Hellenistic thought world to the Jewish way of thinking. The use of "pre-loaded" Greek words in the translation work influenced Jewish diaspora thinking.[47] The document Wisdom of Solomon in particular (originally composed in Greek) shows an awareness of contemporary Greek teachings. Already in this work, one finds the motive of the superiority of the "wisdom revealed by God" over that "attained by man's own powers."[48] It was in line with the sense of God's primacy and the consequential superiority of Jewish thought, that the intimations of the Greek idea of *logos* took on a distinctive outlook within the context of traditional Jewish thought and Greek philosophy. Philo of Alexandria epitomized this outlook in his works.[49]

By the time of Philo's birth in or before 20 BC, Alexandria (founded in 331 BC) was a significant cosmopolitan city under Roman governance and comprised indigenous Egyptians as well as Romans, Greeks, and Jews resulting in a conglomeration of both religious and intellectual ideas.[50] Philo of Alexandria did not so much present a treatise on a *logos* idea as employing it to express his viewpoints. He did not explicitly critique an old or contemporary form of *logos* as per his surviving works. Philo's use of the idea of *logos*, therefore, portrays an assumption of its knowledge among his immediate audiences. In that case he could unreservedly employ the term in his expositions on various subjects. This tendency was apparently in Philo's general attitude in his treatment of philosophers before him and "philosophic problems."[51] It is also possible that Philo's use of *logos* was in itself an attempt to explicate the

---

45. Psalm 33:4 & 6 [32:4 & 6]; Psalm 107:20 [106:20]; Psalm 147:15 [Psalm 147:4]; Isaiah 55:11.

46. Proverbs 3:19; 8:22–3,30; Job 28:12–28; Sirach 1:1, 4; 24:3,8,9; 39:17,28–31; 43:26; Wisdom of Solomon 7:26; 9:1–2; 18:15–16.

47. Walls, *The Missionary Movement in Christian History*, 26–42.

48. Wisdom of Solomon 6:22(23). Wolfson, *Philo* Vol. I, 24.

49. An older contemporary of Jesus Christ and the Apostle Paul, Philo *Alexandrinus* (of Alexandria) or *Judaeus* (the Jew) lived in Alexandria in Egypt between about 25 or 20 BC and AD 45 or 50. Scholer, "Foreword—An Introduction to Philo Judaeus of Alexandria," xi. Schwartz, "Philo, His Family, and His Times," 10. Philo belonged to a prominent Jewish family in Alexandria. His brother, Alexander the Alabarch, for example, served as a Roman leader of the Jews in Alexandria. With considerable wealth, Alexander is known to have contributed silver and gold in the decoration of the temple gates in Jerusalem. Josephus, *Jewish Antiquities* 18.259. Josephus, *Jewish Wars* 5.205.

50. Runia "Philo, Alexandrine and Jew," 1–2.

51. Wolfson, *Philo I*, 97–98.

right nature of the phenomenon or entity that had prominently featured in the Greek philosophical tradition as it reached him.

Josephus' impression of Philo was that of "a man eminent in all accounts ... and one not unskillful in philosophy."[52] Philo saw philosophy as given from heaven, which for him was "the fountain of all blessings [good], of all things which are really good."[53] Philo's view of Philosophy and his endeavor in such discipline served him in his expositions.[54] Though the influence of other religious and intellectual ideas on Philo in Alexandria is not denied, the two streams of his ancestral religion and the Greek philosophical tradition remain paramount.[55] Philo's thoughts as a Jew born and educated in Alexandria reflect the mutual interplay between Judaism (via the LXX) and Greek philosophical and religious tradition. Hence Philo's significance rests on his "Judaism in the biblical tradition and his Hellenism in the tradition of Greek philosophy" and it is impossible to set one over the other.[56]

The importance of the LXX to Diaspora Jews whose first language had become Greek was evidently exemplified in Philo of Alexandria. The LXX was a sourcebook of philosophy for Philo. The Pentateuch, for example, expressed a worthy philosophical view point with "philosophical and beautiful" commandments which are of benefit to humankind in correcting lives.[57] Philo considered Judaism as a religious philosophy (predating

---

52. Josephus, *Jewish Antiquities* 18.259.

53. *De Specialibus Legibus* III, 185–6.

54. Some modern commentators have found it difficult labelling him a philosopher or as one exhibiting the characteristics of an original philosopher. Goodenough, *An Introduction to Philo Judaeus*, 94–95. For Wolfson, Philo was a philosopher in his own right with the characteristics of "any great and original philosopher in the history of philosophy" who ushered in that kind of philosophy which held as paramount revelation (as "embodied in Scripture"). Wolfson, *Philo I*, 114; Wolfson, *Philo II*, 439–60. David Runia, however, sees Philo as a "philosophically orientated exegete" and, with respect to Greek philosophy, an eclectic "with a clear rationale and a strong leaning toward Platonism." Runia, "God the Creator as Demiurge in Philo of Alexandria," 44. The testimony of Josephus and Philo's own view of the discipline makes him, as Kenneth Schenck rightly notes, "fit in his own description of philosophy." Schenck, *A Brief Guide to Philo*, 5.

55. Runia, "Philo of Alexandria and the Timaeus of Plato," 446. For a discussion on Philo's attitude towards the polytheism, mythology and mysteries of Greek religion, see Wolfson, *Philo I*.

56. Runia, "The Theme of Flight and Exile in the Allegorical Thought-World of Philo of Alexandria," 23–24. The juxtaposing of the two streams of Jewish and Hellenistic thoughts in Philo is also discernible from his views of Moses and Plato, calling both "holy" at different times. *Quod Omnis Probus Liber Sit*, 13; *Quod Deus Sit Immutabilis*, 140.

57. *De Opificio Mundi*, 8; *De Vita Mosis*, II, 36.

traditional Greek philosophical thought) and thus his largely philosophical interpretation of the LXX.[58] It seems that Greek as a first language of Philo naturally endeared him to the LXX. Any knowledge of the Hebrew language might have been of domestic importance since his extant works were originally composed in Greek.[59] If, however, Hebrew was the language at home and the literary demands had given Greek the priority, it remains curious how his mother tongue then shaped his theological thinking.

To "philosophize" is the ability to see things exactly as they are.[60] This sight of exact things is directed to God to whom those accustomed to seeking knowledge could be granted such a vision or at least his image (εἰκόνα), the "sacred" or holy *logos*.[61] Thus, in whatever Greek philosophy presented as leading to an understanding of God and his relation to humans and humans' responsive relation to God and relation with one another, Philo saw no contradiction. There is invariably in Philo a Scriptural basis for affirming a truth or principle expressed in Greek philosophy and thus his philosophical vocabulary is determined by the "language of Scripture."[62] Yet a literal reading of the LXX in most cases proved a challenge for the philosophically oriented Philo. The allegorical method of interpretation enabled Philo to explicate what he considered the "underlying" meaning of Scripture texts.[63]

Philo's use of allegory was key in his *logos* theology.[64] His understanding of *logos* is rooted in his conception of God as one without "qualities, one, imperishable and unchangeable" such that God alone can say anything right about himself.[65] God's incomparable perfection and transcendence

---

58. According to Wolfson, the interpretation of "Scripture in terms of Greek philosophy" did not begin with Philo but with the translators of the LXX. Wolfson, *Philo I*, 94.

59. Wolfson, *Philo I*, 88–90. For Wolfson, Philo knew enough Hebrew to "read Scripture in the original and to check up the Greek translations whenever he found it necessary" and that some of Philo's interpretations use original Hebrew wording rather than the LXX, as well as his etymologies of proper Hebrew names.

60. *De Confusione Linguarum*, 97. Philo referred to the contemporary meeting of the Jews for "philosophical" discussions, where the "philosophy of their fathers," alongside the knowledge and theory of things concerning nature, were considered. *Mos.*, II, 216.

61. *Conf.*, 97. Mackie, "Seeing God In Philo of Alexandria: The Logos, The Powers, Or The Existent One?" 25–47.

62. Wolfson, *Philo I*, 97.

63. *De Abrahamo*, 200. *Contempl.*, 28. The Alexandrian Jewish philosopher Aristobulus is regarded as the first to apply the allegorical method of interpretation to the Pentateuch. Tripolitis, *Religions of the Hellenistic-Roman Age*, 78. Runia, "The Theme of Flight and Exile in the Allegorical Thought-World of Philo of Alexandria," 6.

64. *Quis Rerum Divinarum Heres Sit*, 118–19.

65. *Legum Allegoriae, I*, 51. *Leg. III*, 206.

warrants an intermediary in his contact with the created world. The *logos* is neither uncreated like God nor is created as humankind but is the middle of these (two) extremes as a hostage.[66] The intermediary role of the *logos* is explained in one instance with an allegorical interpretation of Numbers 16:48.[67] Here God graciously gave the role of standing between the created and the creator to the archangel and eldest *logos* by whom also mortals are not destroyed.[68] Thus, the function of the *logos* as an intermediary is a two-way activity; preventing humankind from totally being cut off from God and preventing God from despising his own work because of corruption by leading humanity to a state of confidence in God.

God's "right" *logos* is his first-born son, archangel and the eldest of angels, whom he has set as leader over his creation and who directs those yet to be designated "son of God."[69] The *logos* is both in the universe and in human nature.[70] In humans there is *logos* that resides in the mind (ἐνδιάθετος) and one that is uttered (προφορικός).[71] In relation to the universe there is *logos* which concerns the incorporeal or bodiless and archetypal *ideas* (ἰδεῶν) from which the intelligible world was put together and another which concerns things visible which are copies and representations of those *ideas* from which this sensible or perceptible world was produced.[72]

Harry Wolfson proposed a three-stage existence of Philo's *logos* understanding.[73] The *logos* as Philo's substitute for *nous* corresponds to a first stage of its existence as "the mind of God" and, in accordance to God's "absolute

---

66. *Her.*, 206.

67. In the literal text Aaron "stood between the dead and the living; and the plague was stopped."

68. *Her.*, 201–5.

69. *De Agricultura* 51. *Conf.*, 146. According to Philo, the *logos* beginning with many names is also addressed as (first) principle (ἀρχὴ), word, according to (the) image (of God) man, the one who sees, Israel, and "name of God." The "image of God" is his eldest or "ancient" *logos*. *Conf.*, 147. The divine *logos* is the "image of God," "manna," "high priest." *Fug.*, 101; *Her.*, 79; *Somn.*, I, 215. The *logos* is "second (δεύτερον) God" (the pattern after which mortal man was made). *QG*, II, 62. Greek text from Philo, *Questions and Answers on Genesis* (Translated from the Ancient Armenian Version of the Original Greek by Ralph Marcus) (Cambridge: Harvard University Press, 1953), 150 note n. The sense of the *logos* as second to God is found in *Leg.* II, 86.

70. *Mos.* II, 127.

71. *Mos.* II, 127.

72. *Mos.* II, 127. Elsewhere the divine *logos* is the location of the (intelligible) world which consists of the *ideas*, that is, the world which God "thought out" first as a model (παραδείγματι) from which the world as we (are able to) see it was formed. *Opif.*, 19–20. Cf. Wolfson, *Philo I*, 229.

73. Wolfson, *Philo I*, 231, 232 and 327. Wolfson, *The Philosophy of the Church Fathers*, 177. Also Tripolitis, *Religions of the Hellenistic-Roman Age*, 79.

simplicity" implies the *logos* is "something identical with the essence of God."⁷⁴ In its second stage of existence, Philo's *logos* is "as an incorporeal mind created by God," having its "existence outside of God's essence and containing within itself the intelligible world" wherein also consists "the myriads of ideas."⁷⁵ It is in its stage as having its own existence that the *logos* as the image of God is seen as the archetype of things created and hence as an instrument in creation.⁷⁶

God is not the instrument but rather the cause (of creation) who brought to existence the four elements (στοιχεῖα), the matter (material) from which it was composed, and his *logos* the instrument through which it was established.⁷⁷ Hence the instrument employed in creation is itself from God. As God's instrument, the *logos* is that "through which" the "whole world" was "framed" or made.⁷⁸ The sense of "instrument" does not necessarily imply a delegation of creation to the *logos* and this presents a difficulty in reconciling how the *logos*, which existed as the mind of God, is now, in its own existence, an instrument of God in creation. This seems to suggest two separate entities involved in creation and the Stoics could have no such difficulty since the *logos* was God. In attempt to clarify this difficulty in Philo's *logos* in relation to God, Runia asserts that the two are "conceptually, [and] not actually separable."⁷⁹ Conceptually Philo's *logos* could contain the archetypal *ideas*, which will then be at the service of God in the *actual* act of creation and thus gives a sense of "pattern" with the view of the *logos* as an "instrument."⁸⁰

After creation the *logos* assumes another role with things visible in its third stage of existence.⁸¹ The everlasting *logos* of the eternal God is the most secure and firm support of the whole (world) stretching from the center on

---

74. Wolfson, *Philo I*, 230–31. Wolfson sees an influence of Aristotle in this aspect since Aristotle had mentioned that "mind" (νοῦς) as a thinking or intellectual (νοητική) soul "is a place of forms". Aristotle, *De Anima* III, 4, 429a, 27–28.

75. *Sacr.*, 83. Wolfson, *Philo I*, 232.

76. *Leg. All.* III, 96.

77. *Cher.*, 125–7. Philo's discussions here reflect Aristotle's four causes and Wolfson uses that as a basis in arguing that Philo's use of the word ὄργανον is influenced by the sense in which Aristotle used it. Wolfson, *Philo I*, 264–66.

78. *Sacr.*, 8. *Deus*, 57. "Wisdom" also has this instrumental function in Philo: as that "through which" the whole [world] came into existence or being. *Fug.*, 109.

79. Runia, "Philo of Alexandria and the Timaeus of Plato," 370–1. Drummond deduced that Philo's *logos* is the "expressed Thought of God, which takes up into itself all inferior ideas, and combines into one force all the powers of nature." Drummond, *Philo Judaeus* II, 171.

80. Wolfson, *Philo I*, 270 & 274.

81. Wolfson, *Philo I*, 331.

to the limits of nature and bringing together (συνάγων) all the parts and binding them together.[82] This is so because the *logos* is the "indissoluble bond" of all the things in existence that the father has created.[83] In consequence then, since the divine *logos* is in position as a boundary between the (four) elements it ensures that none will be dissolved by or into each other and hence "the world is held in perpetual existence."[84] In this way, in Wolfson's analysis, Philo's *logos* is *immanent* in the world.[85]

God, who made the universe and is above all things, "willed" nature to prolong its existence, the species (of plants) being perpetual and sharing in "eternal existence."[86] The "perpetuity of the species" is due to the presence of "seminal essences," which contain in them "hidden and imperceptible" the *logoi* of the universe.[87] The *logos* is the "seminal substance (essence) of existing things."[88] However, unlike the "seminal *logos*" of the Stoics, identified as *God*, Mind (Reason), Fate, and Zeus, which is "the active principle in the primary fire, as the creative principle in the world," the *logos* in Philo is not God. Ultimately it is God who placed down (in the earth) "the seeds (σπέρματα) and roots of all things" and is the cause of the springing up of the greatest of all plants, namely, the universe.[89] The immanent *logos* ensures the "perpetuity of the species" accordingly as God has willed it in nature.

Wolfson's three stages of the existence of Philo's *logos* conception clarify its nature and function in relation to earlier ideas. Philo critically borrows and revises Plato's theory of *ideas* and at the same time takes hold of a key word ὄργανον from Aristotle and uses it in describing the (conceptual) function of the *logos* which differs from that perceived by the Stoics. The *logos* conception was vital in Philo's unequivocal theocentric outlook in its function in the creation and sustenance of the universe. Ultimately, Philo's

---

82. *Plant.*, 8–9.

83. *Plant.*, 9.

84. *Plant.*, 10. Wolfson, *Philo I*, 332. Philo also spoke of the "altogether leader of heaven and the world," God, who without struggle made the vast world long ago and now forever holds it (συνέχων) never to cease (God does this by the instrumentality of "divine *logos*"). *Sacr.*, 40.

85. Wolfson, *Philo I*, 332–43. As immanent in the world, the *logos* is responsible for "three definite laws of nature," namely, "the law of opposites," "the law of the harmony of opposites" and "the law of the perpetuity of the species."

86. *Opif.*, 42 and 44.

87. *Opif.*, 43.

88. *Quaestiones in Exodum*, II, 68 in Harris, *Fragments of Philo Judaeus*, 67. Also Marcus, *Philo Supplement II—Questions and Answers On Exodus*, 116. *Her.*, 119.

89. *Plant.*, 48.

JESUS CHRIST AS LOGOS (INCARNATE)

logos presents itself as "that aspect or part of the divine [mind] that stands in relation to created reality [as an instrument and sustaining agent]."[90]

The conceptual use of *wisdom* and *logos* appear interchangeable or "equivalent" in Philo especially in his thoughts of *logos* as "mind" of God, and yet in some instances are quite distinct from each other. Philo does not indicate the *logos* is *wisdom* or vice-versa. He refers to the "supreme divine *logos*" as "the fountain of *wisdom*."[91] The varied uses of *logos* in the LXX could have resulted in his frequent use of *logos*.[92] The grammatical gender of both *logos* and *wisdom*, being masculine and feminine respectively, seems to have posed a challenge for Philo in his interchangeable use of the terms.[93]

Philo's familiarity with Greek philosophers such as Heraclitus and the Stoics in their technical use of the term *logos* presents a possibility of their influence in his choice of the term in his conception of the relation between the Transcendent and the world. Philo's *logos* theology is at once a critique and an apparent appraisal of traditional and contemporary ideas. The *logos* in Philo's conceptual framework is not the ultimate reality: God is always above the *logos* which functions as his instrument. As an *immanent* principle, however, the function of Philo's *logos* as the "reasoning principle" or mind of the universe is not different from what the Stoics held.[94] Philo's significance is merely as an apologetic attempt to harmonize Greek and Jewish ideas. His is an example of the nature of the challenge of expressing ideas originating from the Jewish traditional world of thought in the Greek world. Hence, he represents a kind of a pre-Christian missionary to the Greek thought world. Philo's example presents a paradigm in expressing biblical ideas in various worlds of thought, which seems inevitable in Christianity. The centrality of Scripture in his primary mission best known to himself, is uncompromising and Wolfson's summary in this regard is apt: Philo's "purpose was not only to interpret Scripture in terms of Greek philosophy but also to interpret

---

90. Runia, "Philo of Alexandria and the Timaeus of Plato," 274–75.

91. *Fug.*, 97. In an allegorical interpretation of Leviticus 21:11, Philo indicates the high priest is not man but the "word of God" and that the *logos* of God has God as the father and *wisdom* the mother "by whom the universe came into existence." *Fug.*, 108–9.

92. For example, as that by which God made the heavens (Psalm 33:6); the term is used in reference to the "ten commandments" and hence the sense that *logos* is revealed in the Law (Exodus 34:27 & 28; Deuteronomy 10:4). Wolfson, *Philo I*, 254.

93. Philo indicates that the name of Rebecca's father, Bethuel (Genesis 28:2), is *wisdom* but when translated is called "daughter of God" and that in addition to being "daughter of God," *wisdom* is both "male and father" in its function. *Fug.*, 50–52.

94. Goodenough, *An Introduction to Philo Judaeus*, 108.

philosophy in terms of Scripture."[95] Such tendency did not end with Philo but found its way in quite a few Hellenistic Christians after him.[96]

The development of the idea of *logos* in the Greek thought world demonstrates how a conceived idea may not be of interest to immediate successors but could be taken up and explored further, quite distinct but not totally discontinuous with the identified source. The personalities highlighted above, and their respective followers shared in the tradition of the Greek thought world. They responded to a reality which the word *logos* seemed to appropriately convey. The expressions given this reality were not the same and this is partly due to the availability of developed ideas. The diverse exploration of the pre-Christian conception of *logos* as a response to the sense of a perceived transcendent, but immanent, reality was akin to its exploration when Jesus Christ was eventually seen as the incarnate Logos in early Graeco-Roman Christian thought. The growth in the understanding of Jesus as the Logos "become flesh" when assessed within the conversion process of Hellenistic traditional thought, correlates to the depth of his penetration in that world.

Christian Apprehension of Logos

By the end of the third century AD Logos Christology had gone through three distinctive but continuous modes of presentation and application in Graeco-Roman Christianity.[97] Seen from the perspective of the three stages of conversion process, the *missionary* stage presents a *suggestive* Logos Christology while the *convert* and *refiguration* stages respectively present an *elucidative* and *innovative* modes.

---

95. Wolfson, *Philo I*, 254. In the assessment of Runia on the link between Philo and Plato's *Timaeus*, for example, the former's "conception of the Logos records the result of important modifications to the doctrines of the *Timaeus*, but at the same time the Platonic dialogue has left its indelible mark on the way that the role and functions of the divine Logos are conceived." Runia, *Philo of Alexandria*, 376.

96. He could still qualify as a "proto-Christian." Runia, "'Where, Tell Me, Is the Jew . . . ?': Basil, Philo and Isidore of Pelusium," 185. However, from a (Hellenistic) Christian standpoint, he represents a fundamental stage of the impact of Jewish thought on traditional Hellenistic (philosophical) understanding. His was a loyalty to an ancestral faith, viz. Judaism, under an unavoidable weight of Hellenistic philosophical thought. In many respects he still was an outsider to the Hellenistic heritage since his primary allegiance was to the faith of his ancestors.

97. The first three centuries gave a firm rooting of the understanding and application of Jesus Christ as Logos (incarnate) such that by the fourth century it had been clearly laid out with its consequential impact on later Christian understandings. Pelikan, *Jesus through the Centuries: His Place in the History of Culture*, 58.

The shared understandings of Jesus Christ that the author of the Fourth Gospel (John) sought to express in the image of *logos* are found in other images in the Pauline corpus. Paul and John as missionaries to the Hellenistic world were suggestive in their reference to pre-Christian Hellenistic concepts in relation to Jesus Christ. A reason for this is that their immediate respective purposes in writing could not accommodate an explication of the full implications of their association of certain *pre-loaded* pre-Christian ideas or concepts to Jesus Christ. Yet the model of the exposition of these early missionaries served as examples to first generation Hellenistic Christian converts. The Septuagint (LXX) as Scripture was their primary "sourcebook" and the way to interpret the LXX in the light of Jesus Christ was cut out for these converts in the writings of the New Testament. With respect to Logos Christology, the converts would eventually work out to a second level the significance of Jesus Christ the Logos (incarnate) to the shared Hellenistic ancestral world of thought. They all had a methodological justification in the New Testament writings.

Second generation Hellenistic Christians such as Origen represent yet another creative stage in the interplay between Christian understanding and Hellenistic traditional ideas: a stage in the conversion process in which Hellenistic ideas were *refigurated* in the light of Christian revelation and understanding. Considering the fact that at the core of "Origen's theological vision" is the "figure of Jesus Christ depicted in the canonical Gospels" and the "central role" of the concept of *logos* in his thought, the creative *refiguration* enterprise of Origen had its root in his Logos Christology.[98] Origen was familiar with the works of Philo,[99] but the extent of any direct influence remains debatable.[100]

The Missionary Stage—A Suggestive Mode

There is no explicit reference to Jesus as Logos in the extant works of Apostle Paul. Paul's cosmic descriptions and functions of Christ are reminiscent of a *logos* understanding.[101] Paul's use of *wisdom* in relation to Christ is reminis-

98. Kannengiesser, "Christology," 73; O'Leary, "Logos," 142.

99. Clement of Alexandria remains "the first Church father" to explicitly reference him by name (as "the Pythagorean Philo"). *Strom.* I, XV; II, XIX. Runia, *Philo in Early Christian Literature*, 7 & 132.

100. Wolfson, for example, asserted that in John the "pre-existent Messiah [of Paul] is identified with the Logos of Philo's philosophy." Wolfson, *The Philosophy of the Church Fathers*, 178–82. Chadwick, "St. Paul and Philo of Alexandria," 286–307.

101. Paul shows a familiarity with prevailing Hellenistic cosmological conceptions as is evident, for example, in his use of the technical word πλήρωμα (*pleroma*)

cent of Philo's *logos* and *wisdom* descriptions and his language in expressing Jesus' pre-existence and earthly ministry demonstrates knowledge of a *wisdom* tradition.[102] This is the closest we get in identifying any explicit Logos Christology in Paul.

Paul's language in describing Christ's nature and role or function in creation (Colossians 1:13–17; 2 Corinthians 4:4) alludes to and is reminiscent of both the function of *wisdom* and *logos* in the LXX (Psalm 33:6; Proverbs 3:19; 8:22–23; Sirach 1:1, 4; 43:26; Wisdom of Solomon 7:26; 9:1–2) and in Philo.[103] In Philo, the *logos* is firstborn, God's image, instrument, binds together all parts of nature.[104] A key word συνέστηκεν ("hold together") in connection with the sense of the latter characteristic in Philo is, however, not used directly with reference to the *logos* as Paul does with respect to "all things" being held together in Christ.[105] In fact, Philo does mention of the body being "held up (or sustained)" (συνέστηκε) and quickened by the "providence of God" as well as God "holding together" (συνέχων) "the whole" (world) such that it is insoluble.[106] If one maintains that God actually does things in the created world through or by the agency of the *logos* in Philo's understanding, then in both instances above, the agency of the *logos* may be assumed and hence an indirect use of the terms with respect to the *logos*.

---

in relation to Jesus Christ. Martin, "Pleroma," 887–89; Delling, "Πλήρωμα," 298–305.

102. Dunn, *Christology in the Making*, 176–96. Among the key Pauline texts that show the influence of the *wisdom* tradition, it is Colossians 1:15–20 that also portrays a knowledge of *logos* speculation. 1 Corinthians 1:24,30; 8:6; 10:4; Romans 10:6–8 and Colossians 1:15–20.

103. The thoughts expressed in Colossians 1:15–20 are taken here as expressive of Paul's view of Jesus Christ. For a discussion on the issue of Pauline authorship see Lamp, "Wisdom in Col 1:15–20: Contribution and Significance," 45–53. In a significant and an apparent careful use of words, Paul acknowledges that there may be "so-called gods in heaven or upon the earth" as indeed there are "many gods and many lords" (1 Corinthians 8:5). However, for Paul and his Christian audience there is "one God the Father, from whom are all things and for whom we [are / exist] and one Lord Jesus Christ, through whom are all things and through whom we [are / exist]" (1 Corinthians 8:6). Thus, while "all things" ultimately come from God the Father, it is through the one Lord Jesus Christ that "all things" become. This source and agent or instrument statement are reminiscent of the agency or instrumentality of *logos* and *wisdom* expressed in the LXX and Philo of Alexandria. If Paul, in this instance, is informed by such language in the LXX or Philo then the "one Lord Jesus" is *wisdom* or *logos*.

104. *Somn.*, 215.; *Conf.*, 146.; *Agr.*, 51; *Conf.*, 97.; *Conf.*, 147. ; *Fug.*, 101; *Immut.*, 57; *Fug.*, 109; *Plant.*, 9–10; *Sacr.*, 40. Wolfson, *Philo I*, 331–32.

105. The other forms of the verb συνίστημι in Paul are in the sense of "commend" (2 Corinthians 6:4; 10:18; 12:11; Romans 16:1), "prove" (2 Corinthians 7:11) and "demonstrate" (Romans 3:5; 5:8; Galatians 2:18).

106. *Her.*, 23 and 58.

JESUS CHRIST AS LOGOS (INCARNATE)

Paul may have shared in "a common stock of Hellenistic Jewish tradition" with Philo and differing only in application and their respective *hermeneutical keys* or historical points of reference.[107] There was a synonymous use of *logos* and *wisdom* at the time of the authoring of the Wisdom of Solomon (9:1–2). Philo's works points to the technical use of *logos* and *wisdom* to refer to a principal agent in the creation and sustenance of the world or universe by the transcendent God, by the beginning of first century A.D. If Paul was familiar with a *logos* doctrine, it remains curious he did not explicitly indicate a Logos Christology. He would have agreed with the author of the Fourth Gospel on all the functions given to the *logos* and also that Jesus Christ is the *logos* incarnate.[108] Even though there is no explicit reference in the Pauline documents that Jesus is God's Wisdom "become flesh" or *incarnate*, such an understanding is not foreign to Paul's Christology. Paul and John both agree in their cosmic source and function of Jesus Christ, which early Christianity explored from the images of *wisdom* and *logos*.

As a missionary, Paul possibly chose not to employ the term *logos* in communicating his cosmological understanding of Jesus Christ for reasons best known to him. It is unlikely that Paul was unaware of the concept and its implications considering his encounter with some Stoics in Acts 17:18, 28. This is not an attempt to "fit in" a *logos* doctrine in Paul, but his eventual projected association with the Stoics and their teaching makes it difficult to conceive of his ignorance of a *logos* concept.[109] Paul's immediate missionary concerns apparently did not warrant a Logos Christology. The explicit starting point of the Christological exploration of the *logos* concept is indeed the Fourth Gospel, an early missionary document to the Greek thinking world.[110]

---

107. Chadwick, "St. Paul and Philo of Alexandria," 290. Fundamentally both were convinced of God's primacy. It is possible Paul's rabbinic association could have curtailed any advance leaning to Hellenistic Judaism. Paul's eventual interest in not only Hellenistic Jews and Gentile proselytes, but also Gentiles or Greeks who had no association whatsoever with Jewish faith and thought came by the "revelation of Jesus Christ" (Galatians 1:12). Philo on his part was keen to present Moses as the true philosopher. Thus, while Philo apparently penetrates the Hellenistic world of thought via Moses, Paul does so in Jesus Christ.

108. Origen, for instance, indicates that Paul and John say the same thing in Colossians 1:16 and John 1:1–2. *Peri Archon* I. VII, 1; II. IX, 4; IV. I, 30.

109. On the relation between Paul and the Stoics, see, among others, Grant, "St. Paul and Stoicism," 268–81.

110. Though in terms of chronology the connection between Christ and "Logos of God" is first encountered in Revelation 19:13. At any rate, the reference in Revelation is to the "exalted" Christ, that is, post-resurrection, whereas in the Prologue of the Fourth Gospel we are presented with the state of affairs prior to the "heavenly" descent.

The Foundational Logos Christology in John's Prologue

The Fourth Gospel is unique among the other canonical Gospel narratives.[111] There is no explicit reference to its author. It is (partly) associated with one of the twelve disciples of Jesus, John, as author or provider of an earlier version.[112] The date of the authorship of the Gospel is usually taken to be between the latter part of the first century and the first two decades of the second.[113] Westcott's summary on the issues of authorship, circumstance, time and place of the Fourth Gospel is satisfactory:

> The fourth Gospel... was written after the other three [Synoptic Gospels], in Asia, at the request of the Christian churches there, as a summary of the oral teaching of St. John upon the life of Christ, to meet a want which had grown up in the Church at the close of the Apostolic age.[114]

That "want which had grown up in the Church" is subject to inconclusive investigations.[115] The Gospel was primarily addressed to a composite Greek speaking Christian and non-Christian Jewish community including Jewish proselytes which eventually served as a missionary document to the wider Graeco-Roman world of thought.

The structure of the Fourth Gospel is broadly in three parts; it has an introduction normally called the Prologue (1:1–18), a body (1:19—20:21) and a conclusion or an epilogue (21:1-25). Commentators have diversely subdivided the body into either two, three or four divisions.[116] The first eighteen verses of the first chapter stand as a unit on its own, though not disconnected from the entire narrative.[117] As a kind of introduction, some scholars hold it to be "an overture" or "a foyer."[118] Rudolf Bultmann highlighted that as an overture, the reader is led "out of the commonplace into a

---

111. Westcott, *The Gospel according to St. John*, lxxvii–lxxxiv.

112. Barrett, *The Gospel according to St. John*. Brown, *The Gospel according to John I-XII*, xxxiv–xxxix. Brown, *The Gospel and Epistles of John*, 9–11.

113. Barrett, *The Gospel according to St. John*, 28; Brown, *The Gospel according to John I-XII*, lxxxiii & lxxxvi. Achtemeier et al., *Introducing the New Testament*, 204.

114. Westcott, *The Gospel according to St. John*, xxxvi.

115. Wind, "Destination and Purpose of the Gospel of John," 26–29.

116. Dodd, *The Interpretation of the Fourth Gospel*, 289–90; Lightfoot, *St. John's Gospel*, 11; Barrett, *The Gospel according to St. John*, 11; Brown, *The Gospel according to John I-XII*, cxxxviii; Ngewa, "Commentary on the Gospel of John."

117. For example, Polland, "Cosmology and the Prologue of the Fourth Gospel," 147–53; Ridderbos, "The Structure and Scope of the Prologue to the Gospel of John," 180–201.

118. Bowen, "The Fourth Gospel Dramatic Material," 298; Köstenberger, *John*, 19.

new and strange world of sounds and figures," and "particular motifs from the action that is now to be unfolded" are singled out.[119] In other words, one needs the rest of the content of the Gospel account to fully understand the import of the use of such concepts as "light," "life," and "truth."

In its relative brevity and hint on the origin or source of fundamental ideas, such as "life" and "light," the Prologue exhibits a philosophical outlook.[120] The Prologue shows a cosmological trait, presenting fundamental ideas about the origin and impact of Jesus Christ in relation to the world (cosmos) and humans who are the chief subjects of the cosmos.[121] Discussions on the origin and literary structure of the Prologue are generally skewed towards a rhythmic piece of a Hebrew (Semitic) origin.[122] My interest is in the Prologue's presentation of a Logos Christology: the eventual association of Jesus Christ with the idea or concept of *logos*. I have therefore not paid much attention to the structure of the Prologue itself.[123]

A technical sense of the use of *logos* in the Fourth Gospel is found only in the Prologue. Here it is employed as representing a living reality and it occurs four times: three times in 1:1 and once in 1:14.[124] The Logos was in the beginning with or towards God and was God.[125] Through or by the Logos "all

119. Bultmann, *The Gospel of John*, 13.

120. Lightfoot, *St. John's Gospel*, 11. For Bernard, the thesis of the Gospel account can be found in the last verse of the Prologue (1:18) that "Jesus is the Revealer of God" and for which the Prologue is "a philosophical explanation." Bernard, *A Critical and Exegetical Commentary*, cxxxviii.

121. Some notable early orthodox Christian writers also make the philosophical and cosmological character of the Prologue evident from their application of its content. Wiles, *The Spiritual*, 98–101. In the case of John 1:9, Wiles has shown how the interpretations of Cyril [of Alexandria] and Theodore [of Mopsuestia] demonstrate respectively a leaning on its "philosophical significance" and on the "incarnational reference." There is an ambiguity with respect to what the phrase "was coming into the world" (ἐρχόμενον εἰς τὸν κόσμος) refers to, either to the "light" or "every man (human)". Cyril interprets with respect to the "man" while Theodore does so with respect to the "light."

122. Bernard, *A Critical and Exegetical Commentary*, cxlv. Lightfoot, *St. John's Gospel*, 78; Barrett, *The Gospel according to St. John*, 150; Brown, *The Gospel and Epistles of John*, 21.

123. Kruse, *John*, 63–75.

124. In the rest of the narrative, the word occurs in the sense of "saying" (4:37) or "word" (8:37; 12:38; 14:24; 15:25; 18:9; "word of God" (10:35); God's "word" (17:17)). In 12:48 ῥήματα "words" also occurs with λόγος "word" or "saying." Greek texts from the United Bible Societies 4th Edition (UBS4) Greek 1993.

125. E. C. Colwell's helpful grammatical approach to rightly observe, "the Word was God" rather than "the Word was divine." Colwell, "A Definite Rule for the Use of the Article in the Greek New Testament," 21. 1:1c is also linked to 20:28 affirming the Logos, Jesus Christ as God. Lovelady, "The Logos Concept: A Critical Monograph on

things" were made (ἐγένετο). In the Logos was life and the life was the light of humans.[126] The Logos is the true light that, according to two variant readings, either enlightens every human coming into the world,[127] or was coming into the world as the one who enlightens every human.[128] The Logos was in the world and yet the world (which was made through or by him) did not know him. The Logos came into his own who did not receive him. The author intimates that as many as received the Logos and believed in his name, the Logos gave them "power" or "authority" to be children of God.

The Logos became (ἐγένετο) "flesh" and dwelt among us. Herein lies the foundation, or rather a crystallization of (foundational) Logos Christology. It is in the manifestation of the Logos in the "flesh" that his glory as the one begotten from the Father was seen. The Logos in his manifestation is full of grace and truth. A contrast between the Logos and Moses is highlighted: while the Law (νόμος) was given (ἐδόθη) through Moses, grace and truth came (ἐγένετο) through Jesus Christ, the Logos (incarnate). The Prologue is climaxed with the ultimate function of the manifestation of the Logos with his position with the Father restated. Indeed, the author indicates, no one has seen God, but the one begotten Son [of God], who is in the "bosom" of the Father, has "declared" or "interpreted" him. The Logos thus became flesh to reveal the unseen Father.

In the Prologue there is no explicit indication that "the Logos is Jesus Christ" or that "Jesus Christ is the Logos become flesh."[129] "Jesus Christ" is mentioned only in relation to Moses (1:17). An indirect connection, however, is made in 1:14 and 1:17 in seeing Jesus Christ as the Logos become flesh. The Logos became flesh "full of grace and truth" (1:14) and while "the Law was given through Moses" "grace and truth came through Jesus Christ" (1:17). Jesus Christ, then, is the "Logos become flesh" "full of grace and truth."[130]

John 1:1 (Abridged by the Author)," 15–24. Brown renders πρὸς τὸν θεὸν "in God's presence" so as to "capture the ambiguity" of the Greek phrase. Brown, *The Gospel according to John I–XII*, 3–5.

126. The association of *life* and *light* with the Logos is taken up variously in the rest of the narrative.

127. ἦν τὸ φῶς τὸ ἀληθινὸν ὃ φωτίζει πάντα ἄνθρωπον ἐρχόμενον εἰς τὸν κόσμον.

128. ἦν τὸ φῶς τὸ ἀληθινόν, ὃ φωτίζει πάντα ἄνθρωπον, ἐρχόμενον εἰς τὸν κόσμον.

129. Cf. Bernard, *A Critical and Exegetical Commentary*, cxxxviii.

130. Though one could agree with Ridderbos, for example, that the "real subject of the Prologue is Jesus Christ" and not "the revelation of the Logos" per se, it really does not amount to anything significant when one considers the later application of Jesus Christ as the Logos incarnate, where Jesus Christ and Logos are almost synonymous. Ridderbos, "The Structure and Scope of the Prologue to the Gospel of John," 191.

On the Source of John's Logos Concept

The idea of the source or origin of the *logos* motif in the Prologue may not have been an issue for the immediate recipients of the Gospel narrative.[131] The possibility of the author having a Hebrew or Aramaic origin or background and whose fundamental purpose points to a presentation of the reality of Jesus Christ to a predominantly Hellenistic audience attests to a diverse nature of the issue of origin.[132]

The opening phrase ἐν ἀρχῇ ("in the beginning") and the association of *logos* with God (θεὸς) and creation (1:1, 3) are reminiscent of the opening phrase and the "speaking" of God in the creation narrative of Genesis 1:1-2 *et al.*) in the LXX. Both works begin with the phrase ἐν ἀρχῇ. The author of the Fourth Gospel apparently alludes to the same historical reference indicated in Genesis 1:1, a beginning when creation was enacted (cf. 1 John 1:1). In Genesis, when God "created" (ἐποίησεν) "heaven and earth" it was by or through his spoken (εἶπεν) "word" that resulted in the coming into being (or existence) of all things. In Genesis, God's *word* is (certainly) not treated as an entity.[133] In the Prologue, the author's interest in *logos* is in connection with (the manifestation and impact of) Jesus of Nazareth. The attempt is apparently to elucidate the pre-existence of Jesus the Christ who is identified as the Logos (incarnate). This can be seen as a combination of two contemporary shared understandings in early Christianity, namely, the "λόγος statement" referring "to the Word [*logos*] of God which is spoken in the event of Jesus of Nazareth" and that of his

---

131. Cf. Brown, *The Gospel according to John I-XII*, 519-24.

132. The authorship by one of the disciples of Jesus, John, does suggest one who read or heard the Scriptures in his mother-tongue Aramaic and Hebrew possibly, heard Jesus in Aramaic, but communicated what Jesus said and what he came to see Jesus to be in a second language, Greek.

133. The primary understanding is that God "said" and things "became" (ἐγένετο) as directed (1:3 *et al.*). The word ἐγένετο occurs twenty times in Genesis 1. Apart from its association with "evening" and "morning" (twelve times), it occurs eight times following the directive of God (εἶπεν ὁ θεός) (1:3, 6, 9, 11, 14-15, 20, 24, 29-30). Swete (ed.), *The Old Testament in Greek according to the Septuagint—Vol. I Genesis—IV Kings*, 1. The phrase "Word of God" is, however, absent in the Prologue, but apparently implied in the distinct and yet undivided association of Logos with God. The phrase is not found in Genesis either but in later reflections on the event of creation (Proverbs 33:6 *et al.*) so that what is said about the "Word" in John 1:1ff cannot solely rely on Genesis 1. Masanobu Endō has pursued the argument that the description of the identity and the role assigned to the *logos* in the Prologue were on the "basis of the exegetical tradition of the Genesis creation account" and thus the Prologue itself "presented a Christological interpretation of the Genesis creation account." Endō, *Creation and Christology*, 251.

"pre-existence," that "leads necessarily" to the identification of Jesus with "the Word [Logos] of the divine Creator."[134]

The combination of two earlier understandings that led to the (explicit) identification of Jesus as the Logos does highlight the fact that there were Christological developments that led to an explicit Logos Christology expressed in the Prologue. At this stage the "Word of God" was not only "spoken in the event of Jesus of Nazareth" but the "the event of Jesus" was the reality of the "Word of God" in "flesh." In other words, the "λόγος statement" became a Logos Christology in the Fourth Gospel.

The Law is associated with *wisdom* in the book of Sirach where as the "book of the covenant of the Most High God" it overflows with wisdom (24:23 & 25). In the Prologue, Jesus Christ is contrasted with Moses and hence the Law or Torah (John 1:17). This comparison apparently sought to demonstrate the pre-eminence of the Logos Jesus Christ over Moses and the Law.[135] Though the connections between *logos* and wisdom and that of Torah and wisdom were expressed in the Jewish Scriptures, it does not necessarily suggest that the author of the Fourth Gospel had Torah for Logos.[136] The Law, represented by Moses, is apparently on a different plane from the Logos, made manifest in Jesus Christ and whose intimate connection with the Father gives a higher benevolence than the Law ("full of grace and truth").

The Talmud, with its oral foundation and the period of leading Rabbis, offers some clues to first-century views of the Law and wisdom.[137] A saying of Rabbi Akiba (AD 50–135) indicates the Law was "the precious instrument [given to Israel] by which the world was created."[138] In Genesis Rabba 1:1, Torah takes the voice of *wisdom* in Proverbs 8:30, with the emphasis on the word *āmōwn* (primarily interpreted as "workman") and is taken to mean

---

134. Kittel, "Word and Speech in the New Testament," 131.

135. Brown notes the contrast between the Law and Jesus Christ "may indicate that, in part, the Johannine doctrine of the Word [Logos] was formulated as a Christian answer to Jewish speculation on the Law [John 5:39]." Brown, *The Gospel according to John I–XII*, 523.

136. Contrary to David A. Reed who, in his pursuance of the Semitic background of the Fourth Gospel, suggests a reading of Torah for Logos in the Prologue. Reed, "How Semitic Was John? Rethinking the Hellenistic Background to John 1:1," 709–26.

137. Comprising the Mishna (compiled reflections and applications of the (oral) Torah) and Gemara ("commentary on the Mishna"). Williams, *Talmudic Judaism and Christianity*, 13–19.

138. Aboth 3:15 in Danby, *The Mishnah*, 452. Also in the Babylonian Talmud, the Torah is one of the seven pre-world creations with Proverbs 8:22 as proof text. The other created things prior to creation of the world are Repentance, the Garden of Eden, Gehenna, the Throne of Glory, the Temple, and the name of the Messiah. *Pesachim* 54a; *Nedarim* 39b.

"beginning."¹³⁹ Thus, the arguments for the pre-existence and instrumentality of the Torah are taken from texts that originally related to *wisdom*.

The characteristics of the Logos in the Prologue are reminiscent of *sophia* (*wisdom*) in the LXX, particularly Proverbs 8:22, 23, 27–30. The association of life (ζωὴ) with the Logos in John 1:4 echoes Proverbs 8:35 ("whoever finds" *wisdom* "finds life" and "obtains favour with the Lord").¹⁴⁰ Rendel Harris found such apparent parallels between statements about the Logos in the Prologue and those about Wisdom in the LXX particularly in Proverbs 8 as a basis for his thesis that "a more Jewish and less metaphysical Sophia-doctrine" lies behind the Logos conception of the Prologue.¹⁴¹ Harris argued that the transition from *wisdom* to *logos*, which indeed occurred in the Christology of the early church, can be traced to the ninth chapter of the Wisdom of Solomon, itself "a pendant to" Proverbs 8 in Harris' estimation.¹⁴² In the Wisdom of Solomon 9:1 & 2, the Lord by his *logos* and *wisdom*, respectively, "made (ποιήσας) all things" and "formed (κατασκευάσας) humankind." The link between the Logos and "all things" in the Prologue is, however, with ἐγένετο ("came into being") and not "made" or "formed." In Psalm 33:6, "the *logos* of the Lord" established the heavens and Sirach 43:26 talks of the Lord's *logos* which "holds together" (σύγκειται) all things. The verb ἐγένετο is not associated with *logos* or *wisdom* with respect to "all things" coming to existence in the LXX apart from its association with what "God said" in Genesis 1.

Though a "Sophia-doctrine" possibly informed the Prologue, and indeed the entire narrative, it cannot solely account for its *logos* intimation.¹⁴³ The words σοφία and σοφός (and their associated forms) are ironically strikingly absent in the entire Gospel narrative. Whether this was a deliberate plan or not is still subject to conjecture and though the challenge of "a feminine figure" associated with *sophia* is not in doubt, the issue is not merely a gender conundrum.¹⁴⁴ The existence of a Sophia Christology

---

139. *Bereshith Rabbah* 1:1 in Freedman et al., *Midrash Rabbah Translated Into English with Notes, Glossary, and Indices—Volume 1*.

140. Luke 2:52 where "Jesus increased in wisdom (σοφίᾳ) and in stature, and in grace or favor (χάριτι) with God and humans."

141. Harris, *The Origin of the Prologue to St John's Gospel*, 57.

142. Harris, *The Origin of the Prologue*, 15 & 23.

143. O'Collins, *Christology*, 39–40.

144. Hengel, *Studies In Early Christology*, 73–117; Brown, *An Introduction to New Testament Christology*, 205–10. Grant, *Jesus After the Gospels*, 32–33. James Scott, for example, has pursued the view "that the Logos in the Prologue is none other than Sophia" (p. 125) and that the author consciously uses the title Logos to resolve the gender issue. This remains a possibility. Scott, *Sophia and the Johannine Jesus*.

vis-à-vis the "*logos* statement" leading eventually to a Logos Christology cannot be totally ruled out. It would have obviously taken some time for the early Christian community to affirm Jesus as the Wisdom of God and not just as the mouthpiece of God's *wisdom*. Since Jesus is not seen to have explicitly indicated that he is either *wisdom* or *logos* of God, it is difficult to ascertain which one came first in the thoughts of the early disciples.[145] In the New Testament, the association of *wisdom* with Jesus Christ was on the primary conviction that he was at once obedient to the "word (=will) of God" and delivered that as well. Hence, seen as the one through whom God is speaking or has spoken his *logos*, Jesus then would rightly be held as *wisdom* from or of God.[146]

The Aramaic word *memra,* which translates the Greek *logos,* is also employed dynamically in the Targum as is *logos* in the LXX.[147] Though the extant Targumim are relatively of a later date than the Fourth Gospel, there is the possibility of reliance on a shared earlier tradition known to the author of the Prologue. Vries has shown some of the "linguistic connections" between the Prologue and extant Targumim on creation, the themes of life and light, the coming of and accepting the *memra*, the name of the *memra*, the glory of and seeing the glory of the *memra*.[148] The Targumim background to the Prologue is in no wise exclusive.[149] The *logos* in the Prologue is not qualified in the possessive sense as *memra* is in most cases (as "*memra* of God"). If the Apostle John, who was familiar with the idea of the "*memra* of God,"[150] is granted as author and the work itself was originally composed in Greek,[151] then the Logos Christology of the Prologue becomes a Hebrew and Aramaic conception expressed in Greek.[152]

The extent of the influence of Philo of Alexandria's technical use of *logos* on the Prologue is not clear. Wolfson suggested that the doctrine of

145. Harris, *The Origin of The Prologue*, 10–11.

146. Proverbs 28:7; Jeremiah 8:9. Matthew 12:42; 1 Corinthians 1:24.

147. Boyarin, "The Gospel of the Memra: Jewish Binitarianism and the Prologue to John," 255.

148. Vries, "The Targumim as Background of the Prologue of the Gospel according to John," 7.

149. Vries, "The Targumim as Background," 22 & 24.

150. So, Vries: "we may rightly assume that John, the son of Zebedee, had been familiar with the Hebrew Bible Testament in the form of a targum since he was a child. Later he probably also became acquainted with written forms of the targumim." Vries, "The Targumim as Background," 24.

151. In our present concern, this has little to do with whether the Gospel was originally composed in Aramaic and then translated into Greek. The level is not so much literary as mental. Burrows, "The Original Language of the Gospel of John."

152. Brown, *The Gospel according to John I-XII*, 524:

JESUS CHRIST AS LOGOS (INCARNATE)

Incarnation is only an "addition" to and "not exactly a departure from Philo": "in its ultimate formulation the Incarnation became a new stage in the history of the Philonic Logos—a Logos made immanent in a man after its having been immanent in the world."[153] While traces of Pauline thoughts in the Prologue are not denied, Wolfson's assertion that the author of the Prologue attempts a rewrite of Paul's thoughts in the language of Philo is rather mechanistic.[154] The growth of Christian thought in the continual appreciation of the universal scope and significance of the ministry of Jesus, was proportional to the increase in Gentile Christians. Thus, the presence of an early tradition of the Church concerning Jesus and the *logos* of God ("*logos* statement") leading to a crystallized expression of Logos Christology in the Prologue should not be overlooked.[155] In essence, the starting point for the author of the Gospel is the impact of Jesus of Nazareth out of which the reality of his pre-existence and cosmological function then becomes apparent.

As primarily a missionary to the Greek world of thought, the author of the Fourth Gospel may have been fully aware of the technical use of *logos* in both the Jewish and Graeco-Roman senses. The choice of *logos*, though a subjective preference, may also give insight to the possible immediate issue or problem that the author sought to address or resolve. To counter any alleged insufficient association of Jesus Christ with the *logos*, the author may have set out to show the full humanity and superiority of the Logos in flesh without any contradiction to his divine nature or essence. There might even have been no immediate problem but rather, among other things, a reiteration of a shared known fact or truth of the reality of the life of Jesus Christ as the Logos in flesh, *interpreting* God to humanity (John 1:18). The impact of the use of *logos*, however, on immediate recipients and subsequent generations in their working out of a distinctive Christian identity is quite another thing from what influenced the missionary. The missionary's immediate concerns are invariably outlived especially if the concept has such a history as the *logos* in traditional thought. Logos Christology in the Fourth Gospel may be exhaustive, but as far as the wider Graeco-Roman context is concerned it remains introductory and hence foundational.[156]

---

153. Wolfson, *The Philosophy of the Church Fathers*, viii.

154. Wolfson, *The Philosophy of the Church Fathers*, 178–82.

155. It is a helpful insistence when G. Kittel indicates that it is not in the "speculative sense" of "a mythical or theological idea" that the Evangelist asserts the pre-existence of the Logos, who is Christ. According to Kittel, it was rather out of "the historical process of seeing and hearing Jesus in faith" and from which the pre-existence also gains significance. Kittel, "Word and Speech in the New Testament," 130–31.

156. The relation between Jesus, the Logos incarnate, and pre-incarnation figures such as Abraham and Moses are hinted at in the Gospel narrative. The Logos is "before

The Convert Stage—A Clarificatory or Elucidative Mode

By the end of the first century, non-Jewish Christians were in the majority in the Graeco-Roman world.[157] Following the New Testament writers, the application of the idea of Jesus the Logos (incarnate) is not as profound among the Apostolic Fathers[158] as it is in the subsequent group of writers from the middle of the second century, the Apologists.[159] The Shepherd of Hermas, for example, speaks of the "Son of God" as being old and older than all of God's creatures or creation by virtue of he being "the Father's counsellor in his creation."[160] Ignatius of Antioch submitted that "God manifested Himself through Jesus Christ His Son" who is "His *logos* that proceeded from silence."[161] The word *logos* is in the sense of "word" and used possessively as God's *word*: Jesus Christ is God's Logos.

The Apologists were mostly first generation converts, having had previous religious or philosophical affiliations before turning to Jesus Christ. Though Christianity had been recognized as a distinct religious movement from Judaism after the first century, Christians were still a minority.[162] Christianity did not enjoy the recognition from the Roman state that Judaism had.[163] Belonging to a relatively minority group, Graeco-Roman Chris-

---

Abraham became" (8:58). There is no claim that Abraham and Moses are "Christians before Christ" (as Justin Martyr proclaimed). By their obedience to God in faith they were indeed believers of his Christ who was to come into the world (8:56). What then is the significance of Jesus the Logos incarnate for those not sharing in the Jewish heritage? The Fourth Gospel did not set out to fully address this, but certainly did set the path for its exploration.

157. Latourette, *A History of the Expansion Christianity (Volume I)*, 74. Justin, writing in about the middle of the second century, also indicated that there were more Gentile Christians who were also more true than those from among the Jews and Samaritans; Justin Martyr, *First Apology*, LIII.

158. Collectively the writings of Barnabas, Clement of Rome, Hermas, Ignatius of Antioch, Polycarp of Smyrna, *Epistle to Diognetus*, the *Fragments of Papias* and Quadratus. Holmes (ed.), *The Apostolic Fathers*, 1 & 3.

159. Quasten, *Patrology, Volume I*, 188.

160. The Shepherd of Hermas, *Parable* 9.12 in Holmes, *The Apostolic Fathers*; translation of Lightfoot and Harmer. The agency of the "Son of God" in creation is expressed here in a manner which echoes John 1:3 and Colossians 1:15–16.

161. Ignatius, *Magnesians* VIII in Holmes (ed.), *The Apostolic Fathers*. Reading λόγος . . . and not λόγος ἀΐδιος οὐκ. . . . The Loeb Classical Library (tr. Lake), 204 n.1.

162. Bruce, *The Spreading Flame*, 164; Frend, *The Rise of Christianity*, 165; Markus, *Christianity in the Roman World*, 15.

163. Daniélou, *A History of Early Christian Doctrine before the Council of Nicaea Vol. Two*, 8. Also Bediako, *Theology and Identity*, 18.

JESUS CHRIST AS LOGOS (INCARNATE)

tians in general were "constantly in danger of denunciation."[164] Essentially the Apologists' responses to the charges on the legal status of Christianity did not only give them a missionary outlet, but also created the avenue for the working out and expression of a "Christian self-awareness and identity in the context of Graeco-Roman tradition."[165]

The "Apologies" of the Apologists are "the missionary literature of the second century," presenting the message of the gospel while working out a Christian identity as members of Graeco-Roman world.[166] The Apologists were primarily converts, who, sharing in the Graeco-Roman cultural heritage, engaged their tradition with the gospel message. Their Christian efforts were primarily built on New Testament writers, the Apostolic Fathers and the LXX as sourcebook. Thus, in terms turning the ideas and sentiments of the Graeco-Roman world towards Christ it is helpful to consider their thoughts as constituting a *convert* stage.

Among the Apologists, the ambiguity of the word *logos* in the senses of "word" and "reason" and its close association with "wisdom" were exploited. Jesus Christ the Logos incarnate, accordingly, is not only the "Word of God" but the "Reason of God" and expressing God's Wisdom. Aloys Grillmeier's summary of the ways or aspects in which the Logos conception of Christ were applied, though briefly stated, can serve as a helpful background. Grillmeier notes five aspects:

> 1. Cosmological (as creative Word). 2. Noetic (as the basis of knowledge and truth). 3. Moral (as the basis and embodiment of the moral law). 4. Psychological (as the original form of thought (*verbum mentis*)). 5. Saving-historical (as Word of revelation and mediator of salvation).[167]

---

164. Daniélou, *Gospel Message*, 8. Nero's deliberate attack on the Christians after the conflagration in Rome in A.D. 64 is regarded as the first attempt of Roman officials to take actions against the Christians. John Stambaugh, Balch, *The Social World of the First Christians*, 61. Also Bruce, *The Spreading Flame*, 165.

165. Quasten's "three objectives" of the Apologists in their response to critics all point to a missionary outlook: 1. Refuting the calumnies concerning Church being "peril to the State" and showing the contrary. 2. Exposing the "absurdities and immoralities of paganism and the myths of its divinity" and showing the uniqueness of the Christian view of God and the universe. 3. Challenging the views of (ancestral and contemporary) philosophers and demonstrating Christianity's possession of "absolute truth." Quasten, *Patrology* Vol. I, 186–87. On the issue of identity, see Bediako, *Theology and Identity*, 15–63; Rhee, *Early Christian Literature*.

166. Daniélou, *Gospel Message*, 9.

167. Grillmeier, *Christ in Christian Tradition*, 109.

While the cosmological and saving-historical aspects proved suitable for interpreting the work of God in humanity in general ("in the creation of the world and the incarnation of the Logos"), the noetic and psychological aspects helped in "solving the relationship of Logos and Father within God."[168] Grillmeier helpfully observes further that in the Christian opposition to Hellenism, the cosmological, noetic and moral aspects were highlighted and the psychological aspect came into play in transferring to God the human distinction of unexpressed thought (*logos endiathetos*) and that expressed (*logos prophorikos*).[169] The emphasis of these aspects was certainly distinct among the Apologists.

Logos Christology in its *convert* stage was essentially aimed at clarifying the nature and significance of Jesus Christ in relation to Graeco-Roman traditional religio-cultural thought. The exploitation of the dual sense of *logos* as "word" and "reason" among Graeco-Roman converts was founded on the *personal* impact of the reality of Jesus Christ on their respective lives resulting in a consequential conviction and affirmation of his universal significance. The groundwork of recognizing Jesus Christ as the Logos had been laid in the Prologue of the Fourth Gospel and in pursuance of its implications these converts "expounded and developed" this conviction invariably with the instrument of a critical appraisal of Graeco-Roman traditional thought (as part of their heritage).[170] Certainly the task of clarifying the Christian claim of the incarnation of the Logos was not taken for granted and Justin in particular offered an in-depth explanation of the activity of the Logos in the Hellenistic traditional past in his application of Jesus Christ as the Spermatikos Logos. Logos Christology offered these Hellenistic converts both the remedy for the "quest" for integrating "Hellenistic self-consciousness" and "Christian commitment."[171] In the process of this Christian vocational task is the taking of the Christian faith to the very heart of Graeco-Roman thought world.

It is in the above perspective that we can further appreciate the place of Logos Christology in the vocation of figures such as Justin Martyr (c. AD

---

168. Grillmeier, *Christ in Christian Tradition*, 109.

169. Grillmeier, *Christ in Christian Tradition*, 110.

170. Aimé Puech's thoughts on the foundation of the Prologue of the Fourth Gospel of the Logos Christology of the Apologists remain significant: "For the doctrine of the Word in particular, they (the Apologists) could not have expounded and developed it without the aid of philosophy; but they found it in the Prologue of the Fourth Gospel . . . (The decisive step was made before them by the mysterious author of the Prologue) it is highly doubtful whether any of them would have dared to take such a bold initiative on his own." Puech, *Les Apologistes grecs du deuxième siècle de notre ère*, vi. Bediako's translation in Bediako, *Theology and Identity*, 168 n.111.

171. Bediako, *Theology and Identity*, 146.

100–165), Tatian (AD 120–180), Athenagoras of Athens (AD 133–190), Irenaeus of Lyons (AD 135–200), and Tertullian (c. AD 160–225).[172] In Tatian's *Oratio ad Graecos* (*Oration to the Greeks*), the name "Jesus" and the title "Christ" are absent, but the use of "Logos" alludes to the personality of Jesus Christ.[173] He states the incarnation thus, "God has been born in the form of man."[174] Though this may allude more to the language of the Epistle to the Philippians 2:6 & 7, Tatian also shows a familiarity with the Prologue of the Fourth Gospel. He indicates God is "without beginning" but initiated "the beginning" which is the "power of the Logos."[175] The Logos "springs forth by the will of God's singleness."[176] Tatian then endeavors to clarify that the Logos did not "spring forth" in "vain" or "emptiness," but rather by "becoming the firstborn work of the Father" and is thus "the beginning of the world." The Logos and the father are united in essence, with the Logos "partitioned" (μερισθὲν) rather than "cut off" (ἀποτμηθὲν) in relation to the father.[177] It is the Logos, also as the "light of God," who gives order to disordered matter and thus in imitating the Logos, Tatian brings "order" to the apparent "disorder" in the Graeco-Roman traditional thought.[178]

Tatian portrays an insufficient application of Logos Christology in the *Oration*, and that may have contributed to his largely unsympathetic

172. There is no precise dating for Irenaeus' life. The consensus, however, is before the middle of the second century to the end or beginning of the third century. Robert Grant put Irenaeus' birth to AD 140, Grant, *Irenaeus of Lyons*, 2.

173. Bediako, *Theology and Identity*, 65–66. His exploits in the *Oratio ad Graecos* [Πρὸς Ἕλληνας] (*Oration to the Greeks*), reveals much of his endeavor as a Christian apologist and his later association with Encratism should not overshadow that. Bediako, *Theology and Identity*, 88; Hunt, *Christianity in the Second Century*, 177. His view of Greek philosophy, as a student of Justin Martyr, was essentially negative. Quasten, *Patrology* Vol. I, 197 & 220. He refers to his teacher as the "most admirable [or wonderful] Justin" (*Oratio ad Graecos*, XVIII). Tatian was born in the "land of the Assyrians" (*Ad Graec.*, XLII). Having done away with "arrogance of Romans and the idle talk of Athenians, and all their ill-connected opinions," he embraced this philosophy of the Christians (XXXV). Tatian indicates that Christians, both rich and poor, "pursue philosophy" and he even speaks of "all men willing to pursue our philosophy" (XXXII). Christian women also "pursue philosophy (knowledge)" and are "wise" (XXXIII).

174. Tatian, *Ad Graec.* XXI.

175. Tatian, *Ad Graec.* IV–V.

176. Tatian, *Ad Graec.* V.

177. To further illustrate his point, Tatian gives the example of a single fire which gives rise to many others without it lessening its light (Justin, *Dialogue with Trypho*, 61). Similarly, Tatian insists, the Logos "having come forth from the power of the Father" (προελθὼν ἐκ τῆς τοῦ Πατρὸς δυνάμεως), "does not deprive the begetter of the power of rational speech" [Molly Whittaker's translation in Hunt, *Christianity in the Second Century*, 69] (οὐκ ἄλογον πεποίηκε τὸν γεγεννηκότα) (*Ad Graec.* V).

178. Tatian, *Ad Graec.* V and XVIII.

view of the Hellenistic traditional thought world.[179] He shows knowledge of the Prologue of the Fourth Gospel and it is most likely he was familiar with his teacher Justin's exposition of Logos Christology. However, there is not much in Tatian's Logos Christology beyond its exploration in creation and the relation between the transcendent God and creation as expressed in the Prologue.[180] It could well be that Greek and Latin were Tatian's second languages, being of Syrian origin. He shows no sense of attachment to the Graeco-Roman intellectual past. Tatian's effort to demonstrate the anteriority, and hence the superiority, of "barbaric [Christian] philosophy" over against Graeco-Roman philosophy, could have been explored with a conscious Logos Christology.[181] There is a connection between a developed Logos Christology and a critical affirmation of the Graeco-Roman past as I argue below, especially in the case Justin.

The primary concerns of Athenagoras' *Embassy for the Christians* is a call for a just and reasonable treatment of Christians by refuting charges levelled against them, and also to prove, by way of exposition of their fundamental beliefs and teachings, their innocence.[182] It is in this context that one gleans Athenagoras' appropriation and application of a Logos Christology. When Christians were charged as "atheist," Athenagoras insisted that Christians shared the belief in the one uncreated God with the poets and philosophers of Roman-Roman antiquity.[183] However, while the poets and philosophers spoke from their own human efforts the prophets (of the LXX) were inspired by God's Spirit, taught about things of God from God himself.[184] Athenagoras argues that if Plato is not an atheist for conceiving God as one (ἕνα), uncreated and the "maker of the universe," then neither are the Christians who "acknowledge and firmly hold" God, "who by the Logos has framed" all things and by his Spirit holds (συνέχεται) them in being.[185] The Logos is God's Son.[186] Athenagoras clarifies this understanding of *sonship*

---

179. From the fragments of Tatian's other notable work in Syrian Christianity, the *Diatessaron* (a harmony of the Synoptic Gospels and the Fourth Gospel), the genealogy of Jesus begins with the Prologue of the Fourth Gospel (1:1–5). Surprisingly, though, that "the Logos became flesh" (1:14) is missing in this section but taken up later in the narrative (III:54).

180. Hunt, for example, is prepared to see it as an echo of, and refinement of what we find in the Fourth Gospel. Hunt, *Christianity in the Second Century*, 127–28.

181. Tatian, *Ad Graec.* VII.

182. Athenagoras, *Leg.* I & XXXVII.

183. *Leg.* V, IV & VI.

184. *Leg.* IV and VII.

185. *Leg.* VI.

186. *Leg.* X.

indicating that God having a Son is not in the biological manner of the poets. The "Son of God" in Christian understanding is the Logos of the father "in idea (ἰδέᾳ) and in operation."[187] The "Son of God" is not first to be born or produced (γέννημα) in the sense of being brought into "existence," but God, "being eternal mind" and possessing reason (λογικὸς), always had the Logos in himself and brought forth the Logos as the "idea and active force" of all material things to give them life and order.[188]

While the names "Jesus," "Christ," and "Jesus Christ" are absent in the entire treatise and there is no explicit connection between the Logos and Jesus, the person of Jesus Christ unequivocally lies behind Athenagoras' use of Logos. As a Christian convert, Athenagoras could appeal to what he found to be intimations from the Graeco-Roman past concerning the one God in defending Christian beliefs and refuting false charges against Christians. Athenagoras does not comment on the role of the Logos of God among the poets and philosophers of Graeco-Roman antiquity, though he acknowledges a feeling after God among some of them. The same is true of the Syrian theologian Theophilus of Antioch in his *Apologia ad Autolycum* (Apology to Autolycus) in which also a Logos Christology is given in the context rebuttal of (false) charges against Christians.[189]

Logos, as one of the several attributes of God, depicts his sovereignty.[190] God, as Physician, heals through his Logos and Wisdom the "blindness of the soul and the hardness of heart."[191] Logos and Wisdom came forth from God who made (ἐποίησεν) all things from nothing and had his internal Logos in his "inner parts" (σπλάγχνοις).[192] The Logos was at God's service (ὑπουργὸν) as things were brought forth and through him

---

187. *Leg.* X.

188. *Leg.* X. These thoughts concerning the Logos, the Son of God, according to Athenagoras, agree with what the "prophetic Spirit" says in Proverbs 8:22 (LXX). The voice in the original text is that of Wisdom but in this context Athenagoras makes it the voice of the Logos. The son is also the "mind" of God. *Leg.* XXIV.

189. Theophilus was bishop of the church of Antioch (in Syria) (the "sixth from the apostles"). Eusebius, *Historia Ecclesiastica (HE)*, IV.20 and 24. English translation by Arthur C. McGiffert in Schaff and Wace, *A Select Library of Nicene and Post-Nicene Fathers of the Christian Church, Second Series, Volume I*. Rogers, *Theophilus of Antioch*, 3.

190. *Ad Autol.* I.3. The attributes of "mind," "wisdom," and even "spirit," respectively, depict God's "intention or thought" (φρόνησιν), "work" (γέννημα) and "breath" (ἀναπνοὴν).

191. *Ad Autol.* I.7.

192. *Ad Autol.* II.10. Robert Grant has suggested the Greek mythology of the generation of Athena as a background to Theophilus' use of the term *splanchna* in relation to the Logos and God. Grant, *Jesus after the Gospels*, 73–74.

all things have been made.¹⁹³ The Logos is also the "Spirit of God," and "the power of the Most High" who "descended" upon the prophets (in the LXX) and spoke through them concerning the creation of the world.¹⁹⁴ The Logos was God's command for "light" in the Genesis (1:1–5) creation account.¹⁹⁵ The three days in the creation account constitute types of "triad" or "Trinity" (Τριάδος): of God, of his Logos, and of his Wisdom.¹⁹⁶ Consequently, the directive ("let us") prior to the creation of man was from God to his own Logos and Wisdom.¹⁹⁷ The Logos was God's representative in the interaction between God and Adam (and Eve) in Paradise after the disobedience.¹⁹⁸ Theophilus also sought to clarify the nature and meaning of the Christian understanding that the Logos is God's son and this was in the context of his discussion of God's interaction with Adam after the disobedience. God who always had his Logos within (ἐνδιάθετον) his heart, uttered (προφορικὸν) his Logos as "first-born of all creation" and not by any mythical intercourse (συνουσίας).¹⁹⁹

Logos Christology was employed not only in Christian refutations against external charges, but it needed clarification against (unorthodox) Christian misunderstandings. The Logos is explicitly and emphatically Jesus Christ in Irenaeus (Bishop) of Lyons, as he set out to refute the teachings certain Christian individuals ("falsely called Gnostics") who had "departed far and wide from the truth (*veritate*)."²⁰⁰ Among some of the Gnostic

---

193. *Ad Autol.* II.10.

194. *Ad Autol.* II.10.

195. *Ad Autol.* II.13.

196. *Ad Autol.* II.15. There is no consensus as to this being a first reference to the doctrine of Trinity. J. N. D. Kelly translates 'Triad' and adds that Theophilus "was the first to apply the term 'triad' to the Godhead," and thus a primal reference to the doctrine of Trinity. Kelly, *Early Christian Doctrines*, 102. Rick Rogers, however, disputes this sense of "triad" in Theophilus and maintains, with his view of *logos* and *wisdom* as God's agents, that Theophilus' use of the term is "rather arbitrary, referring to the first three days of creation as a type for the work of God and his two hands." Rogers, *Theophilus of Antioch*, 79. Grant, *Gods and the One God*, 156.

197. *Ad Autol.* II.18.

198. *Ad Autol.* II.22. Grant, "The Bible of Theophilus of Antioch," 173–96.

199. *Ad Autol.* II.22. Theophilus is regarded as the first Christian writer to apply the terms ἐνδιάθετον and προφορικὸν to the Logos. Philo also applied the terms to the *logos*. Cf. Grant, *Jesus after the Gospels*, 76.

200. Irenaeus, *Adversus Haereses*, I.XI, 1; II.XXX, 9. Gnostics as an umbrella term represents several individuals and respective followers who apparently synthesized, both Christian and non-Christian, contemporary Graeco-Roman religious and philosophical ideas. Wolfson, *Philosophy of the Church Fathers*, 503; Grant, *Irenaeus of Lyons*, 8–14; Burkitt, *Church and Gnosis*, 8; Rudolph, *Gnosis*, 149 and 308–9; Pearson, *Gnosticism, Judaism, and Egyptian Christianity*.

systems, *Logos* is one of the beings or entities found between the "unborn father" (*innato Patre*) identified with God, and the angels.[201] While *Logos* sprang from Nous, Anthropos and Ecclesia sprang from *Logos* and Zoe in the Gnostic system. Irenaeus points out that such views are a misinterpretation of the Fourth Gospel and especially the Prologue in which certain (key) words such as "life," "grace," "monogenes," and "truth" are used in relation to Jesus Christ the Logos incarnate.[202] In the Gnostic system "Jesus," "Christ" and "Logos" are considered as distinct entities.[203] Jesus is called "Saviour," "Christ," and patronymically "Logos."[204] In this sense the Logos did not become flesh in Jesus for the Gnostics.

Irenaeus insists the Logos could not proceed from Nous and though in human terms one can speak of *logos* as proceeding from *nous*, with regard to God this is not possible since God is "all Nous and all Logos."[205] Irenaeus appeals to the Prologue to show that the "one Jesus Christ . . . the Son of God . . . [is] He that came to His own . . . that became flesh and dwelt among us."[206] John 1:14 is a key text for Irenaeus that the Logos (indeed) is Jesus Christ. Since the implication of the Gnostic system is that the *Logos* did not become flesh but rather the Saviour who came after the *Logos*, Irenaeus restates correctively, "Jesus who suffered for us, and who dwelt (κατασκηνώσας) among us, is Himself the Word [Logos] of God."[207] The Logos is the Son of God and God's salvation (*salutare*) (for humankind).[208] The Incarnation of the Logos of God was primarily for the salvation of humankind, a fact reiterated against the Gnostics. Irenaeus insists, "all things had appeared new" with the Logos (*Verbo*) "setting in order anew having come (in) the flesh, so he might bring

---

201. Such as Valentinus (*Adv.*, I.I, 1–2; I.II, 5–6), Basilides (*Adv.*, I.XXIV, 3), and the Barbelo-Gnostics (*Adv.*, I.XXIX, 1–4). Cf. Irenaeus, *Adv.*, I.XXIV, 3. *Logos* (in italics) represent that of the Gnostics.

202. *Adv.* I.I, 1. Cf. I.XI, 1. Also II.XVII, 9; *Adv.* I.I, 1. Cf. *Adv.* I.VIII, 5. In fact, Irenaeus later indicates that (the apostle) John wrote the Fourth Gospel in response to the false teaching of Cerinthus (*Adv.* III.XI, 1), a contemporary of John (*Adv.* III.III, 4), who held Gnostic views (*Adv.* I.XXVI, 1).

203. Cf. *Adv.* III.XVI, 1.

204. *Adv.* I.II, 6.

205. Adv. II.XIII, 1ff. Cf. *Adv.* II.XXVIII, 5. In this other context, Irenaeus indicates "God both speaks exactly what He thinks, and thinks exactly what He speaks. For His thought is Logos, and Logos is Mind, and Mind comprehending all things is the Father Himself. Also *Adv.* II.XXVIII. 4.

206. *Adv.* I.IX, 2. English translation by Alexander Roberts in Roberts and Donaldson (eds.), *The Ante-Nicene Fathers, Translations of the Writings of the Fathers down to A.D. 325—Volume I*.

207. *Adv.* I.IX, 2. *Adv.* III.IX, 3.

208. *Adv.* III.IX, 1. *Adv.* III.VIII, 2. *Adv.* II.XXX, 9.

back to God, humanity which had departed from God."²⁰⁹ Thus, knowledge of the Son is the knowledge of salvation.²¹⁰

The Logos, prior to the Incarnation, was active in the lives of the patriarchs before Moses with whom the Logos "was in conversation, according to (his) divine nature and glory."²¹¹ Thus, the activity of the Logos of God in the lives of those in the Hebrew Scriptures (LXX) in leading them in pursuing the will of God is acknowledged. However, there is no explicit indication of the activity of the Logos in the lives of those outside the LXX even though the Logos "is always present with the human race, united to and mingled with His own creation, according to the Father's pleasure."²¹² The immediate concern of Irenaeus in refuting the claims of those falsely known as Gnostics may not have given him the opportunity to express his view on the activity of the Logos in pre-Christian Graeco-Roman thought as one finds with Justin Martyr.

In a similar fashion, Tertullian's application of the understanding of Jesus Christ as the Logos is an explication from the "rule of faith" (*regula fidei*) against (heretic) Gnostic speculations of principally Marcion and Valentinus.²¹³ Valentinus had maintained a complete separation of his Aeons, to which also belonged *Logos*, from the Father in such a way that there is no association between the Father and the *Logos*.²¹⁴ However, for those following the "rule of truth," "only the Son knows the Father" (Matthew 11:27).²¹⁵ The Logos (*Sermo*) of God has received (*accepit*) the special or unique (*proprie*) designation of Son and has "heard and seen all things with the Father" and following the Father's command has accomplished (through his Incarnation), not his own will but, the Father's will.²¹⁶ The Son or Logos has always been with the Father, he is an inseparable prolation (*prolatum*) from the Father.²¹⁷ Writing in Latin, Tertullian explains that the Father, Son and Holy Spirit are

---

209. *Adv.* III.X, 2.

210. *Adv.* III.X, 2.; *Adv.* III.XVI, 2. Cf. III.XVI, 6. In becoming flesh, the Logos "passed through every stage of life, restoring to all community (*communionem*) with God." *Adv.* III.XVIII, 7.

211. *Adv.* III.XI, 8; *Adv.* IV.V, 3; *Adv.* IV.IX, 7.

212. *Adv.* III.XVI, 6; *Adv.* IV.VI, 7.

213. Tertullian observed that heresies stemmed from (Hellenistic) philosophy, indicating also that Marcion and Valentinus, respectively, followed Platonism and Stoicism and hence erred in their Christian reflections. Tertullian, *De Praescriptione Haereticorum*, VII and XXX. Tertullian, *Adversus Praxeam*, III.

214. *Adversus Praxeam*, VIII.

215. *Adversus Praxeam*, VIII.

216. *Adversus Praxeam*, VIII.

217. *Adversus Praxeam*, VIII; *Apology*, XXI.

one but not necessarily the same person as some Gnostic held, but God is rational (*rationalis*) and first had Reason (*ratio*) in him which the Greeks call "logos" and in Latin is rendered *sermonem* ("word").[218]

Tertullian highlights the ambiguity of the word *logos* to designate "reason" or "word" in understanding Jesus Christ as the Logos of God and this also gives an interesting aspect of the translational use of the word, since Tertullian wrote (his extant works) in Latin. As part of the general response to the false teachings of Praxeas (*Praxeam*), that the Father, Son, and Holy Spirit are one and the same person,[219] Tertullian examines the question of "who the Son is" and "in what manner (*quomodo*)" is the Son (also as Logos).[220] Certainly, Tertulllian asserts, "God is rational, and Reason (*ratio*) was first in Him; and so all things were from Himself." It is this "reason," which is God's own "thought [or faculty] (*sensus*)," that, Tertullian indicates, the Greeks call "*logos*" and which in Latin is also rendered "word" (*sermonem*). Hence, it is appropriate to regard "reason" as prior to "word" since God had "reason" and not "word" before the beginning and that "word" itself consists of "reason."[221] Thus, before the beginning in which the "word" was, God had his "reason." Nevertheless, Tertullian points out that this distinction is (really) nothing since before God sent his Logos, the Logos was with him and he had the Logos within his "reason" (*ratione*).[222] The Logos also had God's "wisdom" within.[223] Tertuallian attempts to resolve any question of ambiguity by explaining that "wisdom, reason and word" are appellations representing the one "power" (*vim*) or reality of God, that God has made second to himself, and who has been rightly designated Son (*Filius*).[224] This understanding of the multiple imageries of the Logos as Son of God is shared by both Justin Martyr and later Origen.

Justin Martyr's Logos Christology and the Hellenistic Past

Although chronologically Justin Martyr is prior to the above figures highlighted, I have presented him last here as a representative of Logos

---

218. *Adversus Praxeam*, II and V. Tertullian indicates "we designate" (*appellamus*), thus referring to the language (Latin) in which he wrote.

219. *Adversus Praxeam*, II.

220. *Adversus Praxeam*, V. Though God was alone prior to the creation of "all things," he had within himself his "reason" (*rationem*).

221. *Adversus Praxeam*, V.

222. *Adversus Praxeam*, V.

223. *Adversus Praxeam*, VI.

224. *Adversus Praxeam*, VII. Tertullian, *Apology*, XXI.

Christology within the *convert* stage of Graeco-Roman Christianity. Justin's application of Logos Christology is primarily in his response to contemporary charges against Christians as well as his defense of Christian teachings.[225] Essentially, in Justin, Jesus Christ as Logos becomes the *key* for a critical appropriation of his Greek past.[226] Justin's uniqueness primarily lies in his effort to connect the Graeco-Roman past with the activity of God via his Logos: an initiative that we apparently first meet in Justin.

Prior to his conversion to Christianity, Justin indicates his quest for the truth from notable philosophical schools by meeting respective famous teachers.[227] With the view of philosophy as the "greatest possession" honorable before God and whose end leads to God, Justin continued to wear the popular philosopher's cloak (the pallium) to demonstrate his understanding of how the Christian is indeed the "true philosopher."[228] Justin linked his conversion to the reading of the LXX in which a "love of the prophets" was kindled.[229] Scripture (or the Scriptures) for Justin is primarily the deposit of the truth that the prophets, through the agency of the Holy Spirit and the Logos, saw and heard.[230] Justin's measure of truth is the Logos of God, Jesus Christ and so prophecy becomes the utterance of the truth of God to humans.[231] Since the prophets uttered the truth of God with the assistance of God's Spirit and the Logos, they are differentiated from the philosophers of the Graeco-Roman tradition who simply spoke their human opinions.[232]

Logos is one of the names or titles of "a certain rational (λογικὴν) power" that God had begotten from himself before all creation, not by "mixing"

---

225. According to Eusebius, Justin's *First Apology*, as it is known, was "in defense of our doctrine," the *Second Apology* was on "behalf of our faith" and the *Dialogue with Trypho* was a "dialogue against the Jews." Eusebius, *HE* IV, XVIII.2 and XVIII.6.

226. Osborn, *Justin Martyr*, 15; Bediako, *Theology and Identity*, 145; Bates, "Justin Martyr's Logocentric Hermeneutical Transformation of Isaiah's Vision of the Nations," 548.

227. *Dial.*, II.

228. *Dial.*, II. Justin's definition of philosophy is; "the knowledge of that which really exists, and a clear perception of the truth; and happiness is the reward of such knowledge and wisdom." *Dial.*, III. Osborn, *Justin Martyr*, 7.

229. *Dial.*, VIII. For a treatment of Justin's view and use of Scripture (LXX) see, Osborn, *Justin Martyr*, 87–98. Skarsaune, *The Proof from Prophecy*.

230. *Dial.*, XXIII. The singular and the plural are both employed in this section of the *Dialog*.

231. Osborn rightly observes that for Justin "the word of truth is not an abstract thing but a living person, Jesus Christ." Osborn, *Justin Martyr*, 80. Though the early Stoics had associated truth with *logos*, Justin's distinction, as with the Christian understanding, is primarily that the Logos is "a living person, Jesus Christ."

232. *I Apol.*, XXXVI; *Dial.*, XLVIII.

or "sexual union," but "by an act of will."[233] The name "Logos" is given Jesus Christ because he "carries tidings" from the Father to humans, being "the first power after God the Father and Lord of all" and distinct in number but not in purpose (γνώμη).[234] The Logos is the only one entitled to be designated Son and through him God created and arranged all things.[235] It is through the Logos (the "first-born of God") that "every race of men were partakers (μετέσχε)" and by the power and the will of the Father "was born of a virgin as a human, and was named Jesus, and was crucified, and died, and rose again, and ascended into heaven."[236] There is "the [or a] seed (σπέρμα) of the Logos implanted in every race of humans," and for Justin everyone who strived to live in accordance to reason (or Logos) is a Christian, since Christ is the Logos.[237] These, however, lived according to a measure (μέρος) of the "Spermatikos Logos," while Christians live according to "the knowledge and contemplation of the whole Logos," Christ, who appeared for the sake of humanity.[238] Christian teachings are therefore superior.[239]

Justin's understanding of Jesus Christ as the Logos incarnate is clearly linked to his conviction that the whole of truth is only to be found among Christians.[240] Justin's unprecedented association of Spermatikos Logos with Jesus Christ and the application thereof, make his Logos Christology a step

---

233. *I Apol.*, XXI; *Dial.*, LXI. Other names include Holy Spirit, Lord, Son, Wisdom and Angel. The name "Logos" stands unique for Justin, and Osborn is of the view that it "suggests an explanation which even names like Christ or Son cannot supply. It is less materialistic and less pluralistic." Osborn, *Justin Martyr*, 30.

234. *Dial.*, CXXVIII; *I Apol.*, XXXII; *Dial.*, LVI, LXII, CXXVIII, CXXIX. The distinction between the Father and the Logos, according to Barnard, "meant for Justin 'different in person'" and hence this "sharp personality" that Justin ascribes to the Logos distinguishes his use from that of the Fourth Gospel and Philo. Barnard, *Justin Martyr*, 89. Goodenough, *The Theology of Justin Martyr*, 146. In repeating the "numerical distinction" Justin's concern seems to essentially clarify how that the Logos who is "one in will or purpose with the Father" from the beginning would eventually become human.

235. *II Apol.*, VI.

236. *I Apol.*, XLVI.

237. *I Apol.*, XLVI. *II Apol.* VIII. Daniélou, *Gospel Message and Hellenistic Culture*, 41. Socrates, Justin insists, "was more zealous" among such pre-Incarnation individuals accused of the same crime as the Christians are, namely, he was said to "introduce new divinities" and not to consider as such those the state acknowledged as gods. *II Apol.*, X; *I Apol.*, V.

238. *II Apol.*, VIII, X and XIII.

239. *II Apol.*, X. The "right Logos" has come to prove that not all opinions or doctrines are good. The "bad" doctrines are the result of "laws" that "wicked angels" had appointed after their wickedness. *II Apol.* IX.

240. Holte, "Logos Spermatikos," 113. Daniélou, *Gospel Message and Hellenistic Culture*, 41–42.

further from that of the missionary indication of the Fourth Gospel. Justin's use of "Spermatikos Logos" is distinct from its application among the Stoics and in Philo. Though Justin probably last followed Middle Platonism prior to his Christian conversion, his "immaterial interpretation" of the term is not strictly borrowed from that system of thought.[241] Justin's application of "Spermatikos Logos" to Jesus Christ gives a revelatory dimension with its associated "ethical and religious knowledge" and is thus different from the Stoics material conception of "an organic physical development" or Philo's symbolic use as a "principle of Man's spiritual life."[242] Though Justin could have been influenced by the Parable of the Sower in Matthew 13:3–23, he actually does not reference the text.[243]

I agree with Holte that Justin makes use of Logos Spermatikos, as an "innovation" on his part in Christian circles, to "translate St. Paul's doctrine on natural Revelation, to the language of contemporary philosophy" and not strictly as an attempt to "reconcile Christianity with Ancient Philosophy or even to create a synthesis between them."[244] However, considering the *logos* intimation in the Greek (philosophical) tradition and the Christian claim of the Incarnation of the Logos, Justin may have not only echoed Paul's vision of the universal significance of Christ, but also offered

---

241. Barnard, *Justin Martyr*, 96–98. Bediako, *Theology and Identity*, 147–48. Dillon, *The Middle Platonists*, 182. Holte, "Logos Spermatikos," 128, 145–46. M. J. Edwards is rather of the view that Justin's Logos Christology on the whole is a further development of the understanding of Christ the Logos as the embodiment of the Law (Torah) as is evident in Justin's considerable use of the LXX, particularly in the *Dialogue with Trypho*. Edwards "Justin's Logos and the Word of God," 279.

242. Holte, "Logos Spermatikos," 125–28. Bernard, *Justin Martyr*, 97. Goodenough's comment in reference to Philo's use of *logos* in relation to the word 'spermatikos' in *QE* II, 68, the germinal (σπερματική) substance of all things, is a helpful summary in this regard: "The Logos as spermatic had to do with creation and providence, was at once a spiritual principle of life (πνεῦμα) and a regulating principle which could rule the world." Goodenough, *The Theology of Justin Martyr*, 162. R. Marcus translates σπερματική as "seminal substance." Marcus, *Philo—Questions and Answers on Exodus*, 116.

243. Holte, "Logos Spermatikos," 128. Holte helpfully distinguishes "Logos Spermatikos" from "the seed of the Logos" in Justin; "[the seed of the Logos] does not mean that Logos or some part of him is sown in Man . . . [rather] "a seed is sown in Man by the personal Logos, a seed that is clearly distinguished from him but is nevertheless an imitation of Logos, a knowledge in which he is reflected" (133 & 146). Daniélou maintains that "the seeds of the Logos . . . are a participation by the Logos in the human spirit; they derive from the action of the Logos, which in this way sows the individual mind." *Gospel Message and Hellenistic Culture*, 43–44.

244. Holte, "Logos Spermatikos," 164.

a clarification and consequential implication of the Christian claim of the incarnation of the Logos.[245]

The Refiguration Stage—An Innovative Mode

Origen's Christian vocation begins where the Apologists ended. However, his approach in demonstrating the universal significance of Jesus Christ even in the Graeco-Roman tradition has a background in Clement of Alexandria, although Origen makes no mention of him in his works.[246] The tradition in the "catechetical" school of Alexandria that Origen highlights was exemplified by Pantaenus was surely to found in Clement.[247] Clement does not mention Justin but his familiarity with the writings of the latter is generally acknowledged.[248] Clement's Logos Christology highlights profoundly the work of Jesus Christ in the salvation of humanity. William Wilson's remarks on Clement's three major works in relation to his Logos Christology are a helpful summary,

> The three compositions are really parts of one whole. The central connecting idea is that of the Logos—the Word—the Son of God; whom in the first work [Protrepticus] he exhibits drawing men from the superstitions and corruptions of heathenism to faith; in the second [Paedagogus], as training them by precepts

---

245. Bediako, *Theology and Identity*, 146. For, as Holte rightly notes, Justin's Logos Christology enabled him to make the distinction between the Logos among the Christians and his pre-incarnation activity among the Greeks and Jews. Holte, "Logos Spermatikos," 166.

246. For Eric Osborn, the gap between the period of their respective activities and Origen's martyrdom enthusiasm might have limited his appreciation for Clement, who apparently fled Alexandria during the persecution that saw the demise of Origen's father. Osborn, "Clement of Alexandria," 81. Clement is regarded as a teacher of Origen. Eusebius, *HE*, VI, 6. Titus Flavius Clemens was probably born and was likely a Christian convert by the time he met Pantaenus in Alexandria.

247. According to Origen, ". . . as I was devoted to the word (λόγῳ), and the fame of our proficiency was spreading abroad, there approached me sometimes heretics, sometimes those conversant with Greek learning and especially philosophy, and I thought it right [it seemed right] to examine both the opinions of the heretics, and also the claim that the philosophers make to speak concerning truth. And in doing this we followed the example of Pantaenus, who, before us, was of assistance to many, and had acquired no small attainments in these matters." Eusebius, *HE* VI, 19. English translation by J. E. L. Oulton in the Loeb Classical Library edition. In Bediako's assessment, such retrospective remarks point to "an orthodox tradition and a context" in Alexandria "which exemplified the sort of comprehensive synthesis that Clement was seeking" and must have found Pantaenus as "an embodiment for such a reality." Bediako, *Theology and Identity*, 177.

248. Chadwick, *Early Christian Thought and the Classical Tradition*, 40.

and discipline; and in the last [Stromata], as conducting them to that higher knowledge of the things of God, to which those only who devote themselves assiduously to spiritual, moral, and intellectual culture can attain.[249]

The centrality of a Logos Christology in Clement cannot be a source of "a shortcoming of his theological thought."[250] It rather points to an essential fulcrum in his achievement at giving a cohesive view of humanity's (religious) quest for truth.[251] The Logos is the common denominator of Old Testament faith (the spiritual ancestral tradition of Christianity) and the Graeco-Roman tradition in the epitome of philosophy. The activity of the Logos is to be found in both traditions and although Clement consciously makes specific remarks regarding Graeco-Roman philosophy, his view of philosophy goes beyond that tradition.

The Logos as Son reveals the Father (God) in the scheme of the salvation of humanity, being the "face of God" by or through him that "God is manifested and made known."[252] While God remains indemonstrable and hence cannot be "the object of science," the Son (Logos) is capable of being made known and described.[253] The Son is all that can be ascribed to him, but none of such ascriptions is exhaustive.[254] Clement keeps in check the unity in essence and the distinction in manifestation between God and the

---

249. Wilson, "Introductory Note to Clement of Alexandria," 166. Tollinton felt the doctrine of Logos played a pivotal role for Clement in securing the copious Graeco-Roman sources into a "unified system." Tollinton, *Clement of Alexandria*, 334.

250. Karavites, *Evil, Freedom, and the Road to Perfection in Clement of Alexandria*, 12.

251. John Ferguson, for instance, has argued that Clement is the "real founder of a Christian philosophy of religion." Ferguson, "The Achievement of Clement of Alexandria," 80.

252. *Paedagogus*, I, 7; 57,2. The Divine Logos, "omnipotent and paternal," with all his power and using "all the resources of wisdom" is devoted to the salvation of humanity in "curbing" its "irrational impulses." *Paed*. I, 9; 75, 1–2 & 84, 1. Clement keenly notes that "the greatest and most regal work of God is the salvation of humanity" and it is ultimately to this end that the Logos became human. *Paed*. I, 12; 100, 1.

253. *Strom*. IV, 25; 156, 1. Cf. Through Christ, knowledge of the Almighty is approached, not what he is but what he is not. *Strom*. V, 11; 71, 3. Also *Strom*. V, 12; 82, 1–2.

254. The Son, according to Clement, "is neither simply one thing as one thing, nor many things as parts, but one thing as all things," therefore he is "all things" and "the circle of all powers rolled and united into one unity." Accordingly, he is wisdom, knowledge and truth. Clement further notes, this time speaking of the Son as Logos, that he is "the Alpha and the Omega," both the beginning and the end without any break and faith in him secures [an indissoluble] unity in him while unbelief results in the opposite. *Strom*. IV, 25; 156, 1–2.

Logos.²⁵⁵ Clement, thus, held a sense of the insufficiency of language in the conception of the unseen God that is aided in the right response of faith through the manifestation of the Son, the Logos.

The Divine Logos became human for the salvation of humanity.²⁵⁶ He is "perfect," begotten in perfection from the perfect Father.²⁵⁷ Clement allegorically notes that the flesh and blood respectively point to the Holy Spirit and the Logos and the union of both is the Lord Jesus.²⁵⁸ Jesus Christ, the Logos of God and Spirit made flesh, is the "heavenly flesh sanctified" who nourishes Christians as infants.²⁵⁹

The salvific work of the Logos involves a rescue of humans from "the custom of this world in which [they have] been reared" and the training in "the one salvation of faith in God."²⁶⁰ As the "heavenly guide," the Logos is named Protrepticus in calling humans to salvation. The Logos as "at once both curative and preceptive," can also appropriately be designated Paedagogus because he makes as his subject of persuasion what had been prescribed with the promise to cure our passions.²⁶¹ As "the all-benignant," the Logos is a Teacher or didactic and hence his threefold exercise of first exhorting (from on high), training and teaching.²⁶² As the Instructor, the Logos is God with the "form (σχήματι) of God" and "God in the form of (hu)man" in his incarnation.²⁶³ The Logos "was in the beginning, and

---

255. Osborn, *The Philosophy of Clement of Alexandria*, 40. Hägg observes that this mark of distinction is a consequence of Clement's "epistemological apophaticism" and thus the "inaccessible Father needs a mediator, a Logos or a *dynamis*, that is accessible and comprehensible." Hägg, *Clement of Alexandria*, 262.

256. *Paed.* I, 5; 24, 4; *Paed.* I, 8; 74, 4.

257. *Paed.* I, 6; 25, 3.

258. *Strom.* VI, 16; 145, 7. *Paed.* II, 12; 118, 5. Also, the "holy God (θεὸς) Jesus" is the Logos, the Paedagogus. *Paed.* I, 7; 55, 2. *Paed.* I, 6; 43, 2.

259. *Paed.* I, 6; 43, 3. The knowledge of the "divine essence" is also metaphorically regarded as the "meat and drink" of the divine Logos. *Strom.* V, 10; 66, 3–4.

260. *Paed.* I, 1; 1, 2.

261. *Paed.* I, 1; 1, 3.

262. *Paed.* I, 1; 3, 3. Clement distinguishes from the Paedagogus (Instructor) who being "practical and not theoretical" aims to improve the sickened soul by training to a virtuous life, and the Teacher whose it is "to train and guide the soul to all requisite knowledge when it is made able to admit the revelation of the Word [Logos]." Also *Paed.* III, 12; 97, 3, where the Teacher continues from where the Instructor stops in the exposition of the largely symbolic nature of the sacred words of Scripture. Osborn, *The Philosophy of Clement of Alexandria*, 5. Tollinton took note of the fact that the office of the Logos as educational is Christian and "peculiarly" Clement's. Tollinton, *Clement of Alexandria*, 353.

263. *Paed.* I, 3; 9, 4.

before the beginning"²⁶⁴ and is "common to all" and "made all things for all."²⁶⁵ By his admonishing, the Logos (as the "great General" and "Commander-in-chief of the universe") effects the release of those in "slavery, error, and captivity of the adversary."²⁶⁶

Clement clarifies that the Logos of the Father of the universe "is not that which is uttered (προφορικός)" but rather the wisdom and most manifest kindness of God, and his power, which is almighty and truly divine.²⁶⁷ As the "supramundane Wisdom," the heavenly Logos is "the all-harmonious, melodious, holy instrument of God."²⁶⁸ The Incarnate Logos is a "manifest mystery" of God-human, and being "common to both" is the Mediator (μεσίτης) who "executes the Father's will."²⁶⁹ The Logos is the "image of God," and the human mind is the image of this image of God.²⁷⁰ The "true man, the mind which is in man" is the image of the Logos, intimately "assimilated" to the Divine Logos and hence rational.²⁷¹ Faith in the Christian system of thought for Clement is linked to the Logos: it is the "obedience to reason" which the Logos incarnates and everything done contrary to "right reason" is sin .²⁷² The Christian life, then, is a "sys-

---

264. *Protrepticus*, I; 7, 3.

265. *Paed.* II, 12; 120, 3. The Logos is "everywhere" (πανταχοῦ) *Paed.* III, 5.

266. *Paed.* I, 8; 65, 3.

267. *Strom.* V, 1; 6, 3. This has not been a straightforward passage and commentators differ in interpretation. Edwards provides two possible readings, "logos which is prone to display itself in utterance" or "this logos prophorikos of ours" either reading points to the caution of conceiving the Logos as an offspring of God. Edwards, "Clement of Alexandria and his Doctrine of the Logos," 169–70. Wolfson saw this passage as part of the general dissatisfaction of the analogy of *logos endiathetos* and *prophorikos* in speaking of the generation of the Logos from the Father to avoid the misunderstanding of the Logos as "a mere empty word." Wolfson, *The Philosophy of the Church Fathers*, 299–300. In the preceding sentences, however, Clement speaks about Providence and prophecy and it is likely he seeks to draw a line between the uttered logos (= word) of prophecy and the Logos of God (*Strom.* V, 1; 6, 2). The latter, at any rate, is responsible for the former.

268. *Protr.* I; 5, 4. The Logos is also the "one instrument of peace" by which God is honored. *Paed.* II, 4; 42, 3. In reference to Isaiah 2:3, the Logos is the "New Song," heavenly, Clement's "Eunomos," the "true [real] athlete crowned in the theatre of the whole universe." *Strom.* VII, 3; 20, 3.

269. *Paed.* III, 1; 2, 1–2. The Logos is thus, respectively, the Son of God and his Servant and the Savior of humanity and our Teacher.

270. *Strom.* V, 14; 94, 5. Clement's views are here related to the creation of humans in God's image. Furthermore, contrary to the "Olympian Jove," which is "an image of an image" and a "senseless work of Attic hands," the Divine Logos being the image of God is the "genuine Son of Mind" and the "archetypal light of light." *Protr.* X; 98, 3.

271. *Protr.* X; 98, 3.

272. *Paed.* I, 13; 101, 1. He later also notes "whatever is done through error of

tem of reasonable actions" of the things that are taught by the Logos, "an infallible activity" called faith.[273]

The Logos is "to be contemplated by the mind" since he says "I am the truth" (cf. John 14:6), and indicating that Plato spoke of the truth as "an idea," Clement asserts that "an idea is a conception (ἐννόημα) of God" and this is what the "Barbarians" call the Logos of God.[274] Since the activity of philosophy is linked to the Logos, Graeco-Roman philosophy itself is a partial attainment of truth.[275] Indeed, both Graeco-Roman and Barbarian philosophies are fragments "of eternal truth . . . from the theology of the ever-living" Logos.[276] Accordingly, to bring back together the separate parts and make them one is to contemplate the perfect Logos who is the Truth.[277] The partial nature of Greek philosophy, with respect to the Logos as the Truth, makes it preparatory and renders the philosophers children "unless they have been made men by Christ."[278]

Commenting on John 1:17, Clement indicates the Law "given through" Moses by the Logos was temporary but eternal grace and truth were or came by the incarnate Logos.[279] Thus, just as the Logos gave the Law to the Jews as a covenant, so did he provide philosophy as a covenant to the Greeks by which he is glorified among them.[280] Christianity then, as the new covenant, comprises a people "trained in different Covenants of the one Lord" by his Word (ῥήματι).[281] Consequently, the Incarnation

---

reason is transgression, and is rightly called, sin." Elsewhere it is faith, "the key of faith," that unlocks the gates of the Logos which are "intellectual". *Protr.* I; 10, 3.

273. *Paed.* I, 13; 102, 4. The system itself is the "commandments of the Lord," "being divine statues and spiritual counsels." *Paed.* I, 13; 103, 1.

274. *Strom.* V, 3; 16, 1–3.

275. *Strom.* VI, 17; 160, 1.

276. *Strom.* I, 13; 57, 6.

277. *Strom.* I, 13; 57, 6.

278. *Strom.* I, 11; 53, 2. The discipline of philosophy in general for Clement, however, is anterior to the Greeks and is universal. *Strom.* I, 15; 71, 3ff; *Strom.* I, 16; 80, 5. *Strom.* I, 19; 94, 1–3. *Strom.* V, 1; 10, 1–3. Daniélou, *Gospel Message*, 49–68; Wolfson, *The Philosophy of the Church Fathers*, 21–22.

279. *Paed.* I, 7; 60,1–2. The Logos himself can also be regarded as Law and his "commands and counsels as the short and straight paths to immortality" since his "precepts are full of persuasion, not of fear." *Paed.* I, 3; 9, 4.

280. *Strom.* VI, 5; 42, 1.

281. *Strom.* VI, 5; 42, 2. Apostle Paul had spoken of the Law as παιδαγωγὸς until Christ came in Galatians 3:24. The Incarnation, therefore, ushered in "the universal calling to be a peculiar people of righteousness through the teaching which flows from faith, brought together by one Lord, the only God of both Greeks and Barbarians . . . of the whole race of men." *Strom.* VI, 17; 159, 9.

has brought to a halt the Greek quest for human learning in the conviction that the fullness of wisdom is in Christ the Logos ("the whole world, with Athens and Greece, has already become the domain of the Logos ... [since] that which the chiefs of philosophy only guessed at, the disciples of Christ have both apprehended and proclaimed").[282]

My interest so far has been in Clement's application of his Logos Christology (that is, the impact of the incarnate Logos on humanity) and not so much on his views about the "origin" of the Logos.[283] Although Clement uses metaphorical language and diverse imagery in his description of Jesus as Son of God, the dynamism of the image of Logos creatively served his immediate concerns. Clement offers some clarification in his Logos Christology but his application is however relatively more elaborate with respect to the Apologists before him. He does not explicitly refer to Justin Martyr but "there can be little doubt that he had read his writings" and that though some of Justin's "unsophisticated theses are dropped ... the essential pattern is recognizably the same."[284] The Fourth Gospel is foundational to Clement's Logos intimations, which highlights the matchless role of the Logos in the pedagogical journey of the salvation of humanity. In Clement's efforts there is relatively more depth in the use of pre-Christian Graeco-Roman thought. Clement stands, then, between the *convert* and *refiguration* stages in his application of Logos Christology as part of the process of the conversion of Hellenistic thought. Clement's (eclectic) influence on his younger contemporary Origen (though he does not explicitly affirm that) is significant at least at some literary points.

---

282. *Protr.* XI; 112, 1–2.

283. For example, Lilla agrees with Wolfson that Clement adopts Philo's theory of the Logos as a metaphysical principle where the Logos is first encountered as God's reason [or mind] and later becomes a distinct being in his agency in creation and finally represents "the immanent law of the universe." The stages of being in God and later as a distinct being is termed the "twofold stage theory" in contrast to the "single stage theory" or "eternal generation" of the Logos in which there is no time separation between the two stages of being in God and as a distinct being. In other words, the Logos has existed from eternity even in his generated state. Wolfson takes the view that Clement had earlier in his Christian vocation taken the line of the twofold theory only to revise to the single stage possibly under the influence of his younger contemporary Origen. Lilla, *Clement of Alexandria*, 199–212; Wolfson, *The Philosophy of the Church Fathers*, 193–232. More recently, however, scholars such as M. J. Edwards and Henny F. Hägg have argued that Clement originally held a single stage theory. Edwards, "Clement of Alexandria and His Doctrine of the Logos," 159–77; Hägg, *Clement of Alexandria*, 189–93.

284. Chadwick, *Early Christian Thought and the Classical Tradition*, 40.

Origen of Alexandria: Logos Christology and Universal Knowledge

The vocation of Origen reveals other aspects of the conversion of the Greek way of thinking by the third century AD. Origen's spiritual and intellectual fervor was acknowledged in his own time and its influential impact felt by his contemporaries and those of later centuries. By the time of his birth in about AD 186 in Alexandria, Pantaenus was possibly leader of the famous Catechetical school. Eusebius notes that during Origen's childhood, his Christian Father, Leonides, instructed him first in the Scriptures before the Greek sciences.[285] Taking Eusebius' account, Origen remains a second-generation Christian.[286] Origen's life, work and legacy have attracted varied interpretations and conclusions and he is best judged in the circumstances of his own time.[287] Considering Origen's convictions as an uncompromising follower of Jesus Christ, with the affectionate designation, "my Jesus" (ὁ ἐμὸς Ἰησοῦς), his view of the Christian faith in relation to his Graeco-Roman tradition remains exemplary.[288]

Our examination of Origen's Logos Christology is linked to Andrew Walls' missiological assessment of him as indeed the "father of mission studies" akin to what is ascribed to Eusebius as the "father of church history."[289] Walls arrives at this conclusion because Origen "illustrates so vividly the continued interaction of faith and culture that forms the raw material of mission studies and the dedicated and devout intellectual application of those issues that provides its processes."[290] Origen's Logos conception of Christ proved essential in this vocation.[291] Origen, like Clement before him,

---

285. Eusebius, *HE* VI, 2. Eusebius also refers to a testimony of the anti-Christian philosopher, Porphyry, who was appalled at how Origen being "a Greek educated in Greek learning," having achieved significant fame, would eventually drive "straight toward barbarian recklessness." *HE* VI, 19.

286. Chadwick notes that it is possible Origen's parents were not Christians at the time of their son's birth. Be that as it may, they were Christians before Origen could identify himself as one, having had a desire to be martyred with his father. Chadwick, *Early Christian Thought*, 66–67. It is likely Porphyry takes for granted Origen's Christian training alongside his Greek (traditional) education early in his life as Eusebius indicates, and would wish Origen had just stayed with his Greek learning.

287. Chadwick, *Early Christian Thought*, 121.

288. *Contra Celsum* (*Against Celsus*) III, 31 & 32. Tzamalikos regards the translation as 'the Jesus of *mine*,' to be "a more accurate rendering of the spirit of" the Greek phrase. He argues for the originality of Origen as the theologian to introduce the expression into Christian scholarship though the credit has been reserved for Gregory of Nazianzus. Tzamalikos, *Origen: Philosophy of History and Eschatology*, 435–38.

289. Walls, "In Quest of the Father of Mission Studies," 98–105.

290. Walls, "In Quest of the Father of Mission Studies," 98.

291. So, for example, Rebecca Lyman notes, "the accommodation of the incarnate

participated in the contemporary Graeco-Roman intellectual space and his Logos Christology enabled him, within the framework of the "rule of faith," to respond to issues that particularly affected Christian credibility.[292] The Logos as mediator, for example, enabled Origen in his approach to one of the basic philosophical problems of "the relation of the One to the Many."[293] Origen alludes to the idea of the development of *one* to *many* and the return to *one* when he observes that "the end (*finis*) is always like the beginning (*initiis*)" and that from "one beginning" sprang "many differences and varieties" which, in the benevolence and unity of God, Christ and the Holy Spirit, "are recalled to one end."[294]

Christ the Son of God is principally Wisdom and Logos although there are "many different names" ascribed to him according to people's "circumstances or views."[295] These two conceptions (ἐπίνοια) of Christ enable Origen to show how Christ relates to the Father and to the world or created order.[296] The only-begotten Son of God is his Wisdom "hypostatically existing" (*substantialiter subsistentem*).[297] In other words, Wisdom has been with God the Father as long as he has existed. This Wisdom was generated even before any beginning and in its existence or reality contained all the power (*virtus*) and representation of [the intended] creation, the beginnings or forms or species of the whole of creation.[298] The proof text for Origen in this instance is Proverbs 8:22.

Similarly, just as the Son is Wisdom he should be understood as Word (*verbum*) of God: being called Word by status as interpreter or explainer of the secrets of the mind [of God].[299] Origen notes that John, as author of the Fourth Gospel, alluded to this understanding more excellently and very clearly in an appropriate definition defining God to be the Word in

---

Logos as the essential, intellectual, spiritual link between the uncreated Father and the various levels of created being was the centre of his thought and method." Lyman, *Christology and Cosmology*, 39. Daniélou, *Origen*, 251.

292. Studer, *Trinity and Incarnation*, 80.

293. Studer, *Trinity and Incarnation*, 80. Wiles, *The Christian Fathers*, 33–37. Dillon, *The Middle Platonists, 80 B.C to A.D 220*, 45–46.

294. Origen, *Peri archōn* I 6.2. Latin text of Rufinus' translation in Redepenning, *Origenes—De Principiis*. English translation by Frederick Crombie in Roberts et al., *The Ante-Nicene Fathers Volume 4—Fathers of the Third Century*.

295. *Peri archōn* I 2.1. Also as "first-born of God," "power of God"; "light of the world," "the door." Cf. *CommJn* I 21(23)ff.

296. Cf. *Commentary on John* I 28(30); *CCels* II 64.

297. *Peri archōn* I 2.2.

298. *Peri archōn* I 2.2.

299. *Peri archōn* I 2.3.

the beginning of the Gospel account (John 1:1). Origen warns against those who assign both the Word and Wisdom of God a beginning, thereby denying the "unbegotten Father" as having always been Father who had "generated [begotten]" the Logos and had always "possessed" Wisdom.[300] In fact, the Son is "only-begotten" of the Father not by receiving or taking the latter's breath or any external act but from his nature and his generation is "eternal and everlasting" just like the brilliance generated from light.[301]

Origen's explication of the Son of God as both Wisdom and Logos and the respective functions as "containing" and "revealing" the mysteries of God is akin to the view of the "internal" (*endiathetos*) and "external" (*prophorikos*) Logos held by the Apologists.[302] Hence, taking Wisdom to be that "beginning" mentioned in John 1:1, Origen indicates that the Logos was, in effect, in Wisdom.[303] The Logos has always been in the beginning in Wisdom with God.[304] Christ is Logos or can be reckoned as such because he strips off from us "all that is irrational" and equips us in accordance with true reason so that all things, both the common and higher or advance works of life, are done to the glory of God.[305]

By the time of Origen, the Christian understanding or recognition of Jesus Christ as the Logos (incarnate) had reached a stage of common or popular knowledge. Its implications, however, were pursued diversely and the backdrop of pre-Christian conceptions of the *logos* contributed to various views that Origen and others before him saw as contrary to the received "rule of faith." In Origen, the responses to such unorthodox Logos conceptions move further to the root of the misconceptions, namely, the pre-Christian appropriation of the *logos* concept. In his reading of John 1:1, Origen notes that the arrangement of the three sentences are so set out to enable one to perceive that it is by the Logos being with God that he becomes God (Divine).[306] The author of the Gospel account is aware of his use of the article ὁ ("the") before θεὸς and λόγος in conveying an understanding, while adding and omitting it at some points.[307] When θεὸς is with the article, Origen indicates, it is in reference to the "uncreated cause of all things," the "true God." Similarly, ὁ λόγος refers to the source or fountain (πηγή) of the *logos*

---

300. *Peri archōn* I 2.3.
301. *Peri archōn* I 2.4.
302. Cf. Ronald E. Heine, "Epinoiai" in McGuckin (ed.), *WHO*, 93–95(94).
303. *CommJn* I 19(22).
304. *CommJn* I 39(42). Tzamalikos, *Origen*, 31–32.
305. *CommJn* I 37(42).
306. *CommJn* II 1.
307. *CommJn* II 2.

(=reason) in each rational being and that *logos* in each being is not like the first (Logos) "properly termed and called" the Logos.[308]

God (the Father) is "divine by himself" ["very God"] with all others beside him being made divine through participation or sharing (μετοχῇ) in his divinity or divine nature.[309] The Son of God, as "the firstborn of all creation" and first to be with God and to "attract" divinity to himself, is more honorable than the "gods" beside him. It is through his "ministering" that they became gods. These "gods" formed after God, the images' (εἰκόνες) prototype, are apparently "images" and the Logos is the archetypal image, who being with God always remains divine.[310] In anticipation of a reaction to his earlier assertion of other "gods" beside "(the) God" who derive their divinity from the Logos, Origen explains further that the *logos* (=reason) in each rational being occupies the same position in relation to "God the Logos [=Divine Logos]."[311] The Father is the source of "divinity" and Son (Logos) of *logos* (reason).[312] Thus, just as there are many gods and many lords and many *logoi*, Christians pray for the presence of "God the Logos" [Divine Logos].[313]

Origen indicates four types of human responses or approaches to the Logos. There are those who "partake of" the Divine Logos as was the case with such men as Hosea, Isaiah, and Jeremiah and any other who showed or proved that the Logos came to him.[314] The second group comprise those who have known nothing except "Jesus Christ and him crucified" and only know Christ according to the flesh. These are the multitude of those regarded as having believed [the gospel].[315] The third group comprise those have devoted themselves to λόγοις (words or reasons) and partake of the Logos (who they regard to be above all [others]). Among those in the fourth group are people who follow the popular or distinguished and prevailing schools in philosophy

308. *CommJn* II 2.

309. *CommJn* II 2.

310. *CommJn* II 2. Cf. *CommJn* II 1, where Origen observes, the Logos "was always (ἀει) with (συνεῖναι) the Father" and puts emphasis on the verb "was" (ἦν) that the Logos "was in the beginning at the same time when He was with God, neither being separated from the beginning nor being bereft of His Father."

311. *CommJn* II 3. Ronald E. Heine's translation in Origen, *Commentary on the Gospel according to John Books 1–10*, 99.

312. *CommJn* II 3. The dual sense of *logos* as 'word' and 'reason' is apparently taken for granted in these discussions.

313. *CommJn* II 3.

314. *CommJn* II 3. Cf. *HomJr* 9.1–2. [Origen, *Homilies on Jeremiah: Homily on 1 Kings 28*, trans. John Clark Smith (Washington: Catholic University of America Press, 1998), 85–86. http://www.questia.com/read/86025281.]

315. *CommJn* II 3.

among the Greeks. These believe in λόγοις that have been corrupted and godless or ungodly in every way and do away with [divine] Providence (πρόνοιαν), which is visible [manifest or self-evident] and perceptible. These have also accepted another end besides the good.[316] In these categories, Origen demonstrates his understanding of the universal activity of the Logos as being present in rational creatures.[317] It is through the inspiration of the Holy Spirit in the Scriptures [Old and New Testaments] that one can recognize the "higher and diviner reason (*rationem*)" as God's Son.[318]

Indeed, "all things were made by God through Christ."[319] Origen emphasizes the agency of "through whom," as always being mentioned second [with respect to God], to show that God the Father is the originator of all things.[320] It is God who promised his own gospel (Romans 1:1–5) through the prophets and through (his Son) Jesus Christ (the Savior) that he gave the grace and apostleship to Paul and the rest (like him). God made the "ages" through his "Only-begotten" Son (Hebrews 1:2).[321] Thus, if all things "came into existence" (ἐγένετο) through the Logos then, it is not by the Logos that they came into existence but by [one] "superior" and "greater" beside the Logos, the Father.[322] An extension to this understanding of all things "coming into being" through the Logos is for those who hold the Holy Spirit to have an origin to necessarily admit that the Holy Spirit through the Logos "became." In this way, the Logos is older compared with the Holy Spirit.[323] In showing that the Holy Spirit came through the Son

316. *CommJn* II 3.

317. Cf. Tzamalikos, *Origen*, 105. In response to Celsus' charge on God's apparent silence before sending his Son, the Logos, Origen asserts in the process, "For nothing good has happened among men without the divine Logos who has visited (ἐπιδημήσαντος) the souls of those who are able, even if for a short time, to receive these operations (ἐνεργείας) of the divine Logos (θείου λόγου)." *CCels* VI, 78. Translation is by Chadwick, who also sees a connection here with Justin, *Apol.* I, 46. *Origen, Contra Celsum*, 392.

318. *Peri archōn* I 3.1. In the *Contra Celsum*, Origen indicates that while Celsus sees the "logos of all things" to be God himself, to the view of Christians (ἡμᾶς) he is "His Son" and goes on to cite John 1:1. *CCels* V 24.

319. *Peri archōn* I 7.1. Origen supports with quotations from John 1:1 and Colossians 1:16. Cf. *Peri archōn* II 6.1

320. *CommJn* II 10(6). It was to the Logos that, according to Origen, God (the Father) instructed, "let there be . . ." and also "let us create man" and the Logos obeyed and made everything according to the will of the Father. *CCels* II, 9.

321. *CommJn* II 10(6).

322. *CommJn* II 10(6).

323. *CommJn* II 10(6). The subject of the Holy Spirit, according to Origen in another context, is comprehensible only to those familiar with the LXX (the Law and the Prophets) or who have come to faith in Jesus Christ. Furthermore, unlike the Logos

(Logos), Origen submits that the Holy Spirit has no "substance / essence" of his own beyond the Father and the Son.³²⁴

While the Son is considered next beside the Father and is "one in agreement" with him, there is a distinction between the Son and the Holy Spirit evidenced in the respective consequences of blasphemy against the Son and Holy Spirit.³²⁵ The three are "hypostases" and the Father remains uncreated.³²⁶ Hence, of all the things coming forth through the Logos, the Holy Spirit is "more honorable" and first [in] rank.³²⁷ Yet within the sphere of the Trinity [or Triad] (*Trinitate*) nothing, Origen indicates in another context, can be said to be greater or less, "since the fountain of divinity alone holds all things by His Word and Reason, [and] sanctifies by the Spirit of His mouth [cf. Psalm 33:6] those worthy of sanctification."³²⁸

Origen's fundamental concern to defend, as well as explicate, the Christian "rule of faith" and his openness to all that is best and uncontradictory in

---

who is present in all rational beings, the Holy Spirit is found only among the righteous who turn to the good life, move in the direction of Jesus Christ and abide in God (*se ad meliora convertunt . . . vias Christi Iesu incedunt . . . in bonis actibus . . . in Deo permanent*). Cf. *Peri archōn* I 3.1ff.

324. *CommJn* II 10(6).

325. Cf. Matthew 12:32.

326. *CommJn* II 10(6). Hypostases in "the sense of individual subsistence, and so individual existent." Kelly, *Early Christian Doctrines*, 129.

327. *CommJn* II 10(6). Grillmeier's description on the relationship between the three, Father, Son and Holy Spirit is helpful, although his choice of pronoun seems to defeat the understanding of hypostasis: "The Holy Spirit is neither unbegotten like the Father, nor begotten as is the Son, nor is it created like other creatures. It issues from the Father and becomes a subsisting hypostasis by means of the Logos. Thus it belongs on the side of God, but it is in third place after the Father and the Son." Grillmeier, *Christ in Christian Tradition*, 140.

328. *Peri archōn* I 3.7. G. L. Prestige renders the phrase *unius divinitatis fons* as "one fount of deity." Prestige, *God in Patristic Thought*, 132. Origen's language in expressing the distinction and unity of the nature and function of the Father (God), Son (Logos), and Holy Spirit appears ambiguous at certain points to later readers and modern commentators. He has been labelled retrospectively as a "subordinationist" (that is, maintaining a strict distinction of the substance or essence of each of the members of the Trinity and hence indicating a sense of superiority and inferiority in the Trinity) or as a definitive source of "the subordinationist tradition" (Prestige, *God in Patristic Thought*, 249). Prestige opines that, even though "Origen's thought was sufficiently clear," the lack of a "clear, formal definition [of the terms] left the subject [of subordination] still involved in some obscurity and difficulty" (p. 138). Crouzel intimates that Origen's "subordinationism" is "quite equivocal," the Father's initiative is emphasized as well as the "unity of will and of action" [with the Son] and that "it is wrong to confuse the subordinationism of the Ante-Nicenes with that of the Arians." Crouzel, *Origen*, 188. Cf. Kelly who sees the influence of contemporary (middle) Platonism as accounting to Origen's subordinationism in his views on the Trinity. Kelly, *Early Christian Doctrines*, 129–32.

the Greek world of thought,[329] inevitably meant a reworking of such thoughts of Plato and Philo concerning the Logos and associated "invisible" and "incorporeal" forms or ideas.[330] Tzamalikos has argued that there is a contrast between Origen's views on the conceptions of Christ and Plato's notion of ideas. Tzamalikos notes that apart from Wisdom and Logos, which "have always existed in the atemporal being of God," the other conceptions, which for him are what Origen refers to when he says the Son is "many good things," had a beginning and exist in the mind.[331] Thus, unlike the ideas in Plato that have "a real and undisputable existence as beings in themselves," Tzamalikos asserts, the "conceptions" in Origen neither "have any essential existence in themselves" nor "introduce any essential distinction in the Son of God."[332] The Christian understanding of the Logos becoming flesh ultimately accounts for Origen's apparent review of any pre-Christian conceptions of the *logos* concept at his disposal.

Origen's Logos Christology was pivotal in his response to Celsus' unfair accusations regarding Christian piety and ultimate honor of virtue in his *True Word [Doctrine]*:

> For we ought not to imagine that because of the feminine (θηλυκόν) name wisdom and righteousness are feminine in their being. In our view the Son of God is these things, as his genuine disciple showed when he said of him: "Who was made unto us wisdom from God, and righteousness, and sanctification, and redemption" [1 Corinthians 1:30]. Therefore, though we may call him a second (δεύτερον) God, it should be understood by this that we do not mean anything except the [V]irtue which includes all virtues, and the Logos which includes every logos whatsoever of the beings which have been made according to nature, both those which are primary and those that exist for the benefit of the whole. We say that this Logos dwelt (ᾠκειῶσθαι) in the soul (ψυχὴν) of Jesus and was united with it in a closer union than that of any other soul, because he alone has been able perfectly (τελείως) to receive the

---

329. *Epistula ad Gregorium (Letter to Gregory)* I.

330. Wolfson, *The Philosophy of the Fathers*, 274–80.

331. Tzamalikos, *Origen*, 60–61. *CommJn* I 19(22).

332. Tzamalikos, *Origen*, 61. Tzamalikos also sees a contrast between Philo's 'world of ideas' [=intelligible world] and Origen's "models" or "patterns": while in Philo the 'world of ideas' act not only as models but also as "*efficient causes*" and therefore necessarily have to "exist beginninglessly in a timeless world," in Origen the models are present in the world and are not transcendent beings, being part of creation "*out of nothing (ex nihilo)*" (pp. 142–43).

highest participation (μετοχὴν) in him who is the very Logos and the very Wisdom, and the very Righteousness himself.³³³

From the above, the Incarnation is explained as constituting the meeting of soul of Jesus and the divine Logos and that it is the divine in the man Jesus, of whom God also bore witness, that is rightly termed "Son of God," "divine Logos," "God's power and wisdom," and "Christ."³³⁴ However, the explanation of the composite nature and the constituents of the "incarnate Jesus" was a subject of private investigation among believers (or those who believe).³³⁵

The Incarnation is not to be seen as being "circumscribed" (περιγεγραμμένον) to suggest the Logos had no existence outside Jesus' soul and body.³³⁶ Yet this does not amount to "separating" (χωρίζοντες) the Son of God, the Logos, from Jesus since the Logos of God after the "arrangement" (οἰκονομίαν) [involved in the Incarnation] became one with the soul and body of Jesus.³³⁷ Origen once again rebuts Celsus' charge of impiety in regarding (the mortal) Jesus God, with an assertion on the nature of the Incarnation and even recourse to (popular) Greek view of matter:

> Nevertheless, let our critics know that he, whom we think and have believed to be God and Son of God from the beginning, is the very Logos and wisdom and truth itself. We affirm that his mortal body and the human soul in him received the greatest elevation not only by communion (κοινωνία) but by union (ἑνώσει) and intermingling (ἀνακράσει), so that by sharing (κεκοινωνηκότα) in His [God's] divinity he was transformed into God. If anyone should take offence because we say this even of his body, let him consider what is asserted by the Greeks about matter, that properly speaking it is without qualities, but is clothed with qualities such as the Creator wishes to give it, and that often it puts aside its former qualities and receives better and different ones. If this is right, why is it remarkable that by the providence of God's will the mortal quality of Jesus' body should have been changed into an ethereal and divine quality?³³⁸

---

333. CCels V, 39. Origen, *Contra Celsum* (tr. Henry Chadwick). Greek text from Origenes, *Origenis Contra Celsum libri VIII*, ed. M. Marcovich.

334. CCels I, 66. It was this divine part in Jesus, therefore, that asserted, "I am the way, the truth, and the life" (John 14:6), while the soul of Jesus could also express "But now you seek to kill me, a man who told you the truth" (John 8:40). Cf. CCels II, 9.

335. CCels I, 66.

336. CCels II, 9.

337. CCels II, 9.

338. Wolfson points out how in Origen the term ἀνακράσει "mixing up" [intermingling] is neither in the technical sense of Aristotle nor the Stoics but rather in the sense

The explanation of the nature of the Incarnation that Origen gives is not seen pursued by Justin, or even Clement of Alexandria, for whom, in the echo of John 1:14, the "Logos became flesh and was called Jesus Christ." Certainly, in Origen there is a presented need to respond to Celsus and thus such an elaboration. This, nonetheless, takes his exploration of Logos Christology to a creative stage above the Apologists. Though it is natural a response to such a theme as the "True Logos" should have an emphasis on the use of Logos, the conception of Jesus Christ as Logos remains profound in Origen's Christian thinking against Celsus.[339] Hence, his summary of the Christian movement, foretold by the prophets, is characteristically a vision of the function of the Logos:

> for they prophesied that a certain "effulgence and image" of the divine nature would come to human life together with the holy incarnate soul of Jesus, so that a doctrine (λόγον) might be spread abroad (σπείρῃ) which would make a friend of the God of the universe anyone who received it into his own soul and cultivated it, and which would lead him on to the ultimate goodness, if he possessed in himself the power of the divine Logos who was to come to dwell in a human body.[340]

As with the Apologist before him, Origen's Logos Christology has the basis of the Fourth Gospel. The thoughts of the Apostle Paul in Origen's Logos Christology are also foundational. Indeed, John and Paul agree, for Origen, as far as Jesus Christ the Logos, God's Son, is concerned.[341] Origen was conscious of pre-Christian intimations of the *logos* concept especially in his

---

of "predominance" in which the Logos as the "stronger element" remains unchanged. Wolfson, *The Philosophy of the Fathers*, 392. *CCels* III, 41. Cf *Peri archōn* II, 6.5–6. Origen employs the analogy of an iron heated in fire, which eventually takes on the characteristics of the fire, to show the relationship between the human soul of Jesus Christ and the divine Logos. It is also significant that, as Wolfson's analysis makes evident, the Fathers expressed the inadequacy of analogy in explaining the generation of the Logos. Wolfson, *The Philosophy of the Church Fathers*, 304.

339. And so the frequent emphasis on "the Logos": the "incarnate (ἐναθρωπήσαντα) Logos of God" who wished to do good to the whole human race, II, 33; the "animate and living Logos" who is both living Wisdom and Son of God, III, 81; the "image of the supreme God is His reason (Logos)," IV, 85; the Son of God who is "his Logos and is God (divine)" or "the Logos and God (divine)," VII, 44 & 49.

340. *CCels* VII, 17. The Logos came as a physician or healer of sinners and as teacher of "divine mysteries" for those who are pure and no longer sin. *CCels* III, 62 and 54 & 61.

341. Thus, for example, what John indicated of the cosmological function of the Logos as "the one through whom all things were made" (1:3) Paul expressed in another context (Colossians 1:16). *Peri archōn* I 7.1.

response to Celsus. In this work he shows awareness of Heraclitus' literary output which Celsus references.[342] He does not refer to any *logos* conception of Heraclitus but there is reference to a quote of Heraclitus that relates to his view of everything happening according to *logos*, namely, "But one must know that war is a mutual thing, and justice is strife, and that everything comes into being through strife and necessity."[343] Irrespective of the level of Origen's acquaintance with the views of Heraclitus, Tzamalikos' observation on the contrast between the two in their *logos* conception is apt, viz. that in the latter *logos* is a "cosmic principle" to which rational beings are to ascend to through "meditation" and "intuition," while for Origen, Logos is a personal God "who condescends out of grace and compassion to rational beings, being continuously in them after he brought them into being."[344]

Among the Stoics, the *Logos*, also identified with Zeus, is pervasive in all things and responsible for the regenerative conflagration. Origen contrasts this view with that of the Christians in a somewhat teasing tone,

> according to the opinion of the Stoics, who maintain that the first principles (ἀρχὰς) are corporeal, and who on this account hold that everything is destructible (φθείροντας) and venture even to make the supreme God Himself destructible (unless this seemed to them to be utterly outrageous), even the Logos of God that comes down to men and to the most insignificant things is nothing other than a material spirit. But in the view of us Christians, who try to show that the rational (λογικὴν) soul is superior to any material nature and is an invisible and incorporeal being, the divine Logos is not material. Through him all things were made, and in order that all things may be made by the Logos, he extends not to men only but even to the things supposed to be insignificant which are controlled by nature. The Stoics may destroy everything in a conflagration (ἐκπυρούτωσαν) if they like. But we do not recognize that an incorporeal being is subject to a conflagration, or that the soul of man is dissolved into fire, or that this happens to the being of angels, or thrones, or dominions, or principalities, or powers.[345]

The nature of the Logos is fundamentally different for Stoics (material) and Christians (non-material). Tzamalikos also notes that while the Stoics do not differentiate between the *logos* itself and its action in its immanence

---

342. *CCels* I 5; VI 12, 13 & 42.
343. *CCels* VI 42. Chadwick's translation.
344. Tzamalikos, *Origen*, 171–72.
345. *CCels* VI, 71.

in the world, in Origen it is by "his power" in operation that the Logos is present in the cosmos.[346]

Origen, like Clement of Alexandria, explicitly refers to Philo in three instances and his acquaintance with at least half of Philo's extant writings, was more in the direction of the "exegetical part" than the "philosophical and apologetic treatises."[347] Origen employs such terms as "idea of ideas" (ἰδέαν ἰδῶν) and "second (δεύτερον) God" concerning the Logos that are reminiscent of Philo.[348] Origen, however, states in the *Contra Celsum* (composed in his retreat in Caesarea), that he has not found among the learned Jews he has met the belief that the Son of God is the Logos.[349] Although Origen and Philo, with the basis of the LXX, were mindful of the *logos* idea of particularly the Stoics and associated ideas from Plato and Aristotle, Origen's point of departure is the mystery of the Incarnation, while for Philo it is the Law (through Moses). The personal involvement of the Logos in humanity remains a fundamental source of difference in the *logos* conception of the two native Alexandrians, no matter the similarities at the conceptual level. Philo remains an exemplar in the attempt to appropriate the faith of the Old Testament within Graeco-Roman shared categories of thought. If there were no Philo what Justin, Clement, and Origen would have done, would not have been totally dissimilar to what Philo had attempted. The fundamental stage of working out the common ground between the insights of the Old Testament and that of the Graeco-Roman world of thought was needed. The Greek translation of the Hebrew Scriptures (LXX) had been a necessary first step, but the additional layer of the intellectual output that Philo epitomized was still necessary for these individuals in their eventual vocation. Philo remains a source of a *strand* of Logos Christology crystallized in Origen.

Origen's efforts with his Logos Christology had a considerable share of influence in the subsequent development of Graeco-Roman Christian

---

346. Tzamalikos, *Origen*, 167. The "presence" of the Logos points either to "the spiritual advent of Christ," at the Incarnation or at the Parousia. Tzamalikos, *Origen: Philosophy of History and Eschatology*, 66.

347. Namely, "the works of Philo" *CCels* IV, 51; "Philo also composed a book concerning this ladder" [of Jacob, i.e., Philo's treatise *On Dreams* (*de Somniis*)] *CCels* VI, 21; "And Philo, who enjoys a high reputation among intelligent people for many subjects" *Commentary on Matthew* 15.3. Runia "Philo of Alexandria," 169. Runia "Philo of Alexandria," 171.

348. Respectively, *CCels* VI, 64 and V, 39. Philo, *Opif.*, 25, a seal as "idea of ideas" *Migr.*, 103; "the second God, who is His Logos" *QG.* II, 62. Greek text and English translation from Philo, *Questions and Answers on Genesis* (tr. Ralph Marcus), 150 note n. And, the sense of the *logos* as second (δεύτερος) to God is found in *Leg.* II, 86.

349. *CCels* II, 31. Chadwick notes that the reference is to the Palestinian Rabbis. Origen, *Contra Celsum*, 93 n.3.

thought. Logos Christology enabled Origen to reinterpret received "rule of faith" in the context of contemporary intellectual (scientific) space.[350] Despite some apparent limitations of "certainty and clarity" on subjects such as the difference between creation and generation, Studer observes four themes of theological reflection that has the stamp of Origen's Logos Christology: the Trinitarian formula *mia ousia—treis hypostaseis* [one substance—three persons]; the doctrine of the perichoresis of the two natures of Christ; "the doctrine of the history of salvation as summed up in the mystery of the Logos"; and the teaching of the Holy Spirit as the source of Christian freedom.[351]

The Development of Logos Christology as a Process in Conversion

Regarding the organic nature of Christian mission in the history of Christianity, it is helpful to regard Logos Christology beginning from the Fourth Gospel to Origen as a development. It developed as it was applied in addressing contemporary issues and interests. Logos Christology is in effect a first fruit of the Greek understanding of the Incarnation: God's Logos "became flesh" for the salvation of creation and humanity. The Christian understanding of Incarnation has at once given a legitimate drive (*guarantor*) for the Christological explorations of indigenous cultural concepts and serves as the *critique* for their missiological applications.

Logos Christology had an active lifespan. In many ways it represents the appropriation and explication of Jesus Christ in the Greek language, and way of thinking or experience of reality. It is true that Logos Christology as an initial "model" underwent some clarification and refinement leading to a "paradigmatic" status of informing other models in the development of Graeco-Roman Christian thought.[352] It is inadequate to leave it this sense of paradigm. Logos Christology played a significant role in the whole process of "turning" Greek ways of thinking and behaving to the direction of Jesus Christ. Logos Christology ensured a continuous penetration of the significance of Jesus Christ into Graeco-Roman world of thought and practice.

---

350. Studer, *Trinity and Incarnation*, 86.

351. Studer, *Trinity and Incarnation*, 86–87.

352. Heron, "'Logos, Image, Son': Some Models and Paradigms in Early Christology," 43–62. A "model" is employed to "grasp and describe" that which we seek to understand, and it can be a "picture, analogy or metaphor." A "paradigm" is a model at a stage in which it has interacted with other models and has had to be refined and clarified in the process and thus has become a "dominant" and a "controlling model" in understanding and expressing a given reality (44–46).

In the process, it enabled Graeco-Roman Christians to easily highlight the activity of the one God in their undeniable non-Christian past.

The three stages of the conversion process, therefore, makes it possible to discern the level or stage of engagement of the Christological use of a cultural image. In other words, they offer a convenient scheme in assessing the missiological impact of a Christological image. In the case of Logos Christology, its *ambiguity* at the *missionary* stage is *clarified* at the *convert* stage, while its full *missiological implication* is *innovatively* explored at the *re-figuration* stage. This can be a paradigm for assessing Christological images, which are in effect answers to cultural questions about Jesus Christ. Invariably Christian questions are culture specific and the corresponding answers, if they are to address the heart of the matter, should be in the language of the culture. Christological images are inexhaustive and not without challenges and limitations. However, discerning their role in the process of cultural conversion offers opportunities for clarification, refinement, and innovative explorations. If creatively employed adequately, cultural images linger on and serve as witnesses of the impact of Jesus Christ in the respective cultural world. As Studer has highlighted, the legacy of Origen's (innovative) Logos Christology (resulting from a creative engagement with traditional thought) in subsequent Christian reflections cannot be denied.[353]

Conclusion

Philo could not have conceived of the *logos* becoming flesh (human). Those who encountered the reality of Jesus of Nazareth eventually *recognized* him as the Logos incarnate. It is significant that nowhere in the canonical New Testament documents did Jesus explicitly claim the image of *logos*.[354] The Christological image of Jesus Christ as the Logos (incarnate) should not be taken for granted simply because it is part of the canon of Scripture. It is a *recognition* resulting from a deep cultural engagement with the message and impact of Jesus Christ. Jesus the Logos is an encouragement and a pattern for all other non-canonical titles and images of Jesus Christ. In other words, Jesus the Logos itself justifies other titles such as Ancestor.

---

353. Cf. Studer, *Trinity and Incarnation*, 80. The creative stage that Origen belongs to in his application of Logos Christology was exacting, but the confidence to probe every corner of knowledge and indeed any sustained thought in the light of the Logos (incarnate) must have been refreshing for him. Walls, "In Quest of the Father of Mission Studies," 101.

354. Certainly, according to the author of the Fourth Gospel, not every statement of his is necessarily documented (John 20:30).

Logos Christology has a background in a *logos* concept, and the same is true with Ancestor Christology and the idea of *ancestor*. However, before examining the idea of ancestor, particularly among the Akan of Ghana, I discuss the African experience of Jesus via the journey of Christological explorations in the next chapter.

Chapter 3

The African Experience of Jesus

ALTHOUGH THE ATTITUDES OF early Christian missionaries to sub-Saharan Africa toward the African past was largely unsympathetic,[1] the theological efforts of African Christian converts that, in many ways, responded to this missionary legacy have been significant. The fair appraisal of the pre-Christian African religious tradition, which made manifest the quest for an African Christian identity, paved the way for later Christological reflections, which have embraced images of Jesus Christ from African categories of thought.[2] Written Christology in Africa is a later development in African theology when the issue of the value of the African past in theology had been satisfactorily addressed. The titles and images of Jesus Christ in Africa have been possible because of those earlier theological input.

African Christology and the Process of Conversion

Christianity in Africa is about conversion or transformation of the African experience of reality. Part of the task of Christian scholarship in Africa is to continually reflect and discern the state of the process of conversion. Therefore, when the various Christological efforts in Africa are examined in the context of the conversion process in Africa, it becomes possible to

---

1. Idowu, "The Predicament of the Church in Africa," 425–26. Muzorewa, *The Origins and Development of African Theology*, 21–34. Bujo, *African Theology in Its Social Context*, 37–73. On the issue of the African past in theology see, Walls, *The Missionary Movement in Christian History*, 12–13.

2. See Mbiti, *Concepts of God in Africa*; Idowu, *Oludumaré*.

examine the level of interaction between the message of Christianity and African traditional and contemporary realities. Images of Jesus such as Healer, Chief, Master of Initiation, and Ancestor, proposed as fertile avenues for presenting Jesus in Africa, are then signs of a creative stage in the conversion process in Africa.[3]

Grassroot or oral theological experiences are invariably prior to written articulations. Though grassroot theologies are kick-started with the translation of the Scriptures into indigenous languages, there are mostly signs of theological creativity even in the absence of mother-tongue Bibles. Thus, the viability of academic Christology is dependent on grassroot efforts. The proposed relationship between grassroots and academic Christology in African Christianity is highlighted in this chapter.

Over the past three decades there have been constructive attempts at an African Christology that are mindful of the African primal religious context and the socio-political circumstances of most African societies.[4] It was a matter of time before Christological concerns took a considerable prominence, at least at the academic level. John Mbiti's concern with the lack of "African Christological concepts" was at a time when theological issues concerning the pre-Christian African past were the predominant occupation of most of the early African Christian theologians.[5] Though these theologians recognized the uniqueness of Jesus Christ in their theologizing, associating him with traditional African concepts was not prominent. However, from the point of view of the process in Christian conversion, the eventual emergence of African Christology, or concepts of Jesus Christ, is a sign of the deepening and penetration of the reality of Jesus in Africa.

Christology in the Development of African Theology

African Christology has developed within African theology. The emergence of African theology in the mid twentieth century was a corollary of the impact of Christianity on sub-Saharan Africa in the nineteenth and early twentieth century.[6] The concern of early African theology was largely with the continuity of God in Christianity and African Traditional Religion (ATR). The often negative view of the value of the African religious past expressed

---

3. Stinton, *Jesus of Africa*; Schreiter (ed.), *Faces of Jesus in Africa*.

4. Udoh, *Guest Christology*; Mugambi and Magesa, *Jesus in African Christianity*; Bediako, *Jesus in African Culture*; Ezigbo, *Re-Imagining African Christologies*.

5. Mbiti, "Some African Concepts of Christology," 51 cited in Moloney, "African Christology," 505.

6. Muzorewa, *The Origins and Development of African Theology*, 21–34; Bujo, *African Theology in Its Social*, 37–73.

and pursued by a greater part of European missionaries in Africa necessitated this.[7] The issue of the African past and its treatment in the introduction of Christianity in many parts of Africa was dominant in early African theological discourse.[8] Consequently, the early literature on African theology constituted predominantly theological attempts to interpret the African past. These undoubtedly have been vindicated since later African theologians have pursued their Christological interests in what could be termed as a *theological confidence in the African religious past*. As such the efforts of the later theologians become meaningful as they are related to the achievements of the previous generation of theologians.[9]

In the broader picture of the process of turning the patterns of African thought towards the direction of Christ, there are stages involved. From the point of view of Christological development in African Christianity, therefore, it is as if to say one generation prepared the grounds by its attempt to clarify the nature of the involvement of the God and Father of Jesus Christ in pre-Christian (sub-Saharan) Africa. It has been the task of a later generation to attempt a reflection of the *actual* involvement of the person of Jesus Christ with the African experience of reality. The *Christological* generation has been a necessary follow-up to the *theological* generation.

Diane Stinton in her assessment of the "current Christological trends in Africa" identifies the attitudes of a "Christological crisis" along with that of a "Christological confidence."[10] The former, for Stinton, "refers to a lack of critical and systematic reflection on Jesus Christ by Africans in light of their own cultural inheritance and identity."[11] Yet Stinton notes, "among indigenous [African] believers" there abounds a "Christological confidence" in their views of Jesus Christ "through African eyes" since the arrival of Christianity in both North and sub-Saharan Africa.[12] In sub-Saharan Africa the "critical and systematic reflection on Jesus Christ" was to be taken up by those with the benefit of a theological education. Though Stinton does not explicitly differentiate between the "critical and systematic reflection" as largely *academic* and that of indigenous reflections through songs and poems and even the arts as *oral* or *grassroots*, it may be helpful to see them as such.

---

7. Idowu, "The Predicament of the Church in Africa," 425–26.
8. Walls, *The Missionary Movement in Christian History*, 12–13.
9. Bediako, "Guest Editorial: Lived Christology," 1.
10. Stinton, *Jesus of Africa*, 4.
11. Stinton, *Jesus of Africa*, 5.
12. Stinton, *Jesus of Africa*, 4.

Mbiti had noted a relationship between *written* and *oral* theologies even before the last decade of the twentieth century arguing that "written theology" in African Christianity can only come after "oral theology" to examine its features in retrospect.[13] Mbiti's observation was with the conviction that "the Christian way of life is in Africa to stay" and that "much of the theological activity in Christian Africa is being done as oral theology (in contrast to written theology) from the living experiences of Christians."[14] It was therefore only a matter of time before academic or written Christology would grow in confidence in its "critical and systematic reflection," drawing largely from the "indigenous, oral Christologies" in sub-Saharan Africa.

The attempted distinction between theology and Christology in African Christianity with the latter appearing to have followed the former is not to suggest that one is devoid of the other, as if one can speak of a theology without Christology or vice versa in (African) Christianity. This is not possible in Christianity. Yet the movement of Christian presence and the attempt to assess its impact in retrospect does show the concentration on one over the other at some point in addressing immediate concerns. In the case of Christianity in sub-Saharan Africa, the concentration in earlier written works was on the place of God in the pre-Christian past and hence the value of the African religious past as not (entirely) without the witness of God. This concentration, as Bediako has argued, was in itself an effort at working out an African Christian identity.[15] Thus, for Stinton, Christology was "inherent in African theology from the outset" and considers as "latent Christologies" the Christological concern hidden in the efforts of African theologians from 1950 to 1980.[16]

Written Christological efforts in African Christianity from 1980 to the present (2004) for Stinton has been pursued in an attitude of confidence, that is, in a "critical and systematic" way.[17] Beginning from 1980, therefore, there has been "the shift from crises to confidence" in African Christological reflections.[18] Stinton sees demonstrated in the works of Enyi Ben

---

13 Mbiti, *Bible and Theology in African Christianity*, 229.

14. Mbiti, *Bible and Theology in African Christianity*, 229.

15. Bediako, *Theology and Identity*; Stinton, *Jesus of Africa*, 9.

16. Stinton, *Jesus of Africa*, 7.

17. Mugambi *et al.* (eds.), *Jesus in African Christianity*; this collection is largely an East African contribution. The first edition was published in 1989 resulting from a five-day ecumenical symposium held in Karen, Nairobi, from March 13–17 1989, with participants from Kenya, Uganda and Tanzania. Also for a review of Christology in Africa and some of the African Christological titles as at the late 1980s, see Wessels, *Images of Jesus*, 94–115.

18. Stinton, *Jesus of Africa*, 10.

Udoh, Kwame Bediako, Charles Nyamiti, and Takatso Mofokeng between the years 1983–84, "the rapid rise of Christologies across the sub-Saharan continent and across confessional lines."[19] Stinton's two phases view of the development of Christology in African Christianity is helpful from the "historical and theological" perspective.[20] It is however inadequate from the standpoint of understanding the process of the turning of African categories of thought toward the direction of Jesus Christ. Aside the difficulties in dating the development of a thought, it does not adequately indicate the link between "latent" and "emergent" Christologies and their role in bringing Jesus Christ to the heart of African traditional thought. For example, while in 1968 Mbiti had expressed the lack of "African concepts of Christology" in his own attempt at "Some African Concepts in Christology," Kofi Appiah-Kubi in 1976 could attempt "to outline the basic African concepts of Jesus Christ" from "the life, worship and beliefs of the indigenous African Christian Churches [African Independent Churches]." These Churches had been in existence before 1976 and their "African concepts of Jesus Christ" did not emerge at this date.[21] From the perspective of the process of conversion in African Christianity, following the framework of *missionary*, *convert* and *refiguration* stages, one can appreciate the *suggestive*, *explicative*, and *innovative* stages in African Christology from the onset of theological reflections in sub-Saharan Africa.

Trends in African Christology

The task of developing "a clear conception of the person of Jesus Christ" and making him relevant within the everyday experience of African Christians is not the preserve of one generation.[22] From both "latent" and "emergent" Christologies the concern for the cultural and the economic and political situation of various parts of sub-Saharan Africa has been expressed diversely. Charles Nyamiti, in his helpful survey of the Christological developments in Africa, identified the two broad ways of approach in African theology

---

19. Stinton, *Jesus of Africa*, 13. Udoh, *Guest Christology* [Doctoral dissertation in 1983 published later in 1988]. Kwame Bediako, "Biblical Christologies in the Context of African Traditional Religions," 81–121 [Paper presented in 1982 at conference in Bangkok discussing "the emerging Christologies in the Two Thirds World"]. Nyamiti, *Christ as our Ancestor* [Nyamiti's work published in 1984 is a collection of articles published earlier]. Mofokeng, *The Crucified among the Crossbearers*.

20. Stinton, *Jesus of Africa*, 6.

21. See Mbiti, "Some African Concepts of Christology," 51 cited in Stinton, *Jesus of Africa*, 6; Kofi Appiah-Kubi, "Christology," 69.

22. Orobator, *Theology Brewed in an African Pot*, 74.

and hence Christology, namely, "inculturation" and "liberation."[23] Nyamiti identified them as "types" but they could also be considered as "approaches" since both seek a solution in the one reality of Jesus Christ.[24]

Within "the school" of inculturation Nyamiti further indicated those who take as a point of departure the "biblical teaching about Christ" and work within African culture for "relevant Christological themes."[25] Others within the inculturation approach, Nyamiti observed, begin their Christological quest from the background of African culture, that is, examining "the mystery of Christ" from the general African worldview or from a "particular theme taken from the African worldview or culture."[26] This method for Nyamiti can also be termed the "thematic approach" and has been the "most frequently used" in the African Christological efforts.[27]

Liberation theology in Africa, Nyamiti indicates, has been largely pursued in response to two different concerns of liberation.[28] As a response to apartheid, "South African Black theology" as a kind of African liberation theology was linked with the North American Black theology and was gradually influenced by Latin American theology of liberation.[29] The second kind of "African liberation theology" is simply termed as such and was popular "especially in independent sub-Saharan Africa."[30]

---

23. Nyamiti, "African Christologies Today," 3–23; Also Nyamiti, "Contemporary African Christologies: Assessment and Practical Suggestions," 62–77.

24. For discussions on Inculturation and Liberation in African theology, see Martey, *African Theology: Inculturation and Liberation*; Justin Ukpong also discusses five approaches to the issue of Christology and Inculturation in Africa; Ukpong, "Christology and Inculturation: A New Testament Perspective," 40–61.

25. Nyamiti, "African Christologies Today," 3–4. John Mbiti typifies this method, according to Nyamiti.

26. Nyamiti, "African Christologies Today," 4.

27. Various scholars identified in this second category include E. J. Pénoukou and Nyamiti taking the general African worldview. Those taking specific themes comprise Harry Sawyerr, Kwesi Dickson, Anselme Sanon, Aylward Shorter and Bénézet Bujo. One can further add the works of Kwame Bediako on Ancestor Christology and John Ekem on Priestly Christology [Ekem, *Priesthood In Context*] within this latter group. The present study also falls within the latter approach as it examines the various strands in Ancestor Christology.

28. Nyamiti, "African Christologies Today," 12.

29. The origin of the theology of liberation in Latin America is traced to socio-political developments between 1950 and 1960s. See among others Gutiérrez, *A Theology of Liberation*. Kirk, *Liberation Theology*. Muskus, *The Origins and Early Development of Liberation Theology in Latin America with Particular Reference to Gustavo Gutiérrez*. Also, an anthology on the theology of liberation, Hennelly (ed.), *Liberation Theology*.

30. Nyamiti, "African Christologies Today," 13.

Aside the male dominated expositions of Black theology or Christology which to a large extent have been representative of the theology of liberation in Africa,[31] it is an interesting fact that it is the view of Jesus as "Liberator" that appeals more to African female theologians who consequently have substantially explored this Christological theme.[32] Nyamiti sees both South African Black Christology and African Christology of liberation as having some common features. Both start from the humanity of Jesus Christ as the man of Nazareth who lived in a society "oppressed and exploited" by foreigners.[33]

From an African standpoint, Emmanuel Martey has argued that there was no such thing as a "theological dilemma" between the approaches of inculturation and liberation.[34] The "main challenge" in Africa for Martey is in the struggle for liberation in Africa in the areas of "the socioeconomical and political realms of life" and "the religiocultural spheres of life." Accordingly, for Martey, a "relevant, contextual and authentic theology for Africa must have a unitary perception of inculturation and liberation." Such an integral view for Martey will make way for a "unified theology of cultural and political liberation."[35] One can hardly disagree with Martey on the situational reality of contemporary Africa and illegitimacy of any boundary between the two approaches, which in the final analysis seek to address the same concern, namely, the transformation of the people and societies of Africa through the Gospel of Jesus Christ for the glory of God. Keeping the two in a "unitary" vision, however, may be the challenge and that seems to be a perennial one.

Nyamiti considered as "models" the various Christological efforts in both the inculturation and liberation schools and at the same time used the

---

31. Martey, *African Theology*, 95ff.

32. Martey, *African Theology*, 83. See also Hinge, "Jesus Christ and the Liberation of Women in Africa," 261–68; Thérèse Souga and Louise Tappa express their views on the "The Christ-Event" as African women respectively from the Catholic and Protestant perspectives and both emphasize the liberation Christ brings to African women: Souga, "The Christ-Event from the Viewpoint of African Women—A Catholic Perspective," 22–29 and Tappa, "The Christ-Event from the Viewpoint of African Women—A Protestant Perspective," 30–34. Also, Amoah and Oduyoye, "The Christ for African Women," 35–46. For example, Amoah and Oduyoye insist that Jesus Christ "has become for us, for African women and for Africa, the savior and liberator of the world" and later on that as a "friend and companion" Christ liberates "women from [the] assumptions of patriarchal societies" (44 & 45). Nasimiyu-Wasike, "Christology and an African Woman's Experience," 70–81.

33. Nyamiti, "African Christologies Today," 13.

34. Martey, *African Theology*, 130.

35. Martey, *African Theology*, 131.

plural "Christologies" when he looked at them collectively.[36] For Stinton, the "model approach" was a helpful way to "interpret the highly complex realities" evidenced from the textual and qualitative findings in her survey of African Christology.[37] Stinton explains this is in keeping with the desire to realise Martey's proposal of "a unitary perception of inculturation and liberation" in which both theology of inculturation and liberation in Africa are "integrated" to create a "unified theology of cultural and political liberation."[38] In her graphical representation of the four identified "distinct models corresponding to the central Christological themes," Stinton uses "interlocking circles" which show the "significant overlap that occurs among Christological images."[39]

Christological images and titles do overlap due to their underlying idea or the reality they seek to convey. Stinton did not qualify "Christological images" with the definite article "the" or the adjective "African" in her quote above and she seems to suggest that *all* Christological images overlap. Even if she has in mind the overlap among the African Christological images, Stinton here agrees with Nyamiti in upholding the understanding that "all Christian mysteries [expressed in the various images of Jesus such as Son of God and Healer] are organically interconnected (*nexus mysteriorum*)."[40] The interconnection is such that "it is possible to gain a deeper understanding of one particular mystery (in itself and its relevance for us) in the light of others."[41] This understanding, for Nyamiti, warrants the exploration of "deeper African Christologies and theologies" making way also for an "authentically African Christianity in all sectors of church life."[42] An African image of Christ, therefore, that is "truly Christian and African" can be of relevance to the Church outside Africa.[43] It should therefore not be difficult to appreciate that going into the New Testament to understand Christological models need not be a one-way traffic. African images of Jesus Christ can also illuminate our understanding of the Christological efforts of the evangelists or missionaries of the New Testament.

While some early written African Christological attempts were exploratory and hence prescriptive, others endeavored to examine what was present

---

36. Nyamiti, "African Christologies Today," 14 & 17.
37. Stinton, *Jesus of Africa*, 51.
38. Martey, *African Theology*, 131.
39. Stinton, *Jesus of Africa*, 51 & 52.
40. Nyamiti, "African Christologies Today," 14.
41. Nyamiti, "African Christologies Today," 14.
42. Nyamiti, "African Christologies Today," 15.
43. Nyamiti, "African Christologies Today," 15.

in the liturgy of some African churches. Anselme T. Sanon[44] and François Kabasélé[45] respectively represent such distinct aspects with their Christological treatises on the institution of initiation from the West African standpoint and that of chieftaincy from the East African. Of interest in their efforts is the role of vernacular or mother-tongue Bibles in serving the Christological end. The image and symbolism of particular African trees had also been examined at the written level by 1990 in the works of Thomas G. Christensen[46] and Martin Ott.[47] Though described and analyzed by European missionaries, the expressions in liturgy and visual art reflect the African Christian endeavor in responding to the impact of Jesus via the symbolic significance of traditional imageries such as a tree. Hence these are noteworthy in the view of the complementary association between *oral* and *written* Christology.

The Interplay between Grassroots and Academic Christologies

Mbiti's observation that *written* theology in Africa can only come after *oral* theology in examining the latter's features in retrospect is true also for African Christology. Systematic and written reflection of the activity of God in Jesus Christ follows from the responses of the living experiences of those impacted by that reality. The responses are in themselves vital for the attempted articulation of the "deep" experienced impact of the reality of Jesus Christ. Nyamiti in his survey of African Christological trends before the 1990s was careful to note that:

> Indeed if African theology is the understanding and presentation of the Christ-event in accordance with African needs and mentality, then African Christologies must have existed since

---

44. Anselme T. Sanon, "Jesus, Master of Initiation," 85–102. Sanon's work *Enraciner l'évangile: initiations africaines et pedagogie de la foi* was published in 1982. The English translation by Robert R. Barr in the volume edited by Schreiter is from the original French, "Jésus, Maître d'initiation" which was part of the *Chemins de la Christologie africaine* published in 1986. Kabasélé et al. (eds.), *Chemins de la Christologie africaine*.

45. François Kabasélé, "Christ as Chief," 103–15. The translation of "Christ" as *Mulaba* in the Luba language, according to Kabasélé, began a process that led to "the attribution to Christ of several other traditional titles" (Kabasélé, "Christ as Chief," 103). The title of chief, *Mukalengé*, was predominant among the traditional titles resulting from the translation of *Mulaba*. Cf. Stinton, *Jesus of Africa*, 188–90.

46. Christensen, *An African Tree of Life*.

47. Ott, *African Theology In Images*.

the beginning of evangelization on the Black continent (although mainly in a latent, oral, and unsystematic form).[48]

One of the ways to unveil such "authentically [latent, oral and unsystematic] African Christologies," for Nyamiti, is through a "serious scientific research" among African Christian communities.[49] Yet care should be taken not to set one level of Christology, in this case the grassroots form, over against another as being "the only valuable type."[50] Despite the fact that both have their own strengths and limitations, Nyamiti instructively notes that each has need of the other for a "useful mutual complementarity."[51] I understand this to mean that each level needs to learn from and listen to the other to arrive at an "informed" and authentic expression of the response to the impact of Jesus Christ in the lives of African Christians.

Since the presence of "systematic or academic" Christologies do not imply the absence of grassroots reflections, we have deemed it suitable to refer to both as *levels*. In the sense that both have need of each other and not one "crowning" or "making better" the other. Written Christology, with the benefit of the historical developments in the Christian tradition, can *inform* Christology at the grassroots level. An *informed* grassroots Christology can then feed the "systematic or academic" efforts in articulating an "authentic" expression of the African response to Jesus Christ.

Nyamiti did not reference the *oral* Christological articulations of the Ghanaian Christian (Pentecostal) woman, Christina Afua Gyan (Madam Afua Kuma), which had been published in 1980.[52] Afua Kuma's inability to write did not hamper her oral indigenous reflection on Jesus, falling on her biblical knowledge as well as traditional and contemporary social and religious concepts. Her attempt could have been brought to support Nyamiti's observation of the presence of oral Christology or indeed even inform the articulation of some of his points. Afua Kuma's Christology did however inform Kwame Bediako in his "critical and systematic reflection" on the massive presence of Christianity in Africa[53] as evidence of a *reflective* "theological articulation."[54] Nyamiti's view of the "mutual complementarity"

---

48. Nyamiti, "African Christologies Today," 19.
49. Nyamiti, "African Christologies Today," 19.
50. Nyamiti, "African Christologies Today," 19.
51. Nyamiti, "African Christologies Today," 19.
52. Both the Twi and English translation by Jon Kirby; Kuma, *Kwaeberentwu Ase Yesu—Ayeyi Ne Mpaebɔ*.
53. Kwame Bediako, "Cry Jesus! Christian Theology and Presence in Modern Africa," 3–19.
54. Bediako, "Cry Jesus!" 8. Emphasis mine.

between grassroots and written Christology is demonstrated by Bediako's interaction with Afua Kuma's "images of Jesus."

Bediako found in Afua Kuma, whose effort he considered as a "reflective theology," evidence that showed the legitimacy of speaking of the Christian faith "as having become a non-Western religion."[55] That is to say, for Bediako, Christianity is "seen for what it truly is, a universal religion"[56] in which Western and African responses and contributions to the Christian faith are not to be taken for granted. So, for Bediako, a Christian African woman in the freedom of her mother tongue could also equally express the universal significance of Jesus, "the Lord and Saviour of all the nations."[57] This Bediako sees in Afua Kuma's exaltation:[58]

> O great and powerful Jesus, incomparable Diviner,
> the sun and moon are Your *batakari* [robe]
> it sparkles like the morning star.
> *Sekyere Buruku*, the tall mountain,
> all the nations see Your glory.[59]

Jesus is *Sekyere Buruku* for Afua Kuma; a title that, Bediako notes, evokes an indigenous deity (*obosom*) who is associated with "the tall mountain" in the Kwahu mountain ridge in the Eastern Region of Ghana.[60] The splendor of the mountain above the morning clouds, for Bediako, enables an easy transition of the "'power' of a local deity. . . . To the glory and power of the true Lord of the land, come into his realm."[61] Afua Kuma's oral Christology then, for Bediako, is "very elevated," showing the imprint of an "authentic African Christian religious experience and meditation" in the response to Jesus in Africa.[62] The distinction between oral and written Christology is thus blurred in Bediako's reflection.

Bediako explains it "may even be misleading" to speak of academic theology or Christology coming to examine retrospectively the features of African Christianity as expressed in oral theology, as Mbiti observed.[63] Further on, this carries with it a sense of "an oral phase" in transition to an academic or written theology that becomes "the real theology." I have

55. Bediako, "Cry Jesus!" 8.
56. Bediako, "Cry Jesus!" 3.
57. Bediako, "Cry Jesus!" 13.
58. Bediako, "Cry Jesus!" 13.
59. Kuma, *Jesus of the Deep Forest*, 6.
60. Bediako, "Cry Jesus!" 13.
61. Bediako, "Cry Jesus!" 13.
62. Bediako, "Cry Jesus!" 15.
63. Bediako, "Cry Jesus!" 17.

attempted to see both as levels, which can and should overlap each other. Bediako is yet still helpful in insisting that oral theology positively viewed "as theology which comes from where the faith lives, in the life-situation of the community of faith," is "an abiding element of all theology" and "essential for academic theology."[64] The two then become "aspects" of one reality, for Bediako, whose ensured contact enables theology to acquire its "authentic character."[65] Two characteristics of such a theology are evident for Bediako, namely, theology becomes the task of "a community of believers who share in a common context" and not just a specialized few and also where such believers are committed in "bringing the Gospel into contact with the questions and issues of that context."[66]

Once both oral theology and written theology are kept at par with each other, the task of each other is mutual. Oral theology then has a liberating role to play for Bediako in helping the academic theologian to avoid the tendency to "construct a theology" by himself or herself. At the same time it falls on academic theology, in Bediako's estimation, to understand, clarify and demonstrate "the *universal* and *academic* significance" of oral theology.[67] This is Bediako's version of Nyamiti's "mutual complementarity" of oral theology and written theology.

Philip Laryea makes similar conclusions following his comparative study of the theological or Christological imagery of second-century Hellenistic Christian leader Ignatius of Antioch and the twentieth-century Akan Christian woman Afua Kuma. Laryea's analysis reveals that "the phenomenon of Christian imagination" gives rise to "different conceptions of Christ" though it is the same regardless of the (cultural) context. This phenomenon is important in understanding the link, Laryea indicates, "that should exist" between grassroots and academic theology on one hand and the "evolution of Christian doctrine" on the other.[68] Thus, Laryea's reading of Ignatius "through the eyes of Afua Kuma" brings out the significance of Ignatius as a grassroots theologian.[69] Furthermore, "grassroots theology," Laryea insists, is "a credible force in the evolution and development of systematic thought [academic theology]" in which both reflect the "religious experience" of those who encounter Jesus Christ.[70]

---

64. Bediako, "Cry Jesus!" 17.
65. Bediako, "Cry Jesus!" 18.
66. Bediako, "Cry Jesus!" 18.
67. Bediako, "Cry Jesus!" 18.
68. Laryea, "St. Ignatius of Antioch and Afua Kuma of Kwahu," 11.
69. Laryea, "St. Ignatius of Antioch and Afua Kuma of Kwahu," 117–18.
70. Laryea, "St. Ignatius of Antioch and Afua Kuma of Kwahu," 122.

Conclusion

The element of the response to the impact of the reality of Jesus Christ constitutes a primary focus of Christology. This understanding accommodates both systematic written reflection and spontaneous oral expression of the invariably profound impact of the reality of Jesus on individuals and communities. New Testament Christology remains the primary data for subsequent contextual Christological efforts, especially mediated by translated Bibles. African Christological images have not been unrelated to those in the New Testament. For example, both images of Chief and Master of Initiation (though not directly found in the New Testament) have been pursued with New Testament insight, and in the case of the latter particularly the book of Hebrews. African Christology is not only expressed in liturgy, songs, poetry and written texts but also in the visual arts. The symbol of African trees both in their ritual use and physical nature is also a subject matter in Christology. These at the least demonstrate the broad spectrum of concepts diversely employed in African Christology. It is significant that written African Christology has been explored either as a reflection of what has been going on at the grassroots or as an explorative endeavor. Kabasélé and Sanon show these dimensions in their respective efforts with the institution of chief in East Africa and that of initiation in West Africa. The need for both written and grassroots Christologies to complement each other informs my submission that New Testament images of Jesus can complement those in Africa and illuminate the endeavors in both directions. The complementary aspect indicated is in view of the fact of the continuing impact of mother-tongue Bibles in African Christianity.

The exploration of a cultural image in Christology that is mindful of its connection with the whole process of conversion makes it possible to assess its levels or stages of growth and impact. By the time of Justin Martyr, for example, Logos Christology already formulated by the time of the Fourth Gospel, had taken a form that, even though was not discontinuous with its earliest source, differed significantly from it. A reason for this fact is in the diverse pre-Christian views of and application of the idea or concept of *logos* (and its translation equivalent) in the Jewish and Hellenistic world of thought. Ancestor Christology in Africa has been pursued from the (general) sense of the place of the idea of ancestor in traditional Africa and its enduring effects in some contemporary societies. It is helpful to focus on the expression of the concept of ancestor in its local context so its Christological exploration becomes specifically relevant to the context. The next chapter explores the *nana* (ancestor) concept among the Akan of Ghana.

Chapter 4

The Idea of *Nana* (Ancestor) in Akan Traditional Life and Thought

AN ENDURING TRADITION OF the African past in parts of sub-Saharan Africa has been the belief in the existence and influence of deceased kinsmen and kinswomen in indigenous societies. Ancestor Christology has been developed based on the value of the idea or concept of ancestors and its pivotal role in the traditional African society.[1] Among the Akan of Ghana, the religious, philosophical, and ethical dimensions of the concept of ancestors are manifested in such social activities as festivals, funerals, and children naming ceremonies. The Ghanaian writer J. B. Danquah linked the Akan idea of *nana* to what he felt was the portrait of the ideal person in the community and this has implication for Christian missionary engagement. An ancestor survives in the memory of the living and hence John S. Mbiti's designation of an ancestor as the "living-dead"[2] (who though dead is yet alive in the memory of the living). Precisely because of their potency in the memory of the living, ancestors become the representatives of the past for the present generation and therefore also as a source of identity.[3] The reality of the

---

1. I have designated the belief in ancestors and all its consequential activities as the 'concept or idea of ancestors' and this comprises the thinking behind all the (visible) expressions of things done in honor of ancestors during traditional social functions as well as (individual) opinions concerning ancestors and their involvement in private and public life.

2. Mbiti, *African Religions and Philosophy*, 25. Fortes, *Religion, Morality and the Person—Essays on Tallensi Religion*, 68.

3. Cole, "Sacrifice, Narratives and Experience in East Madagascar," 404.

ancestors ensures that inherited "ancestral cultural values" are maintained.[4] Tradition itself is invariably linked to the memory of the ancestors who act as guardians of traditions and history.[5] The concept of ancestors is a worldwide phenomenon that is expressed and applied diversely. Mary Beard *et al.* indicate the Roman festivals for the dead, Parentalia and Lemuria, which focused primarily on family ancestors.[6] Activities for or concerning the dead run from among the Yup'ik people of Southern Alaska,[7] to the Pacific and Asia (with perhaps its most sophisticated forms found in Korea, Japan and China).[8] In Africa, the concept of ancestors survives in many contemporary societies predominantly in the Southern, Eastern, and Western part of the continent. There are slight geographical variations but the underlying components are essentially the same (though it is absent in some places).[9] Several communities in Ghana hold, in varying degrees, attitudes to the (collective) memory of forebears.[10]

The Roots of the Akan Idea of Nana and Its Relation to Akan Society

The concept of ancestors is profound among the Akan.[11] It essentially revolves around the view of the family seen as comprising both the living and

---

4. Gyekye, *Tradition and Modernity*, 217.

5. Parrinder, *West African Religion*, 125; Meyerowitz, *Akan Traditions of Origin*, 21.

6. Beard et al., *Religions of Rome: A History*, 50; Smith "The Religion of Archaic Rome," 32–33.

7. Fienup-Riordan, "Eye of the Dance: Spiritual Life of the Central Yup'ik Eskimos," 181–207.

8. Swain and Trompf, *The Religions of Oceania*, 129–32; Park, "Between God and Ancestors," 257–73; Kumuro, "Christianity and Ancestor worship in Japan," 60–68; Ching, *Chinese Religions*, 17–32; Ahern, "The Thai Ti Kong Festival," 397–425.

9. Moodley, *Shembe, Ancestors and Christ*; Amanze, "Christianity and Ancestor Veneration in Botswana," 43–59; Makwasha, "Not Without My Ancestors"; Brown, "Madagascar: Island of the Ancestors," 14–17; Cole and Middleton, "Rethinking Ancestors and Colonial Power in Madagascar," 1–37.

10. Kröger, *Ancestor Worship among the Bulsa of Northern Ghana*; Der, "God and Sacrifice in the Traditional Religions of the Kasena and Dagaba of Northern Ghana," 172–87; Gaba, *Scriptures of an African People*, 11 & 107; Field, *Religion and Medicine of the Gã People*, 196–205.

11. There are Akan people also in the eastern part of Côte D'Ivoire as well as the western part of Togo but the Akan of Ghana are primarily referred to in this book. The Akan of Ghana form over 40 percent of total national population and thus Akan traditional institutions are a significant aspect of Ghanaian culture. There are several dialects of the Akan language of which the main ones include Akyem, Akuapem, Asante, Brong and Mfantse. Although Asante culture has become definitive of Akan culture, many of

the spirits of dead relatives. The Akan ancestor is primarily an exemplar of the ethical standard conceived by the community. The qualifications for an *opanyin*, who will be an ancestor barring any disgrace prior to death, are that which ensure the health and growth of the community.[12] Among others, an *opanyin* should have started a family with wife and children, he should be in good physical condition and die naturally at a good old age. An *opanyin* is expected to be welcomed in *asamando* (the abode of the ancestors), having led such an exemplary life. Ancestor-hood is for both men and women. Though at the community level, the male forebears appear to overshadow the females, the latter are nonetheless also regarded. There are female leaders within the *abusua* (*obaa opanyin*) and stools for the queen mothers and their predecessors.

Almost every facet of Akan communal life is linked to the revered predecessors known as *nananom nsamanfo* (sing. *nana* [elder] *saman*). The various traditional social functions, which communicates the people's sense of identity, have aspects that are associated with these ancestors. The survival of such functions is intimately linked to the perceived effective presence of the *nananom nsamanfo*. The content of some of the invocations during libation at traditional functions does suggest that the ancestors are held to be in proximity with the Supreme Being, *Nyankopon*. The ancestors are held to have power to influence community life.

On the nature of Ɔsaman

Ɔsaman is the generic name for that which survives after death, either the *sunsum* (spirit)[13] or *ɔkra* (soul)[14] of the departed. There is no consensus as to which of these two components becomes ɔsaman. The *ɔkra* and *sunsum* are parts of the constituents of the Akan concept of the human being, alongside either *nipadua* [*honam*] ("body"), or with *mogya* (*bogya*) ("blood") and

---

the enduring Akan traditions predate the former's ascendancy to prominence. Darkwah, "Antecedents of Asante Culture," 57–79. The following discussion on the idea of ancestors primarily focuses on the Asante, Akuapem and Mfantse. Akan expressions are from these three groups and incorporate the spelling rules indicated by the Akan Language Committee (some quoted references are, however, left as they are in the original). Akan Language Committee, *Akan Orthography—Spelling Rules*.

12. Dzobo, "Values in a Changing Society," 233–34.

13. Christaller, *Dictionary*, 423. Sarpong, *Ghana in Retrospect*, 37. Crentsil, *Death, Ancestors, and HIV/AIDS Among the Akan of Ghana*, 35.

14. Afriyie believes the ɔsaman is the soul of the departed since in Akan belief the soul returns to God and thus it is that which "can mediate between the living and Onyankopɔn." Afriyie, "The Theology of the Okuapehene's Odwira,," 87.

honhom ("breath of life"),[15] or with *ntorɔ*[16] ("fatherhood-deity") and *mogya*.[17] The *ɔkra* (*ɔkara*) is perceived to be the "spark of the Supreme Being" that gives life to the person ("the life force")[18] and is regarded as having a "pre-earthly existence as well as a post-earthly existence."[19] It is the *ɔkra* that distinguishes humans from animals and plants, although all of them have *honhom* (breath). The *ɔkra* is seen as the bearer of the desired destiny, *nkrabea* or *nhyɛbea*, ("destiny" or "fate") which is given by Nyame (God).[20] According to Christaller, in life the *ɔkra* "is considered partly as the soul or spirit of a person" and "partly as a separate being, distinct from the person" and can relate to him or her.[21] Death is thus seen as the separation of the *ɔkra* from the body, at which point also the *ɔkra* is believed to return to God.

The *sunsum*, on the other hand, is thought to derive from the father and thus not divine as Busia and Meyerowitz opined.[22] Danquah saw the *sunsum* to be a "personality or shadow,"[23] and "the matter or physical basis

15. Sarpong, *Ghana in Retrospect*, 37. Danquah, however, considered the three components to constitute "blood," *kra* (soul) and *honhom* (spirit) with *sunsum* as "personality." Both the *kra* and *honhom* returned to God. Danquah, "The Culture of Akan," 363.

16. Also as *Nton*, *ntrɔ* or *Ntorɔ*, is regarded as coming from the father of an individual. It is treated as a "spirit" or "deity" and is worshiped as such with taboos that are to be observed. It is totemic and identified with certain animals, which are not to be killed or eaten, and has a day of the week on which it is ritually "washed." Obeng, *Ancient Ashanti Chieftaincy*, 6.

17. Gyekye, *An Essay on African Philosophical Thought*, 94. Antubam, *Ghana's Heritage of Culture*, 36. See also Afriyie, "A Comparative Study of Akan and Biblical Concepts of a Human Being," 15–16.

18. Gyekye, *An Essay on African Philosophical Thought*, 85 & 88. There is also the Akan expression that links the *ɔkra* with *mogya* indicating the former's life giving nature: *kra ne mogya* "the *kra* is [life] blood." Meyerowitz, *The Sacred State*, .84.

19. Opoku, "African traditional religion: An Enduring heritage," 74 & 75.

20. The two Akan words are synonymously used to express the sense of destiny or fate. Christaller, *Dictionary*, 208. The suffix *bea* in both words is usually rendered "manner" though it could also mean "place." *Nkra* has the senses of "taking leave, [an] errand, [a] mandate, order, commission, word, message, information [or] notice" (Christaller, *Dictionary*, 262), while *(n)hyɛ* has a wide range of meanings and thus with respect to *nhyɛbea* has been rendered as to "fix" or "arrange" (Gyekye), "command" (Meyerowitz), "order [or] make law" (Danquah, *The Akan Doctrine of God*, 202). Gyekye, *An Essay on African Philosophical Thought*, 104–19. The two words are used interchangeably.

21. Christaller, *Dictionary*, 262. Thus such expressions as *Ne kera nedii n'akyi, nkye owui* ("But for his *Kera* that followed him, he would have died") and *Ne kera eye nitira, na nkye ade aye no* ("Had it not been that his *Kera* was good, some calamity would have befallen him"). Antubam, *Ghana's Heritage of Culture*, 37.

22. Sarpong, *Ghana in Retrospect*, 37. Meyerowitz, *The Sacred State of the Akan*, 86. According to Busia, "it perishes" with the individual. Busia, "The Ashanti," 197.

23. Danquah, "The Culture of Akan," 363.

of the ultimate ideal of which the ɔkra (soul) is the form and the spiritual or mental basis."[24] The nature of the *sunsum*, unlike the ɔkra, which originating from the Supreme Being is held to be divine and immaterial or spiritual, is, however, not unanimously held and the debate thereof inconclusive. Gyekye is of the view that if the *sunsum* perished at death, as Busia for instance had maintained, it implies that it is "something physical or material."[25] In his view, however, the *sunsum* is "neither material nor mortal nor derived from the father" judging from its attributed functions or activities.[26] Gyekye agrees with Busia, Meyerowitz, Rattray, and Danquah that the *sunsum* is responsible for the personality of an individual.[27] As an immaterial element, the *sunsum*, Gyekye argues, is part of the ɔkra,[28] it is the latter's "active part," and that though both ɔkra and *sunsum* are logically distinct, ontologically they are not.[29]

The ɔkra and *sunsum*, in Gyekye's analysis, are "constitutive of a spiritual unity, which survives after death" and that the "soul" (which is "ɔkra plus *sunsum*") "does not lose its individuality after death."[30] The *saman*, then, for Gyekye is composite of the ɔkra and *sunsum* and this is contrary to Rattray who thought the *saman* to be *sunsum* without the ɔkra but nevertheless did indicate the uncertainty of what becomes of the ɔkra after death.[31] Christaller on the other hand, used the two interchangeably with regards to *saman*, rendering ɔkra and *sunsum*, respectively, as "soul or spirit" and "a soul or spirit of a man . . . a spirit or ghost."[32] Gyekye's view of the ɔkra and *sunsum* as "constitutive of a spiritual unity," then, seems to explicate Christaller and addresses Rattray's dilemma.

The ɔkra is apparently known by its activating presence in human life, having originated from God. It is indeed an immaterial component unique

24. Danquah, *The Akan Doctrine of God*, 66 & 115.

25. Gyekye, *An Essay on African Philosophical Thought*, 89.

26. Gyekye, *An Essay on African Philosophical Thought*, 89

27. Busia, "The Ashanti," 197. Meyerowitz, *The Akan of Ghana*, 98, 146 & 150. Rattray, *Ashanti*, 46. Danquah, *The Akan Doctrine of God*, 66–67 & 83.

28. Francis Amuzu comes to a similar conclusion in his study of the idea of 'soul' among the Akan and Ewe of Ghana and in Plato's metaphysics: "there is no distinction between Okra and Sunsum or Luvö and Gbögbö, and that the Soul, in essence, is a single non-divisible entity with several and contrary qualities." Amuzu, "The Soul in Akan, Ewe and Platonic Metaphysics," 6.

29. Gyekye, *An Essay on African Philosophical Thought*, 98.

30. Gyekye, *An Essay on African Philosophical Thought*, 98; Oyeshile, "Towards an African Concept of a Person: Person in Yoruba, Akan and Igbo Thoughts," 104–14; Dovlo, *Ancestors and Soteriology*, 50.

31. Rattray, *Ashanti Proverbs*, 25–26 & 36–38.

32. Christaller, *Dictionary*, 262 & 484.

to humans. Since it is that part of the Supreme Being that guarantees His ever-living character, the ɔkra, it appears, continues to give life to the sunsum after death. In other words, the sunsum is actually what results and nurtures from the life-giving element or principle called ɔkra and the material substance of both mother and father. Without the ɔkra there is no sunsum and without the sunsum there is no person (manifested physically in the nipadua [body]). However, while there can be sunsum without nipadua, in which case it is saman (ghost), there can be no sunsum without ɔkra. It is the sunsum that also exhibits the emotions and that may account for the perceived expression of the emotions of the ancestors.[33] An ɔkra without a manifesting sunsum is apparently unknown and remains in the Supreme Being. Thus it may suffice to translate saman as the "spirit of a deceased."

There are three types of saman namely, saman pa ("good spirit"), samantwɛntwɛn ("wandering spirit"[34]) and ɔtɔfo saman ("lit. fallen [unexpectedly]").[35] The saman pa is the one who died a peaceful death (abodwowu) at old age with progeny(ies) or sacrificially in a time of war and is considered in the fold of nananom nsamanfo whose abode is asamando.[36] The samantwɛntwɛn group comprise those spirits that are wandering, and are occasionally sighted by the living, while those who die by suicide or accident are in the ɔtɔfo group. Spirits within these latter two groups are supposedly denied entry into asamando and are thus not considered for remembrance or veneration.[37]

---

33. Sarpong, *Ghana in Retrospect*, 38.

34. The Akan word literally means, Rattray indicates, "a wait-about, wait-about." Rattray, *Ashanti Proverbs*, 36.

35. Christaller, *Dictionary*, 423. Rattray, *Ashanti Proverbs*, 36.

36. Also, as *asamann*. Christaller, *Dictionary*, 423. *Asamando* is that spiritual community of the *nsamanfo*, which is a projection of the physical one, functioning similarly to the present physical one, and is closer to the abode of God. It is held that in *asamando*, chiefs, for instance, continue to reign as chiefs and therefore in need of respective subjects at their service. It is the fulfilment of *nhyebea*, which also fulfils certain physical qualities or standards that guarantee rest for the departed spirit and safe return to *asamando*.

37. Arthur, *Akanfo Amammerɛ Ho Adesua 2*, 27. Crentsil also indicates in addition to *atɔfowuo* (death through suicide, accidents), *ammumuwuo* (death of a pregnant woman or during childbirth); in both cases the spirits of the deceased are not considered as ancestors. In her study on the effect of HIV/AIDS in Akan society, she notes that death resulting from AIDS is considered "bad death" and thus it is a disqualification for ancestor-hood which has had a disrupting effect on the "social organisation among the Akan". Crentsil, *Death, Ancestors and HIV/AIDS*.

Nananom (Ancestors) and Nyankopɔn

The Supreme Being in Akan traditional thinking is aware of and concerned with the activities of the physical world yet appears too remote to be approached directly. Though in crucial circumstances he is inquired directly, in most cases he is reached explicitly or implicitly through entities believed to have special links with him. The *abosom*[38] (deities) are considered his children (*mba*) or linguists (*akyeame*), while the ancestors are deemed to be closer to him. The Supreme Being bears the title *Nana*, among other appellations. He is the creator of all, *Ɔboadeɛ*, and it is from him that humans receive that vital element, the *ɔkra*, for animated life in the physical world. It is the fulfilment of the *nkrabea* carried by the *ɔkra* that guarantees a venerable life in the physical world and makes way for a transition into the world of ancestors, *asamando*, following death.[39]

Being in a spiritual state and, as Opoku observes, capable of speaking both the language of the living and that of those in *asamando*,[40] the ancestors are able to convey requests from the living to the Supreme Being. Libation as a way of communicating with the ancestors originates from this understanding of the "close relationship" between the ancestors and the Supreme Being, whereby "prayers are directed" to the former and "ultimately" to the latter.[41] There is no clear evidence that the relatively close proximity of the ancestors to the Supreme Being guarantees any mediatory function as in the case of Jesus Christ. In the prayers or invocation during libation, in which *Nyankopɔn* and *nananom nsamanfo* are mentioned, no reference is made to the latter to plead or inquire the Supreme Being on behalf of the supplicants. The requests are distinctively either directed to *Nyankopɔn* or

---

38. Singular *ɔbosom*, as Christaller rightly notes is more appropriately not to be rendered "fetish" (though he ends up using it in his own translation). Christaller renders it "*tutelar or guardian spirit* of a town or family; imaginary spirits, subordinate to God ... worshiped or consulted." I use "deity" as an appropriate rendition unless otherwise rendered by a referenced author. Etymologically, the word breaks into *ɔbo* (stone or rock) and *som* (worship or serve) and Christaller gives a native account which seems to suggest that in ancient times it had originated from the worship of stones: *tete abosom no a mpanyimfo som wɔn (anase wɔde nsa ne nguan kogyaw wɔn) no yɛ abo ara nko* "the fetishes which our forefathers served (by bringing them palm wine & sheep) were only stones." Christaller, *Dictionary*, 43. Sarpong, *Ghana in Retrospect*, 14. The *abosom* can be found in trees or rivers.

39. The belief that newly born children are from *asamando*, makes the space between birth and death in Akan thinking a journey of striving to fulfil an otherwise unknown *nhyebea* whose physical manifestations, nonetheless, satisfy the Akan standard of life.

40. Opoku, *West African Traditional Religion*, 36.

41. Opoku, *West African Traditional Religion*, 37.

to the *nananom*. The ancestors are indispensable in the sense that while the *abosom* and other potent protective objects such as *suman* ("charm or amulet") can be dispensed with, the ancestors cannot suffer such fate. The ancestors originate from and remain part of the community. Their distinguished status as worthy *mpanyifo* (elders), having trod the path of the living and their perceived closeness to the Supreme Being, implies that their demands and concerns, as it were, cannot be compromised.

In the logical progression of the belief of the proximity of the *nananom nsamanfo* towards God, one would have expected the former to convey the will or desire of the latter to the living.[42] If indeed this were to be the case then Christian teaching may appear to be redundant to the traditional Akan mind. The ancestors do not either appear to take requests to the Supreme Being or bring responses from *Nyankopɔn*. Their involvement among the living is therefore limited to those things that are envisaged in the Akan ideal of community life hence their call for prosperity, fertility among couples and particularly women. The ancestors are not called so much to show the way to live this life as to bring blessings. This is what the young generally and naturally (should) expect from living elders.

In this perspective, then, Madam Afua Kuma's reflection on the knowledge of the *nananom* concerning *Nyankopɔn* underscores the limitation of the *nananom nsamanfo* in conveying the way(s) of *Nyankopɔn*. Afua Kuma makes her declaration as a conscious Akan Christian who is familiar with the traditional setup. According to her,

> Our ancestors (*Nananom*) didn't know (*anhu*) of Onyankopɔn:
>   the great God
> They served lesser gods and spirits, and became tired.
> But as for us, we have seen (*yekohuu*) holy men, and prophets.
> We have gone to tell the angels
> How Jehovah helped us reach this place.
> Jehovah has helped us come this far;
> With great gratitude we come before Jesus,
> The One who gives everlasting life.[43]

Afua Kuma's use of the verb *hu* has attracted diverse interpretations. Philip Laryea sees Jon Kirby's translation of *anhu* as "didn't know" as

---

42. Perhaps in the sense of the story of Lazarus and the rich man who, in his spiritual state, desired to communicate his present experience to his living relations (Luke 16:19–31). Even in this story, the conversation is between human spirits.

43. Kuma, *Jesus of the Deep Forest*, 30. Twi text from Kuma, *Kwaeberentwu Ase Yesu*, 30.

"misleading."⁴⁴ The literal meaning of the word *anhu* as "did not see" implies that it can be rendered as the "inability to perceive" and hence "Afua Kuma possibly takes for granted the existence of *Nyankopɔn* whose presence *Nananom* (ancestors) were unable to perceive." For Laryea the rendering of *anhu* as "inability to perceive" and thus implying the "inability of Nananom to 'see' God and yet were able to see and experience the lesser gods and spirits presents a theological difficulty." Laryea's concern, then, is what "made it impossible" for the ancestors "to recognise God?"⁴⁵

According to Christaller, apart from its basic rendering as "to see . . . To perceive by the eye . . . To discover, find, find out, invent . . . To recognize" among others, *hu* or *hunu* can also mean "to learn . . . know, understand, be conversant with, be able." Christaller cites some Akan expressions together with his English rendering: *minnhu ne yɛbea* (I do not *know* how to make it); *asɛm yi, yennhu ne kita no, yennhu ne gyaa no* (we do not *know* [are at a loss] how to manage this matter).⁴⁶ Afua Kuma may well be communicating the idea of the ancestors going to see or consult the *abosom* and *nsamanfo* rather than the source of all things Himself, *Nyankopɔn*.⁴⁷ Instead of consulting *Nyankopɔn*, *nananom* did not, but rather consulted the *abosom* and *nsamanfo*.⁴⁸ So, perhaps, then, *nananom* did not consult *Nyankopɔn* because they could not recognize Him, even though they knew of Him. Such knowledge of the Supreme Being in Akan traditional thinking seems innate as it is captured by a rendering of the Akan maxim, *obi nkyerɛ abɔfra Nyame* ("no one shows or teaches a child [about] God").⁴⁹

---

44. Laryea, "St. Ignatius of Antioch and Afua Kuma of Kwahu," 71. According to Laryea, this was drawn to his attention by Prof. J. H. Nketia.

45. Laryea, "St. Ignatius of Antioch and Afua Kuma of Kwahu," 104 n.36. For Gabriel Setiloane, the traditional experience of the ancestors in their experience of God, from Southern Africa may have not presented this "theological difficulty." The ancestors' knowledge of God, Setiloane intimates, is evident from their indigenous names for God such as *Uvelingqaki* "the first one," *Unkulunkulu* "the big big one." Setiloane, "I am an African," 57.

46. Christaller, *Dictionary*, 189–90. Emphasis added.

47. As a conscious Akan Christian who has encountered Jesus Christ and who also fills her praise poetry as a matchless personality, Afua Kuma's knowledge of God as an Akan Christian is (now) from her encounter with the Son of God, Jesus Christ.

48. And as a corollary to that, "we (*yɛn de*) [Christians] went to consult prophets (*nkɔmhyɛfo*) and seers (*adiyifo*) and to show (*yɛkɔkyerɛɛ*) the angels (*ɔsoro abɔfo*) how the LORD (*Yehowa*) has helped us to this end. The LORD has helped us to this end, we will go to the presence of Jesus with tumultuous thanksgiving (*aseda kɛse*), he has given (*ɔno na wama*) us life everlasting."

49. Appiah et al., *Bu Me Bɛ*, 37 no. 563.

Nananom, Life, Birth, Adulthood, Marriage, and the Family

Traditional Akan belief has it that a child comes from *asamando*. The ancestors are invariably requested to enable births among women during typical libation prayers. Among the Mfantse, according to Kofi Antubam's informant, a child is brought by an *Okeragyaa*, one of the seven tutelary beings believed to be in the court of the Supreme Being who bears the respective names of the days of the week.[50] A newly born child is considered an *ɔhɔho* ("a stranger, visitor or guest") and will have to wait for seven days before being given a name.[51] The name eventually given on the eighth day constitutes his or her *kra din* (a name derived from the day of the week the child was born) and the name of a known worthy ancestor. It is believed that the period of seven days ascertains that the child has come to stay on earth and not return to *asamando* prematurely. After giving the child a name, he or she is no more regarded as an *ɔhɔho*. In traditional Asante culture, on the eighth day after birth, an elderly woman takes the baby and places him or her in her arms. She heads towards a refuse dump repeating these words on the way: "*Akokoa yi ni ne ne se a mowɔ asamando, ɛnnɛ akokoa yi ne mo too nkwanta a moapae, enti mommfrɛ no mo ba bio*" ("The baby's father and mother at the land of the dead, your child has today departed from you. Don't call him your child anymore").[52]

An Akan adult is expected to marry and bear children. Marriage (*aware*) is a requisite for both adulthood and subsequently ancestor-hood. The goodwill of the elders of the community, both living and dead, is sought during marriage arrangements and ceremonies. Since it is essential in ensuring the survival of the *abusua*, it is valued and honored in the traditional society. Marriage is considered to be a union not just between two individuals but that of the respective families concerned.[53] Marriage among members of the same *abusua* is prohibited.[54] The desire for its permanence is expressed in the proverb *aware nye nsafufu na woaka ahwe* ("marriage is not like palm wine to be tasted [and spewed out]"),[55] even though an eventual divorce (*awaregyae*) is accommodated (*awaregyae ngu kurow*, "divorce does not destroy

---

50. Antubam, *Ghana's Heritage of Culture*, 39.
51. Opoku, *Hearing and Keeping*, 72–73.
52. Kwadwo, *A Handbook on Asante Culture*, 33–34.
53. Gyekye, *African Cultural Values*, 78–79.
54. Members of *abusua* are blood relations and see themselves as *mogyakoro* (lit. one blood). Meyerowitz, *The Sacred State of the Akan*, 29.
55. Opoku, *Hearing and Keeping*, 25–26.

[end] a town").⁵⁶ The close connection between the sanctity of marriage and the wellbeing of the community (ɔman) is perhaps indicative of the high premium given to sexual intimacy as exclusively within the context of marriage. Pre-marital sexual relations is termed aguamammɔ or adwamammɔ (fornication) literally meaning "that which cuts into pieces [gua or dwa] the community" while the term for extra-marital sexual relations, awareɛe (adultery) literally is "destruction of marriage."⁵⁷ The procreation desired in marriages is to ensure the survival of the family.

One is expected to also contribute to the wellbeing of the family to which he or she belongs since the burial arrangements upon his or her demise is the responsibility of the family.⁵⁸ The Akan traditional community is seen as one big *abusua*: a nexus of family units knitted by matrilineal blood relation. The role of the queen mother is conceptually analogous to that of the mother in the basic family unit. As the mother of the community, the queen mother (symbolically) gives a son to lead the community by nominating a male from the royal matrilineal family, who may also be her own biological son.⁵⁹ In this sense the queen mother appears to "own" the community, as Meyerowitz deduced.⁶⁰ However, since the queen mother is also nominated by a ruling chief, the roots of the Akan traditional political setup actually underscores the Akan's considerable regard for the role of women in the society.

Nananom, Kingship, Festivals, the Community, and Libation Prayers

Traditional festivals have survived among the Akan primarily because of the regard for the *nananom nsamanfo* in the history and religious life of

---

56. Opoku, *Hearing and Keeping*, 27.

57. Christaller, *Dictionary*, 147–49 and 559. The 1909 edition of an English-Twi (Asante) dictionary, however, translates "adultery" as *aguamammɔ* as well as *awareɛe* and *agobone*. "Fornication" is also translated as *aguamammɔ* and *agobone*. *A Dictionary, English-Tshi (Asante)*, 6 & 80.

58. The Akan proverb *Abusua do funu* ("The family loves a corpse"), which thus indicates the attention the family gives to the burial of the dead. Opoku, *Hearing and Keeping*, 29.

59. For the role of the Asantehemma (queen mother) in contemporary Asante society, see, for example, Hagan, "The Ascent to the Golden Stool: Women Make the King," 33–42.

60. Meyerowitz inferred that the Akan community is "owned" by ɔhemmaa (queen mother) and "ruled" by the ɔhene chief or king. Meyerowitz, *The Sacred State of the Akan*, 27.

the communities.⁶¹ Festivals, which are invariably founded on communal traditions, are opportunities to connect the past with the present and provide "a major channel for the expression and renewal of cultural identity."⁶² Traditional festivals are intimately linked with the ancestors, who are either consciously and directly commemorated or indirectly honored by carrying on with what they had begun.⁶³

The ɔhene (chief or king), in whose office Akan traditional society derives its survival, is regarded as that vital link between the living members of the community and the (royal) *nananom nsamanfo*.⁶⁴ He plays an important role in the rituals during festivals because he is considered as the link between the living and the ancestors. The chief's stool, a symbol of his authority, also "symbolises [and represents] the ancestors."⁶⁵ The sacral nature of the chief is linked to the ancestors and his stool is vital for such a link. The stool of a royal ancestor is ritually blackened.⁶⁶ The black stool apparently serves three ends: as a shrine through which communicating with the ancestors is achieved (and without it "the religion of the ancestors" is almost meaningless);⁶⁷ as an object of remembrance and also as "the representative of the ancestor who owned it."⁶⁸ In addition to the black stool being a "living representative of the founder of the state," the leadership of the people of Akropong-Akuapem see it also as "the contract document" between the rulers and the people, whose allegiance is apparently to the stool rather than the person occupying it.⁶⁹ The other reason given is an incentive mechanism

61. Opoku, *Festivals of Ghana*, 4; Nketia, *The Role of Traditional Festivals in Community Life*, 7–9.

62. Nketia, *The Role of Traditional Festivals*, 13.

63. Opoku, *West African Traditional Religion*, 37.

64. By "traditional society" we mean that community that consciously seeks to maintain ancestral traditions even in contact with a wider foreign cultural world that by and large suggests or puts demands on modern ways of doing things.

65. Dickson, *Theology in Africa*, 70–71. Danquah also observed that the stool was the "symbolic and visible link between the ancestors and the living" and that its sacred nature meant the "chief who occupied it was never made to sit on it," he was "suspended over it three times" at his installation. Danquah, "Autopsy on Old Ashanti," 136.

66. Blackening is done with soot and the yolk of eggs. Opoku, *Festivals of Ghana*, 7. The stool of the living chief is not blackened. Sarpong, *The Sacral Stools of the Akan*, 37–38.

67. Sarpong, *The Sacral Stools of the Akan*, 5 & 75. Sarpong, however, observes that though "strictly speaking the stool cannot be an Ɔbosom (shrine)," nevertheless the "treatment given to it is similar to the shrines of the minor deities" (Sarpong, *The Sacral Stools of the Akan*, 46).

68. Sarpong, *The Sacral Stools of the Akan*, 45.

69. The saying goes thus *Yesom Akongua na yensom nipa* which is rendered as "we serve only a chief who is duly enstooled on the original Black Stool." Akuapem Odwira Festival Brochure, 57.

for the living chiefs to "lead exemplary lives," so that their "memories will also be preserved after their death."[70]

The stool is significant during the *Adae* festival which is primarily held in honor of the *nananom nsamanfo* (ancestors).[71] The observance of *Adae* also aids in the calendar calculation for the Akan traditional year. This ceremony is observed twice every forty (or sometimes forty-two)[72] days on a Sunday (*Akwasidae*) and on a Wednesday (*Awukudae*).[73] There are nine successive *Adae* within one Akan calendar year, *Adaduanan*,[74] with the ninth *Adae* known as *Adae Kɛse* (Big [or Great] *Adae*).[75]

At the community level the royal ancestors are the point of interest and the responsibility is on the chief, while at the family level it is the specific family ancestors concerned and the onus is on the *abusua panyin* (family head). In both cases, however, the selected leaders accompany the chief or family head with respective functions. The attention given the royal ancestors is also for "renewing the spiritual and political bonds that allow for the continued participation of the dead in the affairs of the living."[76]

Since the primary focus of the *Adae* festival is the ancestors, the central rites take place in *nkonguafieso* (the stool house or room),[77] the "spiri-

70. Akuapem Odwira Festival Brochure, 57.

71. The word literally means "a place of rest, lying down or sleeping" or "resting-place." Etymologically it derives from the ubiquitous verb *da* which, among other uses, means to lie, to be or live in a certain place, to sleep, to be quiet, to remain or be at rest. The word is also found in *da ase* the Twi for "to thank" which literally means "to lie under." Christaller, *Dictionary*, 56–57 & 60; Opoku, *Festivals of Ghana*, 7; Sarpong, *The Sacral Stools of the Akan*, 56. Nketia, *The Role of Traditional Festivals*, 2; Agyemang-Duah, "The Adae Festival," 4.

72. Dankwa, *The Institution of Chieftaincy*, 101.

73. There are forty days between two Akwasidae and Awukudae; twenty-three days between an Akwasidae and the next Awukudae; and seventeen days between an Awukudae and the next Akwasidae. Agyemang-Duah, "The Adae Festival," 1. Opoku, *Festivals of Ghana*, 7.

74. The *Adaduanan* (forty days) calendar consists of nine sets of forty day periods in which seven days mark one week making a total of six weeks within one forty day period. There are six prefix names given to the days of the week beginning with *Wukuada* (Wednesday) with the seventh day taking that of the first: *Mono, Fɔ, Nwona, Nkyi, Kuru, Kwa*. Thus, a forty-day run, beginning with a *Mono-Wukuo* (*Mono*-Wednesday), ends with a *Nkyi-Kwasi* (*Nkyi*-Sunday) with the Monday and Tuesday taking respectively, *Kuru* and *Kwa*, the Wednesday then takes a *Mono* and the cycle begins anew. It is on a *Kuru* Wednesday or Sunday that the *Adae* is observed. Meyerowitz, *The Sacred Akan State*, 143–45. Also J. B. Danquah, who was full of praise for the findings in Meyerowitz's mentioned work, Danquah, "The Culture of Akan," 365.

75. Nketia, *The Role of Traditional Festivals*, 5. Opoku, *Festivals of Ghana*, 7 & 13.

76. Nketia, *The Role of Traditional Festivals*, 1.

77. Opoku, *Festivals of Ghana*, 7.

tual source of political authority,"[78] where the ritually blackened stools of previous worthy chiefs are privately kept. The significance of the stool in the *Adae* festival also means that every family with a stool does observe the ceremony in honor of its ancestors.[79]

Preparations for *Adae* are made on the preceding day called *Dapaa*,[80] *Memeneda Dapaa* for the Saturday before *Akwasidae* and *Benada Dapaa*[81] for the Tuesday before *Awukudae*.[82] The food items such as yams or plantains, water, drinks, chicken, eggs, sheep, firewood, and all necessary items are made available on the *Dapaa*, since no travelling is permitted on *Adae*.[83] On the evening of *Dapaa* when all preparations have been made, there is drumming at the chief's palace, *ahemfie*, till late in the night.[84] On the day of the *Adae*, people gather at the chief's palace in the morning to present an *adae* gift (*adaekye*)[85] to the chief who is also symbolically called to the day's function by drumming and invocation by the chief's principal drummer.[86]

78. Nketia, *The Role of Traditional Festivals*, 2.

79. Arthur, *Akanfoɔ Amammerɛ Ho Adesua*, 92.

80. There is *dabone*, literally "bad day" or "an unlucky day" on which only domestic work is allowed and thus ultimately serves as a form of a resting day for the community. The opposite of this day is *dapa* "a good, lucky, festival day" (Christaller, *Dictionary*, 59 & 65). *Akwasidae* and *Awukudae* are both considered *dabone* since no communal work or travelling is permitted on such days. In this sense *Dapaa* in contrast to *dabone* will then mean a "good day" or "favorable day." This however appears to be a conceptual correlation since Christaller, for instance, is not explicit on any correlation and did not make any comparison. See Christaller, *Dictionary*, 66. Rattray renders it *adapa*. Rattray, *Ashanti*, 107.

81. It can be noted that the prefix names for both *adae* and *dapaa* days are the Akan names for the day of the week: *Kwasiada* (Sunday), *Dwoada* (Monday), *Benada* (Tuesday), *Wukuada* (Wednesday), *Yawoada* (Thursday), *Fiada* (Friday), and *Memeneda* (Saturday).

82. Opoku, *Festivals of Ghana*, 8.

83. On the day of *Dapaa* there is also cleanup of houses and their environs as well as pathways. Opoku, *Festivals of Ghana*, 8.

84. Opoku, *Festivals of Ghana*, 8. Arthur, *Akanfoɔ Amammerɛ Ho Adesua* 1, 89. Edward Bowdwich, writing in the nineteenth century, gives a brief description of the atmosphere in Asante on the *Dapaa* and the early morn of the *Adae*: "The large drum which stands at the entrance of the palace, adorned with skulls and thigh bones, is struck with great force at sunset the preceding day [*Dapaa*] as a signal; the whole of the establishment of the palace shout, and their shout is echoed by the people throughout the town. Music and firing generally beguile the night. The next morning [on the *Adae*] the King goes to the fetish house (Himma), opposite the palace, and offers several sheep; the blood of this sacrifice is poured on the gold stool." Bowdwich, *Mission from Cape Coast Castle to Ashantee, with a Descriptive Account of that Kingdom*, 230–31.

85. Arthur, *Akanfoɔ Amammerɛ Ho Adesua* 1, 90.

86. Opoku, *Festivals of Ghana*, 10.

The principal drummer's call or invocation is apparently intended to arouse (sɔre) the spirit of the chief to go and meet with his predecessors. Opoku gives an English rendering of the call of a master drummer:

> Great and Valiant Ofori,
> I [principal drummer] am off to Abirm Akyem,
> I am going to the stool house
> Where room encloses room.
> King of hosts
> Who is ever sought for an ally in battle,
> Benevolent great killer
> Vanguard amongst equals
> Unconquerable one,
> Dread of the old and the young
> Grandson of Ofori of the Asona Clan
> He that balances the keg of gunpowder upon his head
> And somersaults over the flames,
> He that bends the sword with ease
> Out, and come with me!
> Out, and come with me![87]

The pilgrimage to the stool house is led by the *nkonnwasoafoɔhene*,[88] the chief of stool bearers (attendants). The black stool plays a significant role in this festival. At the stool house (room), the chief stands before the black stools and "as a sign of humility and respect for his ancestors, he slips off one of his sandals and steps on it" and with his mourning or old[89] cloth slightly lowered off his shoulder he pays homage to his ancestors,[90] with such greeting as *Nananom nsamanfoɔ mema mo akye o!*[91] ("I bring you greetings grandsires [ancestors]"). The chief stool attendant pours water to the ground, to invite the ancestors to wash their hands (*Nananom monnye nsuo nhohoro mo nsa*).[92]

The chief stool attendant gives to the chief in a ladle (*kwankora*) the prepared mashed yam or plantain (*ɛtɔ*) mixed with palm oil contained in the earthenware bowl (*asanka*).[93] The chief then, beginning with the "first

---

87. Opoku, *Festivals of Ghana*, 10–11.
88. Arthur, *Akanfoɔ Amammerɛ Ho Adesua 1*, 90.
89. Opoku, *Festivals of Ghana*, 11.
90. Nketia, *The Role of Traditional Festivals*, 3.
91. Arthur, *Akanfoɔ Amammerɛ Ho Adesua 1*, 90.
92. Arthur, *Akanfoɔ Amammerɛ Ho Adesua 1*, 90.
93. Arthur, *Akanfoɔ Amammerɛ Ho Adesua 1*, 90.

stool of the dynasty" to that of his immediate predecessor, places the ɛtɔ on each black stool uttering the following:

> My ancestors (*nananom nsamanfoɔ*), today is Awukudae
> (or Akwasidae)
> Come and receive this mashed yam or plantain (*ɛtɔ*)
> and eat and make this town good [or well, prosper]
> And let women give birth
> And let the people in this town acquire money [gold, wealth].[94]

The remaining food, after serving the royal ancestors is then taken outside of the stool room and sprinkled in the compound. This is done supposedly for the spirits of the royal courtiers and attendants who are believed to continue in their vocation in *asamando* as servants of the chief.[95] A sheep is brought in at this stage.[96] The sheep is slaughtered first by a cut in the throat such that a small amount of its blood spills to the ground and some collected into a wooden bowl to be smeared on the seats of the black stools.[97] The rest of the collected sheep's blood is used later to "mark the chest and forehead of the chief and all present."[98]

The various parts of the flayed sheep are cut up and taken to the sacred black stools. The fat from the entrails of the sheep is applied to the "center props" of the stools, while the "head and parts of the intestines are placed before the stools."[99] Skewered meat of the sheep is also placed on the stools, and the rest of the meat is used in the preparation of the saltless soup with *fufu* (pounded boiled yam or cassava and/or plantain or cocoyam). The queen mother oversees the preparation of this meal, which is then placed before the stools until late in the evening.[100]

The libation (*hwie* [or *gu*] *nsa*) prayers the chief stool attendant performs, as he pours drink on each of the stools, are also directed to the ancestors for the wellbeing of the community and chief:[101]

94. Arthur, *Akanfoɔ Amammerɛ Ho Adesua 1*, 90. Translation mine. Agyemang-Duah, "The Adae Festival," 2.

95. Arthur, *Akanfoɔ Amammerɛ Ho Adesua 1*, 90.

96. Opoku notes that on some special occasions such as the *Adae Kɛse* (Big Adae), the chief carries the sheep before the stools as a sign of "high respect." Opoku, *Festivals of Ghana*, 13. Arthur, *Akanfoɔ Amammerɛ Ho Adesua 1*, 90.

97. Arthur, *Akanfoɔ Amammerɛ Ho Adesua 1*, 90. Opoku, *Festivals of Ghana*, 13.

98. Opoku, *Festivals of Ghana*, 13.

99. Opoku, *Festivals of Ghana*, 13.

100. The queen mother also has her blackened stools and does observe *Adae* in conjunction with what the chief does. Rattray, *Ashanti*, 105–6. Opoku, *Festivals of Ghana*, 13.

101. Christaller, *Dictionary*, 204. Arthur, *Akanfoɔ Amammerɛ Ho Adesua 1*, 91.

> Nana [so and so], [here is] drink (*nsa*)!
> For the life (*nkwa*) of this nation.
> Whosoever brings evil on this town
> Let calamity [misfortune] be upon him or her.
> Nana [so and so] [here is] drink! [here is] drink!
> For the life of this town
> Let the king last long on this throne
> Let not any evil thing come into this town
> For the life of this town
> Nana [so and so], [here is] drink!¹⁰²

A similar example of the libation prayer directed to the ancestors, and also the *abosom* (deities), for the wellbeing of the community and specifically for the chief is given by Sarpong. This is said at the installation or enstoolment of a chief: after the mentioning of the names of previous deceased chiefs, *nananom*, and *abosom* (deities), the prayer continues,

> We beseech all the gods [*abosom*] whom we have called upon and all the multitudes of ghosts (ancestors) [*nananom nsamanfoɔ*] we have mentioned—we do implore you—we do pray that this chief who is going to occupy the Stool may be able to keep it, and that he may govern his state well and hearken to what his people will tell him, and that his people may pay heed to what he also tells them. . . . We do beg you, we do pray for health for the chief, also for good fortune and blessings . . . .¹⁰³

Though in this example *Nyame* is not called upon, in other instances there is reference to *Nyame* (invariably also along with *Asase Yaa*, the earth deity), which precedes the ancestors.¹⁰⁴ A close look at the prayers offered during the *Adae*, makes it difficult to accept the view that the Supreme Being is worshiped "through" the (revered) ancestors.¹⁰⁵ The perceived proximity of the ancestors to the Supreme Being appears enough to account for their potency to bestow blessings and honor requests. Such requests are essentially for the good of the individual and the community at large. One does not find a request to the ancestors to reveal any will of the Supreme Being. Rather the

---

Peter Sarpong highlights the intent of libation (*nsaguo*) prayer from the indigenous names associated with the act. Libation as *mpaee* or *mpaebo* or *mpaeyie* connotes the prayer to ward off a curse or misfortune, the word *Apaeeyie* being derived from *apaee* (curse) + *yi* (to remove). Sarpong, *Libation*, 15.

102. Arthur, *Akanfoɔ Amammerɛ Ho Adesua 1*, 91. Translation mine.

103. Sarpong, *Libation*, 20. Sarpong's translation.

104. Crentsil, *Death, Ancestors and HIV/AIDS*, 92–93. Rattray, *Religion and Art in Ashanti*, 70.

105. Antubam, *Ghana's Heritage of Culture*, 33–34.

assumption seems to be that the ancestors are mindful of the good things of the community and in their spiritual existence can bestow such boon and certainly also to frown on those acts that are to the contrary.

The significance of libation, for Sarpong, is both religious and social. In addition to revealing the people's belief in God, the Supreme Being and the ancestors and deities, libation brings about unity and brotherliness in the community, ensuring solidarity among the living and between the living and the ancestors.[106] The erstwhile paramount chief of Akuapeman (Akuapem Traditional Area) Oseadeeyo Addo Dankwa III presents an interesting delineation of the traditional understanding of libation. Libation, in the original cultural sense, "was never intended to be a complete religious act."[107] He differentiates between "traditionalists" and "fetish adherents" who are involved in the practice of libation. The second group, whom he also calls "idol worshippers," have (wrongfully) given the impression that the "whole act constitutes a religious performance."[108]

Dankwa argues further that from the perspective of the traditionalist libation constitutes two social acts and one religious act.[109] The first social act comprises the "symbolic gestures" of inviting the ancestors to participate in the given function by the giving of "the liquid substance" to wash their feet. The second is the welcome address and greetings to the ancestors "who are presumed to have responded to the invitation." The prayers consequently offered constitute the third and religious act. These, for Dankwa, are not different from what the living usually do for their living elders, and the ancestors "are considered as the heads, [of] both the living and the dead."[110] Since the social acts are really symbolic for inviting the ancestors, the prayers are, "culturally speaking," "intended for the family deities Abosom, and Asuman, etc., or the supreme God."[111] Thus, in his proposed original form of libation, after the invitation of the ancestor(s), the prayers can be directed to Christ.[112] It is quite obvious from the foregoing that Dankwa has approached the issue

---

106. Sarpong, *Libation*, 23.

107. Dankwa III, *The Institution of Chieftaincy in Ghana: The Future*, 79.

108. Dankwa III, *The Institution of Chieftaincy in Ghana*, 79. Bediako, *Christianity in Africa*, 219–21.

109. Dankwa III, *The Institution of Chieftaincy in Ghana*, 79–80.

110. Dankwa III, *The Institution of Chieftaincy*, 80.

111. During libation in an enclosed surrounding, the doors are open, and no one can stand in the doorway. This for Dankwa further explains the notion that the ancestors are symbolically invited and not "invoked spiritually." If the latter was the case, then the doors would not be left opened. Dankwa III, *The Institution of Chieftaincy*, 80, 82–83.

112. Dankwa III, *The Institution of Chieftaincy*, 81.

of libation from a Christian standpoint,[113] even though he is also mindful of some Christian misconceptions of the act. His differentiation between "traditionalist" and "idol worshippers" or "fetish adherents" within the traditional setup, however, seems oversimplified.

The Akan tradition itself is mindful and reverent of the potency of the *abosom* and adherents, specifically the *ɔkomfo* (priest or priestess). They are not singled out as "idol worshippers" over pure "traditionalists" such as the chief. If the *ɔkomfo* was superfluous and reduced to an optional religious figure within the Akan traditional setup, then Dankwa's concern may well be justified. This is not the case, however, since an *ɔbosom* hardly survives without an *ɔkomfo*.[114] Furthermore, Dankwa rightfully notes that in times past the "best exponents of our culture" were the "mediums or fetish priest,"[115] the adherents of the *abosom*.

Several Akan festivals in which attention to royal ancestors is prominent, as well as those that introduce a new harvest, have their basis in the *Adae* observation and the times for such festivals are determined by the timing of the ninth *Awukudae*.[116] The *Papa* festival held by the people of Kumawu among the Asante is significant not only because it falls on an *Adae*, but that it is also commemorated because of a specific royal ancestor, Barima Tweneboa Kodua.[117] Traditional history has it that Kumawu was one of the two candidate towns to serve as the capital of the nascent Asanteman (Asante nation). The priest-chief of Agona and a close ally of Osei Tutu I, Ɔkɔmfo Anɔkye (Priest Anokye) upon consultation for the site of the capital, planted "Kumanini" trees at the site of Kumawu and what would become Kumasi.[118] The tree at the site of Kumasi flourished while the one at Kumawu died, making Kumasi the eventual capital.

In the wake of the struggle of the Asante states to break free from the Denkyira, Barima Tweneboa Kodua, then chief of Kumawu, responded to one of the three demands of human sacrifices that Okomfo Anokye

---

113. Cf. Bediako's note on Dankwa as a Christian, Bediako, *Christianity in Africa*, 232 n.43.

114. Bowdich, for instance, notes "two orders of fetishmen," that is adherents to the *abosom*: those who dwell with the fetish (the "first class") and those who "pursue their various occupations in society" but do "assist in customs and superstitious ceremonies" (the "inferior class"). Bowdich, *Mission from Cape Coast Castle to Ashantee*, 214.

115. Dankwa III, *The Institution of Chieftaincy*, 83.

116. The Odwira festival, for example, among the Akuapem, Akwamu and Asante (as *Apafram*) and the *Papa* festival of the people of Kumawu as well as the (harvest) Yam Festival of the Aburi. Opoku, *Festivals of Ghana*, 14, 22, 28 & 48. Meyerowitz, *The Sacred Akan State*, 149.

117. Opoku, *Festivals of Ghana*, 48.

118. Opoku, *Festivals of Ghana*, 48.

postulated to ensure victory for the Asante.[119] Tweneboa Kodua was to lead his *asafo* (army) in his full battle regalia but could not protect himself. The sacrificial death of Tweneboa Kodua has thus instituted an annual festival and his burial place on the *Nanankɔ* hill, Opoku points out, "has since become the shrine to which his successors in office and their people go annually to worship and take inspiration."[120]

The Okuapeman's Odwira festival at Akropong also falls within the *Adae* calculation and begins two days before the ninth (or eighth) *Awukudae*, counting from the first *Awukudae* from the previous year's Odwira.[121] Though the ceremony is primarily "not about propitiating *abosom* [deities] or *Nananom Nsamanfo* [ancestors]," but rather a covenant keeping with the *Odosu* (a ritual object), the ancestors are consciously involved.[122] In fact forty days prior to the Odwira festival, that is the eighth (or seventh) *Awukudae*, is declared period of meditation after a ceremony known as *Adae Butuw*.[123] During this period there is ban on communal noise making. The reason given for this period of meditation is to allow for rest, both for the living and the ancestors, in the last month of the traditional calendar. It also serves as a period of preparation for the annual festival. There is also a ban on the eating of yam during this period of meditation.

On the first day of the Odwira festival, which is on the Monday, there is the "clearing of the path" that leads to the royal mausoleum, Amanprobi.[124] The "symbolic value" of the clearing of paths, in the words of Oseadeeyo Addo Darkwa III,

> . . . not only open[s] the gate so that the ancestors may come in and eat but also keeps the lines of communication open between the living and the ancestors so that the ancestors may travel home without hindrances.[125]

Once the path is symbolically cleared, the community of the living and the "living dead" are ready to commence the celebration. On Tuesday there

---

119. Sarpong, *Libation*, 12.

120. Opoku, *Festivals of Ghana*, 48.

121. Barima, *10-Year Calendar of Akuapem Odwira, Awukudae and Akwasidae Festivals 2011–2020*.

122. Afriyie, "The Theology of the Okuapehene's Odwira," 146 & 191. Frank Adams indicates the key role of the attitude towards the ancestors in the Asante Odwira festival. Adams, *Odwira and the Gospel*, 129.

123. Dankwa III, *The Institution of Chieftaincy*, 102.

124. For a more detailed description of the activities of the various days during the Odwira week, see Afriyie, "The Theology of the Okuapehene's Odwira," 130.

125. Dankwa III, *The Institution of Chieftaincy*, 104.

is the official presentation or out-dooring of new yam at the *Krubiihene*'s palace at Akropong. On this day also the *Banmuhene*, *Adumhene* and their team go to Amanprobi to bring the *Odosu*. After the presentation of the *Odosu* to the Okuapehene, the ban on noise making is lifted (*Dapaatu*) and the ancestors are thus ushered into the community. The Wednesday, which turns out to be the *Awukudae Kɛse* (the last *Awukudae* of the traditional year), is a day for the remembrance of the dead and the "suspended wailing" during the *Adaebutuw* could now be expressed.

It is on the Thursday that the black stools are ritually purified at a nearby Adami stream. This rite of purification is "to symbolize the cleansing of the traditional area."[126] On this day also the five divisional chiefs of Akuapem renew their allegiance to the *Ofori Panyin* Stool of the paramount chief. There is general feasting for which also food items such as mashed yam with or without palm oil and drinks are taken to *Nsɔrem*, the sacred burial site of the ancestors. There is a grand durbar of chiefs on the Friday where a high public figure is invariably invited. The whole of the festive activities is climaxed with a church service on Sunday, which customarily takes place at the Christ Presbyterian Church in Akropong. On the Friday following the Odwira Sunday, that is, eight days from the Odwira climax, there is a mini celebration known as *Fida Fofie* (Friday Fofie) or the Octave.[127]

Worship or Veneration

The words expressed in the libation prayers, and in the case of the *Adae* festival the activities held in honor of the ancestors, indicate the nature of the whole institution and hence the need for an appropriate descriptive term. It is always helpful to start with the indigenous terms of description. Cecilia Arthur notes that the Akan observe the *Adae* festival in order to *sɔre wɔn nananom nsamanfoɔ* ("*sɔre* their ancestors").[128] It is instructive that she uses *sɔre* meaning "serve or worship" and not *kae* (remember).[129] Further on in her description of the activities involved in *Adae*, she uses *som* to describe the collective activities towards the ancestors.

Christaller notes that, in addition to the rendering as "to serve or worship," *sɔre* also has the meaning of "taking care or treating something with

---

126. Dankwa III, *The Institution of Chieftaincy*, 105.

127. Afriyie, "The Theology of the Okuapehene's Odwira," 16

128. Arthur, *Akanfoɔ Amammerɛ Ho Adesua 1*, 89.

129. The Sanaahene of Akropong of the Kronti division of Akuapeman, Nana Sanaa Twum Barima does not share the view of *sɔre* or *som* as a descriptive term and insists the whole customary rite is done in remembrance (*kae*) of the ancestors. Barima, Interview, 25 February 2014.

care" as is expressed in the statement "sɔre wo ho oo!; look after yourself or take care of yourself."[130] It is from the word sɔre that the Akan word for church or temple (asɔre) derives.[131] Som on the other hand simply renders as "to serve" and largely implies being a servant to that effect. So, for Arthur to indicate that Adae is to sɔre the ancestors, does suggest something more than "to serve." If one is to strictly abide by her choice of words, then in the process of *serving* the ancestors, the practitioners actually do sɔre their worthy predecessors. It could also mean she uses the words som and sɔre interchangeably and in which cases the primary sense "to serve" would be implied. What the word sɔre practically connotes may be seen from the annual activities done in connection with the ancestors at a special traditional place known as nsɔrem during the Okuapeman's Odwira festival at Akropong-Akuapem.[132] The place is traditionally regarded as the burial place (or somewhere close to it) of the first ancestors of the land and as such the ancestors are symbolically attended to annually with food and drink.

In a sermon on the fundamental nature of Christian worship, originally composed in Akuapem Twi, the notable Ghanaian composer Ephraim Amu keenly observed its connection to the traditional ritual activities at the nsɔrem.[133] According to Amu, sometimes a purification plant sommɛ is planted to ward off (ɛbɛpam) evil spirits (ahonhommone) and the palm fronds (mmrɛnkɛnsono) placed at the nsɔrem indicates its sacredness. The place is called nsɔrem because it is "a place where they sɔre the ancestors (fako a wɔsɔre nsamanfo)." The sɔre of the ancestors constitutes three basic aspects:

> when the worshippers [those involved in the sɔre] bring their things [food and drink] to the ancestors [nsamanfo], they thank them [the ancestors], exalt them or praise them, commit themselves into the hands of their ancestors asking for their help. Thus what is called asɔre (worship), has three fundamental characteristics namely: commitment [ahofama], thanksgiving and praise [aseda ne osebɔ], and petition [adesrɛ].[134]

---

130. Christaller, *Dictionary*, 471.

131. Isaiah 6:1; Acts 3:1; Colossians 1:18.

132. For the people of Akropong-Akuapem this is done during the Thursday of the Akuapemanhene Odwira festival.

133. Laryea, *Ephraim Amu*, 356–57 (Appendix V). Laryea considers this sermon in his treatment of Amu's "theology of worship" (Laryea, *Ephraim Amu*, 39–41).

134. Translation mine. Laryea's translation runs, "the 'asɔrefo' (those who are involved in the activity of revering the dead) bring something of their substance to the ancestors, thank them, praise them and commit themselves into the hands of the ancestors and implore their assistance. And so what is referred to as 'asɔre' involves three elements: commitment, thanksgiving and praise and supplication." Laryea, *Ephraim Amu*, 357.

It is evident that Amu has the sense of "worship" in his understanding of *sɔre*. He notes that it is because of this insight into the activities at the *nsɔrem*, which is "very much similar to or exactly the same as (*sɛ pɛpɛɛpɛ*)" what Christians do at church, that Christian missionaries observed and which informed the use of the indigenous word *sɔre* as constituting what Christians do when they meet; they go to *sɔre Nyankopɔn*.[135] Amu's view that the two forms of "worship" at *nsɔrem* and church were irreconcilable is quite clear in his later expression of the "absurdity" of giving food to his deceased father.[136] Amu's conclusion of "worship" as what is done in regard to the ancestors at *nsɔrem* is not shared by Akan commentators such as Peter Sarpong and Nana Addo Dankwa. Both consider the label "ancestor worship"[137] as inappropriate. The challenge seems to relate to the sense of worship as regarding the object of adoration as an end.

In Sarpong's view the ancestors are "venerated" not "worshipped" and that all that the Ghanaian (Akan) does is to "honor," "respect," "serve" and "remember" them.[138] Thus the invoking of the ancestors "to bear witness" to a truth being expressed, commending and entrusting to their care, as well as praising them all constitute "veneration" and not "worship." According to Dankwa, the "living chief must give reverence and respect to his seniors, the ancestors, conceptually."[139] Though he acknowledges the ambiguity of the Akan word *som*, which translates either "serve or worship," Dankwa considers the sense of "serve" as more appropriate considering the fact that the "African [Akan] only extends to the ancestor the same reverence and performs the services as he would render to the living chief."[140] Furthermore, since "personality cult" is not encouraged among the Akan, there is no deification beyond respect for any individual and thus the term "ancestral-worship" is a misconception.[141] Whether the act is deemed "worship" or "veneration" is subject to the practitioner.[142]

---

135. It is perhaps worth noting that Amu in this instance does not say *sɔre Yesu*.

136. This was part of his response to an interview question of what he found "objectionable about [paganism]." Laryea, *Ephraim Amu*, 254 & 276.

137. "Ancestor worship" has been a blanket term for the general attitude of the living towards their ancestors which in most cases is characterized by elaborate activities such as the giving of food items and gifts, some form of communication and even visit to their graves. It has however been regarded as different from the "worship of the dead." Meyer, "Some Reflections on Ancestor Worship in Africa," 122–42.

138. Sarpong, *Ghana in Retrospect*, 42–43.

139. Dankwa III, *The Institution of Chieftaincy*, 69.

140. Dankwa III, *The Institution of Chieftaincy*, 69.

141. Dankwa III, *The Institution of Chieftaincy*, 71.

142. Barima, Interview, 25 February 2014.

The meeting with the ancestors as manifested in the *Adae* ceremony, exhibits the intricate nature of the amalgam of culture and religion. Dankwa attempts to separate the two with regard to traditional activities such as those in honor of the ancestors, the sprinkling of blood and libation.[143] Such attempts would invariably be arduous, since it is the religious connotations that seem to prolong the traditional institutions. There are rites and rituals that are to be observed in the chieftaincy institution. In the case of the Akan, it is the institution of chieftaincy that ensures the continuity of the cultural elements manifested in the respective traditions. Any dichotomy between the apparently symbolic activities and the tendency towards their religious appropriation would, therefore, be subjective and superficial. A chief may maintain the distinction, but respective subjects and participants in the traditional rites and rituals will not always share that. Hence the question of the worship or veneration of the ancestors is not resolved by the judgement of an individual.

Nananom, Death and Funerals

Funeral rites are occasions for the final physical parting of the dead and the living. Funerals for the advanced in age and elders and chiefs are specially observed with, sometimes, elaborate activities. Sarpong notes that funerals are a duty for the living; "bad funerals," that is those not apparently organized well, are a disgrace while "good" ones are prestigious.[144] Death itself completes the threefold cycle of events in an individual's life, along with birth and puberty.[145] The belief in life after death and the involvement of the spirit of the deceased in the physical world mean that a proper funeral rite is invariably expected for those who have lived through puberty to adulthood. A translated address to a deceased just before his (or her) coffin was finally covered, given by Busia, illustrates traditional Akan thinking about death and the necessity of funeral:

> You are leaving us to-day; we have fired guns; we have given you a sheep; we have performed your funeral. Do not let any of us fall ill. Let us get money to pay the expenses of your funeral. Let the women bear children. Life to all of us. Life to the chief.[146]

---

143. Dankwa III, *The Institution of Chieftaincy*, 67–84.
144. Sarpong, *Ghana in Retrospect*, 26 & 29.
145. Nketia, "Birth, Puberty and Death," 1.
146. Busia, *The Position of the Chief*, 23–24.

Just as the outdooring and puberty rite ceremonies usher, respectively, into life (on earth) and adulthood, death and the befitting funeral usher one into the ancestral world. The dead in the above address is reminded of his or her departure, the befitting funeral and then the expected benevolence now that he or she is at an advantageous position to do so.

Nananom, Knowledge, Wisdom, and Traditional Proverbs

The ancestors are regarded as the source of traditional wisdom. Tempels observed among the Bantu that, not only does the "vital human force" fundamentally depend on the elders, but also "the power to know" depended on the "wisdom of the elders."[147] A key source for accessing a people's traditional knowledge and wisdom is via their indigenous proverbs, most of which the ancestors have bequeathed. Proverbs provide an insight into a people's shared understanding of reality, which encompasses views of and relations to the transcendent or transcendental entities, nature, and fellow humans.[148]

Proverbs (*mmɛ, abebusɛm, mmebusɛm*; sing. *ɛbɛ*) being "accumulated wisdom and experiences of past generations" and also the result of "observation," indeed, deal with the various facets of human life, reflect a people's "mind and philosophy" and also their belief in and influence of the unseen spiritual world.[149] Christaller noted the pervasiveness of proverbs in indigenous languages of the peoples of the Gold Coast (Ghana) when he observed that the languages are "highly figurative" and that "facts or themes of discussion are usually compared with, elucidated by, or judged after certain precedents or self-evident truths substantiated by proverbs."[150]

The Akan words *nimdeɛ* (*nyimdzee*) and *nyansa* both translate as either "knowledge" or "wisdom," but the latter, *nyansa*, seems to connote more of

---

147. Tempels, *Bantu Philosophy*, 48.

148. Mbiti, "Children Confer Glory on a Home," ix–xiv; Mbiti, *African Religions and Philosophy*, 66–67; Gyekye, *An Essay on African Philosophical Thought*, 15–16.

149. The Akan word for the palm (tree) is *abe* and Gyekye, for instance, has maintained that the two words *abe* and *ɛbɛ* are etymologically linked following his field research. Gyekye's observation is that all the products that derive from the palm such as oil, wine and soap all go through processes such as distillation. Thus, the usefulness of the palm is only realized after several processes: all the products "lie deep in the palm tree." Gyekye notes then that similarly, the meaning of a proverb is not immediately obvious but has to be distilled reflectively, as it were. Gyekye, *An Essay on African Philosophical Thought*, 16–17. To utter or create a proverb is to *bu* or *to bɛ*. Both verbs *bu* and *to* have a wide scope of usage with various respective senses such as to "account" or "consider" and to "throw" or "lay." Christaller, *Dictionary*, 11, 48–50 & 519–21. Opoku, *Hearing and Keeping*, xviii. Christaller, *Twi Mmebusɛm Mpensā-Ahansia Mmoaano*, v.

150. Christaller, *Twi Mmebusɛm*, v.

activity and practical application.¹⁵¹ For instance, it is said that *nimdeɛ firi obi ano* ("it is from a person's mouth that wisdom [or knowledge?] comes") and that *obi nhu nimdeɛ nkɔ ayi (ase) na ɔ(kɔ—or—bɛ) sɔre a, waserew* ("No one with any sense [knowledge] goes to funeral and then laughs when she/he gets up to leave").¹⁵² The emphasis placed on applied wisdom is seen in the expression, *nyansa nyɛ sika na wɔakyekyere asie* ("Wisdom is not like gold dust that you can bundle up and store away").¹⁵³ Words and wisdom are not synonymous according to the Akan proverb *asɛm nko, nyansa nko* ("words are not the same as wisdom").¹⁵⁴

Nyansa in Akan thinking is acquired through learning as expressed in the proverb, *nyansa nyinaa ne osuahu* ("all wisdom [knowledge] is acquired by learning").¹⁵⁵ Gyekye, however, attempts to distinguish between two forms of *nyansa*: an inborn "mental faculty" equivalent to *adwen* ("thinking") originating from the *sunsum* (spirit) of the person, and one that connotes "skill, practical knowledge" which is acquired.¹⁵⁶ Gyekye adds that in this way, wisdom, "is not confined to the elders,"¹⁵⁷ although knowledge of "inherited ancestral traditions may be the preserve of the elders."¹⁵⁸ Age, then, has nothing to do with wisdom in the Akan sense, and since everybody in Akan thinking has *sunsum*, "anyone has the potential to be wise."¹⁵⁹

The dynamism of experience as imperative in both knowledge and wisdom, even in the Akan sense, implies a regard for what has been or gone before. No matter how one arrives at wisdom or to a state of being considered wise, it is practically impossible to do so without knowledge of previous ideas. In the Akan perspective, a wise person (*nyansafo*) is not only knowledgeable of traditional proverbs but has the ability to understand a given proverb in the context of its use and application.¹⁶⁰ Thus while a prov-

---

151. Cf. Christaller, *Dictionary*, 342 & 358.

152. Lange's translation. Lange, Christaller, *Three Thousand Six Hundred Ghanaian Proverbs*, 198, n. 2355 & 17. n. 191.

153. Lange, Christaller, *Three Thousand Six Hundred Ghanaian Proverbs*, 214, n. 2554.

154. Lange, Christaller, *Three Thousand Six Hundred Ghanaian Proverbs*, 241, n. 2869.

155. Opoku, *Hearing and Keeping*, 71. Opoku in this rendering, though, associates *nyansa* with both wisdom and knowledge.

156. Gyekye, *An Essay on African Philosophical Thought*, 61–62.

157. Gyekye, *An Essay on African Philosophical Thought*, 63.

158. Gyekye, *African Cultural Values*, 145.

159. Gyekye, *An Essay on African Philosophical Thought*, 63.

160. Proverbs are largely employed as summaries of thoughts that are intended to educate, solve a present challenge or to illuminate the nature and implication of a

erb may suffice for a "wise child" rather than lengthy discourse in a given instance, a fool needs explanation: *oba nyansafo wobu no be, na wonka no asem* ("the wise [child] person is spoken to in proverbs, not in plain [lengthy] talk"); *okwasea na wobu no be a, wokyere no ase* ("when a fool is told a proverb, the meaning of it has to be explained to him").[161]

The close connection between proverbs and tradition mediated by the elders and ancestors is captured in the frequent prefix to proverbs with the phrase *Nananom se* ("the ancestors say") or *Mpanyinfo se* ("the elders say").[162] Proverbs are a means for communicating and maintaining traditions, and hence knowledge and right application of proverbs is a characteristic of a worthy elder. It is more desirable to speak the language of the elders than that of children: *wowu gyaw wo mpanyin kasa a, wonnyae nkoka mmofra kasa* ("if the elders leave you a legacy of dignified language, you do not abandon it to speak childish language").[163] The above proverb also expresses the greater respect given to antiquity over the relatively young present. In such a case, though present experiences may bring insightful observations, they are appropriated in the context of the wisdom of the old, that is, the inherited knowledge of the elders and ancestors.

The Value of the Concept of Nana

It is tradition, Laurenti Magesa notes, that provides the "moral code" for societal life and has the ancestors as the custodians.[164] The medium for the transmitting of tradition is the category of myth.[165] Thus the development

---

problem or situation at hand: an Akan proverb puts it this way *asem ba a, na abebuo aba* ("when a problem/matter/occasion arises, then comes the uttering of a proverb"). Cf. Christaller, *Twi Mmebusem*, 119 no.2859; Christaller's rendering of the proverb: "When a matter (for public and formal discussion, or, as the usual term is, a palaver) comes, then proverb-making comes" (p.v). The meanings of Akan proverbs are thus well appreciated in each relevant context. Opoku, *Hearing and Keeping*, xix–xx; Mbiti, *African Religions and Philosophy*, 2.; Gyekye, *An Essay on African Philosophical Thought*, 17; Finnegan, *Oral Literature in Africa*, 379–411.

161. Opoku, *Hearing and Keeping*, xviii.

162. Opoku, *Hearing and Keeping*, xviii–xix. Cf. Rattray, *Ashanti Proverbs*, 112 n.399 [Christaller, *Twi Mmebusem*, n.2623]. Some animals are purported to have declared certain proverbs: *Akoko se, "Ade ansa a, anka memee'* "The fowl says, 'If it had not got dark, should I have had my fill?'"; *Oguanten se, "Mefwe osebo na mawo no so"* "The sheep says, 'I shall look on a leopard that I may give birth to one like it'" Rattray, *Ashanti Proverbs*, 79 n.203 [Christaller, n.1655] and p. 90 n. 276 [Christaller, n.1232].

163. Opoku, *Hearing and Keeping*, xix.

164. Magesa, *African Religion*, 35–36.

165. Magesa, *African Religion*, 36.

and sustenance of the concept of ancestors, particularly in relation to the keeping of tradition, is linked to the myth-making mechanism of pre-literate traditional societies.[166] The origin or formative factors notwithstanding, the concept of ancestors does have its role in the society. From the Igbo context, Iloanusi notes that the ancestors remain the "custodians of law, customs and morality," they mediate between *Chukwu* (Supreme Being) and humans and also control social relationships that ensure domestic productivity.[167] According to Kwesi Dickson, the (Akan) cult of ancestors presents three values, namely, mediation with the transcendent, providing "a sense of solidarity and security," and serving as a reminder of the virtues defining the "morally good life."[168]

In his study of Akan ethics, C. A. Ackah deduced two main types of moral sanctions in Akan society, namely, public opinion and religious or supernatural sanctions.[169] While the former consists of the opinion of living members of the community in approving or disapproving the actions of members who are eventually traced to their *abusua* (family), the latter is from unseen entities within the community, consisting the *abosom* (gods or deities), *suman* (charms or talismans), *sasa* (spirit of a dead person), the ancestors and taboos.[170] According to Ackah, the concept of ancestors[171] among the Akan commends itself in its moral value, in which the ancestors are considered as "guardians of morality."[172] The living, due to their regard for their ancestors, appease them for any wrong way of life perceived to be disapproved of the ancestors to avoid any consequential punishments in the form of sudden calamity or disaster and even death.

Ackah further outlines five "ethical standards" that both "account for acts which are regarded as wrong" and also embrace duties and virtues which when neglected may incur "social disapproval."[173] Ackah observes

---

166. According to Iloanusi, who speaks of pre-literate societies in general and particularly with regard to the Igbo, "myths are the most general and effective means of awakening and maintaining consciousness of the spirit world of the ancestors." Iloanusi, *Myths of the Creation of Man and the Origin of Death in Africa*, 23. Bediako also shares this view concerning the evolvement of the whole concept of ancestors. Bediako, *Jesus in African Culture*, 40.

167. Iloanusi, *Myths of the Creation of Man and the Origin of Death in Africa*, 100–103.

168. Dickson, *Theology in Africa*, 177.

169. Ackah, *Akan Ethics*, 89.

170. Ackah, *Akan Ethics*, 89.

171. Ackah uses "ancestor worship."

172. Ackah, *Akan Ethics*, 98. Thus as an "important means of social control," Nukunya, *Tradition and Change in Ghana*, 59.

173. Ackah, *Akan Ethics*, 120ff.

that the "Nana standard," though not the only ethical standard, is nonetheless significant and does inform the activities surrounding the concept of ancestors. The "Nana" is

> regarded by his or her descendants as the moral exemplar in many respects, who in his day lived a life that befitted the good name of the family, and so set a standard which his living grandchildren and great-grandchildren should aim at.[174]

Ackah primarily considered the concept of ancestors among the Mfantse. Brian Jennings' consideration of the *Nananom* to be at the head of the Mfantse "moral vision"[175] in his study on *Methodist and Fanti Moral Traditions* is in agreement with the Ackah's "Nana standard." For Kofi Opoku, the ancestral beliefs not only act as a "form of social control by which the conduct of individuals is regulated," but they also underscore fundamental West African (Akan) ideas such as belief in life after death, an unending sense of obligation in African (Akan) society and the sense of community as constituting both the natural and supernatural.[176]

Among the Akan the regard for dead forebears is quite selective. That is, only those who have met both moral and physical conditions are recognized at the community level. At the family level, regard for ancestors is not as pronounced as one would find at the community level and especially during festivals. In this way filial piety, as has been deduced to be the "essence of [Chinese] ancestor worship,"[177] for example, is not fundamental to the Akan idea as moral standard is.

In fact, it is largely the institution of chieftaincy in contemporary Akan societies that ensures the continual rituals associated with the ancestors. As the chief is regarded as both the vital link between the living and ancestors as well as the measure of traditional moral standard,[178] he has a key role to play in keeping the moral standard of the traditional society. This traditional moral standard ensures the religious or cosmic harmony desired to

---

174. Ackah, *Akan Ethics*, 121.

175. Jennings, *Leading Virtue*, 122. The book is essentially the substance of his earlier doctoral thesis titled "Christian Virtue in a West African Context: A Study of the Interaction and Synthesis of Methodist and Fanti Moral Traditions as a Model for the Contextualisation of Christian Ethics."

176. Opoku, *West African Traditional Religion*, 38–39.

177. Shih, "A Study of Ancestor Worship in Ancient China," 189 quoted in Chea, "Some Observations on Parental-Children Ties in the Old Testament and Their Possible Bearing on Filial Piety," 14.

178. I make use of "traditional moral standard" in the sense that this has its own parameters of measure and can thus be distinct, though not essentially discontinuous, from say "Christian moral standard."

guarantee communal prosperity. So long as the honored memory of the ancestors ensures the safeguard of the traditional moral standard, the concept of ancestor remains intricately connected to the fabric of the Akan society, from the family to the community.[179]

Nana as *Discovered* Messiah: J. B. Danquah's Conceptual Portrait of the Akan Ideal Personage

The indigenous names given the ancestors in various communities indicate the respective perception of dead forebears and the consequent attitude towards them. Among the Akan the title *nana* is essentially a moral title.[180] It is gender-neutral and sometimes serves as a personal name but is generally ascribed to elders, as Ephraim-Donkor has captured: "not everyone who bears the title *nana* is an elder, but every elder [*opanyin*] is a *nana*."[181] Living elders, of whom the chief is regarded as foremost in the community, are designated as *nananom* (plural of *nana*).[182] This would mean, then, that a *nana saman*, though not frequently used as compared to the plural form (*nananom nsamanfo*), is an elder *saman* in the sense that he or she, while alive, was regarded as an *opanyin*.

Traditional Akan society was not literate by the time Twi was made literate with the introduction of Christianity. Akan literacy is remarkably a Christian legacy. There were therefore no written accounts, or any speculations for that matter, of Akan ideas and beliefs. Oral tradition, traditional proverbs together with various artefacts such as crafts and Adinkra symbols served as a memory of the past. These also pointed to traditional Akan ideas and beliefs. For people of Akan descent such as J. B. Danquah, who had the benefit of both English and Akan mother-tongue literacy the illiterate traditional past of the Akan was not a limitation to accessing and communicating the values inherent in the Akan tradition.[183]

---

179. In this sense Barrett's observation on the intricate nature of the role of the concept of ancestors among the Bantu is to a fair extent true also for the Akan: "it represents the hierarchical social system carried over into the spirit world; it validates the traditional political structure; it ensures fertility, health, prosperity and the continuity of past and future in family life; it is a sanction for the respect of living elders. To affect it, was to attack the very foundations of tribal and family structure." Barrett, *Schism and Renewal in Africa*, 120.

180. Dzobo, "Values in a Changing Society—Man, Ancestors and God," 231–32.

181. Ephrim-Donkor, *African Spirituality*, 120.

182. Ephrim-Donkor opines that *Nananom mpanyinfo* is the "proper designation" for two or more elders. Ephrim-Donkor, *African Spirituality*, 120.

183. Danquah's varied interests with significant contributions are succinctly

In the process of demonstrating the value of Akan traditional thought, religious belief and ethical understanding primarily via Akan proverbs, Danquah deduced a conceptual portrait of the Akan ideal person. Yet his guides towards this venture were primarily the two works of the Basel missionary to the Gold Goast, J. G. Christaller's Twi Dictionary and the compilation of some three thousand six hundred and eighty (3,680) proverbs.[184] Danquah was keen to note the activity of God's Spirit among the Akan, which was evident from the truth expressed in the proverbs compiled by Christaller (who had referred to "sparks of truth" in the Akan proverbs): "the Spirit of God is abroad, even in the Akan of the Gold Coast [Ghana]."[185]

Danquah's *The Akan Doctrine of God*, which was first published in 1944, shows his theological interests and exploits in a substantial way.[186] The content comprises rewritten sections of the third part of a larger three-volume study originally entitled "Gold Coast Ethics and Religion" (A Theory of Morals and Religion in the Akan Tradition).[187] Danquah indicates that the evidence and findings of the original complete volumes confirmed the thesis "*what the Akan take to be the good is the family . . . .*"[188] Kwesi Dickson,

---

summarized by K. Twum Barima: Danquah was "an illustrious son of Ghana [with] many sidedness, an astute politician, a lawyer, a philosopher, a poet, and ardent nationalist and a scholar" (Twum Barima, "Preface," *Danquah*, 7). Danquah's "many sidedness" was matched with a conscious affirmation of Christian truth. Not only was he the son of a Christian convert with a fond memory of his father's nurturing, it is evident from Danquah's writings, as Joe Appiah has noted, that he believed in God and the Christian teaching, though he was not seen going to church regularly. (Joe Appiah, *The Man J. B. Danquah*, 10).

184. Danquah, *The Akan Doctrine of God*, 185.

185. Danquah, *The Akan Doctrine of God*, 187. Christaller, *Twi Mmebusɛm*, xi.

186. Recognised by Andrew F. Walls as "the first modern African constructive theologian" and his *The Akan Doctrine of God* as a "remarkable book." Walls, *The Cross-Cultural Process in Christian History*, 171. Also as "the first African theologian of the 20th Century . . . the first significant African intellectual to recognise that there was a body of religious wisdom, knowledge and experience in Africa[n] tradition that could be assembled and presented in an organised manner and described as a 'theology.'" Bediako, *Religion, Culture and Language*, 5 & 6.

187. Unfortunately, the manuscript of the first two volumes were destroyed by a fire that "completely consumed" his residence and "everything therein." The "providentially preserved" volume III, Danquah indicates, "aims to elucidate the nature and significance of the divinity whom the Akan call *Nyankopon Kwaame*, the "'Greater' God of Saturday." Danquah, *The Akan Doctrine of God*, xxvii; xxx. That the Chapter one (I) of *The Akan Doctrine of God* was originally Chapter twenty-one (XXI) of Book five (V) of the three-volume work shows the amount of effort and work done which produced a now lost background to *The Akan Doctrine of God*. It is thus useful to assess Danquah's work with an assumed background consumed by fire.

188. Danquah, *The Akan Doctrine of God*, xxvii.

in his introduction to the second edition of Danquah's work, offered a helpful theological critique, particularly his assertion that "Akan knowledge of God teaches that he is the Great Ancestor."[189] For Dickson, the title *Nana* applied to God is not enough to support Danquah's theory since one would have expected "*Nyame* to be spoken of as a deified ancestor . . . [which is] never done."[190] In Dickson's view, amidst debatable conclusions reached from "speculation and etymologisings," there is much that is "valuable" and "authentic Akan Wisdom" with one corrective being the "insistence on the supreme reality of God" at a time when the "role of God in African religion" was "generally underestimated."[191]

Dickson recognized two assumptions underlying Danquah's work and he instructively cautions readers to take note and this I think is significant and demonstrates the depth of Danquah's religious concern in his intellectual vocation. The first is that by their own wisdom, the Akan "have been able to perceive God in a way that gives the west (sic) no basis for a feeling of superiority."[192] Secondly, the "Akan religious doctrine knows only one God" with everything else in the "form of religion . . . [a] superstition."[193] Danquah's methodological tools in demonstrating the first concern as well as his conclusion on the second, in Dickson's analysis, are not without pitfalls.[194] Yet

---

189. Dickson, "Introduction" in Danquah, *The Akan Doctrine of God*, vii–xxv.

190. Danquah, *The Akan Doctrine of God*, xx.

191. Dickson, "Introduction," xxiv.

192. Dickson, "Introduction," vii. Cf. Thompson also observes that Danquah, through this work, succeeded in showing "Akan ethics and theology can stand as equals with any equivalent conceptions in European culture." J. C. Thompson, "Introduction" in Ackah, *Akan Ethics*, 18.

193. Dickson, "Introduction," viii. cf. Danquah, *The Akan Doctrine of God*, 39.

194. According to Dickson, Danquah's overt reliance on his philosophical expertise in his attempt to demonstrate the Akan ingenious perception of God does not avoid "the obvious pitfall of substituting philosophy for theology." Danquah's conviction of the Akan knowing only one God, for Dickson, cannot be justified in view of the available evidence from the significant efforts of such scholars as Christaller and Rattray on Akan religion. Dickson therefore concludes that Danquah's approach may well be considered as a reaction to another type of approach to assessing the Akan religious tradition. Dickson, "Introduction," viii and ix. The difficulties with Danquah's conclusions have been largely due to his methodology. For instance, such reviews as, C. R. Gaba, "Review: Danquah, Joseph Buakye, The Akan doctrine of God: a fragment of Gold Coast ethics and religion. Second edition with a new introduction by Kwesi A. Dickson," 152; Edwin Smith on the first edition of Danquah's work who also cautions other Africans who follow up from Danquah not to write like Hegel. Edwin W. Smith, "Review: The Akan Doctrine of God, a Fragment of Gold Coast Ethics and Religion by J. B. Danquah," 186–87.

when one considers Danquah's overarching concern in *The Akan Doctrine of God*, his efforts remain timeless.[195]

Danquah indicated that the original work ("Gold Coast Ethics and Religion") presented "the Akan idea of the good, or the supreme good."[196] The conclusion was that the family is what the Akan take to be the good and scores of Akan proverbs

> pointed to one truth, that the family, [and] the neighbors, were those of the blood, the group held together by community of origin and obligation to a common ancestor, the Nana, and held together also by the high standard of attainment in goodness and prosperity enshrined in the Nana's memory. It was for this group that morality was of value and, for it, beneficence was truly beneficial and profitable—in both senses; in worth and in increment.[197]

The community (as a family of blood relations) had "the Nana" as both the source of coming to existence and the "standard of attainment in goodness and prosperity." The memory of "the Nana" is essential for the life of the family. The view of the family as "the supreme good" in Akan thinking in consequence made way for Danquah's conception of Nana as an ideal (an idea). The idea of "the Nana" is pivotal in Danquah's exposition of Akan (ethical) theology, holding the Supreme Being to be Father-Ancestor-Creator, the "Great Ancestor."[198]

The Nana or Exemplar—The Discovered Messiah

Danquah discovered eight "irreducible fundamental postulates" that, apart from demonstrating the possession of a "distinctive theory of life and being"

---

195. So Thompson, seeing Danquah as a "prophet before his time," feels that although the latter failed to distinguish clearly "a description of what Akan beliefs and practices are, and his interpretation and expansion and development of these ideas," nevertheless his "systematic development of Akan moral beliefs," for Thompson, was a pointer to the future "when a systematised and rationalised version of Akan ethics will proudly be able to take place alongside the classical ethical systems of western thought." Thompson, "Introduction," 19.

196. Danquah, *The Akan Doctrine of God*, xxvii.

197. Danquah examined the available "anthropological evidence" encompassing the Akan philosophy of life which included their gods, "fetishes," customs, maxims or proverbs, festivals, religious observance, calendars, folklore, family system, social and moral codes, and racial history, fears and hopes. Danquah, *The Akan Doctrine of God*, xxviii.

198. Danquah, *The Akan Doctrine of God*, 27. Cf. Thompson, "Introduction," 11.

among the "Akan-Ashanti," "are also the working tools of the Akan practice of morals and religion."¹⁹⁹ These are, in order of discovery, "E-su, or φύσις [nature]"; "The Nkara or Chosen Soul"; "The Sunsum or Experiencing Soul"; "The Nana or moral and religious exemplar"; "The Nyame or suprasensible E-su of Being"; "The Nyankopon or suprasensible Experiencing Soul of Being"; "The Odomankoma, or the exampled Reality"; and "The Honhom or Mind, Spirit of Reality."²⁰⁰ In an earlier publication, Danquah observed that the term *nana* is a ceremonial appellation and etymologically means "mother-of-mothers, i.e. grandmother or grandfather."²⁰¹ At the time of the *Akan Doctrine of God*, Danquah would assert that the name *nana* "appears to have derived from *e-na*, mother."²⁰² As to why a name of feminine origin is now "applied to the deified ancestor who is in most cases male," one may need to probe further unless one is content with the fact that the *opanyin* who becomes a *nana* "derives his blood by right of [a] female descent."²⁰³

In Danquah's discerned Akan conceptual framework, Nana is the "middle term of the Akan existential logic" and it is the Nana that connects in "a hand of fellowship, or . . . relationship" to the postulates of E-su, Nkara and Sunsum on one hand and on the other that of the "universal postulates of Onyame, Onyankopon and Odomankoma."²⁰⁴ The Nana is "exemplar" of the second group [Onyame, Onyankopon and Odomankoma] and at the same time reflects their "universality . . . in the [Akan] race." It is through the Nana, therefore, that "the Akan family participates in the greater family of the universal whole in one union."²⁰⁵ The Nana is "the example to the ethnic Akan of the universal man, or the divinity in man" and therefore partakes in the two natures of "ethnic" and "universal."²⁰⁶

The idea of Nana is behind the means to realizing "the right ideals to make men live well" and what the Akan offer as "the right way" is the "example

199. Danquah, *The Akan Doctrine of God*, 104 and 106.

200. Danquah, *The Akan Doctrine of God*, 109–10.

201. Danquah, *Gold Coast Akan Laws and Customs and the Akim Abuakwa Constitution*, 24.

202. Danquah, *The Akan Doctrine of God*, 51.

203. Danquah, *The Akan Doctrine of God*, 51.

204. Danquah, *The Akan Doctrine of God*, 110.

205. Danquah, *The Akan Doctrine of God*, 110.

206. Danquah, *The Akan Doctrine of God*, 110. One can discern from Danquah a concern with the link between the local (particular) and universal (general) and this has some affinity with Philo of Alexandria's *logos* as a kind of "shock absorber" entity between God (transcendence) and humanity (physical or perceivable). For in Danquah's thinking the postulates of Onyame, Onyankopon and Odomankoma in a sense transcend the Akan mind contrary to E-su, Nkara, Sunsum and Nana, which are in "their nature absolutely original constructions of [the] Akan mind."

of the dignity of the *opanyin* . . . who is to become a *nana*."[207] Thus, the end or destiny of the head of the family "is to become a *nana*." The assessment of an *opanyin* involves the discovery of whether such a person can be a *nana* or realize the idea of *nana*-ship. The "dignity of the *opanyin*" is the standard or example for the right way to make the Akan live well. This dignity has as its measure the ideal or idea of a Nana, which is traced to the Father-Ancestor-Creator, the Great Nana, the Supreme Ideal, the Supreme Being.[208]

Danquah compares the idea of Messiah in the Hebrew tradition with that of Nana among the Akan. Why he does that he does not explicitly indicate. But perhaps having a level of knowledge in the Judaeo-Christian tradition (quite certainly chiefly in his reading of the Christian Bible in the Twi language) he readily took this path. In Danquah's view the Hebrew conception of a Messiah was "of a personage expected to come as the divine agent to fulfil a promise or covenant of delivery and triumph."[209] The Akan Nana is held "in a certain sense . . . . to be a Messiah, the anointed of the Akan people, king and exemplar."[210] The difference between the Akan Nana and Hebrew Messiah is that while the latter is an "expected personage," the former is a "discovered or revealed Messiah."[211] Because he is not expected, the Nana could be regarded as "produced, invented, fashioned or hewed out by his community."[212] It is the family, therefore, that creates and recognizes or makes manifest the Nana, since a Nana is invariably linked to a family and a family owes its origin to a common *nana*.

The complete discovery of the one elected as head of the community (family, tribe, clan or state) as "the revelation of the ideal good" is or was at the end of his [or her] life, at death and his election is itself by "a gradual process of elimination."[213] By his selection or election, the *opanyin* while alive "had been anointed and . . . worshiped with acts of adoration and reverence as someone like a god, or . . . about to become a god."[214] The discovery, which had taken place in the earlier stage of election, is confirmed at a stage which is fitting for the *opanyin's* deification, namely at his death. If at the *opanyin's* death he was still held in honor, the "revelation became complete." Thus, the *opanyin's* life as a "revelation of the ideal good" is first

---

207. Danquah, *The Akan Doctrine of God*, 109.
208. Danquah, *The Akan Doctrine of God*, 27.
209. Danquah, *The Akan Doctrine of God*, 120.
210. Danquah, *The Akan Doctrine of God*, 120.
211. Danquah, *The Akan Doctrine of God*, 120.
212. Danquah, *The Akan Doctrine of God*, 120.
213. Danquah, *The Akan Doctrine of God*, 120.
214. Danquah, *The Akan Doctrine of God*, 120.

discovered when he is elected as head of the community and is confirmed at his death when, after surviving "the great trial and ordeal of headship," he was still "an honored man."[215]

Danquah explains that the Akan maxim: *Animguase mfata Okanni Ba* "a thing of dishonour and a son of the Akan go ill together" is where the Akan sense of Messiah is "best interpreted."[216] It is the person of dignity, one without disgrace, who, "in nature [is] like a son of Akan," is the "one fit to be called God's anointed."[217] Danquah was convinced that with this form of a moral and religious personage as "a man [or woman] of dignity," the original Hebrew idea of Messiah is irrelevant to Akan traditional thought. The "available moral tradition" of the Akan does not indicate the expectation of "a prophet, a divinely born 'Osei'" as a national or "universal ruler or deliverer," among other functions.[218] Rather Akan society,

> at all times regarded the possibility of discovering an ideal personage living in their community who should embody in his person the positive qualities of a citizen of the moral and civil estates, as a present fact of the "practical" life.[219]

Instead of an expected personage with a divine mandate, the discoverable "ideal personage" among the Akan lived in the community and was expected to embody "positive qualities" of both the moral and civil establishment. Akan society from the foregoing did not "dissociate the religious from the moral" or both from the civil life.[220] The act of doing "good" or "practical goodness" was more of an activity of "beneficence" and less of "a capacity or potentiality" and the "actual life of well doing, [in the] here and now, in every aspect of life" constituted what the Akan held as goodness.[221] The *opanyin's* life as lived in the community was to exhibit such a quality of Akan goodness. It was or is not so much what the person can do as what the person does. Hence the *opanyin's* importance was that he had lived as an "ordinary citizen and had not lost his dignity or honour and not suffered disgrace."[222] Such a person is "fit to rule . . . [an] anointed head of the

---

215. Danquah, *The Akan Doctrine of God*, 120.

216. Danquah's translation. It can also be rendered as "Disgrace is not befitting of an Akan child."

217. Danquah, *The Akan Doctrine of God*, 120–21.

218. Danquah, *The Akan Doctrine of God*, 121.

219. Danquah, *The Akan Doctrine of God*, 121.

220. Danquah, *The Akan Doctrine of God*, 121.

221. Danquah, *The Akan Doctrine of God*, 121.

222. Danquah, *The Akan Doctrine of God*, 121.

people, [a] revelation of God in man, [and] discovered by man."[223] From Danquah's etymology of *opanyin* as "one whose goodness has grown" from the word *pa*, "good" and *nyin*, "grow," the idea of growing in goodness as is expected with physical growth is, perhaps, implicit in the word *opanyin*. He should not or cannot be a child. Christaller's definition, which Danquah also quotes, gives the picture of someone of respectable age and attainment and not necessarily an old person.[224]

When an *opanyin* dies with "honour and dignity in him still at a high level without disgrace," he is "truly deifiable, a proved divinity, bearer of the supreme moral idea, a Nana, the exemplar and paradigm of Nyankopon, what God in Himself is, or ought to be."[225] The *opanyin* becomes a Nana at his death while still being held in honor and dignity. In other words, a Nana (ancestor) is an *opanyin* who at the time of his death was or is still held in honor and dignity by way of the activity of his life and has not suffered disgrace. From the proverb *Obi nhyee da nwoo panyin pen* ("No one by design ever gave birth to *opanyin*"), Danquah deduced that the *opanyin* was not born but made, discovered by his community "as much as he makes his community good."[226] The community is able to discover an *opanyin* by his activity within that community in making it good. The community has its standards or expectations and by satisfying those standards one is, in the process, made into a personage that the community then discovers as a revelation of the ideal Akan (*Okanni*). The *opanyin*, "once so made," is not regarded susceptible to the "temptations of the moral life" and his standard is even preferred to the religious object of a fetish (charm, amulet).[227]

The Nana, as the ideal personage ("the exemplar and paradigm of Nyankopon") to the community, is relevant only in his active involvement in the community. The community makes him, and he is discovered by his activity in the community in making it good. For Danquah therefore, the Akan ideal of a Messiah, the Nana, is closer to the Greek ideal as it did not involve a

---

223. Danquah, *The Akan Doctrine of God*, 122.
224. Christaller, *Dictionary*, 375.
225. Danquah, *The Akan Doctrine of God*, 122.
226. Danquah, *The Akan Doctrine of God*, 122.
227. Danquah sees this as expressed respectively in the maxims *Obi mfa opanyin nhye adanse* ("no one turns an opanyin into his witness" or "nobody makes or takes an opanyin as a witness" [My rendering]) and *Opanyin ano sen suman* ("The Opanyin's word is more potent than fetish [charm, amulet]"). Danquah, *The Akan Doctrine of God*, 122–23. These proverbs, and especially the second one, also demonstrate the value given to the words and activities of *mpanyinfo* (elders). As noted above on the discussion on the ancestors and traditional proverbs, "knowledge of and right application of proverbs" is expected of an *opanyin* and thus his or her words ought to communicate as far as possible the truth in a given situation or concerning a present reality.

man's detachment from the world or his community for personal attainment. The Greek and the Akan ideal "was made for human nature."[228] Danquah agrees with the British sociologist and politician Leonard Hobhouse's contrast of the Christian saint in the "spiritual religions" with that of hero or statesman in the Greek (philosophical) ideal.[229] Hobhouse addressed the contemporary question on what constituted the "moral standard," by comparing the idea of the Christian saint and the Greek hero statesman in his general study on "the theory of ethical evolution."[230] Hobhouse asserts that though Plato and Aristotle will put the life of the philosopher above that of the statesman, both of them were mindful of the obligation of the philosopher and statesman as citizens of a "self-governing community." He adds,

> . . . the first duty of man, whether in the Republic [of Plato] or in the Ethics [of Aristotle], is to be a good citizen. . . . The good citizen is one who can both rule and be ruled. He has the self-discipline which enables him to submit to others when their turn comes, and the wisdom which enables him to direct, not only his own affairs, but those of the state when his own turn comes. . . . He should have an adequate measure of self-respect, and a great-souled man, who is in a sense the perfect type of this kind of character, being worthy of great things, should deem himself worthy of great things. He should know himself for what he is, and do nothing to belittle or demean himself. . . . He should feel a proper pride in himself, and trust to that pride to keep him from anything degrading. He is thus the direct antithesis of the holy and humble man of heart whom the Christian teaching holds up to esteem. The antithesis is inevitable; the Christian saint is conscious of a sinfulness from which the divine grace alone has raised him, and which nevertheless still tinges and stains all that he does when it is matched against the white radiance of infinite perfection. The great souled Greek has learnt to govern his own nature; he measures himself with his equals, and if he owes a debt it is to his country and her laws, which he repays in the capacity of faithful and upright magistrate and citizen. And thus the Greek ideal is cast rather in the mould of the hero or the statesman than in that of the saint.[231]

Danquah insists that because the Greek idea of hero or statesman is the "true parallel" with the Akan idea of *opanyin* or Nana, the answer that

---

228. Danquah, *The Akan Doctrine of God*, 122.
229. Danquah, *The Akan Doctrine of God*, 123. Hobhouse, *Morals in Evolution*.
230. Hobhouse, *Morals in Evolution*, 558.
231. Hobhouse, *Morals in Evolution*, 559.

both the Greek and Akan will give to the issue of moral standard is in this one proposition; "The practical expansion of patriotic devotion to a personal ideal of dignity that sustains the common life."[232] A citizen who can be a king and also a subject was expected to actively participate in society. Contrary to the picture of a saint whose goodness is in his withdrawal from society because of a sense of sinfulness and reliance of "divine grace to lift him from the natural sinful state," the *opanyin's* or Nana's significance or goodness was in his involvement in all aspects of societal life.[233] Two characteristics contrasts the "Christian saint" with the Akan Nana. First, the idea of Nana gives a place in the society for the "operation of basic human nature to expand in a harmony of common development with those who agree to share the common life," rather than the "unrealizable rule of self-expression" found in the case of a saint.[234] The saint in this sense prevents the moral and religious growth of others within the community by his (or her) recoil from the society. Second, in place of the value attached to the withdrawal from society as a means of fortifying the carnal nature of man in the case of a saint, the Nana ideal offers the challenge to "courageously face" the potentials for perfection within the society so members "may live well."[235] Consequently, the Nana ideal "enables the fitter man, or the supremely good man, to rise above the prevailing standard, setting forth new values for further expansion."[236] Danquah therefore sees a more corporate benefit of the Nana ideal as compared to that of the saint ideal exposed by Hobhouse. Danquah found the German Diedrich Westermann's (general) view of African religious life as primarily concerned with the "here and now" and enabling the African to "live well," as a further clue of his thesis that the idea of Nana, as with the Greek hero, in its religious and moral strivings was for the good of the society, that men [and women and children] may live well.[237]

Danquah's view of Hobhouse's saint was further informed by the nature of Christianity he found within his Akan (Gold Coast) context. Finding

232. Danquah, *The Akan Doctrine of God*, 123–24.
233. Danquah, *The Akan Doctrine of God*, 124.
234. Danquah, *The Akan Doctrine of God*, 124.
235. Danquah, *The Akan Doctrine of God*, 124.
236. Danquah, *The Akan Doctrine of God*, 124.
237. Westermann, *Africa and Christianity*, viii, 93–94. Westermann, *The African To-day*, 204. One weakness Danquah notes in the Geek ideal as exposed by Hobhouse is that it excluded women, children, and slaves in its definition of full citizenship. The strife towards this ideal occasionally involved "extreme self-sacrifice" and an "extreme expectation" that was significantly cruel. For the African (Akan), Danquah agrees with Westermann that his religion was not of "high blown moral aspirations" but demanded merciless sacrifices. Yet, for Danquah, the Greek and Akan effort in the religion and moral ideal had not been in vain. Danquah, *The Akan Doctrine of God*, 125.

a parallel of the significance of a "headman" in Nyasaland (Malawi) to that of the Akan Nana, Danquah was convinced the Akan is not alone in regarding the *opanyin*, Nana, as the ideal that informed the moral strivings.[238] He then puts a challenge in this way,

> If the Akan Nana is of the right sort and served his age and community by living well and aiding them also to live well, cannot a greater community, equally disciplined, discover a greater Nana as their Messiah to serve his age and aid the greater, or even the universal community equally to live well?[239]

God as Nana and the Christological Construction

In Christian terms, the above is Christological challenge. Danquah observed that the revelation through the Apostle Paul's assertion that "God made all men of one blood" implies that "all men are of one family."[240] This teaching is profound because,

> [it is] an actual living principle of the possibility of one human harmony of life, that all men *are* one family, and can only see God or be like God when they live as members all of one body, descendants of one Great Ancestor.[241]

The Akan designation for the Supreme Being, *Nana Nyankopon* ("Grandfather Nyankopon") demonstrates the fatherhood of *Nyankopon*.[242] Akan knowledge teaches that the Supreme Being is the "Great ancestor"; the "true high God and manlike ancestor of the first man."[243] He therefore "deserves to be worshipped, and is worshipped in the visible ancestral head, the good chief of the community."[244] Danquah maintains

---

238. Danquah, *The Akan Doctrine of God*, 126. Cf. Smith, *African Beliefs and Christian Faith*, 176.

239. Danquah, *The Akan Doctrine of God*, 126–27.

240. "He has made from one blood every [or all] nation of men (ἀνθρώπων) to dwell on all the face of the earth" Acts 17:26 (NKJV).

241. Danquah, *Akan Doctrine of God*, 22.

242. Also, *Ataa Naa Nyonmo* among the Ga, as Danquah indicates although his translation as "Old One Grandfather 'Nyonmo'" fails to convey the gender-neutral character of God that the title hints at. *Ataa* is father and *Naa* is mother, hence "Father Mother Nyonmo [God]." Danquah's trace of the origin of *nana* to the female, nana = "*ena* [ne] *ena*" (mother's mother), however, shows that the title Nana is itself gender-neutral. Danquah, *Akan Doctrine of God*, 22.

243. Danquah, *Akan Doctrine of God*, 27.

244. Danquah, *Akan Doctrine of God*, 22–28.

it is in the line of the "Great Ancestor" that ancestors, who "must live according to the dignity of the first," are honored and deified, a process that makes them "worshipful" as the "Great Ancestor."[245] Implicit in the "Great Ancestor" is his [or her?] capacity as creator, by which he is known as the "Odomankoma, the creator *par excellence*."[246]

Harry Sawyerr found Danquah's ideas on God as Ancestor and Creator as the basis for his enquiry into the traditional concepts of the Supreme Being among selected people groups in Ghana (Akan), Nigeria (Yoruba) and Sierra Leone (Mende).[247] Sawyerr deduced two concepts relating to the pattern of a creative process that constituted the idea of the ancestor-ship of God among the three sub-groups, namely, the idea of a birth-process and that of the "artificer [craftsman] concept."[248] Thus, the ɔkra as the "spark of fire" coming from the Nyame among the Akan, the Yoruba belief of humans receiving breath from Olu after the form had been moulded by Ɔbatala and among the Mende *Ngewɔ*'s speech making the human, are all linked to the idea of God as the "Great Ancestor." Sawyerr then remarks in his conclusion:

> In man's state of helplessness, God and God alone, by whatever name He is called is man's last resort in times of crisis and so by analogy becomes their ultimate ancestor. He also created the world and all that is in it. As such He is creator and Great Ancestor.[249]

These sentiments are also with the conviction of an understanding of the divine as "human with all its potentialities fulfilled."[250] Both Danquah and Sawyerr did not attribute the title *nana* in its ancestral sense to Jesus Christ. Danquah, from an apparent Christological perspective, sought to distinguish between the Judeo-Christian idea of Messiah as an "expected" one and the Akan idea of Nana as a "discovered" personage. Sawyerr considered Jesus Christ as the "elder Brother" but his preoccupation to find God in the African past, may have limited his use of Ancestor to God.[251] In the case of Danquah, his concentration was on Akan idea of God and how

---

245. Danquah, *Akan Doctrine of God*, 28.

246. Danquah, *Akan Doctrine of God*, 28.

247. Sawyerr, *God Ancestor or Creator?* 95. Sawyerr also noted at the time of his current study that Danquah continued to "elude" him having read the *Akan Doctrine of God* "intensively at least twenty-times during the last three years" (x).

248. Sawyerr, *God Ancestor or Creator?* 96–97.

249. Sawyerr, *God Ancestor or Creator?* 105.

250. Sawyerr, *God Ancestor or Creator?* 103.

251. Sawyerr, *Creative Evangelism*, 72 and 133.

that has informed the Akan view of life and thus explicit Christological concerns could not surface.

Christological explorations making use of African cultural concepts, at the written level, generally became manifest in the late 1970s and early 1980s. Charles Nyamiti, for example, as Danquah and Sawyerr had done before him, began exploring the image of ancestor in his Christian view of God (as Father) before his Christological explications. Nyamiti did not seem to have any challenge in transferring the image of ancestor from God (Father) to Jesus Christ (Son), and the triune God has certainly been key in his Ancestor Christology. Kwame Bediako, however, writing at the time when ancestral Christologies were emerging, did express some concerns with the attribution of the term *ancestor* to God.[252] Bediako intimates that the designation of God as Ancestor "has a tendency to marginalise Christ" who, quoting Nyamiti, "is the one through whom God becomes 'the true progenitor of the (Christian) community,'" and thus "from the Christian viewpoint the term Ancestor is more meaningful when confined to Christ."[253] Bediako further clarifies his view with an analogy to the idea of *logos* in early Christian usage where it would have meant designating God as Logos and then Christ as "God's Logos."[254]

The issue of *right* designation seems to revolve around the use of the word "ancestor." If one is to take the Akan titular word *nana*, for example, which is constitutive of both an elder (*opanyin*) and ancestor (an elder *saman*), the attribution to both God and Jesus present no such difficulty. Pre-Christian Akan religious thought already expressed Nana Nyankopon which is expressed also in the proverb; *Asaase tre na Nyame ne panyin* ("the earth is vast [yet] Nyame is head [oldest]"). Designating Jesus as Nana, which Akan mother-tongue Christian expression readily affirms [Nana Yesu] will then mean to clarify any difference and significance between such assertion and that of Nana Nyankopon. Bediako, in the above instance, did not comment on the mother-tongue expression of *nana*.

Conclusion

Ancestors cannot be forgotten. The ancestors represent the memory of a people and since memory is vital to one's identity, the issue of ancestors is

252. Kwame Bediako, "Christian Tradition and the African God Revisited: A Process in the Exploration of a Theological Idiom." Prior to this essay, Bediako had also explored the image of ancestor in Akan in relation to Jesus Christ. Kwame Bediako, "Biblical Christologies in the context of African traditional religions," 96.

253. Bediako, "Christian Tradition and the African God Revisited," 90.

254. Bediako, "Christian Tradition and the African God Revisited," 90.

linked to the past and identity. The Akan concept of *nana* informs their identity at the family and community levels. History, tradition, communal ethical standard, and political configuration are all linked to this concept. The Akan *nana* remains a blood related member of the family and community. The concept does not concern itself with the relationship between the Akan community and other non-blood related communities. The concept projects the community as an end. Everything done in honor of the ancestors and the help desired from them is in the final analysis to make the community good and prosperous.

Danquah's conceptual portrait of the Akan ideal person from the idea of *nana*, though it appears problematic in its approach, is important for Akan (African) Christology. There is no pre-Christian Akan literature giving a systematic account of the concern behind the Akan view of ancestors. Danquah's reconstruction efforts, relying as they do on Akan proverbs, can be likened to Philo of Alexandria's philosophical use of the LXX. Danquah made use of what he knew in his day: a fair exposure to the European (British) intellectual currents and a firsthand knowledge of Ghanaian (Akan) cultural values. Danquah's view of the *nana* as a "*discovered* Messiah" in contradistinction to Hebrew "*expected* Messiah" is significant and has implications for an Akan Ancestor Christology.

Christian presence cannot ignore the reality of the concept of ancestors in contemporary societies in Ghana and in particularly Akan communities. There is need for continuous engagement between the gospel message and the ancestor concept or construct. This requires more than one Christian generation. The expectation of the continuous engagement is the transformation of the ancestor concept and associated religious practices. A transformed ancestor concept in turn serves as an avenue for Christian proclamation within the respective cultural world. In other words, proclaiming Jesus as Nana means the concept Nana is now understood in Christian terms without any major severance of its cultural roots and becomes an avenue for Christian witness. Such has been the concerns of the Ancestor Christology explored in African Christianity. In the next chapter I examine the efforts so far within the framework of the three stages of conversion.

Chapter 5

Ancestor Christology and the Process of Conversion in African Christianity

THE EXPLORATION OF ANCESTOR Christology within African Christian theology has taken place in discernible stages. My treatment of Logos Christology within Walls' three stages of (cultural) conversion (*missionary*, *convert*, and *refiguration*) highlighted three corresponding stages or levels in its lifespan, namely, *suggestion*, *clarification* or *elucidation*, and *innovation*. Hence it is possible and helpful to examine theological activities making use of pre-Christian ideas or concepts within these three stages of the process involved in the conversion of traditional thought. Ancestor Christology, from the perspective of the conversion process of African traditional thought, has gone through a similar three-stage process. That is, the Christological exploration of the concept of ancestor has had its initial *suggestive* stage, then an *elucidative* phase, with an *innovative* phase yet to be comprehensively exploited. In this section I explore the journey of Ancestor Christology within the framework of the process of conversion in African Christianity. The journey highlights more of the state or mode of reflection on the subject than a chronology, even though some of the scholars have built on the ideas of predecessors.

The Missionary Stage—A Suggestive Mode

The *missionary* stage constitutes suggestive remarks for Jesus to be reckoned as Ancestor with little or no sustained attempt to clarify any implication of such an assertion. The views of John Pobee and Kwesi Dickson on Jesus as Ancestor reflect the *missionary* stage.

John S. Pobee and Kwesi Dickson

John Pobee suggested the image of Jesus Christ as Ancestor in the context of his proposal of the nature and function of an African theology that would express "essential Christianity into African categories and thought forms."[1] Pobee attempts a Christology from the Akan worldview, with a Christological question: "Why should an Akan relate to Jesus of Nazareth, who does not belong to his clan, family, tribe, and nation?"[2] The divinity and humanity of Jesus is imperative in any Christological reflection.[3] The divinity of Jesus implies "his authority and power" over humans.[4] Pobee notes that it is the Supreme Being (God) who grants the authority to the ancestors to influence society. Thus if Jesus is to be looked on as Ancestor he would be "the Great and Greatest Ancestor" or *Nana* and even if he is *Nana* like other "illustrious ancestors," who also bear that title, he is superior by virtue of "being closest to God and as God."[5] Pobee, however, does not suggest an Akan title for Jesus that will convey his superiority over other "illustrious ancestors."

Dickson made his suggestion in the context of appropriating the cross of Christ (the symbol of suffering, death and resurrection power) from the African context.[6] The area of sacrifice in African life and thought for Dickson can be employed. Christ who was the "perfect victim" of the supreme sacrifice of God, by his death merits the African image of ancestor; "the greatest of ancestors."[7] For Dickson, Christ "never ceases to be one of the 'living-dead'" since "there always will be people alive who *knew* him, whose lives were irreversibly affected by his life and work." The physical Cross, therefore, Dickson opines, becomes Christ's symbol as "*the ever-living*" one just as the traditional staffs and stools are considered as symbolic representations of the presence of ancestors.

---

1. Pobee, *Toward an African Theology*, 18.
2. Pobee, *Toward an African Theology*, 81.
3. Pobee, "In Search of Christology in Africa: Some Considerations for Today," 17.
4. Pobee, *Toward an African Theology*, 94.
5. Pobee, *Toward an African Theology*, 94.
6. Dickson, *Theology in Africa*, 185.
7. Dickson, *Theology in Africa*, 197–98. Edusa-Eyison, "Kwesi A. Dickson: The Bible and African Life and Thought in Dialogue," 113–14.

The Convert Stage—An Elucidative Mode

At the *convert* stage there is adequate clarification of the use of the concept in Christological reflection with the possible problems associated anticipated and addressed. The efforts of François Kabasélé, Charles Wanamaker, Peter Sarpong, Abraham Akrong, Uchenna Ezeh, and recently that of Benhardt Quarshie reflect the *convert* stage.

François Kabasélé

Kabasélé applies to Jesus the various characteristics of the Bantu concept of ancestors: as the transmitters of *Life*, their *Presence* everywhere, being the *Eldest* and their role in *Mediation*.[8] Analysing these along with some selected New Testament texts, Kabasélé demonstrates how these characteristics are fulfilled and transcended by Jesus Christ. Thus, for example, Jesus' assurance "And behold, I am with you always" (Matthew 28:20b) is linked to the fact of the ancestors as the "principal "allies" of earthly beings" in Bantu traditional thinking.[9] Kabasélé also argues that "Christ as Ancestor" does not abolish the role of the Bantu Ancestors and indicates their limited role as exemplars for values which, though "not originally Christian, can become Christian."[10]

Charles Wanamaker

Wanamaker's Ancestor Christology is in response to the challenge posed by the prevailing idea of ancestors in South Africa.[11] He notes that while the European Christian interpretation of God resonates with Bantu "vague notions of deity," the issue is in fitting Christ in a world view that attributes his role as "judge, mentor, and intermediary" to the ancestors.[12] The effort concerns the possibility of "Africanizing Christology through connecting it with both traditional and Christianized understanding of the ancestors."[13] Though the idea of "Africanizing Christology" seems to take Christology itself as a

---

8. Kabasélé, "Christ as Ancestor and Elder Brother," 116–27. Kabasélé has also justified the incorporation of the concept of ancestors in church liturgy particularly with respect to the Eucharist. Lumbala, *Celebrating Jesus Christ in Africa—Liturgy and Inculturation*, 35–41.

9. Kabasélé, "Christ as Ancestor and Elder Brother," 121.

10. Kabasélé, "Christ as Ancestor and Elder Brother," 124 & 125.

11. Wanamaker "Jesus the Ancestor," 281–98.

12. Wanamaker "Jesus the Ancestor," 281.

13. Wanamaker "Jesus the Ancestor," 282.

ready-made proposition that needs "Africanizing," Wanamaker's effort in reading the New Testament from an African ancestral perspective to illustrate the ancestorship of Jesus is significant. The social and religious functions of ancestors, in the South African Bantu context, as guardians of the social and moral order, givers and sustainers of life, and as mediators are iterated.[14]

Wanamaker rightly cautions that the development of Ancestor Christology "cannot provide African Christians with a total Christology" but promises to "link an important dimension of many African Christians' identity and experience with a significant aspect of Christ's function."[15] In his ancestral reading of the story of Jesus Christ, Jesus' family life, which the Gospel writers emphasize in their respective genealogies, is an important pointer considering the fundamental imperative of family membership for the African. Matthew's link to king David, from an African perspective, is significant since it points to Jesus' "authority and power" within his social group.[16] Luke's tracing of Jesus Christ to the first human, Adam, means his "human ancestry links him to all the tribes of the earth."[17] John's presentation of him as the "Son of the Primogenitor of all the living and the living dead" implies for traditional African cosmology that "he is the one in whom all of the creative interactive power of the Supreme God has been present and through whom it has been active in creating and sustaining the world and all that is in it, including human beings."[18] Furthermore, the formation of the nascent Christian community comprising people from disparate cultural, socio-economic, and family backgrounds (which resulted from Jesus Christ's work), also makes Jesus the "eldest brother," who in (traditional) African families is responsible for the ritual of the ancestor cult.[19]

Wanamaker, from the viewpoint of (Bantu) ancestor religion, indicates that Jesus' life and public activity as well as the nature of his death are unimportant but the fact of his death is.[20] The quality of one's human existence is not decisive for whether the person becomes an ancestor or not.[21] Jesus as a "member of the living-dead" can be seen as realizing the three social and religious roles of the ancestors from an African reading of his New Testament story in Wanamaker's assessment. Jesus is presented as

14. Wanamaker "Jesus the Ancestor," 286–91.
15. Wanamaker "Jesus the Ancestor," 291.
16. Wanamaker "Jesus the Ancestor," 291.
17. Wanamaker "Jesus the Ancestor," 292.
18. Wanamaker "Jesus the Ancestor," 292.
19. Wanamaker "Jesus the Ancestor," 292.
20. Wanamaker "Jesus the Ancestor," 293.
21. Wanamaker "Jesus the Ancestor," 284.

the eventual judge of "all humanity at the end of the current world order" (cf. Matthew 25:31–46 *et al.*), of which Wanamaker observes is not what an African would expect from an ancestor since ancestral punishment is more immediate.[22] However, incidences in the Book of Acts show the influence of Jesus the Ancestor (Acts 5:1–11; 13:6–12; 19:11–20).[23] Jesus is the source of benefit and a "giver and sustainer of the life of his descendants (the members of the Church)."[24] Jesus' mediatory role between God and the living and living-dead, for Wanamaker, is expressed in John 14:6 and he notes that "neither living humans nor ancestors have direct access" to God.[25] With the incorporation of "beliefs and practices" of the Bantu into Christianity via Bantu Christians, Wanamaker's hope is that such a New Testament reading in the light of the "nature and function of ancestors for African people" may foster the understanding and expression of Bantu Christians so that ultimately the idea of ancestors, echoing Bishop Mutlanyane Stanley Mogoba, "may be 'one of the great contributions African Christianity can make to world Christianity.'"[26]

Peter Sarpong

Peter Sarpong, describing Asante Christology as that based upon the Asante's "conception of leadership in their traditional political setup," namely, chieftaincy, remarks that Jesus is "a kind of special ancestor" in relation to four chiefs in Asante history whose deaths are considered to be sacrificial.[27] A traditional leader who would eventually become an ancestor is "a man for others" chosen not for himself but for his people whom he leads to a "successful end."[28] Thus in his assessment, Jesus "puts forward in his personality" the qualities desired in a traditional ruler "in a supernatural way," by exhibiting in "a more perfect way" those qualities the ancestors endeavored to practice.[29] In this sense for Sarpong, Jesus is not only a kind

---

22. Wanamaker "Jesus the Ancestor," 293–94.

23. Wanamaker "Jesus the Ancestor," 294.

24. Wanamaker "Jesus the Ancestor," 294–95.

25. Wanamaker "Jesus the Ancestor," 295.

26. Wanamaker "Jesus the Ancestor," 296.

27. Sarpong, *Dear Nana—Letters to my Ancestor*, 143 & 152. The four chiefs are Nana Asenso Kofo (Adwumakesekese), Nana Dikopim I (Edweso), Nana Tweneboa Kodua (Kumawu), Nana Boahen Anantuo (Mampong) (Sarpong, *Dear Nana*, 149).

28. Sarpong, *Dear Nana*, 141.

29. Sarpong, *Dear Nana*, 143.

of ancestor but also a "model ancestor" superior to an ancestor; the "greatest possible ancestor imaginable."[30]

One significant distinction of Jesus' Ancestorship, Sarpong asserts, is in the fact that while in the case of the four Asante chiefs their sacrificial death was for their nation and those they love, Jesus died also for his enemies and thus "stands out shoulder and head above the ancestors and becomes a proto-ancestor, a very highly respected and respectable ancestor."[31] Jesus' resurrection in itself, for the Asante is "an indication that he was an ancestor."[32] The following Akan ancestral epithets, Sarpong indicates, are rightly applied to Jesus, which encapsulate the Asante view of him as "an ancestor": *Osagyefo, Kantamanto, Kurotwiamansa, Oduyefoɔ, Paapa, Ahummɔbrɔ, Daasebrɛ, Daaseɛnsa* and *Nyaamanekɔse*.[33]

Abraham Akrong

Abraham Akrong explains that Jesus Christ is "an ancestor because of his status as saviour of the world": combining both the function of God as "the great ancestor" and that of "human ancestors" since he is "God-man."[34] Akrong regards Jesus Christ as a parent: being an ancestor, the head or chief of the Church as a "new community" and therefore as a chief he can receive all the traditional titles depicting such status.[35] Akrong identifies three categories of ancestorhood that Jesus assumes in his role as savior and God-man nature, namely, hero, mediator and tutelary.[36] The ancestorhood of Jesus Christ not only transforms our conception of ancestors,[37] but also "implies a change in the religious world model for the understanding of Jesus Christ."[38] Hence

30. Sarpong, *Dear Nana*, 143 & 160.
31. Sarpong, *Dear Nana*, 152.
32. Sarpong, *Dear Nana*, 153.
33. Sarpong, *Dear Nana*, 157–60. *Osagyefo*—"a great chief who never fails in war, he conquers and can be relied upon," *Kantamanto*—"one who does not deceive you" and who is "not weak" but "has the power to do anything," *Kurotwiamansa*—"the leopard or the tiger king of the forest," *Oduyefoɔ*—"the doctor or medicine man," *Paapa*—(affectionate) father, *Ahummɔbrɔ*—"one who has a very soft heart for people, very merciful, very compassionate," *Daasebrɛ*—"the fatigue of the person who wants to thank Jesus [because his benevolence is unlimited]," *Daaseɛnsa*—"you never stop thanking him because he never stops doing good to you," *Nyaamanekɔse*—"the refuge of those in trouble."
34. Akrong, "Christology from an African Perspective," 119–30 (122).
35. Akrong, "Christology from an African Perspective," 123.
36. Akrong, "Christology from an African Perspective," 125.
37. Akrong, "Christology from an African Perspective," 125.
38. Akrong, "Christology from an African Perspective," 126–27.

from the standpoint of the idea of ancestor, Jesus Christ is the "preeminent member" of the family of God on earth [the Church] and as Ancestor, he is the agent of salvation and "sole protector of the human family."[39]

In a later article, Akrong proposes a "Christology of empowerment"[40] that, presenting Jesus Christ with the face of "our ancestor," reinterprets the "functions and role of Jesus Christ from the perspective of the salvation issues of post-colonial Africa." Akrong's expectation is to realize a "spiritual and an existential conversion and transformation" by presenting an image of Christ "that gives the oppressed power and the knowledge to reinterpret reality in the light of the Christ event which can give them access to new life and a new way of viewing themselves."[41] There is need to have "access to a power source that can protect, empower and preserve life," just as experienced with the idea of ancestors, which is "the foundation of the salvation concerns of African Christians."[42] Thus, Christ in the fashion of the ancestors "should be the key spiritual resource that can empower the individual and community to work for the creation of conditions that will support the fulfilment of the God-given purposes for human beings in all aspects of life."[43]

Akrong recognizes the need to develop "a more rigorous methodological procedure for ancestral Christology."[44] His attempt has been based on what he considers as an "analogical correlation," that is, on the premise that "God deals with us in our various cultural contexts in plural forms."[45] Thus, Jesus Christ "becomes an ancestor in the context of the offices and functions related to the ancestors and elders" (in the Akan traditional setup) when the correlation of his work of salvation is set in analogy with the "traditional roles and functions that deal with salvation."[46] Jesus Christ, then, becomes the "norm and standard," the basis on which the roles and offices of ancestors are "judged and evaluated."[47] In this connection, some of the Akan traditional praise titles that Madam Afua Kuma ascribes to Jesus Christ

39. Akrong, "Christology from an African Perspective," 127. Jesus also becomes the "hero ancestor" assuming the title *Okatakyi birempong* "the great incomparable hero" in view of a correlation between the functions of Jesus Christ and those of the hero and founding ancestor of the Akan people. Akrong, "An Akan Christian View of Salvation from the Perspective of John Calvin's Soteriology," 250.

40. Akrong, "Jesus with the Face of an Ancestor," 29.
41. Akrong, "Jesus with the Face of an Ancestor," 28.
42. Akrong, "Jesus with the Face of an Ancestor," 28.
43. Akrong, "Jesus with the Face of an Ancestor," 24.
44. Akrong, "Jesus with the Face of an Ancestor," 29.
45. Akrong, "Jesus with the Face of an Ancestor," 29.
46. Akrong, "Jesus with the Face of an Ancestor," 30.
47. Akrong, "Jesus with the Face of an Ancestor," 30.

become a point of departure for Akrong in his exploration into the "office and function" of Jesus Christ as Ancestor. Jesus Christ as the "first ancestor" whose life benefits all human beings earns the title *Edikan Brempong* and God is the "ultimate ancestor of the human race."[48] However, Akrong appears to apply the title *Ebusua Dupon* (the root of the family of humankind) to both God (Father) and Jesus Christ. Jesus Christ, the "first ancestor" represents all of humanity before God the "ultimate ancestor and our elder (Ebusua Dupon)" and then makes a note on the "priestly and mediatorial role of Jesus Christ as Ebusua Dupon."[49] Moreover, Jesus Christ the Son of God, Akrong indicates, "becomes our chief (nana) who rules in the shoes of God the ultimate ancestor of the human race."[50]

Akrong's use of ancestral titles in the mother tongue for Jesus Christ in his ancestral Christology is significant. Certainly, the space of an article may not have guaranteed in-depth discussions on the implications of the traditional titles ascribed to Jesus Christ as Ancestor. Such an exercise is beneficial to Ancestor Christology if the latter is to have a continued impact on traditional thinking.

Uchenna Ezeh

Uchenna Ezeh examines Ancestor Christology in the light of the eventual council formulations of the Christological developments of the first five centuries of Christianity.[51] The implications of the respective decisions of the councils of Nicaea, Ephesus, and Chalcedon in resolving the challenges in communicating the person of Jesus as both divine and human are linked to the effort of Ancestor Christology in Africa.[52] For example, one implication for Ancestor Christology of the Council of Chalcedon's expression of Christ as "one person in two natures" is in the area of Christ's mediation, since, in his assessment, it is mediation that makes the cult of ancestors pre-eminent in African religion and culture.[53] Therefore observing that there is that "quest for unity between God and man" in African Cosmology, Ezeh asserts,

> In the African ancestral Christology, we want to maintain that the incarnate state of the Son of God, as "true God and true man," is an ancestral status par excellence. The ancestral role of

48. Akrong, "Jesus with the Face of an Ancestor," 30 & 34.
49. Akrong, "Jesus with the Face of an Ancestor," 33.
50. Akrong, "Jesus with the Face of an Ancestor," 34.
51. Ezeh, *Jesus Christ the Ancestor*.
52. Ezeh, *Jesus Christ the Ancestor*, 139–256.
53. Ezeh, *Jesus Christ the Ancestor*, 251 and 253.

mediation between God and man is what Jesus Christ perfectly achieved as God-man through the union of divinity and humanity in his person at incarnation.[54]

Furthermore for Ezeh, since the Chalcedonian Christological definition in expressing the mystery of Christ employed pre-Christian Hellenistic terms "*prosopon* and *hypostasis* to explain on the personal level the unity of the divine and the human natures in the one Christ," the pre-Christian concept of ancestor "recommends itself, in interpreting the mystery of Christ."[55] Ezeh clarifies Christ's mediatorship as God-man in relation to his status as Ancestor. Jesus Christ is "ancestor analogously through unique or special mediatorship based on the mystery of his incarnation. He is more than a mere mediator."[56] By "making immanent the transcendent God" (cf. John 1:18), Jesus also achieves the ancestral role of mediating God's presence in the world.[57]

The "communication or interchange of attributes," *Communicatio Idiomatum*, in which is the understanding that divine and human attributes can be applied to either of Jesus Christ's respective natures as human and divine, for Ezeh also justifies Ancestor Christology. In "the incarnate Christ [the Logos], the idea and value of the African ancestorship is (sic) stretched to an absolute point."[58] Jesus Christ is both "God and man" as the Ancestor and since no human language can exhaustively articulate this mystery of Jesus Christ, Ezeh notes, Ancestor Christology can confidently endeavor to articulate from the African perspective.[59] Here Ezeh is in line with Nyamiti and in addition does not see the issue of stretching the humanity of Jesus over his divinity any major concern since in his ancestorship Christ's divinity is assumed. This is an implication from the Council of Ephesus, for Ezeh, that insisted that the two natures of Christ can afford him both "divine and human attributes."[60]

Ezeh essentially affirms the efforts of Bujo and Nyamiti. His distinctiveness lies in the assessment of Ancestor Christology in relation to the early Christological definitions. However, before the eventual definitions of the respective councils, the efforts of Christian writers in applying their conception of Jesus Christ in relation to their shared Hellenistic heritage have features that are equally helpful to the Christological attempts in

54. Ezeh, *Jesus Christ the Ancestor*, 252.
55. Ezeh, *Jesus Christ the Ancestor*, 252 & 253.
56. Ezeh, *Jesus Christ the Ancestor*, 254.
57. Ezeh, *Jesus Christ the Ancestor*, 255.
58. Ezeh, *Jesus Christ the Ancestor*, 238.
59. Ezeh, *Jesus Christ the Ancestor*, 238.
60. Ezeh, *Jesus Christ the Ancestor*, 238–39.

contemporary Africa. Thus, his study suggests a need for a comparative Christological examination of *logos* and *ancestor* images for the present context of Ancestor Christology.

Benhardt Y. Quarshie

Reassessing Kwame Bediako's thoughts on Ancestor Christology based primarily on the Epistle to the Hebrews, Benhardt Quarshie has also offered a further clarification on and an extended view of Jesus Christ as Ancestor.[61] Quarshie makes note of Bediako's apparently limited preoccupation with the religious aspect in addressing the significance of Jesus Christ for the African in the latter's Hebrews based Ancestor Christology.[62] Thus highlighting the African's (Akan) "deepest yearnings" which are essentially concerned with the here and now and are ultimately aimed at attaining ancestorhood, Quarshie elaborates on an (Hebrews based) Ancestor Christology. Quarshie helpfully highlights a fundamental functional difference between the view of ancestors presented in Hebrews (1:1; 3:9; 8:9; 11:2) and in Africa in that while in the former the ancestors are "passive onlookers" without any activity on behalf of the living, in the latter they remain the "most potent force" after the Supreme Being actively involved in the affairs of the living.[63] Jesus is Ancestor functionally and not ontologically (just as in the Epistle's view of him as High Priest) and, primarily from the text of Hebrews 12:2, insightfully submits the view of Jesus as indeed the "Super-Ancestor" who is also the Ancestor-Maker; the one who actually "makes ancestors."[64] It would be equally stimulating, however, if Quarshie were to indicate the Akan or Ga equivalent of "Super-Ancestor" and "Ancestor-Maker" with any respective significance for traditional thought.

The Refiguration Stage—An Innovative Mode

At the *refiguration* stage, two primary aspects may be realized. Here the Christological use of the ancestor concept is innovatively applied to other subject areas aimed at giving further grounding of the Christian faith in Africa. Furthermore, there is opportunity for the eventual transformation of the concept to an extent that one could say Jesus Christ now rightly owns

---

61. Quarshie, "'Jesus, Pioneer and Perfecter of Faith' (Heb. 12:2): Kwame Bediako's Hebrews-based Ancestor Christology Revisited," 21–37.

62. Quarshie, "'Jesus, Pioneer and Perfecter of Faith' (Heb. 12:2)," 25.

63. Quarshie, "'Jesus, Pioneer and Perfecter of Faith' (Heb. 12:2)," 28–30.

64. Quarshie, "'Jesus, Pioneer and Perfecter of Faith' (Heb. 12:2)," 33–35.

it, just as he owned the *logos* concept so much so that now when Logos is mentioned, Jesus Christ is invariably associated with it.

Emmanuel Martey's recommendation of the view of Jesus as the "Ancestor who liberates" or "liberating Ancestor" as a way of keeping in tension the "religiocultural and politico-socioeconomic concerns" in Africa in a dynamic and creative way is an agenda for the *refiguration* stage.[65] Such an exercise calls for a clear and sustained view of Ancestor Christology, which is then applied in addressing or engaging with those concerns identified. Kwame Bediako, Bénézet Bujo, Charles Nyamiti, and lately Gift Makwasha, have all pursued a sustained Ancestor Christology with such concerns in view, though, quite understandably, with respective overarching personal interests. In Bediako, Ancestor Christology is on the verge of a *refiguration* stage, having been in the *convert* stage. In Bujo and Nyamiti, however, there is a transition from the *convert* to the *refiguration* stage. Makwasha's effort in proposing a tripartite view of Jesus as family, tribal, and national Ancestor, conceiving them in the indigenous language in the Zimbabwean context is a *refiguration* attempt.[66]

Kwame Bediako—Jesus Christ, The Only Real and True Ancestor

Bediako's approach to Ancestor Christology is primarily informed by his concern for an authentic African (Akan) understanding and affirmation of Jesus Christ.[67] This concern follows up on John V. Taylor's incisive question as to what Christ would look like when he emerged "as the answer to the questions that Africans are asking."[68] In pursuing such concerns, Bediako could not escape the pervasiveness of the concept of ancestors, which, for him, "represent a more enduring reality in the African world-view" and requires a Christian response.[69] Bediako's concern is twofold: the place of ancestors, both pre-Christian and Christian, in Christian thinking in Africa

---

65. Martey, *African Theology: Inculturation and Liberation*, 84–86.

66. Jesus the Family Ancestor (Jesu Mudzimu Wepamusha); Jesus the Tribal Ancestor (Jesu Mudzimu Wedzinza); Jesus the National Ancestor (Jesu Mudzimu Wenyika). Makwasha, "'Not Without My Ancestors,'" 10.

67. Bediako, *Jesus in African Culture (A Ghanaian Perspective)*, 9. Bediako was born in Ghana and received doctorate degrees from the University of Bordeaux (French Literature) and University of Aberdeen (Theology). He was an ordained minister of the Presbyterian Church of Ghana (PCG) and the founding rector of the Akrofi-Christaller Institute (ACI) in Akropong-Akuapem in the Eastern Region of Ghana.

68. Taylor, *The Primal Vision—Christian Presence Amid African Religion*, 16.

69. Bediako, *Christianity in Africa—The Renewal of a Non-Western Religion*, 216.

and the presentation of Jesus Christ as the one who fulfils and transcends the roles perceived for the ancestors.[70] A theology of ancestors, for Bediako, attempts to interpret the African past to show that Africans had anticipated the Gospel of Jesus Christ in their quests and responses to God in former times.[71] It is the Scriptures, particularly the Old Testament, that make such a theology of ancestors relevant in Africa since it provides a model for understanding the African pre-Christian past.[72] The pursuit of Ancestor Christology itself, Bediako contends, "helps to clarify the place and significance of 'natural' ancestors."[73]

Jesus Christ, Bediako observes, bridges that "gulf between the intense awareness of the existence of God and yet also of his 'remoteness' in African Traditional Religion and experience."[74] Bediako asserts that, Jesus Christ as "our Elder Brother" has shared in the African experience in all spheres except in sin and separation from God. However, now in God's presence, Jesus "displaces the mediatorial function of our natural 'spirit-fathers'" since "these themselves need saving . . . [having] originated from among us."[75] Though from the standpoint of Akan traditional beliefs, Jesus' resurrection and ascension imply that he has gone to the sphere of the ancestors and "gods," he has not gone there as one of them but as their Lord.[76] Jesus in this way assumes "all their powers and cancels any terrorizing influence they might be assumed to have upon us."[77]

Jesus as Ancestor, Bediako notes, does not belong to the category of human ancestors since he is divine.[78] He is "the only real and true Ancestor and Source of life for all mankind" who fulfils and transcends the "benefits believed to be bestowed by lineage ancestors."[79] The Epistle to the Hebrews serves well for Bediako for this assertion. Jesus has secured "eternal redemption" (Hebrews 9:12) for those who acknowledge and receive him, having achieved that "perfect atonement through his own self-sacrifice" and by "effective eternal

---

70. Bediako sees the need for the recognition of African traditional ancestors and Christian ancestors in Christianity in Africa. See Fotland, "The Christology of Kwame Bediako," 44. Also Fotland, "Ancestor Christology in Context—Theological Perspectives of Kwame Bediako," 189–202.

71. Bediako, *Christianity in Africa*, 224–25.

72. Bediako, *Christianity in Africa*, 226.

73. Bediako, *Christianity in Africa*, 217.

74. Bediako, *Jesus in African Culture*, 16.

75. Bediako, *Jesus in African Culture*, 18.

76. Bediako, *Jesus in African Culture*, 18.

77. Bediako, *Jesus in African Culture*, 19.

78. Fotland, "The Christology of Kwame Bediako," 44.

79. Bediako, *Jesus in African Culture*, 41–42.

mediation and intercession as God-man in the divine presence."[80] Jesus is also the mediator of "a new and better covenant between God and humanity (Hebrews 8:6; 12:24)," Bediako indicates, and thus "brings the redeemed into the experience of a new identity," linking their human destinies to the eternal will and purpose of God (Hebrews 12:22–24).

The potency of the cult of ancestors, according to Bediako, is that of myth.[81] The cult itself, in Bediako's assessment, is in the category of myth "from the intellectual point of view" and the ancestors are "the product of the myth-making imagination of the community."[82] That does not mean, however, that the cult of ancestors should be taken for granted, Bediako insists, but rather it underscores its "functional value."[83] Seen from the perspective of myth, therefore, Bediako implies that "ancestral function . . . have no basis in fact."[84] The suggestion of myth and "basis in fact" have raised some concerns for Victor Ezigbo, who thinks Bediako's suggestion tends to "eclipse the historical reality of the cult" and is thus misleading.[85]

Though Ezigbo's concern is understandable, I think he has not looked deeper into Bediako's interest here. To begin with, Ezigbo does not comment on Bediako's understanding or use of the word "myth" in this connection. Considered closely, Bediako in his use of the category of "myth," and from the intellectual or rational point of view, seeks to convey his conviction that since "ancestral spirits" are really "human spirits" who have not "demonstrated any power over death" they "cannot be presumed to act in the way tradition ascribes to them,"[86] whereas Christ has demonstrated this in his resurrection. The challenge remains, though, as to who or what then is behind the "power" felt by practitioners of the cult, who would have abandoned such practices had there been no experiential power.

Once Jesus Christ is shown to be superior to the ancestors, what happens to the institution of the chief who in Akan thinking is the mediator between the ancestors and the living? Bediako was keenly aware of this and his observation in this regard over two decades ago remains significant:

> What happens to the position of the chief who "sits on the stool of the ancestors" when it becomes evident that Christ himself

---

80. Bediako, *Jesus in African Culture*, 41–42.
81. Bediako, *Jesus in African Culture*, 40.
82. Bediako, *Jesus in African Culture*, 39.
83. Idowu, *African Traditional Religion—A Definition*, 84.
84. Bediako, *Jesus in African Culture*, 41.
85. Ezigbo, *Re-Imagining African Christologies*, 77 & 78; Aye-Addo, *Akan Christology*, 109.
86. Bediako, *Jesus in African Culture*, 41.

is the Great Ancestor of *all* humankind, the mediator of *all* divine blessing, the judge of *all* mankind and that access to him is not dependent on inherited right through royal lineage, but through grace and faith, and repentance from the heart? Will the chief be a man among men, respected and honoured, but not venerated or worshipped?[87]

The chief continues to define traditional politics in contemporary Akan societies. Therefore Bediako's suggestion of a Christian contribution to politics, which presents the "non-dominating" characteristic of Jesus' conception of power, is relevant since the institution of chief remains central in Akan societies.[88] There is thus a need for a sustained reflection on the implications of Ancestor Christology in the field of politics, perhaps both within the institution of church and the wider community. Such an endeavor will most likely lend itself to a new conception of ancestorship in the light of the impact of Jesus Christ.

The application of Ancestor Christology in Bediako is not given a sustained treatment under any particularly identified theme such as one finds in Bujo and Nyamiti. Several factors such as the author's or proponent's immediate interest or prevailing ecclesiastical demands may account for this. Bediako's view of Jesus as Ancestor, notwithstanding, served him in his overall concern for the appropriation and deepening of the Christian message in Africa. Moreover Bediako's remark on the need for the "experience of the reality and actuality of Jesus" to inhabit the "world of 'Nana' in the same way that it could inhabit the Greek world of 'Logos,'" does show a possible roadmap for a further reflection on Ancestor Christology. The "experience of the reality and actuality of Jesus" in contemporary Akan societies cannot ignore the world of the idea of ancestors. Ancestor Christology remains an important component of Akan Christian thinking in its endeavor to nurture Akan Christianity and thereby ensuring growth, and in its witness to Jesus Christ in the contemporary Akan society.

Bénézet Bujo—Jesus Christ as Proto-Ancestor

Bénézet Bujo's[89] Ancestor Christology also stems from a similar concern as that of Bediako, namely, "In which way can Jesus Christ be an African among

---

87. Bediako, *Jesus in African Culture*, 26 & 28, with the emphasis.

88. Bediako, *Jesus in African Culture*, 29.

89. Bujo is a Catholic priest originally from the Democratic Republic of Congo. He obtained a doctorate degree from the University of Wurzburg (Germany), taught for some time in both Congo and Kenya and has been a moral theologian with the

the Africans according to their own religious experience?"[90] Bujo's contention is that African Traditional Religion possessed a "liberating dimension" that was severely distorted under the period of colonial rule in many parts of Africa. The task of African theology, Bujo observes, is to rediscover this "liberating dimension" and demonstrate how Jesus "provides it with a new, purifying and total stimulus."[91] Conceiving a new Christian community in Africa therefore, according to Bujo, cannot take lightly the concept of ancestors and hence his proposal of the Proto-Ancestor model for how we both speak of Jesus (Christology) and how we view the community of Jesus (Ecclesiology).[92] Bujo is convinced of a moral motive behind the concept of ancestors as well as its salvific potency in Africa. Accordingly, the "particular words, actions and rituals associated with the ancestors, and with the elders in general . . . constitute a rule of conduct for the living."[93] The "remembering and reenactment of the deeds of ancestors and elders" is thus "a memorial-narrative act of salvation designed to secure total community, both before and after death, with all good and benevolent ancestors."[94]

This "cultural phenomenon" of ancestors, according to Bujo, could be used to find a new "Messianic" title for Jesus Christ with a "new theological way of speaking of him" ensuing.[95] Under such conviction Bujo proposes the title "Ancestor Par Excellence" or "Proto-Ancestor" for Jesus.[96] It is apparent that the primary motive for Bujo in naming Jesus Christ as Proto-Ancestor is for an avenue to bring him to the very heart of the African tradition. In this way his concerns are not different from that of Bediako. Nevertheless, whereas Bujo speaks generally of African culture, Bediako is specific in his focus on the Akan culture.

Bujo observes that the title "ancestor" is to be applied to Jesus in an "analogical, or eminent, way."[97] Inherent in the title "Proto-Ancestor" is that Jesus both realized the "authentic ideal (model) of the God-fearing African ancestors" and also "infinitely transcended that ideal and brought it to new completion."[98] As Proto-Ancestor, Jesus Christ is the "ultimate embodiment

---

University of Fribourg in Switzerland. Cf. Parratt, *Reinventing Christianity*, 122.

90. Bujo, *African Theology in Its Social Context*, 12.
91. Bujo, *African Theology in Its Social Context*, 75.
92. Bujo, *The Ethical Dimension of Community*, 19.
93. Bujo, *African Theology in Its Social Context*, 77.
94. Bujo, *African Theology in Its Social Context*, 78–79.
95. Bujo, *African Theology in Its Social Context*, 79.
96. Bujo, *African Theology in Its Social Context*, 79.
97. Bujo, *African Theology in Its Social Context*, 80.
98. Bujo, *African Theology in Its Social Context*, 80. Stinton, *Jesus of Africa*, 120.

of all the virtues of the ancestors, the realization of the salvation for which they yearned."[99] According to Bujo, his proposal of a Proto-Ancestor has to do with the "very essence" of the Incarnation, the "Word's becoming human."[100] Through the mystery of the Incarnation, God has identified with humanity in a unique way. Jesus Christ is not only "the explanation of God" but also the "explanation of humankind."[101] Jesus the Christ is thus Proto-Ancestor for the African, having become the explanation of God and humanity.[102]

It is through Jesus Christ, the Proto-Ancestor, that the concept of ancestors can fully be understood, according to Bujo.[103] With reference to Hebrews 1:1–2, Bujo observes that God indeed spoke to (pre-Christian) African ancestors and that in these last days he speaks to us through his Son, whom he has "established as unique Ancestor, as Proto-Ancestor, from whom all life flows for God's descendants."[104] It is in Jesus, as "new source of life," Bujo asserts in another context, that we have "a new Ancestor" who is beyond all ancestors and who reunites all the different clan ancestors to make of them "a single clan and a single ethnic group."[105] Bujo remarks that a translation of the title "Proto-Ancestor" for Jesus Christ into a corresponding theology and catechesis will have "much more meaning for Africans" than the titles of "*logos* (Word) and *Kyrios* (Lord)."[106] Bujo, however, offers no example of such a translation even from his own mother-tongue. Though a translation of the title Proto-Ancestor into African languages is desirable, a more appropriate approach would be to construct such an indigenous title for Jesus primarily from the African languages themselves and then, where possible, translate it into any desired language.

The significance of the translated Bible in African Christianity implies that mother-tongue readers of the Bible do not meet, in most cases, the words "*Logos*" or "*Kyrios*," but rather indigenous equivalents such as, respectively, in the case of the Akan, *Asem,* and *Awurade*. The translation of Proto-Ancestor from English (or French) into indigenous African languages may bypass the creative process of the engagement from within in arriving at the ancestral image of Jesus Christ in the light of Christian thought and tradition. What may be worth exploring is the pre-Christian usage of translation equivalents

---

99. Bujo, *African Theology in Its Social Context*, 81.
100. Bujo, *African Theology in Its Social Context*, 82.
101. Bujo, *African Theology in Its Social Context*, 82–83.
102. Bujo, *African Theology in Its Social Context*, 83.
103. Bujo, *African Theology in Its Social Context*, 83.
104. Bujo, *African Theology in Its Social Context*, 83.
105. Bujo, *Christmas*, 33–34, Cited in Ilo, "African Christology," 67.
106. Bujo, *African Theology in Its Social Context*, 83.

with their influence in both Christian reflection and mother-tongue exegesis. With respect to the pursuit of Ancestor Christology in its *refiguration* stage, the indigenous conception of the idea of ancestor can then be complemented with the insights acquired from the analysis of the pre-Christian usage of the biblical equivalent respective terms and concepts.

Jesus Christ the Proto-Ancestor becomes the "model" of the moral life in Africa. Jesus Christ becomes the model in the sense that, according to Bujo, those who contemplate him "can find values and norms" which by integrating into their lives can "provide inspiration for responsible conduct."[107] Jesus affirms all the positive elements of the African ethical vision arising from its anthropocentrism but, however, provides a wider scope beyond the family and friends to the "whole human race, in loving service of the Father."[108] Proto-Ancestor Christology, Bujo notes, can also inform the morality of, what he terms, "post-ancestral" Africa which is stricken with corruption and abuse of power, when Christ is given the priority as Proto-Ancestor.[109] With Bujo, as also with Bediako, is a suggestion of Ancestor Christology in the area of politics.

Bujo's proposal of an African ecclesiological model also revolves around Jesus the Proto-Ancestor. The model of the Church in Africa has the Eucharist (The Lord's Supper or Communion), which is considered as "the proto-ancestral meal," as its foundation stone.[110] Bujo's thoughts in this area have the intent of reviewing the situation of the Roman Catholic Church in Africa in its own activities and relation to Rome. This naturally limits his reflections on Church life to the Roman Catholic tradition. Bujo's Christological exploration and ethical suggestions, however, go beyond the Roman Catholic tradition in Africa. The application of Jesus the Proto-Ancestor has creatively informed Bujo's conception of African Christian life and thought and specifically its ethical foundation. Bujo's suggestion of the translation of "Proto-Ancestor" into African languages remains to be exploited.

Charles Nyamiti—Jesus Christ the Brother-Ancestor

Charles Nyamiti's Christian reflections from the perspective of ancestors have relatively been intensive and extensive.[111] Nyamiti's effort has been to expound

---

107. Bujo, *African Theology in Its Social Context*, 87.

108. Bujo, *African Theology in Its Social Context*, 88. Bujo, *Foundations of an African Ethic*, 132–134.

109. Bujo, *African Theology in Its Social Context*, 90.

110. Bujo, *African Theology in Its Social Context*, 94.

111. Nyamiti was born in Tanzania and spent much of his academic career in Kenya

Christian teaching from the perspective of the African way of thinking. An observation Nyamiti made, over some four decades ago, is revealing in seeking to understand his Christological intentions. According to Nyamiti,

> Up to the present moment the African Catholic Church still belongs to the Latin Rite. I would not go so far as to call this state of affairs "ecclesiastical colonization," as some have called it; but it remains true that at an epoch when the African Church is supposed to have surpassed the missionary phase, it is no longer fitting that she should still be considered as a Latin Church.[112]

The desire for a genuine "African Catholic Church" also means that the church in Africa should have an African way of understanding fundamental doctrines. In a later observation, Nyamiti notes that the Christology of the early councils, per historical factors, mainly concentrated on the Incarnation at the expense of the other mysteries revealed in the New Testament.[113] The "Christology of Catholic traditional manuals [which] is poorly limited" followed suit by taking the teachings of the early councils as their main point of departure and thus primarily concentrated on the Incarnation as well as the salvific value of Christ's sacrificial death.[114] Nyamiti's attempt has therefore been to avoid taking as point of departure the Christology of the Catholic manuals but rather has "taken [them] seriously as a partner in dialogue" in his ancestral Christology.[115] In his Christological quest, Nyamiti sees the concept of ancestors in Africa as not only appropriate in understanding the person of Christ and what he means to the African, but also in understanding the mystery of the Trinity (the relation between the Father, Son, and Holy Spirit) and also the Church. He defines "Ancestral Christology" thus, "a theology on the mystery of Jesus Christ expressed in terms of African conceptions on traditional ancestors."[116]

Nyamiti identifies five main elements of the African conception of ancestorship.[117] There is a "natural relationship" or "consanguineous kinship"

---

with the Catholic University of East Africa (CUEA) after receiving doctorate degrees from Louvain (Leuven) University (Belgium) and the University of Vienna (Austria). Wachege, "Charles Nyamiti," 149–51. Vähäkangas, *In Search of Foundations for African Catholicism*, 289.

112. Nyamiti, *African Theology: Its Nature, Problems and Methods*.
113. Nyamiti, *Jesus Christ, the Ancestor of Humankind*, 49.
114. Nyamiti, *Jesus Christ, the Ancestor of Humankind*, 49–50.
115. Nyamiti, *Jesus Christ, the Ancestor of Humankind*, 50.
116. Nyamiti, *Jesus Christ, the Ancestor of Humankind*, 259.
117. Nyamiti, *Christ as our Ancestor* 15–16. Nyamiti, *Jesus Christ, the Ancestor of Humankind*, 3–4.

between the ancestor and his earthly relatives which limits ancestorship to blood relations. The ancestor, through death, acquires a "supernatural (superhuman) sacred status" and comes with "magico-religious powers"[118] that earthly relatives can benefit from because of the proximity to the Supreme Being. The supernatural status of the ancestor is also the basis of the former's "exemplarity": as a "model or exemplar of conduct in society, and as a source of tribal tradition and its stability."[119] The ancestor, in most cases, is considered as a "mediator" between the Supreme Being and kin members. The ancestor is thus entitled to "regular sacred communication" through prayers and "ritual donations (=oblation)."[120] These characteristics provide for Nyamiti a framework in his ancestral explorations.

Nyamiti's working "metaphysical" definition of ancestorship, therefore, takes into account the above elements but is further "purified" from all "superstitious connotations" as well as "other forms of limitation, so as to make the definition applicable to God in his inner life."[121] In other words, the idea of ancestor has been *re-figured* in the light of Christian teaching. Accordingly, "ancestorship is a sacred kin-relationship which establishes a right or title to regular sacred communication with one's own kin through prayer and ritual offering (oblation)."[122] Thus in Nyamiti's analysis, the mystery of the Trinity can be given an ancestral interpretation in which "analogically speaking, God the Father is the Ancestor of God the Son," the Son being the "Descendant of the Father," and the two are "entitled to a mutual sacred communication in the Holy Spirit."[123] The Holy Spirit, Nyamiti notes, is the result (product) of the "reciprocal love" of the Father and Son through whom they communicate to one another "as expression of their mutual love . . . and Eucharist [thanksgiving]."[124]

118. Nyamiti, *Jesus Christ, the Ancestor of Humankind*, 3.
119. Nyamiti, *Jesus Christ, the Ancestor of Humankind*, 3.
120. Nyamiti, *Jesus Christ, the Ancestor of Humankind*, 4.
121. Nyamiti, *Jesus Christ, the Ancestor of Humankind*, 4.
122. Nyamiti, *Jesus Christ, the Ancestor of Humankind*, 4.

123. Nyamiti describes "analogy" as "the attribution of one particular term to two or more realities according to a meaning which is similar and dissimilar at the same time" and that the "expression *analogia entis* (= analogy of being) implies the idea that when the term 'being' is applied to God and to a creature, the term 'being' is neither univocal nor equivocal, but analogical." Thus "analogy" "entails the conviction that between God and his creatures there is some similarity which enables us to gain a deeper understanding of divine mysteries by examining them in the light of our natural knowledge gained from our observations of his creatures in the world." Nyamiti, *Jesus Christ, the Ancestor of Humankind*, 259.

124. Nyamiti, *Jesus Christ, the Ancestor of Humankind*, 4.

God (the Father) qualifies as "our Ancestor" and as Parent-Ancestor, since the above "essential elements" apply to Him and also by the fact of Christ's "Ancestorship to us."[125] As "our true Brother in Adam" as well as "elder Brother to the Father (kinship)" in "common divine sonship" through the "grace of filiation," Jesus Christ also satisfies the other "essential elements" of ancestorship: as "God-man" and Saviour he is "supremely holy (sacred)," "our unique Mediator (mediation)" and "unsurpassable Model of Christian conduct (exemplarity)" as well as having "absolute claim to our unbroken attachment to him through regular prayer and ritual (right to our regular sacred communication)."[126] Thus as both our Brother and Ancestor, by virtue of his *"divine Sonship, humanity, redemptive activity and our participation in the divine nature,"*[127] Christ is designated Brother-Ancestor[128] by Nyamiti; indeed, a Brother-Ancestor *par excellence*.[129]

Jesus Christ, the Logos incarnate, did not become our ancestor only through his Incarnation and redemption work, Nyamiti observes. Before the Fall and, for that matter, also the Incarnation all the ancestral qualities were found in the relationship between the Logos and Adam and Eve as well as the angels and was thus their "true Brother-Ancestor":

> In fact, before the Fall of human beings the Logos was the true Brother (*kinship*) of Adam and Eve and of the angels. For, thanks to his divine Sonship, he was the source of their life of adoptive filiation in him. He was, moreover, their holy (*sacredness*) Model (*exemplarity*) of spiritual life and, in a certain sense, he was their Mediator, in that it was in him and through him that they became God's children and obtained the capacity to enjoy the beatific vision. In addition, by virtue of his status as their Creator and divine Brother, the Logos was *entitled to their regular sacred communication with them* through prayer and in—case of Adam and Eve—through some form of ritual offering.[130]

---

125. Nyamiti, *Jesus Christ, the Ancestor of Humankind*, 5.
126. Nyamiti, *Jesus Christ, the Ancestor of Humankind*, 5.
127. Nyamiti, *Christ as our Ancestor*, 32.
128. Nyamiti is gender conscious in his terminology and indicates that the definition of the term applies to a female also. A brother-ancestor "is a relative of a person with whom he has a common parent, and of whom he is mediator to God, archetype of behaviour and with whom—thanks to his supernatural status acquired through death—he is entitled to have regular sacred communication." Nyamiti, *Christ as our Ancestor*, 23.
129. Nyamiti, "African Christologies Today," 12.
130. Nyamiti, *Jesus Christ, the Ancestor of Humankind*, 6, with the emphasis.

Logos Christology was a helpful avenue in communicating the activity of the Logos prior to creation and the significance of the eventual Incarnation; the Logos who is God and was in the beginning with God was the one through whom all things were made (John 1:1–3). Nyamiti applies an understanding of Logos Christology while making use of the ancestral concept to interpret the "nature" of the relationship between the Logos and humanity and the angels. This becomes a latent example of a complementary use of Logos and Ancestor Christologies.

After the fall of Adam and Eve, and prior to the Incarnation, God's promise of the salvation of humankind through a "divine Redeemer (Genesis 3:15)," Nyamiti opines, made the Logos the "*redeeming Ancestor* of all human beings in the sense that all those men and women who were saved after the Fall before the Incarnation were saved through the Logos as their future incarnate Messiah."[131] Through his redemptive work after the Incarnation Christ, the Logos incarnate, became "our *incarnate redeeming Ancestor*."[132] Nyamiti's concentration has been on this stage of the Ancestorship of the Logos incarnate, as God-man and Redeemer.

Nyamiti explains further that the Ancestorship of Christ "begins to be, operates, grows, reaches its full maturity, and is factualised" through the Holy Spirit.[133] The biblical evidence for Nyamiti includes Jesus' conception (Luke 1:35), baptismal sign (Mark 1:10), "messianic activity" and acts (Luke 4:14) with the eventual offering of himself on the cross to the Father (Hebrews 9:14). The Holy Spirit is involved in the resurrection making Jesus Christ a "life-giving spirit" (1 Corinthians 15:45) and thus, Nyamiti infers, acquires the fullness of his saving function and destiny as the "Son of God in power" according to "the spirit that was in him" (Romans 1:4). The event of Pentecost for Nyamiti "completes" Jesus Christ's "messianic work and factualises his Ancestorship."[134]

Our ancestral relationship with Jesus Christ is brought about and lived through the Holy Spirit. According to Nyamiti, just as the ancestral relationship between the Father and the Son in the Trinity is that of communication through the "mutual giving" of the Holy Spirit "in token of love, veneration and thanksgiving," Christ also gives us his Spirit in order to communicate ancestrally to us.[135] A difference, however, between the two ancestral relationships, Nyamiti indicates, is that whereas Christ communicates the Holy Spirit

---

131. Nyamiti, *Jesus Christ, the Ancestor of Humankind*, 6–7, with the emphasis.
132. Nyamiti, *Jesus Christ, the Ancestor of Humankind*, 7, with the emphasis.
133. Nyamiti, *Jesus Christ, the Ancestor of Humankind*, 158.
134. Nyamiti, *Jesus Christ, the Ancestor of Humankind*, 158.
135. Nyamiti, *Jesus Christ, the Ancestor of Humankind*, 158.

to the Father "most spontaneously" as "that which is due" him, with regard to Christians he gives the Holy Spirit as "free Gift . . . as gratuitous and spontaneous donation of love."[136] If we [Christians] are to love Christ ancestrally as we should, Nyamiti argues, then we would inevitably communicate to Christ, and by extension to the Father also, the totality of what we are and possess (which includes the Holy Spirit).[137] In this we share in Christ's "immanent activity of giving the same Spirit to his Father [in the Trinity]."[138]

In our ancestral link with the Father, Nyamiti explains, the Father together with the Son "sends us the Spirit as Gift of his love and ancestral faithfulness" but "our communication of the [Holy] Spirit to the Father," in this instance, "takes place through the Logos."[139] Though God was our Ancestor even "without the mediation of the *incarnate* Logos . . . he chose to be our Ancestor also through Christ and thereby deepened our descendency in him."[140] Nyamiti, however, maintains that the Ancestorship of the Father is the "ultimate foundation" of Christ's Ancestorship. It is through Christ that God assumes to "himself human qualities of ancestorship" and thus makes the Ancestorship of the Father "closer to the African type."[141] Nyamiti does not comment here, though, on any relevance of his assertion to the belief in some African societies, such as the Akan of Ghana, where the Supreme Being was already regarded as Ancestor (Nana) even before the introduction of Christianity.

The Incarnation is given an (African) ancestral description as "the unsurpassable and irrevocable descendantisation of the man Jesus with the immanent Descendancy of the Logos in the Trinity."[142] In other words, at the Incarnation is found the meeting of the man Jesus as *descendant* of Adam and the Logos as *descendant* of God the Father in the Trinity.[143]

---

136. Nyamiti, *Jesus Christ, the Ancestor of Humankind*, 158.
137. Nyamiti, *Jesus Christ, the Ancestor of Humankind*, 159.
138. Nyamiti, *Jesus Christ, the Ancestor of Humankind*, 159.
139. Nyamiti, *Jesus Christ, the Ancestor of Humankind*, 159–60.
140. Nyamiti, *Jesus Christ, the Ancestor of Humankind*, 163.
141. Nyamiti, *Jesus Christ, the Ancestor of Humankind*, 163.
142. Nyamiti, *Jesus Christ, the Ancestor of Humankind*, 58–59.
143. Bujo expresses his hesitation towards Nyamiti's insistence of the Adamic origin of Jesus, as a basis of His ancestorship "for all Africans." For Bujo, an argument appealing to the historical Adam "raises controversy in contemporary theology" and would thus rather see, as central point in Christ's ancestorship, the fact that "Christ, God-man born from God" must "transcend all racial, tribal, clan-barriers in a definite way." Bujo, *African Theology in Its Social Context*, 94 n.40. Nyamiti has, however, maintained that Christ's Adamic origin is not essential to His Ancestorship and that His Brother-Ancestorship is on account of "His divine-human structure." Nonetheless the fact of Christ's status as "our fellow-Descendant in Adam" deepens His relationship to us as

Nyamiti's "metaphysical" definition of ancestorship highlights a "sacred kin-relationship" and a "right or title to regular sacred communication" and as a result declared analogically the Father as the Ancestor of the Son and the Son the Descendant of the Father.[144]

Nyamiti not only attempts to interpret the Incarnation in ancestral terms, but also identifies the Incarnation with Christ's Ancestorship. According to him,

> When the Incarnation is understood in African ancestral terms, the Logos' becoming flesh and all his redemptive activity (the analogous parallel to the African ancestral mediatory function)—together with the descendantisation of his members through grace (the analogous parallel to the African descendants' loving and respectful sacred communication with their ancestor)—must be considered as inseparable constitutive elements of the Incarnation. At the same time, this implies also that all the Christological items found in the New Testament teachings on Christ's mode of being and salvific activity are particular dimensions of his Incarnation understood in the African ancestral sense.[145]

Furthermore, from the standpoint of the idea of ancestorship, the Incarnation, as well as Christ's Ancestorship, becomes "*an entirely holistic and dynamic mystery, comprising Christ's hypostatic union, together with his entire salvific work and the life of grace as lived by his members in union with the Church.*"[146] In Nyamiti's assessment, both the Incarnation and Ancestorship of Christ "gradually grow" to their respective definitive "maturity" and "fulfilment" at the Parousia (end of time).[147]

Nyamiti's attempt to re-evaluate the traditional conception of the mystery of the Incarnation in African ancestral terms is significant. He demonstrates the dynamism and, to an extent, the fecundity of the Christological application of a prevailing traditional or indigenous concept. His

---

our "supernatural Brother-Ancestor." Nyamiti, *Christ as our Ancestor*, 28. In a later response to Bujo' sentiments, Nyamiti draws attention to the fact that his approach to the multi-dimensional mystery of Jesus Christ is from the "perspective of his membership in the human race originating from Adam and Eve" as against the "perspective of his divinity alone." Nyamiti, *Jesus Christ, the Ancestor of Humankind*, 26–27.

144. Cf. Nyamiti, *Jesus Christ, the Ancestor of Humankind*, 4.

145. Nyamiti, *Jesus Christ, the Ancestor of Humankind*, 59, (emphasis in the original).

146. Nyamiti, *Jesus Christ, the Ancestor of Humankind*, 60–61, (emphasis in the original).

147. Nyamiti, *Jesus Christ, the Ancestor of Humankind*, 61.

preoccupation with his sense of the viability of the concept of ancestor in Africa is equally impressive and exemplary. Wachege wittingly remarks, "where Nyamiti will stop in his ancestorship will be perhaps when he himself will qualify as an ancestor in life after this life."[148]

As with my general critique on the efforts in Ancestor Christology, Nyamiti's thoughts await a further mother-tongue exploration or application rooted also in the translated Scriptures. Nyamiti even proposes an outline for a treatise on African Ancestral Christology, which shows his commitment to further discourse on the subject.[149] The indigenous language appropriation of Nyamiti's Ancestor Christology may well also provide the needed platform for its engagement with traditional thought forms and institutions intricately linked to the idea of ancestors.

Gift Makwasha—Jesu Mudzimu Wepamusha, Wedzinza, Wenyika

There is use of indigenous terminology and a link to the political space in Gift Makwasha's address of the "theological problem" of the issue of ancestors among Shona Christians in Zimbabwe.[150] Makwasha focuses on the responses of mainline churches as an Anglican priest but does acknowledge the exponential growth of Pentecostal churches in Zimbabwe who are mainly "anti-ancestor."[151] Makwasha's assessment of the responses of the mainline churches as well as the AICs and the *Kuyera KweDzimbabwe* (The Holiness of Zimbabwe) movement's critical incorporation of the issue of ancestors leads him to formulate a tripartite Ancestor Christology which corresponds to the three categories of ancestors in Shona traditional thought.[152] The goal of this Christology is "to contribute to a wider Shona understanding of Jesus as their ancestor par-excellence in whom all their physical and spiritual needs—including those of their own ordinary ancestors fail to meet—get 'fulfilled.'"[153]

According to Makwasha, there are three socio-political subdivisions among the Shona, namely, the kraal (sing. *musha*, pl. *misha*, family), chiefdom

---

148. Wachege, "Charles Nyamiti," 159.

149. Nyamiti, *Jesus Christ, the Ancestor of Humankind*, 189–98.

150. Makwasha, "'Not Without My Ancestors.'"

151. Makwasha, "Not Without My Ancestors," 8.

152. This includes, family ancestors (*midzimu yepamusha*), tribal ancestors (*midzimu yedzinza*) and national ancestors (*midzimu yenyika*). Makwasha, "Not Without My Ancestors," 21.

153. Makwasha, "Not Without My Ancestors," 10–11.

(*ushe*, tribe), and the nation.[154] Petitions at the family level are directed, via the head of the kraal, to the *midzimu yepamusha* (ancestors of the family).[155] At the tribal level, it is the chief's responsibility for any engagement with the *mudzimu wedzinza* or *mhondoro* (tutelary or tribal ancestor). The tribal ancestors are active in politics especially in the election of a new chief and are also vital in rainmaking rituals to *Mwari* (Supreme Being).[156] The potency of the *mhondoro* (lit. lion) among other tribes, Makwasha indicates, earns them the respect of a *mudzimu wenyika* (national ancestor).[157] It is noteworthy that the title *mudzimu wenyika* was eventually applied to those who had been instrumental towards the independence of Zimbabwe.[158]

Indicating the supremacy of Jesus Christ as Mediator (the Mediator of mediators) between the Supreme Being and humanity, Makwasha points out that in the Shona context Jesus becomes the *Mudzimu Mukuru* ("the Greatest Ancestor, the Supreme one of our supreme ancestors") through whom a *kusuma* ("plea or representation") can reach *Mwari*.[159] Jesus as a family Ancestor (*Jesu Mudzimu Wepamusha*), in line with the demand of filial piety by Shona ancestors, according to Makwasha, "fosters unity and harmony" among believers considered as his family.[160] As "an Ancestor," Makwasha rightly notes, Jesus "challenges traditions that endanger human life" (cf. Luke 6:1–10) and is the "moral example for those who seek to live a righteous life at its best."[161] Proclaiming Jesus as *Mudzimu Wepamusha* implies, for Makwasha, a Christian liturgy that replaces the traditional funerary rite of *kurovaguva* with *Bira Rerumuko Rwevakafa* ("The Celebration, Feast or Eucharist for the Resurrection of the Dead").[162] Since the primary aim of the traditional *kurovaguva* rite is *kumutsa mudzimu* ("the invitation of the spirit of the dead to come back home as an ancestor"), Makwasha notes, it can be accommodated within the Christian belief of the resurrection of the dead. Similarly, the traditional concept of *kusuma midzimu* ("appealing to the ancestors to accept and accommodate the spirit of the dead") can now be directed to *Jesu Mudzimu Wepamusha*.[163]

---

154. Makwasha, "Not Without My Ancestors," 50.
155. Makwasha, "Not Without My Ancestors," 50.
156. Makwasha, "Not Without My Ancestors," 68 & 75.
157. Makwasha, "Not Without My Ancestors," 51.
158. Makwasha, "Not Without My Ancestors," 51.
159. Makwasha, "Not Without My Ancestors," 302.
160. Makwasha, "Not Without My Ancestors," 309.
161. Makwasha, "Not Without My Ancestors," 311.
162. Makwasha, "Not Without My Ancestors," 314.
163. Makwasha, "Not Without My Ancestors," 314. Cf. John 14:1–3.

Once the Church is seen as the Clan of the *Mhondoro* Jesus, his role as *Mudzimu Wedzinza* (Tribal Ancestor) also becomes apparent, for Makwasha. As the *Mhondoro*, Jesus upholds the good and confronts what is evil in tribal laws or politics.[164] Proclaiming Jesus the *Mhondoro* also makes, in Makwasha's assessment, the Church his *rushanga* (shrine) where people come with their pleas through him to *Mwari*.[165] The role the Churches played in the struggles toward Zimbabwe's independence, according to Makwasha, accords Jesus the title *Jesu Mudzimu Wenyika* (Jesus the National Ancestor) who demanded (political) liberation for the people.[166] In post-independence Zimbabwe, Makwasha argues, the Church in Zimbabwe is challenged to pursue the liberating influence of Jesus the *Mudzimu Wenyika*. For example Makwasha makes a polemic plea that,

> Since national *mhondoros* were concerned about gaining back the lost land and returning it to its original Shona owners, Jesus the *mhondoro* should be interested in sorting out the land crisis by restoring the national economy totally wrecked by Mugabe and his cronies.[167]

Not all Zimbabwean Christians may fully agree with Makwasha in his assertion, but it does underscore his desire to take the discussion of Ancestor Christology into national politics.

Expressed Limitations of Ancestor Christology

There have been several dismissive remarks on the designation of Jesus Christ as Ancestor as well as critical responses to the claims of Ancestor Christology. Unlike Diane Stinton, I have not endeavored to classify them under any church denomination or geographical area but to treat the various critiques broadly under "academic" and "grassroots" categories.[168] The former comprises those with theological education including the clergy while the latter includes non-academic laity. One major concern has been that Ancestor Christology is an *academic* preoccupation with little or no patronage at the *grassroots* everyday African Christian experience. In highlighting the various concerns distinctly from the grassroots and academic

---

164. Makwasha, "Not Without My Ancestors," 351.
165. Makwasha, "Not Without My Ancestors," 352.
166. Makwasha, "Not Without My Ancestors," 352.
167. Makwasha, "Not Without My Ancestors," 377.
168. Cf. Stinton, *Jesus of Africa*, 130ff.

levels, I seek to show the common ground on which any further work on Ancestor Christology can proceed.

Grassroots Responses

The erstwhile Omanhene (Paramount Chief) of Akuapem traditional area in the Eastern Region of Ghana, Oseadeeyo Nana Addo Dankwa III, in a lecture titled "The Black Stool and Ancestral Worship" gave his critique of (Akan) Ancestor Christology.[169] Addo Dankwa sees the phrase "ancestor worship" as a misconception and as such an inscription as "Christ the ancestor" presupposes a misunderstanding on the question of ancestor worship.[170] An ancestor for the Akan should have had "all the human qualities of the Akan and interacted with others in the normal way" while in the first degree of existence (that is while in the present world) "as a mortal being," before entering into the second degree of existence (second state of being beyond this present world). In this regard "God and Christ are not ancestors" in the Akan understanding of ancestors.[171] These assertions are apparently based on Addo Dankwa's understanding of the nature of God and Christ. God is creator and though He is believed to be everywhere, He "has never stayed physically on this world."[172] Christ's "body never saw corruption in the grave," Nana Addo Dankwa notes, even though He once stayed physically on earth. The Spirit of Christ, being part of the Trinity, Nana Addo Dankwa adds, "is not part of the living community" in the way other ancestors are considered as part of the community.[173] Thus, God's transcendence and Christ's divinity and resurrection prevent both from being considered as ancestors in Akan thought.

According to Stinton, the reasons given for the image of ancestor reflect the interplay between biblical and African concepts and elucidate how Jesus fulfils the traditional roles of the ancestors in Africa.[174] The four main functions include: mediation, founder of a community, participation in the life of the community, and as provider of life. For example, a Kenyan

---

169. Lecture delivered on November 16, 1987 as part of a series of four lectures given at the Trinity College (now Trinity Theological Seminary). Lectures subsequently published as *Christianity and African Traditional Beliefs;* Dankwa, *Christianity and African Traditional Beliefs.*

170. Dankwa, *Christianity and African Traditional Beliefs*, 33.

171. Dankwa, *Christianity and African Traditional Beliefs*, 33.

172. Dankwa, *Christianity and African Traditional Beliefs*, 33.

173. Dankwa, *Christianity and African Traditional Beliefs*, 34.

174. Stinton, *Jesus of Africa*, 126.

Catholic lay man explained, "Jesus fits exactly as the supreme ancestor, because he comes and he founds a new community," adding further,

> His ancestry is so physical, in the sense that not only was he there, at that time, but he continues. So you can see Jesus present himself as an ever-present ancestor—he's actually there all the time, and he was there before, and now he continues. So this makes the people feel very much at home.[175]

The challenge that Stinton's respondents had with the issue of Jesus as Ancestor, in her analysis, ranged from historical and missiological issues, theological problems and the challenge of contemporary relevance.[176] According to one Kenyan Protestant lay woman, there has been a severance of any link to the idea of ancestors because it has been associated with "worship." Her grandparents rejected completely the idea after becoming Christians (presumably at the insistence of missionaries or church leaders).[177] According to her, she does not "know too much about" her ancestors and that makes it difficult for her to associate Christ with ancestry.[178]

A Ghanaian Protestant layman, expresses his view on the limitation of the idea of ancestor when applied to Jesus,

> I would picture him as rather much bigger than an ancestor. I see ancestors as, in the traditional concept, living in ghost land—vaguely alive, but hardly having bodies and not being able to interact with people. Jesus as ancestor would only mean to me that he's died and gone, but my difficulty with the use of the word *ancestor* for Jesus Christ has to do with my understanding of who Jesus is. You see, he died, but rose again! and therefore I can't relate with ancestors, I can relate with Christ.[179]

It is significant that the difficulty for the above respondent is in his understanding of who Jesus is. Certainly, who Jesus is and eventually becomes to us, is "much bigger" than any image or title we can attribute to him. The understanding of ancestors as *just* "living in ghost land," *asamando* for the Akan, is, however, limited and underestimates any perceived influence they are known to have in traditional societies. Personal knowledge of

---

175. Stinton, *Jesus of Africa*, 127. Stinton notes that Kiarie in the course of his response referred to Johannine teaching on rebirth and Pauline teaching on the mystical body of Christ.

176. Stinton, *Jesus of Africa*, 130.

177. Stinton, *Jesus of Africa*, 131.

178. Stinton, *Jesus of Africa*, 131.

179. Stinton, *Jesus of Africa*, 133–34.

the ancestors is also a concern for one Kenyan Catholic layman for whom Jesus as Ancestor makes little impact because "we know Jesus much, much better than we know our ancestors."[180]

The theological issue of Jesus' divinity in the application of the image of ancestor was also expressed. One of such remarked, "I think I have reservations, maybe because I view him more in terms of his divinity than his humanity!"[181] A Ghanaian scholar and laywoman significantly raises the issue of the uniqueness of Jesus among the numerous ancestors of a particular people group if he is claimed to be an Ancestor. According to her, when in the libation prayer all the ancestors and gods, far and near, are being summoned and Jesus is mentioned among such a host that would *take out* his uniqueness (as being divine).[182]

The Akan word, *nana*, as we have mentioned is a honorific title applied to the living chief and also to the elders both living and dead (the ancestors, *nananom nsamanfo*).[183] It appears that while technically the "ancestors" are *nananom nsamanfo* an Akan would hardly refer to an ancestor as *nana saman* X but rather simply as *nana* X. Thus, in claiming the title Nana for Jesus, as we are advocating for a mother-tongue Ancestor Christology, would also imply his "chiefly" and "elder" status. From Stinton's survey, in naming Jesus as Chief, it is interesting that a few respondents were ambivalent. For example, while a Catholic layman was ready to designate Jesus as Nana, though for him the nature of traditional chiefs does not make the image fit Jesus,[184] a female Christian group leader was not convinced to accept the title Nana or even see Jesus as chief because for her, Jesus is "king of kings and lord of lords."[185]

Academic Responses

The written responses to the endeavor of Ancestor Christology have challenged both its method and the extent of its relevance. One common argument is in its discerned inadequacy in communicating the divinity of Jesus Christ in the African context. Nyamiti has responded to some of the

---

180. Stinton, *Jesus of Africa*, 134.
181. Stinton, *Jesus of Africa*, 134.
182. Stinton, *Jesus of Africa*, 134–35.
183. It soon becomes a personal name, however, as the holder's name is eventually overshadowed by it. For example, the chief would be called by his full name mostly on special occasions, but mostly in everyday referrals *nana* is commonly employed.
184. Stinton, *Jesus of Africa*, 188.
185. Stinton, *Jesus of Africa*, 189.

critiques of his Brother-Ancestorship and Ancestor Christology in general. Nyamiti responds to nine areas of objection to Ancestor Christology. I will consider the first seven and later that of Volker Küster and Diane Stinton under respective sections. Sebastian Karotemprel, an Indian Catholic theologian, had questioned the extent of, what he calls, the "theological *myth*" of ancestor in revealing the "whole person of Jesus Christ," indicating,

> How do we exploit this concept to capture all the richness of Traditional Christology within the context of the theology of the Trinity? Socio-culturally, is this myth still valid today, and how long will it have relevance in Africa given the momentum of the process of modernization, urbanization and universalization of education?[186]

Nyamiti takes issue with the classification "theological myth" and disagrees with any associated implication of "myth" as "something fictitious without real existence" and thus also to suggest the non-existence of "ancestral veneration" in contemporary Africa.[187] On the issue of the survival of the idea of ancestor in the midst of modernization and urbanization, Nyamiti, though accepts the possibility of a disappearance, remarks that "human culture is given to us also as a *TASK*"; not only to develop but also to "preserve their authentic values by consciously and assiduously combating all that threatens the survival of such values."[188] Accordingly, Nyamiti rightly affirms, in Bujo's words, "even if the African would start forgetting [those values], it is imperative and it is the duty not only of theology, but also of the Gospel to restore them back to the minds of the Africans."[189] Finally, on Karotemprel's concern of the adequacy of the concept in capturing "all the richness of Traditional Christology within the context of the theology of the Trinity," Nyamiti believes he has addressed in his writings and reiterates that "no single human category" can make known all there is on the person of Jesus Christ.[190]

According to Nyamiti, Jean Galot's concern that the idea of Christ as Ancestor would render Christ an old man who will be unattractive to young people implies a non-African conception of ancestor.[191] In Africa,

---

186. Karotemprel, "Introduction: Christology and Mission Today," 19 as cited in Nyamiti, *Jesus Christ, the Ancestor of Humankind*, 211.

187. Nyamiti, *Jesus Christ, the Ancestor of Humankind*, 211–12.

188. Nyamiti, *Jesus Christ, the Ancestor of Humankind*, 214.

189. Bujo, "La Christologie Africaine n'est-elle qu'une archéologie culturelle?" 363 as cited in Nyamiti, *Jesus Christ, the Ancestor of Humankind*, 214.

190. Nyamiti, *Jesus Christ, the Ancestor of Humankind*, 214.

191. Jean Galot, "Le Christ, notre ancêtre?" 214–15 & 257.

Nyamiti notes, old-age is regarded as "a sign of wisdom and God's blessing" and while the term is applied *analogically* to Christ, even if it contains the idea of old-age, for Nyamiti, that "would have to be purified" since the term is "meant to designate Christ as Logos before and after his Incarnation."[192] In both stages Christ was not "an old man" and when this is well explained to the young, Nyamiti opines, the danger of an unattractive old being would be removed. It is curious why Nyamiti in responding to the issue of the appropriateness and adequacy of the use of the English term "ancestor" did not in any way propose a mother-tongue or indigenous-language exploration. Nyamiti rather argues that what "really matters is whether the elements it is meant to signify are really found in African religious beliefs and practices, and whether the Christology based on such elements is usefully relevant for the African Churches and elsewhere."[193] Furthermore for him, a "wiser and more constructive criticism would be to suggest a better title to such Christology, rather than to disqualify it altogether."[194] In this case a Nana Christology (that is, a mother-tongue Ancestor Christology) may address Nyamiti's second point.

Nyamiti reiterates the issue of "analogy" and the need to "modify" and "purify" in responding to Adam Wolanin's concern on the "risks" and "difficulties" in applying the concept of ancestor to Christ. According to Nyamiti, Wolanin apparently overstates the fact in declaring that in African societies the following three serve as conditions for ancestral status, namely, "abundant offspring," "a *natural* death," and death at a "venerable age."[195] These three, Nyamiti notes, are not required *everywhere* for ancestral status in black Africa and more so where the Supreme Being is regarded as Ancestor. Wolanin, Nyamiti observes, also sees the "risk" and "difficulty" in the sense that while the ancestors intercede exclusively for their relatives, Christ is the universal Mediator and Intercessor and again while the ancestors are subordinate to the Supreme Being, Christ is of the same nature as God the Father. Nyamiti's stand is that human terms can only be applied to creatures and to God only analogously, implying similarities and differences and thus invariably require "modification and purification."[196] Therefore, the "risk" and "difficulties" do not only apply to the African concept of ancestor but also to the application of any human categories to the divine mysteries.[197] It can also be noted that

---

192. Nyamiti, *Jesus Christ, the Ancestor of Humankind*, 215.
193. Nyamiti, *Jesus Christ, the Ancestor of Humankind*, 215.
194. Nyamiti, *Jesus Christ, the Ancestor of Humankind*, 215.
195. Wolanin, "Teologia africana: tra fede e cultura, 230.
196. Nyamiti, *Jesus Christ, the Ancestor of Humankind*, 216.
197. Nyamiti, *Jesus Christ, the Ancestor of Humankind*, 217.

even the application of *logos* to Christ needed some clarification especially in contradistinction to the Stoics.

The fifth response has to do with the existence of the idea of Nyamiti's "brother-ancestorship" in Africa. Some authors (he does not mention) argue that brother- or sister-ancestorship does not exist in black Africa.[198] Nyamiti acknowledges "brother-ancestorship" is a rare phenomenon, but nonetheless is found in some localities such as among the Kikuyu when Jomo Kenyatta indicated three types of ancestors among them: parent-ancestors (*ngoma cia aciari*), clan ancestors (*ngoma cia muherega*), and ancestors of an age-group (*ngoma cia riika*).[199] Accordingly for Nyamiti, a clan or an age-group ancestor can have earthly individuals who are his [or her] brothers [or sisters]. Since Christ's brotherhood is "clearly taught in the Bible" (cf. Hebrews 2:11–13 *et al.*), Nyamiti asserts, African theology would be "completely false" if the title "brother" is suppressed in the view that it is "incompatible with the African conception of ancestor."[200]

Related to the above concern, is the relevance of Christ's Brother-Ancestorship to those contexts in which "a brother (or sister) can never play an ancestral role after his (her) death.[201] This objection is on a false basis implying that the relevance of the Christian mysteries depends on "their correspondence to or agreement with African mentality and customs."[202] Such a line of thought, Nyamiti argues, may render the fatherhood of God and the mysteries of the Incarnation and Trinity irrelevant in Africa since "none of their traditional religious teachings corresponds entirely to the Christian doctrine on those mysteries."[203]

There is also the concern that the function of an ancestor is primarily "to provide protection and communication in the world of spirits" and not reconciliation between God and human beings. Therefore, Christ's "reconciling function" is "not easily captured" in the mediatory role of Brother-Ancestor, according to Carl F. Hallencreutz.[204] Nyamiti asserts that "ancestor" in the African sense is not "directly opposed to Christ's reconciliatory function" and cautions that the "theologian should avoid reducing . . . [revealed] mysteries to the level and scope of the philosophical categories"

198. Nyamiti, *Jesus Christ, the Ancestor of Humankind*, 217.

199. Nyamiti, *Jesus Christ, the Ancestor of Humankind*, 217. Cf. Kenyatta, *Facing Mount Kenya*, 226–27.

200. Nyamiti, *Jesus Christ, the Ancestor of Humankind*, 218.

201. Nyamiti, *Jesus Christ, the Ancestor of Humankind*, 218.

202. Nyamiti, *Jesus Christ, the Ancestor of Humankind*, 218.

203. Nyamiti, *Jesus Christ, the Ancestor of Humankind*, 218.

204. Hallencreutz, in *Swedish Missiological Themes*, 305 as cited by Nyamiti, *Jesus Christ, the Ancestor of Humankind*, 219 & 257.

used to interpret and express them.²⁰⁵ Two ways to avoid "this error" is to, on the one hand, study thoroughly "the revealed truths in the Bible and Church Tradition" and, on the other, integrate "harmoniously the human category in the totality of the divine mysteries."²⁰⁶ This, for him, would invariably involve transcending the human categories "as well as their modification and purification and even—in some cases—the complete transformation of their original meaning."²⁰⁷ The realization of this agenda is in that stage which we have termed *refiguration*, where pre-Christian cultural concepts are *refigured* in the light of the reality and impact of Jesus Christ.

Volker Küster

According to Küster, Nyamiti's "dogmatic remarks which follow the construction of an analogy between Jesus Christ and African brother-ancestor are substantially independent of the title ancestor" which at one point remains a "formal translation."²⁰⁸ Furthermore, Küster is unconvinced whether Nyamiti's Ancestor Christology "can be described at all adequately with the categories of accommodation and inculturation."²⁰⁹ Accordingly, for Küster, the "African notion of ancestors and the gospel do no enter into an inner dialogue" and neither does Nyamiti give "the gospel" an "African garb."²¹⁰ Nyamiti responds to Küster's concerns by indicating that the latter does not give "concrete examples" to show how the "dogmatic remarks" are independent of the title "ancestor" and that leaves Nyamiti to speculate on the reasons behind such concerns.²¹¹ Nyamiti is first of the view that Küster is "partly influenced" by Heribert Rücker who maintains that the African way of thinking is essentially symbolic and therefore prefers the use of symbols over "analogy and metaphysics" in African theology.²¹² However, one cannot empty symbols adequately without analogy.

It is possible, Nyamiti opines, Küster's criticism is directed against his "firm support of the *dogma* on Christ's true divinity and humanity personally united in the eternal Logos, as was defined by the early councils."²¹³ This

205. Nyamiti, *Jesus Christ, the Ancestor of Humankind*, 220.
206. Nyamiti, *Jesus Christ, the Ancestor of Humankind*, 220.
207. Nyamiti, *Jesus Christ, the Ancestor of Humankind*, 220.
208. Küster, *The Many Faces of Jesus Christ: Intercultural Christology*, 74.
209. Küster, *The Many Faces of Jesus Christ*, 74.
210. Küster, *The Many Faces of Jesus Christ*, 74.
211. Nyamiti, *Jesus Christ, the Ancestor of Humankind*, 220–21.
212. Nyamiti, *Jesus Christ, the Ancestor of Humankind*, 221.
213. Nyamiti, *Jesus Christ, the Ancestor of Humankind*, 221.

appears so because Küster has expressed the need to "keep investigating the conceptions which lie behind" the "terminological clarifications of the early church, which are steeped in the cultural and religious world of Hellenistic ideas."[214] For Nyamiti, this seems to be an invitation to "third-world theologians to question, or even to deny, the validity of the dogmas or teachings of the early councils" and that Küster could well be one of those who regard the councils as Hellenizing the gospel message and thus *"falsified* that message."[215] If these are Küster's informing concerns, then, for Nyamiti, the issues of "inner dialogue," "formal translation," and "African garb" are understandable. However, Nyamiti points out that it is accepted today that the early Christian formulation of the biblical message on Christ in Hellenistic categories "was a legitimate and even necessary effort to *inculturate* the gospel teaching in the Graeco-Roman cultures," something that is present even in the later writings of the Old Testament and in the New Testament itself.[216]

These notwithstanding, it could be that Küster also accepts the conciliar dogmas and seems to suggest that the "inculturation of that theology" is not a mere "translation" into African categories. This, Nyamiti subscribes to and notes that "although the African theologian may go beyond what was taught by the councils, his or her interpretation should not contradict or ignore the original meaning of the dogmas as defined by the Church."[217] Nyamiti invites Küster to "be more concrete in his criticism" by taking, for instance, the various points mentioned in his earlier book *Christ as our Ancestor* and refuting them one by one.[218] For him, most of the points are intended to demonstrate the "African originality" of his Ancestor Christology and thus indicate an "inner dialogue" between the African idea of ancestor and Christian teaching and hence giving the latter "an African garb."[219]

Küster also acknowledges the "close connection" between the ideas of ancestor and that of chief and master of initiation.[220] While Jesus Christ under the ancestor model is shown (following Kabasélé) to communicate life, being present among the living, as an elder brother and mediator between God and humans as well as among humans, he nonetheless does not "correspond to the vitalistic criteria of African ancestor worship" not having

---

214. Küster, *The Many Faces of Jesus Christ*, 84.

215. Nyamiti, *Jesus Christ, the Ancestor of Humankind*, 221–22.

216. Nyamiti, *Jesus Christ, the Ancestor of Humankind*, 222 (emphasis in the original).

217. Nyamiti, *Jesus Christ, the Ancestor of Humankind*, 222–23.

218. Nyamiti, *Jesus Christ, the Ancestor of Humankind*, 223. See Nyamiti, *Christ as our Ancestor*, 74–78.

219. Nyamiti, *Jesus Christ, the Ancestor of Humankind*, 223.

220. Küster, *The Many Faces of Jesus Christ*, 66.

fathered any children and dying a violent death.²²¹ In terms of the various approaches to Ancestor Christology, Küster considers Bujo to be "more aware of the problem" of African ancestor worship in the Christological endeavor than the various authors he examines.²²² Bujo's "proto-ancestor" designation, for Küster, shows the discontinuity from natural (traditional) ancestors and that Bujo has worked out the revaluation needed in giving the title "ancestor" to Jesus Christ.²²³

Küster's conclusions are, however, not beyond question. Nyamiti, to be sure, has also been keen in demonstrating the manner of his use of the "Brother-Ancestor" terminology. Rather than seeing Bujo's Ancestor Christology as "incidental," as Küster indicates, and thus as peripheral to the former's interest in "negro-African-christocentric morality," it is helpful to note that Bujo is convinced it is the idea of ancestor that informs the African sense of morality. Thus for any morality that is Christ-centred to be relevant to the African, it ought to begin from a meaningful engagement between Christ and the idea of ancestor. Bujo's interest in African Christian morality is fundamentally linked to his Ancestor Christology.²²⁴ Moreover, with respect to Nyamiti, Bujo's eventual absence from Africa, it may be noted, could account for the relative limited further reflection on Ancestor Christology as one finds in the case of his former colleague, Nyamiti.

Diane B. Stinton

Stinton reflects, relatively more extensively, on the proposals of Pobee and Bujo with an apparent full affirmation of the latter.²²⁵ According to her, in the formulation of Ancestor Christology, following Pobee's indication, inadequate attention is given to the "thorny issue" of Jesus' link with African lineage ancestors, which was inherent in Pobee's "Christological query."²²⁶ With respect to Pobee's effort, Stinton notes that a "further consideration of Jesus' role as ancestor, beyond functions of power and authority to judge, would enhance his presentation of the image."²²⁷ In my view Pobee's

---

221. Küster, *The Many Faces of Jesus Christ*, 67 & 68.
222. Küster, *The Many Faces of Jesus Christ*, 71 & 75.
223. Küster, *The Many Faces of Jesus Christ*, 76.
224. Cf. Stinton, *Jesus of Africa*, 123.
225. Stinton, *Jesus of Africa*, 116–23.
226. Stinton, *Jesus of Africa*, 118.
227. Stinton, *Jesus of Africa*, 118.

missionary suggestions have been diversely taken up for further clarification and application.[228]

Bujo, for Stinton, essentially satisfies her expectation of the nature and function of Ancestor Christology in the demands of contextual theology in Africa. She practically sees no limitation in Bujo's method and assertion in her assessment of his Proto-Ancestor Christology. For example, Bujo is able to complement an "ascending Christology" or "Christology from below" (in the sense that from the example or model of the life of the historical Jesus of Nazareth one can learn how to be human) with an emphasis on his supraterrestrial status as Proto-Ancestor through his death and resurrection.[229] Bujo's remark that the "way of the Cross" is imperative in understanding Jesus as Proto-Ancestor, for Stinton, shows that the strength of Bujo's Ancestor Christology is not only its content but also the method advocated.[230] Furthermore, Bujo, according to Stinton, demonstrates a clear focus on the inculturation and liberation concerns and thus supersedes any divide between the two models.[231]

Stinton, however, takes note of the "new insights" Nyamiti offers in articulating, from an African perspective, the "identity and significance of Christ." Yet Nyamiti's attempt, according to her, "to develop an African scientific or systematic theology" that favors "metaphysics and philosophical speculation over sociocultural analysis," diminishes any impact of his Christology in the contemporary context. Accordingly, though Nyamiti provides some pastoral implications, Stinton continues, "he draws criticism for writing abstract reflections without adequately addressing the contemporary situation in keeping with current priorities for contextual theologies in Africa."[232] Nyamiti takes these concerns to mean either Stinton is negative towards African scientific or systematic theology, or her concern is about the bias towards metaphysics and philosophical speculation over "sociocultural analysis." In the case of the former, the argument against Küster suffices for him.[233]

On the latter (possible) concern of Stinton, Nyamiti notes he would not claim to have *adequately* addressed the priorities of the "contemporary situation" in his writings and believes no theologian can claim to have

---

228. For example, Bediako comments on Pobee's "Christological query" and Nyamiti, in his 1984 *Christ as our Ancestor*, shows awareness of Pobee's suggestion.
229. Stinton, *Jesus of Africa*, 120.
230. Stinton, *Jesus of Africa*, 123.
231. Stinton, *Jesus of Africa*, 123.
232. Stinton, *Jesus of Africa*, 12
233. Nyamiti, *Jesus Christ, the Ancestor of Humankind*, 223–24.

done so.[234] Though Stinton does not give indication of having examined his other works (citing five of his essays), Nyamiti asserts there are no criteria for what is a priority for "contextual theologies in Africa." Moreover, for Nyamiti, sociocultural analysis does not necessarily have to be "more important or more urgent than metaphysics and philosophical or theological speculation in African theology."[235] Accordingly, there is the need for philosophical speculation in the articulation and expression of African Christology, for the "theological reflection on Christ's mystery in its intimate link with the Trinity" in African theology requires philosophical and metaphysical apparatus.[236]

Furthermore, Nyamiti intimates there is *"hierarchy of priorities"* in the focus or emphasis in African Christologies, namely, human duty in seeking "material" welfare and that of fulfilling spiritual obligations such as "regular prayer, frequent devout reception of the sacraments."[237] These two priorities are not on the same level for Nyamiti and asserts, arguable though, that the human material aspect is "inferior in importance" to that of the spiritual tasks.[238] Thus his priority on the "spiritual tasks" has led to his interest mainly in expounding the mystery of Christ using the category of the concept of ancestor. Nyamiti notes in his concluding remarks that "for a Christian of authentic faith, the fruits of spiritual tasks are inalienable animating factors for a fruitful and meritorious performance of worldly duties."[239]

With hindsight, however, I think Stinton's choice of "sociocultural" rather than "socioeconomic" with the basic understandings of social and cultural or economic factors, leads to a misjudgment of the relevance of Nyamiti's Ancestor Christology in the social and cultural sides of communal life. Nyamiti remains an African Christian. The African context is not only about the priorities of socio-economic conditions of poverty or of poor governance. There are African intellectuals taking solace in the philosophical undergirding of African traditional religious thought. They too need the witness of the Gospel. Nyamiti's method may well be one of the ways at systematizing African Christian thought for witness in such contexts. There are certainly cultural implications from Nyamiti's effort, though his concentration appears to be more towards church life than the wider community. For example, if we claim Jesus as the Ancestor (Nana) of our community, then we continue to remind

---

234. Nyamiti, *Jesus Christ, the Ancestor of Humankind*, 224. Nyamiti's emphasis.
235. Nyamiti, *Jesus Christ, the Ancestor of Humankind*, 224–25.
236. Nyamiti, *Jesus Christ, the Ancestor of Humankind*, 225–26.
237. Nyamiti, *Jesus Christ, the Ancestor of Humankind*, 226.
238. Nyamiti, *Jesus Christ, the Ancestor of Humankind*, 226.
239. Nyamiti, *Jesus Christ, the Ancestor of Humankind*, 227.

ourselves that everyone in the community, those who have received him and those yet to, belong to him and it remains the responsibility of (spiritual) elders, that is Christians, to lead the young ones (non-Christians) to Christ. This also means that all communal service and action should ultimately be pleasing to Nana (Ancestor) Jesus.

Nyamiti's response to Stinton seems to touch more on economic demands and he is even ready to argue there is a tendency towards secularism in most African Christologies.[240] Nyamiti's priority of the spiritual over the human "socioeconomic" situation also raises a concern: was this the strict way of Jesus?[241] Stinton's critique and Nyamiti's concerns in his responses do make it evident that Ancestor Christology is not exhaustive yet: the working out, in this case, of the balance between the supernatural and natural needs is desired.

Victor Ezigbo

Victor Ezigbo highlights some limitations of Ancestor Christology in his argument towards a "Revealer" Christology in the Nigerian context. Ezigbo identifies three foundations from which he sees the arguments of the proponents of Ancestor Christology ensuing, namely, the "humanness," "mythological" and "soteriological and ethical."[242] In the "humanness (biological) argument," Ezigbo sees the emphasis on the Ancestorship of Christ as stemming from the fact of the Incarnation, that is, Christ "taking on a human nature."[243] Nyamiti and Ezeh represent this line of argument for Ezigbo.[244] Even though this approach highlights the genealogy of Christ and is thus helpful in expressing his universal significance, Ezigbo's sentiment is that this "underestimates" the relevance of the question of Jesus becoming an African ancestor when he was biologically a non-African.[245] According to Ezigbo, the fact that traditionally ancestors are regarded as owners of land and custodians of customs, and also the criteria of raising a family and living an exemplary life in obedience to family or societal laws to qualify as

240. Nyamiti, *Jesus Christ, the Ancestor of Humankind*, 226.

241. In his earthly ministry, Jesus clearly demonstrated the need for and nature of the balance between spiritual and economic needs. For example, the feeding of the multitude first, became a launchpad for the need to seek the food that lasts, the bread of life (John 6:1–14, 22–58).

242. Ezigbo, *Re-Imagining African Christologies*, 75ff

243. Ezigbo, *Re-Imagining African Christologies*, 75.

244. Ezigbo relies primarily on Nyamiti's *Christ our Ancestor* and Ezeh's *Jesus Christ the Ancestor*.

245. Ezigbo, *Re-Imagining African Christologies*, 76.

an ancestor, make the question of the eligibility of Jesus' ancestorhood as a non-African important.[246] Ezigbo is however not convinced by the arguments set so far by Nyamiti and Ezeh in addressing this issue and calls for a "meaningful theological response."

I have indicated Ezigbo's concern over the "mythological" foundation. Bujo's approach, for Ezigbo, has as premise the "soteriological and ethical" argument. Bujo has argued that Jesus as Proto-Ancestor is believed to be the "firstborn of all the ancestors" on a soteriological level, rather than biological, to a "mystical and supernatural life and mode of existence."[247] Similarly, Ezeh has maintained that the African "cult of ancestors epitomizes" the quest of salvation (soteriology) and the goodness of life (ethics) and that through his Incarnation Christ, as "perfect God and perfect man," "perfectly fulfilled" these African values (of soteriology and ethics).[248] Ezigbo contends it is "enigmatic" to situate the relationship between Jesus and the (African) ancestors on a soteriological ground as this "overloads" the cult of ancestors with "redemptive concepts" mainly derived from Christianity.[249]

The mediatory work of the ancestors, Ezigbo argues, is "didactical and ethical" and not redemptive, since the "primary concern" of the ancestors is obedience to ancestral laws, which leads to "wellbeing" and the avoidance of any destructive wrath of the gods or Supreme Being.[250] Ezigbo is also right in observing that rather than being "redeemers (buying back the freedom of someone or something held captive)," the ancestors are "guides to the knowledge of the spirit world,"[251] even though they are not alone in this function.[252] There is, nonetheless, common ground on the mediatory role of Jesus Christ and the ancestors in that in both cases the belief in the proximity to God is fundamental even though the degree and nature of function are clearly different. It is with respect to this common ground of being close to God that Bediako, Bujo, and Nyamiti, for example, consider the area of mediation as a point of contact but are also keen on clarifying its nature in both cases.

Nevertheless, Ezigbo's concern with the emphasis on "the mediatory work" of Christ and the ancestors as exhibited in Ancestor Christology is

---

246. Ezigbo, *Re-Imagining African Christologies*, 76.
247. Bujo, *African Christian Morality at the Age of Inculturation*, 82–83.
248. Ezeh, *Jesus Christ the Ancestor*, 316.
249. Ezigbo, *Re-Imagining African Christologies*, 78.
250. Ezigbo, *Re-Imagining African Christologies*, 79.
251. Ezigbo, *Re-Imagining African Christologies*, 79.
252. The deities or *abosom* in the Akan context are also involved in the knowledge of the spiritual world.

that it can lead to the view of Christ as "a mere middleman who connects God and humans."[253] Ezigbo's challenge for proponents of Ancestor Christology is, therefore, to consider "seriously" the "ontological question" of Jesus' identity, since it is "Christologically inadequate" to isolate Jesus' person from discussions on his work.[254] Nyamiti in his essays on the ancestral interpretation of Jesus' person and work, apart from the 1984 *Christ our Ancestor*, has shown awareness of this latter concern and Ezigbo in his assessment here appears to be unaware of them. Furthermore, Ezigbo seems to ignore, though aware of, an equally important premise for these proponents, namely, reckoning Jesus Christ as ancestor "analogically." Perhaps his concerns may be given an additional dimension when the "analogical" argument is also critiqued.

Stanislaus C. Ilo

Stanislaus C. Ilo in his comparative study on the Christological efforts of Nyamiti and Bujo draws attention to some weaknesses in their respective ancestral models and also suggests some guidelines for the future of Ancestor Christology. According to Ilo, Nyamiti does not adequately take into consideration the limitation of his use of analogy when in some African traditional societies the term is a "proper mode of being for God."[255] Not only is the use of "analogy" inadequate in showing Christ's "unique divine identity," Nyamiti's "formal and analytic" use of "ancestral language" in his Christology poses difficulties since African religious discourses are not "propositional or regulative" but "more intuitive and concrete" stemming from a "memorial culture."[256] For Ilo, Nyamiti is not clear when exactly Christ is Ancestor, whether before or after his resurrection and indicating the *natural* or *physical* limitation of qualifying Jesus as Ancestor, such as his violent death at a relatively young age, notes,

> There is thus the problem of the theological interpretation of the identity of African ancestors and how this is applied to Christ without qualification and the problem of the place of Christ as the sole mediator between humanity and God.[257]

---

253. Ezigbo, *Re-Imagining African Christologies*, 80.
254. Ezigbo, *Re-Imagining African Christologies*, 80.
255. Ilo, "African Christology," 131.
256. Ilo, "African Christology," 131–32.
257. Ilo, "African Christology," 132.

Nyamiti's infrequent use of or reference to biblical material is also of a concern for Ilo, who opines that the former could well have mitigated some of his limitations had he "given greater attention to the biblical evidence on the nature and person of Christ."[258]

According to Ilo, Bujo's "idealistic notion of African ancestry and African past" overlooks its shortcomings.[259] For Ilo, Bujo overlooks the serious issue of the oppression of women, minorities, and children in African cultures. For instance, he questions, "if the wisdom of the ancients should guide the present day Africans, how can they meet new challenges of today with worn-out idealized sapiential tradition which Bujo attributes to African ancestors."[260] Ilo also takes issue with the absence of "due attention to women liberation" in Bujo's Christology and that he has no place for women ancestors.[261] Accordingly, a "failure to construct an inclusive theology that finds an equal place for women shows an androcentric bias, which challenges his theology."[262] Both Nyamiti and Bujo use "African theology" in the singular and hence, according to Ilo, fail to recognize the plurality of African realities.[263]

The above shortcomings notwithstanding, Ilo proposes some points for consideration on the future agenda of Ancestor Christology. First, it should wrestle with or relate the Incarnation of Christ to African cultural practices.[264] It should be dependent on the changing context of African anthropology and history. A third point is on the adequacy of the language of its "theological formulation."[265] Finally, it should show awareness of its limitation in symbolizing the divinity of Christ. According to Ilo, the limitations of both Bujo and Nyamiti can be met by a "deeper cultural hermeneutics, deeper recourse to the New Testament Christologies and integration of the dogmatic formulations of the Church on the nature and person of Christ (Nicea, Chalcedon, etc)."[266]

---

258. Ilo, "African Christology," 133. Perhaps as a response to such concerns, Nyamiti pays attention to the *Relevance of New Testament Christologies and the Mysteries of Christ's Life* in a later reflection on Ancestor Christology: Ilo does not cite this particular volume in his study in question. Nyamiti, *Jesus Christ, the Ancestor of Humankind*, 49ff.

259. Ilo, "African Christology," 134.

260. Ilo, "African Christology," 134.

261. Ilo, "African Christology," 135.

262. Ilo, "African Christology," 135.

263. Ilo, "African Christology," 136.

264. Ilo, "African Christology," 137.

265. Ilo, "African Christology," 138.

266. Ilo, "African Christology," 140.

Robert Agyarko also opines that within the Akan (African) context the image of ancestor does not "adequately express the Nicene affirmation" of Jesus Christ as "truly God" and "truly human" and consequently his "atoning work."[267] Accordingly, Agyarko argues that Bujo's Proto-Ancestor model, despite highlighting Christ's role as saviour, nonetheless reduces his person "to a mere human being, or at best a divinised person" and hence cannot express the Nicene affirmation of his person and work adequately.[268] Agyarko regards Nyamiti's' position on the "supernatural (superhuman) sacred status" that an ancestor (usually)[269] acquires through death,[270] as implying that the ancestors are "sacred" and therefore (become) "divine beings."[271] Agyarko contends that, "not all sacred entities are necessarily divine" which is a false assumption he finds Nyamiti to have made.[272] Thus, arguing for Jesus Christ's divinity, according to Agyarko, "along this path of ancestorhood [from sacred status to divinity] . . . would lead to a heresy comparable to Arianism."[273]

Agyarko contends with Bediako's thoughts on the nature and function of the (Akan) ancestors, particularly, their "terrorizing" influence for good or ill.[274] Bediako has made the assertion that through the resurrection and ascension, Christ has "now returned to the realm of spirit, and therefore of power" and that from the point of view of "Akan traditional theology and cosmology" this also means to the "realm of the ancestor spirits, and the gods."[275] However, since Christ has gone to such a realm as "Lord over them [ancestors and gods]," "he sums up in himself all their powers and annuls any terrorizing influence they might be assumed to have upon us."[276] Associating any "terrorizing influence" with the ancestors will be contrary to the definition of ancestor as a "good human spirit"

267. Agyarko, *God's Unique Priest (Nyamesofopreko)*, 69.
268. Agyarko, *God's Unique Priest (Nyamesofopreko)*, 73.
269. Cf. Nyamiti, *Jesus Christ, The Ancestor of Humankind*, 3.
270. Nyamiti, *Christ as Our Ancestor*, 15.
271. Agyarko, *God's Unique Priest (Nyamesofopreko)*, 75.
272. Though in the Akan worldview the ancestors are regarded as "mere human spirits," Agyarko notes, the ancestors who become divinities in the Yoruba context are still considered among the "lesser divinities." Agyarko, *God's Unique Priest (Nyamesofopreko)*, 75.
273. Agyarko, *God's Unique Priest (Nyamesofopreko)*, 75.
274. Agyarko, *God's Unique Priest (Nyamesofopreko)*, 80–81.
275. Bediako, *Biblical Christologies*, 104.
276. Bediako, *Biblical Christologies*, 104.

as there is no such thing as a "bad ancestor."[277] Agyarko is right to note that there are other ghosts or spirits of the deceased who are not regarded as "good" ghosts or spirits (ancestor, *saman pa*). However, in the context of Bediako's assertion, he seems, whether incidentally or not, to refer to the "spirit world" in general which comprise ghosts (good or bad) and the deities.[278] Furthermore, Agyarko observes, for Bediako to maintain a de-sacralization of the ancestors by restoring their humanity on the one hand and on the other make the king first among his fellow humans, means the "ancestors are or have become divinities."[279] Since the ancestors are not regarded as divine, at least among the Akan, and thus are not "worshipped" but "venerated," "one cannot use the image of the ancestor to account for Christ's divinity."[280] Thus the limitation in this case is in the concept itself as inadequate to convey divinity and not the approach.

Robert Aboagye-Mensah had also raised concern regarding the issue of conveying divinity. He observed that the human status of the ancestors, who are seen to have no "divine powers," poses a challenge in expressing the divinity of Jesus when the concept is applied to him. He notes,

> A positive Christological inference to be drawn from the concept of ancestors is that Jesus is one of us in that he once shared in this-worldly life and is now in the sphere of the spirits and power. In this realm he is able and willing to help the living. Negatively, the ancestral concept has a serious defect when applied to Jesus Christ. It cannot be used to speak of His divinity, since ancestors are never considered divine. In view of this it seems to us that the idea of making Jesus the Great and Greatest of Ancestors must be taken cautiously.[281]

Aboagye-Mensah's caution is what Agyarko seems to reiterate by highlighting the Nicene affirmation. Agyarko, however, also enumerates six points he sees Ancestor Christology to rightfully express: Jesus founds a new and universal community; he participates in the life of human community; he is custodian of public morality; he is a "role model" or exemplar; revering him as Ancestor deepens the African spirituality which was linked to the reverence of ancestors; declaring Jesus as Ancestor also ensures credibility

---

277. Agyarko, *God's Unique Priest (Nyamesofopreko)*, 81.

278. Bediako first refers to "ancestor spirits, and the gods" and then a few lines below he indicates "Jesus has gone to the realm of 'spirits and the gods.'" Bediako, *Biblical Christologies*, 104.

279. Agyarko, *God's Unique Priest (Nyamesofopreko)*, 82.

280. Agyarko, *God's Unique Priest (Nyamesofopreko)*, 82.

281. Aboagye-Mensah, "Socio-Political Thinking of Karl Barth," 444.

and respect for Christianity.[282] According to Agyarko, his challenge, however, is with the intermediary role ascribed to the ancestors between God and humans and subsequently summarizes his contention as follows,

> Firstly, the notion of "Jesus as ancestor" does not capture adequately what is at stake in the doctrine of Trinity. Secondly, if Jesus is not truly God, it then follows that it is inappropriate to worship him, because the Christian faith accords worship only to God. Thirdly, and on a more serious note, categorising Jesus as being amongst the ancestors leads to some serious confusion between the (Nicene) Christian understanding of Jesus' resurrection as one "risen from the dead" or as one who merely made "appearances beyond death."[283]

Agyarko's concern to safeguard the Nicene and Chalcedon understanding of Jesus as truly God and man is paradoxically the point from which Ezeh, for example, takes his departure in his assessment and affirmation of Ancestor Christology. There is no interaction with Ezeh in Agyarko's arguments here. Nyamiti in particular has applied extensively the ancestral concept in his explication of the mystery of the Trinity and one can hardly say he is not abreast with what is "at stake in the doctrine of Trinity."

Clifton Clarke on Ancestor Christology Among Akan AICs

Clifton Clarke's work on the Christology among African [Akan] Indigenous [Independent] Churches [AICs] in Ghana shows how the image of Jesus as Ancestor is of little importance in these churches.[284] The Akan title of *nana* ("ancestor") when applied to Jesus presented "a different level of engagement."[285] For Clarke, even though the term *nana* would be favorable, "it appears that this is down to language familiarization not theological appropriation."[286] In view of this, Clarke questions Pobee's suggestion of Jesus as Nana, arguing that "the centrality of the Bible within the context of Akan AICs would make it unlikely that such a traditional and non-biblical title

---

282. Agyarko, *God's Unique Priest (Nyamesofopreko)*, 97.

283. Agyarko, *God's Unique Priest (Nyamesofopreko)*, 98.

284. His doctoral thesis "Faith in Christ in Post-Missionary Africa (Christology Among Akan African Indigenous Churches in Ghana)" (University of Birmingham, 2002), subsequently published as Clarke, *African Christology—Jesus in Post-Missionary African Christianity*.

285. Clarke, *African Christology*, 92.

286. Clarke, *African Christology*, 92.

ANCESTOR CHRISTOLOGY AND THE PROCESS OF CONVERSION

be applied to Jesus."[287] Clarke rather suggests an approach that applies "the nature of the ancestral relationship" of the Akan to the relationship of Jesus as "Son of God" or "Servant of God" as well as "other such terminology that can engage with both the Akan worldview as well as the Bible and indigenous African Christians."[288] In other words,

> it is not theological legitimation and proposition of African terminological usage of traditional concepts that gives validation, but scriptural affirmation, and therefore any terminology that will be employed by AICs must be one that can mediate between the biblical worldview and that of the African.[289]

Though Clarke's concerns are understandable, his view of "scriptural affirmation" seems limited. To begin with, the images of Jesus Christ, in the New Testament, such as Lord and Logos had Hellenistic meanings at the time of Christian preaching. The benefit of the LXX made the transition into Christian proclamation less problematic, while at the same time their contextual appropriation needed some working out. For example, proclaiming "Lord Jesus" in the religious context of Hellenistic "lords many" though scriptural needed a clarification of how he is not *like* the "lords" in that context. If, for instance, the Akan translation of honorific titles in the Bible takes *nana*, would proclaiming Nana Yesu then be a "scriptural affirmation" in the end? Scriptural affirmation is not limited to titular equivalents but also conceptual as well as dynamic associations.

In terms of method, Clarke raises a fair concern when he indicates that, "*ancestor* is a concept that is familiar to the African, but the discourse in which Christ is inculturated as ancestor is foreign to the African setting."[290] He thereby points to the foundation of *oral* Christian reflections for eventual *systematic* Christology. A concluding remark, however, that Clarke makes on the Christology of the Akan AICs is quite interesting. Clarke notes further how "Akan AICs have defined Christ as the empowering one to whom they can address their questions and concerns like *their benevolent ancestor*."[291] If the Akan AICs can relate to Jesus like "their benevolent ancestor," why is it that he cannot be seen as their Ancestor?

---

287. Clarke, *African Christology*, 92.
288. Clarke, *African Christology*, 92.
289. Clarke, *African Christology*, 92–93.
290. Clarke, *African Christology*, 171.
291. Clarke, *African Christology*, 174. Emphasis added.

Conclusion

Ancestor Christology in Africa is in a *refiguration* stage; it has gone through the modes of suggestion and clarification and it is in a mode of innovative application. What is apparent is that the various proponents have taken distinctive points of departure in communicating the one *reality* of Jesus Christ with the category of the concept of ancestor. Apart from informing the doctrine of the Church in Africa (theology and Christology) and its existence (ecclesiology), Ancestor Christology is to specifically inform her preaching (kerygma). For example, what is the significance of proclaiming Jesus as the Nana (implicit in all its connotations) in the Akan context? Akan Christians must continually demonstrate the relevance of Nana Yesu (Jesus) to their shared inherited tradition and the contemporary social and political challenges.

The various critiques of Ancestor Christology are necessary signposts for its journey in the Christian conversion of Africa. On the issue of divinity, I submit that one does not lose sight of the development of Logos Christology and that it was not *easy* for the early Christians to communicate the humanity of Jesus Christ once they affirmed him to be the Logos. This was a challenge to non-Christian minds such as Celsus and undoubtedly would have also been for the Hellenistic-Jewish mind of Philo. Writers such as Justin, Clement and Origen diversely worked out the implications of the bold missiological stroke "and the Logos became flesh" in their respective vocations. The general recourse was to the fact that if it was not impossible for the Greek gods to have human offspring, then it was much less impossible for the Almighty God to have his Son become human (for the sake of humanity). Logos Christology essentially did not deny the humanity of Jesus Christ. Justin and Clement in their clear view of Jesus' nature and capacity as the Logos did not see his humanity as being at stake. Origen took an alternate path in addressing the "Logos became flesh" by indicating the eternal inseparable union of the soul of the man Jesus and the Logos. The fact that Jesus Christ is the divine Logos did not make him less human in his Incarnation.

It seems to me that the *fear* of diminishing the divinity of Jesus Christ with the endeavor of Ancestor Christology stems largely from the deposit of the creedal formulations. However, one cannot take for granted the Christological endeavors prior to the respective councils. Ezeh rightly sees some implications of these councils for Ancestor Christology. If, as Nyamiti observes, we take the approach to the "mystery of Jesus Christ" from the standpoint of his humanity to show his superiority and transcendence over all human institutions, we may certainly assume but not deny his divinity.[292] In any case, we speak of divinity from our humanness. The Fourth Gospel harmoniously expresses this traffic between Jesus' divinity and humanity: he did what he did because he is the Logos and because he is the Logos, with an unfailing love for his creation, he did what he has done.

Is it impossible to arrive at the divinity of Jesus by exploring his ancestorship? If the answer is in the negative, then Ancestor Christology can be an ongoing project, requiring generational inputs.[293] If, however, one answers in the affirmative, then we may further question his or her view of the experience of the first disciples of Jesus Christ. For Jesus is not seen, per the Gospel accounts, declaring "I am the Son of the living God, believe in me!" Rather, in the wisdom of God, the Logos chose to dwell among his people, in the everyday encounter of human challenges so that through that experience he may show them, and us, what God is *truly* like. Out of this experience of his humanness was met with the revelation from God, so Peter could declare, "You are the Messiah, the Son of the Living God."

At the *refiguration* stage, there is the need for a more conscious mother-tongue approach to the innovative application of Ancestor Christology in respective communities in Africa. This can give adequate attention to any nuances of the indigenous terminology of "ancestor" for further exploration in Christology. In view of the importance of the mother-tongue Scriptures in Christian apprehension and its related sense of identity, a pursued contextualized biblical image can serve as a model and complement to the Christological exploration of an African image. In the next chapter, I propose a dialogue between a contextualized (Akan) apprehension of the foundational Logos (Asɛm) Christology in the Fourth Gospel and the pursuit of a Nana (Ancestor) Christology. I see as vital for a Christology that seeks to be biblical and relevant for the Akan, an Akan Christian apprehension of Jesus as the Asɛm with the backdrop of this same Jesus as the Nana. After all, the Graeco-Roman Christian and the Akan Christian are both members of one body, which is Christ.

---

292. Nyamiti, *Jesus Christ, the Ancestor of Humankind*, 27.

293. Walls, *The Cross-Cultural Process in Christian History*, 75. "Christian faith, therefore, is necessarily ancestor-conscious, aware of the previous generations of faith. It cannot divinize the ancestors, however, for their continuing significance comes only from God's activity in and towards them. The work of salvation is cross-generational, and never completed in one generation."

Chapter 6

The Logos as Nana (Ancestor)
Towards a Logos-Ancestor Christology

My inference from the thoughts of the various proponents of Ancestor Christology, examined in the previous chapter, is that the basis of Jesus Christ's Ancestorship is an emphasis on his death.[1] The significance of his death, in my judgment, guarantees any attempt to conceive of him in the light of the concept of ancestor. The fact of his resurrection does not nullify his Ancestorship, no more than his Incarnation belittles the fact that he is the Logos. The Logos became flesh; he lived among us and died for our sins and was raised from the dead to become the "firstborn from (among) the dead" (*ewufo mu abakan*).[2]

The Translated Bible and Indigenous Christology

The creative stage of African Christian reflection requires an innovative use of the everyday indigenous languages of African Christians.[3] Certainly there are areas where European languages such as English and French are actively employed in Christian worship. Yet African traditional institutions

---

1. Kwesi Dickson's remark that Christ the "perfect victim" of the supreme sacrifice of God merits the African image of ancestor by his death remains significant. Dickson, *Theology in Africa*, 197–98.

2. Colossians 1:18; Revelation 1:5 (ὁ πρωτότοκος τῶν νεκρῶν).

3. Philip T. Laryea's work on the association of Jesus Christ with the Ga traditional festival *Hɔmɔwɔ* primarily in the Ga language is a worthy example in this connection. Laryea, *Yesu Hɔmɔwɔ Nuntsɔ*.

such as chieftaincy continue to operate in the indigenous language as for example among the Akan of Ghana. There can hardly be an enduring impact if Akan Christians attempt any creative engagement with the institution of chieftaincy in any other language than say Mfantse or Twi. Akan Ancestor Christology remains an essential avenue to reach the heart of Akan traditional thinking. The pursuit of an Akan Ancestor Christology therefore requires a continuous effort in using the Twi language in related discourses. Although language may not be the only issue at stake, nevertheless it remains essential. The Akan ancestors, after all, do speak Twi. The translated Christian Bible is a veritable component in indigenous Christian theological reflections. It grants that common ground needed for the encounter between Christian and traditional (indigenous) thoughts and hence also a viable means to the cradle of traditional institutions.[4] Christian affirmation ensuing from the interaction of biblical thought and indigenous thinking essentially ought to be expressed in the "host" language. Logos Christology enjoyed this privilege in the Greek language. Its suggestive stage and working out, through to its innovative application were all in the language in which the pre-Christian understanding had been explored.

Having examined distinctively the ideas of *logos* and *ancestor* and their respective exploration in Christology, my focus in this section is an exploration of an Akan Ancestor Christology pursued in conversation with an Akan reading of the foundational Johannine Logos Christology. J. B. Danquah's exploration of the Akan idea of *nana* is our point of departure here.[5] This complementary exercise remains relevant considering on the one hand, the need for an indigenous expression of Ancestor Christology and on the other, the fundamental role of biblical thought in subsequent Christian expressions. In the process I also seek to address some of the hitherto expressed limitations of Ancestor Christology.

---

4. Bediako, "Scripture as the Hermeneutic of Culture and Tradition," 2–11. Bediako, "Biblical Exegesis in Africa," 12–20. Bediako, for instance, drawing from the example of the Liberian Christian prophet William Wade Harris' use of the Bible as being in line with the African pattern of "participation in" the truth, intimates that the Scriptures be reckoned as "context, so that persons of varied cultural backgrounds can enter and participate in them, bringing their own cultural worlds of meaning with them" (Bediako, "Biblical Exegesis in Africa," 16). It can also be noted that as these "cultural worlds of meaning" are brought into the interpretation of the translated Scriptures, the common ground of language allows for the opening up of the "cultural world" to the reality of truth inherent in the Scriptures.

5. Though Danquah used the capitalized 'Nana,' we will employ an italicized "*nana*" and use "Nana" when it is applied to Jesus Christ. I retain the form of the word in verbatim quotes from Danquah's work.

Jesus Christ as the Expected and Discovered (Revealed) Messiah

It is quite evident that Danquah's exploration of the *nana* concept was done with a conscious indigenous thinking on the matter, although the eventual write up was in English. His suggestion of the Akan idea of *nana* as a "discovered" Messiah in contradiction to the Judeo-Christian "expected" Messiah is already a form of the critical engagement of Christian understanding with indigenous Akan thought, at least at a certain degree. Danquah did not approach his subject as a technical Christian theologian. Nonetheless his theological efforts as a conscious believer of Christian teaching certainly led him to such a comparison.[6] In my view, this is a necessary step for further exploration.[7] My engagement with Danquah's views in the light of an Akan reading of the Prologue of the Fourth Gospel does reveal that Jesus Christ, the Nana, can be looked on as both the expected and discovered Messiah who at once brings near to us the knowledge of God and its consequential transcendental moral vision for the Akan community.

Danquah did not make extensive use of biblical references, particularly the New Testament, in his exposition of the Akan idea of *nana*. However, that he was familiar with the Fourth Gospel and its Prologue is shown in his reference at two separate instances to John 1:1[8] and John 1:14.[9] The reference to John 1:1 is of immediate relevance at the present. There is an indigenous Akan song, a "mythical ditty" according to Danquah,[10] which talks of a beginning of creation:

> Hena kɔse, hena kɔse, hena kɔse?
> Hena na okɔsee 'Te,
> Maa 'Te kɔsee Ananse,
> Maa Ananse kɔsee Odomankoma,
> Maa Odomankoma bɔɔ adee?
> . . .

---

6. For instance, in his concluding statements in the *Ancestors, Heroes and God*, Danquah indicates "I think of religion, and see a blurI think of Jesus and I see a person, a lovable person. I think of God and I see Jesus. God is like Jesus. He is the Father, and he the Son, and we are all his sons, through Jesus." Danquah, *Ancestors, Heroes and God*, 46.

7. Danquah, for all that could be said for or against his method, attempted to reconstruct Akan religious and philosophical thought primarily through its proverbs, relying on the work of an earlier Christian missionary. From a Christian missiological perspective, the *Akan Doctrine of God* remains an indispensable deposit.

8. Danquah, *Gold Coast Akan Laws*, 250 n.1.

9. Danquah, *The Akan Doctrine of God*, 175.

10. Danquah, *The Akan Doctrine of God*, 43.

> Who said, who said, who said?
> Who said to Hearing (te—to hear),
> That Hearing told Ananse,
> That Ananse told the Creator,
> That the Creator made the World?[11]

Danquah referred the reader to "compare the idea behind the sentence ['Who said to Hearing'] with 'In the beginning was the Word, and the Word (λόγος) was God.'"[12]

According to Danquah, one becomes an *opanyin* (elder) before becoming a *nana* (ancestor). A *nana* is an *opanyin*, Danquah asserts, who at the time of his death was or is still held in honour and dignity by way of the activity of his life and has not suffered any disgrace.[13] An *opanyin* is not born as such, according to Danquah, judging from the proverb *Obi nhyee da nwoo panyin pen*, which Danquah renders as "No one by design ever gave birth to opanyin." He is made, discovered by his community, according to Danquah, "as much as he makes his community, good," and having satisfied all requirements at death is then "truly deifiable, a proved divinity, bearer of the supreme moral ideal, a Nana, the exemplar and paradigm of Nyankopon, what God in Himself is, or ought to be."[14] In this sense, for Danquah, the *nana* is a "*discovered* or *revealed* Messiah" in contradistinction to the Hebrew "*expected* Messiah."[15]

The Akan ancestor is primarily an exemplar of the ethical standard conceived by the community. The qualifications, therefore, for an *opanyin*, who will be an ancestor, barring any disgrace prior to death, are that which, as far as the Akan are concerned, ensure the health and growth of

---

11. Danquah, *Gold Coast Akan Laws*, 250 with Danquah's translation.
12. Danquah, *Gold Coast Akan Laws*, 250 n.1.
13. Danquah, *The Akan Doctrine of God*, 122.
14. Danquah, *The Akan Doctrine of God*, 122.
15. Danquah, *The Akan Doctrine of God*, 120. Emphasis mine. Danquah used the words "discovered" and "revealed" interchangeably to apparently indicate the sense of "finding out." For instance, he notes that "by a gradual process of elimination the elected head of the community generally called *opanyin*—who had survived the great trial and ordeal of headship, was, on his death, discovered as a revelation of the ideal good The discovery had, in fact, taken place at an earlier stage, when as a member of the general mass of the family, he had been selected the fittest person to rule and lead his community. The revelation became complete, the discovery confirmed, when the Opanyin reached a stage fitting him for deification; when, that is, overtaken by death, he still was an honoured man. He had proved himself a ruler well and truly anointed of his people, an Opanyin became a Nana." I have maintained this sense of both words in our discussion herein.

the community.¹⁶ Among others, an *opanyin* should have started a family with wife and children and should be in good physical condition and die naturally at a good old age. An *opanyin* is expected to be welcomed in *Asamando*,¹⁷ the spiritual society, which is a projection of the physical one, having led such an exemplary life.

Towards an Akan Reading of the Prologue of the Fourth Gospel

The incipient Logos Christology of the Prologue can be accessed in any language following the principle of the translation of the Christian Scriptures.¹⁸ Respective expressions and subsequent application may differ from one language to another. Nevertheless, the fundamental fact remains that God's principal reality in operation from the beginning "became flesh" in the person of Jesus of Nazareth. This can be expressed in any language though not necessarily in the same way. Once this is granted, it paves the way to think of an indigenous Logos Christology. An Akan Logos Christology, therefore, can ensue, attempting to express in the Akan languages and with Akan categories of thought the fundamental facts of the Prologue. Our attempt here is not for its own sake, but as a complement to an indigenous expression of associating Jesus Christ with an idea that is fundamental to the traditional Akan thought, namely, the idea of *nana*.

I allude to Danquah's views, whenever possible, in my Akan (mainly Mfantse) reading of parts of the Prologue under four themes with the Logos as the subject matter. These themes and their related verses, I deem, are more related to the concerns of Danquah in his exposition of *nana*, namely, "expected," "discovered" and "exemplar." The discussions are more "expositional" than "exegetical," contrary to, for example, M. S. Tshehla's reading of the Prologue in Sesotho, which is more "exegetical."¹⁹

Logos Incarnate, Asɛm a abɛyɛ honam , vss. 1–5, 14

1. Mfitiaseɛ no, na Asɛm no wɔ hɔ, na Asɛm no ne Onyankopɔn na ewɔ hɔ, na Asɛm no yɛ Onyankopɔn.
2. Ɔno ara na mfitiaseɛ no na ɔne Onyankopɔn wɔ hɔ

16. Dzobo, "Values in a Changing Society," 233–34.
17. Also as *asamann*. See Christaller, *Dictionary*, 423.
18. See chapter two above for the view of the foundation of Logos Christology in the Prologue of the Fourth Gospel.
19. Tshehla, "Reading John 1:1–18 in Sesotho," 54.

3. Ɛnam ne so na wɔyɔɔ ade nyinaa, na wɔankwati no anyɔ biribiara a wɔyɔeɛ.
4. Ne mu na nkwa wɔ, na nkwa no ne nnipa hann;
5. na hann no hyerɛn esum mu, na esum no anni no so.
. . .
14. Na Asɛm no bɛyɛɛ honam, na ɔbɛtenaa yɛn mu, na yɛhunuu n'animounyam sɛ agya no no ba a wɔwoo no korɔ animuonyam, na adom ne nokorɛ ayɛ no ma.[20]

1. Ahyɛse no na Asɛm no wɔ hɔ, na Asɛm no nye Nyankopɔn wɔ hɔ, na Asɛm no yɛ Nyame (Nyankopɔn).
2. Ɔnoara na ahyɛse no ɔnye Nyankopɔn wɔ hɔ.
3. Wɔnam no do yɛɛ adze nyina na woennkwetsi no annyɛ biribiara a wɔyɛe.
4. No mu na nkwa wɔ, na nkwa no nye nyimpa ne kan.
5. Na kan no hyerɛn wɔ sum mu, na sum no annkyer (na sum no nntum nnhyɛ do)
. . .
14. Na Asɛm no bɛyɛɛ honam, na ɔbɔsoeɛ hɛn mu (na ɔnye hɛn bɛtsenae), na yehun n'enyimnyam dɛ Egya no ne Ba kortoo no n'enyimnyam a adom nye nokwar ahyɛ no mã.[21]

Logos (λόγος) appears four times in the Prologue: three times in 1:1 and once in 1:14. In all instances it refers to a being and thus is not used in the ordinary sense. It is worth noting that in the Gospel narrative Jesus does not refer to himself as Logos or "Logos of God" and neither does the author.[22] The connection is however indirectly made in between two verses (1:14 & 17).

In 1 John 1:1 the author speaks "concerning the word of life" as "what was from the beginning . . . heard . . . seen . . . looked at and touched with our hands." The author writes concerning Jesus Christ with whom there has been a close association. The other New Testament reference with a close association of Jesus (the Son) and God and "his powerful word [or word of power]" is Hebrew 1:3 (though *rhema* is used in this instance). In Revelation 19:13 the name of him who sat on the white horse is "the Logos of God" which evidently is (the glorified) Jesus Christ.

There is nowhere in the Prologue or even in the rest of the narrative that we are told explicitly that the Logos is Jesus or that the Logos "become

---

20. UBS Asante Twi, 1964.

21. UBS Mfantse 1974. The alternative reading in parentheses is the UBS 1982 renderings.

22. Bernard, *A Critical and Exegetical Commentary*, cxxxviii.

flesh" is Jesus.[23] In the Prologue "Jesus Christ" is only mentioned in relation to Moses (1:17). But there is an indirect connection made in 1:14 and 1:17 in seeing Jesus as the Logos that became flesh. The Logos became flesh "full of grace and truth" and while the Law was "given" (*mae*) through Moses, "grace and truth" "came" (*bae*) through Jesus. It is noteworthy in 1:17 that whereas the Law was "given" to Moses by God, that is, the Law came from God and was given through Moses, "grace and truth" "came" through Jesus Christ. Thus, also it can only be from Jesus' fullness (πληρώματος, *amayɛ*) that we all receive "grace upon grace." Here too the connection between Jesus (Son) and God (Father) is alluded to, namely, that Jesus does what the father does and hence sharing in the Father's essence as 1:1 put it emphatically.

The essential thought behind the Logos in the Prologue may well be the active prophetic word of revelation, *Dabar YHWH* (the word of the LORD), in Hebrew thought and its synonymous Aramaic rendering *memra*. The Akan word "*asɛm*" translates the word *logos* as well as the equivalent *rhema* and the Hebrew *dabar*.[24] Thus, the Akan reading of the association of *asɛm* and Nyankopɔn would have the background of "Nyankopɔn *asɛm*" as we meet in the Old Testament.[25]

The *Asɛm* was (*wɔ*, "existed") in the beginning (*ahyɛse*) with (*nye*) Nyankopɔn and was (*yɛ*, "existed as") Nyankopɔn (Nyame). The Asɛm therefore cannot be dissociated from Nyankopɔn and hence is as old as Nyankopɔn, in that as long as Nyankopɔn has been from the beginning the Asɛm has been (*wɔ hɔ*).[26] The Akan translation renders the Greek ἐγένετο (aorist indicative middle of γίγνομαι "come into being") in its instances in 1:3 & 10 as *yɛɛ* (made).[27] Thus *wɔnam no do yɛɛ adze nyina* or *wɔnam no do yɛɛ wiadze* brings out the instrumentality of the Asɛm; through the Asɛm "all

---

23. Bernard, *A Critical and Exegetical Commentary*, cxxxviii.

24. Where the word *logos* refers to Jesus the word is capitalized (*Asɛm*) in the Akan version of the Bible. Although it is difficult to indicate capitalization in an oral presentation (unless of course one uses stress in pronunciation), the reader is guided to recognize the significance of the word in context and not to treat it as he or she would ordinarily.

25. Psalm 33:6 "*Ewuradze n'sɛem na ɔdze yɛɛ ɔsor; Na n'anomu ehuhuw na ɔdze yɛɛ no mu dɔm nyinara.*"

26. Brown's rendering of πρὸς τὸν θεὸν as "in God's presence," which in Mfantse would be *Nyankopɔn n'enyim* (lit. 'in front of God'), may also carry this sense of the Asɛm being with God from the beginning. The picture of the Asɛm in God's presence waiting to execute his command seems quite vivid in this sense of πρὸς τὸν θεὸν (in Akan thinking) than the sense 'with'. Brown, *The Gospel according to John I–XII*, 3–5. Genesis 3:8; Exodus 18:12; 33:14 *et al*.

27. Christaller, *Dictionary*, 583–85, 586–87: *Yɛ* "to come or enter into existence, be created or produced"; *ɔyɛ* "the act of making, doing, performing"; *yɛbea* "manner of making"; *ɔyɛfo* "maker, doer, author" or even "mischief maker."

things were" or "the world was" made. An alternate reading with the rendering of ἐγένετο as *bae* would run *wɔnam no do na adze nyina / wiadze bae* or *beyɛɛ hɔ* ("all things" or the world came or became through him, πάντα / ὁ κόσμος δι᾽ αὐτοῦ ἐγένετο).[28] It is the Asɛm, then, superior to *Ananse*, who both heard and gave expression to Odomankoma's creative activity.[29]

In the (*no mu*) Asɛm was (*wɔ*) *nkwa* (ζωὴ, "life"). The *nananom* are considered sources of biological and communal life. The Asɛm, as Nyankopɔn, is the source of life of even the *nananom*. The *nkwa* of the Asɛm is linked to humanity as its light (*kan*). In some sense, the *nananom* become the *kan* of their communities, since their directives are desired in times of difficulties. As Nana, then, the Asɛm is the primary source of *kan* for *nyimpa* (humanity) since from the beginning the Asɛm was with Nyankopɔn. The link between *kan* and *sum* (darkness) also points to Genesis 1:2–3 where, at Nyankopɔn's directive, *ekan bae* ("there was light") in the midst of *isum* (darkness).

The word *asɛm* itself is ambiguous in meaning as Johannes Christaller might have observed in his six sub-definitions.[30] Interestingly, Christaller did not cite John 1:1 as an example in his definitions of *asɛm*. He rather referred to John 19:19, where *asɛm* renders the Greek τίτλον ("title") as that which Pontius Pilate placed on the cross of Jesus which read "Jesus of Nazareth, the King of the Jews." According to Christaller, *asɛm* can mean, among other things, "word, talk, speech, saying, tale, story, history . . . matter [thing, problem, issue] . . . transaction in words . . . manners, demeanour."

The following proverbs and expressions demonstrate the dynamism of *asɛm*:

> ɔkāā me asɛm bi
> He or she told me something [news, story][31]

> asɛm no nyɛ me hõ asɛm
> This matter [thing] is no concern of mine[32]

> Asɛm a ɛsene ɔhene wɔ hɔ[33] / Asɛm a esen hene wo ho[34]
> There is a problem [matter] which is beyond even the chief[35]

---

28. John 1:17 renders *bae* for ἐγένετο. Cf. Genesis 1:3 *et al.*
29. Cf. Danquah, *The Akan Doctrine of God*, 44.
30. Christaller, *Dictionary*, 437–38.
31. Christaller, *Dictionary*, 437.
32. Christaller, *Dictionary*, 437.
33. Appiah et al., *Bu Me Bɛ*, 247 no. 5485.
34. Christaller in Danquah, *Akan Doctrine*, 196. no.2857.
35. Appiah et al., *Bu Me Bɛ*, 247.

There is a reality greater than the King[36]

Asεm ba a, na abεbuo aba
When the occasion arises, a proverb comes to mind[37]
When a matter (problem, issue) arises there is opportunity for proverbs (my translation)

Asεm bi nni adanseε a, yεtwa ho bi yε danseε
If an affair [matter] has no witness, we cut part of it as a witness[38]

Asεm is not only used in relation to humans and everyday life but also with respect to the Supreme Reality. Two proverbs that relate the words *asεm* and Nyame or Onyame (God), as does John 1:1 in its literal reading, are considered here.[39] The first proverb indicates the sovereignty and omnipotence of God and the limitation of humans in that humans cannot undo what God does. With its variant forms, it runs,

Asεm a Onyame adi abua no, ateasefoɔ ntumi nsesa no[40]
A case which God has tried and judged cannot be changed by living persons[41]
Men cannot change God's decision[42]

Asεm a Onyame adi asie no, Oteasefo nnan no[43]
The order God has settled living man cannot subvert[44]

Asεm a Nyame edzi esie no, dasanyi nndan no[45]
A matter that Onyame has settled cannot be changed by the living (my translation).

The other proverb with *asεm* and Nyame, *nsεm nyinaa ne Nyame*, has attracted a few renditions. The challenge is not just because it contains the

---

36. Danquah, *Akan Doctrine*, 196.
37. Appiah et al., *Bu Me Bε*, 247 no. 5492.
38. Appiah et al., *Bu Me Bε*, 247 no. 5498.
39. These two proverbs are taken as predating the coming of Christianity among the Akan.
40. Appiah et al., *Bu Me Bε*, 247 no. 5483.
41. Appiah et al., *Bu Me Bε*, 247 no. 5483.
42. Bannerman, *Mfantse—Akan Mbεbusεm Nkyerεkyerεmu*, 51.
43. Christaller in Danquah, *The Akan Doctrine of God*, 196. no.2855.
44. Danquah, *Akan Doctrine*, 196. no.2855.
45. Annobil, *Mbεbusεm Nkyerεkyereemu*, 55.

ambiguous *asɛm*, it also has the quite tricky verb *ne* ("to be"). Christaller's note on *ne* in relation to a similar verb *yɛ* is a helpful background:

> When *ne* is used, the subject coincides with the predicate, or entirely absorbs the characteristics of the predicate; when *yɛ* is used, the subject partakes of the characteristics of the predicate.[46]

Christaller provides the following as examples; *ɔne hene* translates "he is the king (the one reigning from the time in the country of the speaker)," while *ɔyɛ ɔhene* means "he is a king (as there are other kings beside him)."

The proverb *nsɛm nyinaa ne Nyame* may well be literally rendered into English as "All things (matters) [or the sum of all things] is God." There are various renderings from the standpoint of linguists, philosophers, and theologians. In his comment on the proverb, C. A. Akrofi, a notable Christian Akan linguist, indicated the meaning of the proverb as *nyansa nyina fi Nyame* ["all wisdom is from Nyame"] and thus rendered it as "All wisdom is from God."[47] The *nsɛm* (issues) of life (*abrabɔ mu nsɛm*) are what proverbs largely capture and as Laryea rightly notes, "the totality" of the happenings in life "is grounded in God and hence the proverb."[48] In this regard Laryea also indicated a possible parallel between the proverb *Nsɛm nyina ne Nyame* and the Akan rendering of John 1:1c "*Asɛm no yɛ Onyankopɔn (Nyame).*"[49] I shall return to this shortly.

According to the Ghanaian (Akan) philosopher, Kwame Gyekye, *Nsɛm nyina ne Nyame* is one of such Akan proverbs that "indicate that Onyame [God] is the ultimate or absolute reality" and he thus rendered it as "All things are dependent upon Onyame."[50] Kwame Bediako also follows Gyekye's translation and has argued that this proverb "held a particular and

---

46. Christaller, *Dictionary*, 332. See also Laryea's application of this understanding of *ne* in his comment on Ephraim Amu's expression *Yesu ne nhwɛso* ["example," (something) "to look upon" or "imitate"] where he maintains that "Jesus has absorbed in himself those elements that constitute *nhwɛso*." Laryea, "Christianity As Vernacular Religion," 173–74.

47. Akrofi, *Twi Mmbusɛm*, 169. Bediako sees a Christian influence in Akrofi's translation. Bediako, *Religion, Culture and Language*, 4.

48. Laryea, "Christianity As Vernacular Religion," 154.

49. Laryea also indicates the possibility of formulating an "Asɛm" Christology "using categories from Akan sources" following his discussion on Ephraim Amu's composition from a reflection on Luke 2:8–20. He maintained that the "Asɛm" (*rhema*) of Luke 2:15 is about Jesus, the "Asɛm" (*logos*) that became flesh (John 1:1). Laryea, "Christianity As Vernacular Religion," 178.

50. Gyekye, *An Essay on African Philosophical Thought*, 71.

greater significance" in Danquah's "intellectual scheme and argument."⁵¹ Bediako's justification is that Danquah regarded the proverb as "the last of all the [Akan] maxims" and hence rendered it as "God is the justification (End-Cause) of all things."⁵² Danquah made use of this proverb in his discussions on the relationship between his perceived triad of *Onyame, Onyankopon* and *Odomankoma*.⁵³

Asɛm, therefore, from the proverb in question, is associated with "all things" and "wisdom." So that whether "all things are dependent upon Onyame" or that Onyame is "the justification of all things," the fact is "all things" (*nsɛm nyina*) result from "a-thing" (*asɛm*); an *asɛm* leads to *nsɛm*.

Bediako's comment on the (Akuapem) Twi of John 1:1 (*Mfiase no na Asem no wo ho, na Asem no ne Nyankopon na ewo ho, na Asem no ye Onyankopon*) in the light of *Nsɛm nyina ne Nyame* is instructive especially when considered in conjunction with Danquah's vision of the Akan idea of *nana*. Taking the sense of *asɛm* as referring to "reality as experienced or observed,"⁵⁴ Bediako notes that to an "Akan mind that is exposed to Christ," this verse points to Christ who "appears to signify precisely this kind of self-evident truth or reality as *Asem*" [which is associated with God from the beginning].⁵⁵

To this I submit that for the Akan Christian who shares, more or less, Danquah's portrait of the Akan ideal personage enshrined in the idea of *nana* as revealing the "self-evident" reality of the Akan people, Jesus Christ as the Asɛm, existing with Nyankopɔn from the beginning and being Onyankopɔn can *naturally* be said to embody the idea of *nana*. In a similar way, the non-Christian Akan is also invited to experience the one "self-evident reality or truth" who has been from the beginning with Nyankopɔn with the guarantee of realizing that "self-evident truth or reality" that both fulfils and transcends what the Akan envisages in the *nana*. The Asɛm is thus the Nana.

An understanding of the Incarnation was key in the development and application of Logos Christology. According to Justin Martyr, the Logos who "took shape, and became man, and was called Jesus Christ" is the one

---

51. Bediako, *Religion, Culture and Language*, 5.

52. Bediako, *Religion, Culture and Language*, 5. Cf. Danquah, *The Akan Doctrine of God*, 63.

53. Danquah, *The Akan Doctrine of God*, 63.

54. For example, the proverbs (*Asɛm a ɛsene ɔhene wɔ hɔ*, "There is a reality greater than the King') and (*Asɛm bi nni adansee a, yetwa ho bi yɛ dansee*, "If an affair [matter] has no witness, we cut part of it as a witness')

55. Bediako, "Biblical Exegesis in Africa," 16.

"of whom every race of men were partakers."[56] Of importance to the explorations in Ancestor Christology is the fact that the Logos became flesh and dwelt among humans.[57]

How can the Asɛm become *honam* [or *onipa*]?[58] The question of this mystery of the Logos becoming "flesh" is one that not only the Akan, but also every "cultural world" in its encounter with Christianity is invited to give an answer to. The Logos is primarily interested in humanity: *Ɔwɔ wiadze, na wɔnam no do yɛɛ wiadze, na wiadze ennhu no* ("He was in the world, and the world came into being through him; yet the world did not know him" [1:10]). In his relation to humanity, the labor of the Logos is to make humans children of God (*Nyankopɔn mba*) (1:12).

The importance of the family (*abusua*) in Akan traditional thinking is expressed in the notion that every human (born of a woman) belongs to a family and hence, especially among the males, is a potential "opanyin to become a nana." The Asɛm qualifies, on this score, to be looked upon as the Nana because he became flesh and took his dwelling (*ɔbɔsoɛɛ*) among humanity (both Jews and Gentiles) in an *abusua*.

The Expected One vss. 6–9

A further theme in the Prologue that connects with Danquah's understanding of *nana* is the sense of the Logos incarnate as the expected one.

6. Nyimpa bi bae a Nyankopɔn somaa no a ne dzin dze John.
7. Ɔnoara na ɔbaa adasedzi, dɛ oribedzi kan no ho dase, ma nyimpa nyina eedua no do agye edzi.
8. Nnyɛ ɔno nye kan no, na obedzii kan no ho dase.
9. Nokwar kan no a ɔma nyimpa nyina mu yɛ kan na ɔreba wiadze. [Mfantse]

Jesus came as the expected Messiah and the understanding is that prior to his manifestation God sent a witness to that effect.[59] John (the Baptist), sent from God, preceded Jesus (the Logos) who is the "true" or "real" (ἀληθινόν) Light. In the Akan society this may be akin to the *adawubɔ* [or *adawurubɔ*] before the king meets with the community or prior to the invocation *nana 'ba o* ("the king comes or is coming!") before he is

---

56. Justin, *First Apology*, V & XLVI.

57. See previous chapter.

58. The 1977 UBS Ga New Testament translates *Ni Wiemɔ lɛ tsɔ gbomɔ adesa* ('And the Word became a human being').

59. Cf. John 1:41, 45.

introduced or presented at a gathering.[60] John in his *adasedzi* (witnessing) could well be proclaiming *kan no (r)eba o* ("the light is coming!"). The *Asεm*, as it were, needed an introduction.

John came in order to witness to this "true" Light so that "all might believe through him." This "true" Light that "enlightens everyone was coming into the world." There are two variant readings of 1:9 where the coming (ἐρχόμενον) is either taken with human (ἄνθρωπον) or light (φῶς). The Mfantse rendering takes the *coming* with *light* (*Nokwar kan . . . na ɔreba wiadze*).[61] This gives a back translation of "enlightens everyone" a noteworthy import: *nokwar kan no a ɔma nyimpa nyina mu yε kan* can literally mean "the true light who / which makes the inside of all people to be light or to be full of light." Thus, bringing out a sense of a working from within.

Realized, Discovered, Recognized—vss. 10–12

10. Ɔwɔ wiadze, na wɔnam no do yεε wiadze, na (naaso) wiadze ennhu no.
11. Ɔbaa dza ɔyε nedze hɔ (ɔbaa nankasa nedze hɔ), na hɔn a wɔyε (nankasa) nedze no anngye no.
12. Na dodow a wɔgyee no no, ɔmaa hɔn tum dε wɔnyε Nyankopɔn mba, mekyerε hɔn a wɔgye ne dzin dzi no a (Na dodow biara a wɔgyee no na wɔgyee no dzii no, hɔn na ɔmaa hɔn tum dε wɔnyε Nyankopɔn mba).

The idea of recognition that for Danquah forms part of the process of the making of a *nana* can also be observed in these verses. The world was made through the Logos who was in the world (1:3) but the world did not recognize him. The world came into existence through the Logos and he was in the world (from the beginning)[62] but the world (as the sphere of humans and their thought systems) failed in *recognizing* him. Not only did the world fail to recognize him, his own (Jewish people) did not receive him. Coming to his own implies a belonging to a family and a community

---

60. Christaller, *Dictionary*, 67. Christaller gives as example a saying with the English rendering, *εsono dawuro, εsono dawuro, na εsono Akonɔ-kumaa dawuro* ("there are many words alike, yet each has its own meaning" (Christaller, pr. 3013). This apparently shows a connection between *dawuro* and *asεm* (word).

61. See Westcott, *The Gospel according to St. John*, 6–7 for a discussion on the possible readings.

62. Westcott, for instance, maintained that "[i]t is impossible to refer these words [He was in the world] simply to the historical Presence of the Word in Jesus as witnessed to by the Baptist. The whole scope and connexion of the passage requires a wider sense." Westcott, *The Gospel according to St. John*, 8.

from which the Logos incarnate acquired or assumed a "definite humanity." Jesus' (Jewish) Messiahship was a product of his participation in Jewish family and community life. His Messiahship was "hewed out"[63] from his Jewish community.

The Logos incarnate needed to be "discovered" by or "revealed" to men and women whose vision was on God and not on themselves (John 6:45). This is contrary to Danquah's *opanyin* who is to become a *nana* that is "discovered by man." Jesus Christ coming as the "expected" Messiah was "revealed" to or "discovered" by men and women whose vision was on God. God's family is beyond the Jewish community and thus even though his family and community failed to receive Jesus (in faith), "to all who received (or receive) him . . . believing in his name, he gave (or gives) power to become children of God." It is thus possible to fail to recognize and receive the Logos who became flesh.

I have earlier on discussed the Akan verb *hu* that translates *egno* with the senses, among others, "to see or perceive with the eyes," "discover" or "recognize." That the world "did not know" the Logos implies the need for an effort on the part of those to whom the Logos manifests in the person of Jesus Christ to recognize and receive him in order to be made "children of God." Also, Jesus Christ should be realized or discovered in the community from the lives of those who have received him. He gives the grace and power or strength (*tum*) to the Akan to be what Akan traditional thought seeks after in its view of *nana*, as Danquah deduced and envisaged.

If the *nana* is an "exemplar of the Supreme Being,"[64] the image of God, so to speak, that Akan thought (in Danquah's view) envisages, then it is only the Son of God who perfectly fits this image of God who actually embodies or in a sense incarnates the idea of *nana*. This view of Jesus as Nana does not compromise the divinity of Jesus Christ over his humanity. In his essence with the Father, in his becoming flesh and in his living among humans the Akan can see clearly how close Jesus as the "exemplar of the Supreme Being" is to him or her.

Interpreter or Revealer of God—vs. 18

The view of the *nana* as the "exemplar and paradigm of Nyankopɔn" also carries with it the sense of the *nana* showing us "what God in Himself is, or ought to be," according to Danquah.[65] A final theme and role common to

---

63. Danquah, *The Akan Doctrine of God*, 120.
64. Danquah, *The Akan Doctrine of God*, 122.
65. Danquah, *The Akan Doctrine of God*, 122.

Danquah's *nana* and the Logos of the Prologue to the Fourth Gospel is that of an "Interpreter of God."

> 18. Obi nnhun Nyankopɔn pɛn; Ɔba a wɔwoo no kor no a ɔwɔ
> Egya no bo mu no, ɔno na oeyi no akyerɛ (Ɔba kortoo no a ɔda
> Egya no n'akoma ho no, ɔno na ɔada no edzi akyerɛ hɛn).

The author of the Fourth Gospel recalls the idea of recognition in 1:14, 18. One will hardly fix his or her eyes on an object for a very long time if he or she has failed to recognize its value or worth. The author indicates a sense of community recognition: "we beheld" ["*yehun*" or "*yehuu*"] "his glory (*enyimnyam*), the glory as of a father's only son, full of grace (*adom*) and truth (*nokwar*)." The Logos in flesh came to "interpret" (ἐξηγήσατο, *oeyi no akyerɛ*) God to us. Our Nana, the Asɛm, who is the "real" image of the Father, coming in to live and work among us, "explains" or "reveals" or "makes known" (*yi kyerɛ, da edzi kyerɛ*) him to us. It is he who, as Son (*ba*) of Nyankopɔn, fulfils the anticipated role of the *nana* as the "exemplar and paradigm" of Nyankopɔn in Akan traditional thought. In this sense, the Asɛm as Nana gives us the right vision of Nyankopɔn and *nyimpa* (humans) (so far as the end of *nyimpa* is to become a *nana*). In other words, he reveals to us who Nyankopɔn is and what *nyimpa* should be in the light of the vision of Nyankopɔn.

Nana Yesu and the Akan Primal Imagination

The "expected Messiah," who was with God from the beginning, in the very bosom of the Father, has been revealed among us. He became flesh and lived amongst us so we may recognize him and discover that in his fullness of grace and truth we will be able to see God who is unseen.

Danquah's view of *nana* can help in the articulation of an Akan Ancestor (Nana) Christology. The image of *nana* when placed alongside the image of Logos beginning with the Prologue of the Fourth Gospel can help resolve some of the expressed challenges and limitations of Ancestor Christology; notably the compromise of the human-divine nature of Jesus Christ. For the Nana was with Nyankopɔn in the beginning and is Nyankopɔn.

Jesus the Nana is the one who also enables the Akan to be a *nana* before God, an exemplar of God. If "children of God" applies to a "likeness of God," then the Akan idea of a "child of God" is in the sense of a *nana*. Danquah did not connect the idea of *nana* to Jesus but found it convenient to reckon God as the Nana. However, if Danquah had attempted to see Jesus in the light of his view of the Akan concept of Nana he would not have hesitated to reckon him as the promised and expected Messiah who the Akan can discover or realize as his or her *true* Nana. This will not contradict his observation in a different work that "Christianity is the fulfilment of the religious conception of our own people."[66]

Putting together Danquah's portrait of the Akan idea of *nana* and the image of Jesus Christ the Logos in the Prologue discussed above, the following thoughts may ensue, captioned as *Nyame N'Asɛm a ɔabɛyɛ hɛn Nana* or *Nana a ɔyɛ (Nyame na) Asɛm* ("God's Logos who has become our Nana" or "The Nana who is [God's] Logos"),

> Ahyɛse no na hɛn Nana no wɔ hɔ
> Na hɛn Nana no nye Nyankopɔn wɔ hɔ
> Na hɛn Nana no yɛ Nyame (Nyankopɔn)
>
> Adze nyina fi hɛn Nana yi mu
> Wɔnam no do na Ɔdomankoma bɔɔ adze nyina
> Nyimpa nyina fi no mu
> Ɔno nye nkwa Wura osiandɛ no mu na nkwa wɔ
>
> Hɛn Nana yi baa hɛn ntamu / Hɛn Nana yi bɔsoɛɛ hɛn
> Na yennhu no anngye no annto mu / Na yennhu no anngye no dɛ
> Ɔdze Nyame Asɛm brɛɛ hɛn
> Ɔnoara nye Asɛm no a adom nye nokwar ahyɛ no ma no
>
> Na dodow a wɔgye no no
> Ɔma hɔn tum dɛ wɔnyɛ Nyankopɔn mba
> Ama wɔaayɛ nananom atseneneefo wɔ Nyame mu
> Tse dɛ Nana Jesus [Yesu] a ɔyɛ Nyankopɔn Ba kor no
>
> In the beginning our Nana was
> Our Nana was with God
> Our Nana was God
>
> All things came from our Nana
> It is through him that the Creator made all things
> Humanity springs from him
> He is the Lord of life for in him is life
>
> Our Nana came into our midst / came to visit us
> But we did not see him to receive him
> He brought us God's Word

---

66. Danquah, "Religion in Ghanaian Society," 16 quoted in Bediako, *Religion, Culture and Language*, 17.

> He is himself the Word full of grace and truth
>
> But to all who receive him
> He gives them power to be children of God
> So they become righteous ancestors before (or in) God
> Just like our Nana Jesus God's only Son

So, the Akan mind can have his or her sense of Nana in the background as he or she appropriates the thoughts on the Logos in the Prologue. The Asɛm, the subject matter of the Prologue, is also the Nana in every possible essence of the Akan imagination and at the same time also in a transcendent sense since the Akan is but an expression of humanity.

I have maintained the expression the "Asɛm as Nana" or "Nana as Asɛm" hitherto. The two words can be put together as *Asɛmnana* or *Nanasɛm* which would mean, in the light of the above discussions, *Hen Nana a ɔyɛ Nana Nyame n'Asɛm* (Our Nana who is God's Word [Logos]). Thus, we meet him as the Nana and soon discover that he is in fact the Asɛm of Nyankopɔn or we meet him as the Asɛm and soon discover that he is also our Nana. This is certainly not discontinuous with the various thoughts on Ancestor Christology, chiefly those of Bediako, Bujo and Nyamiti. Translating Bujo's Proto-Ancestor as Dikan-Nana, Nanakan (Nana *a ɔdikan*) or Nyamiti's Brother-Ancestor as Onua-Nana, Nananua (Nana *a ɔyɛ hɛn Nua*) would have similar implications as Nanasɛm, though that has not been pursued here.

Nana Yesu, Asɛm, Nyansa, Tum(i)

In the New Testament, the image of Jesus Christ as Logos (Asɛm) is related to that of Wisdom (Nyansa). There is a close connection between *asɛm* and *nyansa*, aside from the proverb indicated earlier, in the Akan expression *aka asɛm paao / wa ka asɛm paa o* (lit. "you have really said something") which suggests *nyansa* in what has been said (be it a proverb or inference from a situation at hand). The Akan proverb *asɛm nko, nyansa nko* (lit. "spoken word is one thing, wisdom another") as, Gyekye rightly notes, does show that words in themselves "do not constitute wisdom."[67] So also is the expression *onyansafo wubu no bɛ na wɔnka no asem* (the "wise person is spoken to in proverbs, not in words"). However, to Akan traditional thought, *asɛm kyɛ a, nyansa ba ho* (lit. "when a situation keeps long, wisdom comes to it"), which may also point to the fact that the wisdom of a

---

67. Gyekye, *An Essay on African Philosophical Thought*, 63.

situation or even a spoken word may take some time in coming.[68] In other words, it is time that brings out all the revealing facets of an *asɛm* before any inherent *nyansa* can be discerned.

If Jesus as the Nana is the *Asɛm* of God, that is God's "self-evident reality," then in Akan thinking he is also Nyansa. The operation of the *Asɛm* of God has made him also God's Nyansa to us. Paul's reflection in this sense is thus affirmed in Akan thinking: Christ Jesus "became (ἐγενήθη, *ayɛ*) for us wisdom from God" (1 Corinthians 1:30).

Paul's close association of "wisdom" and "power" (δύναμις, *tum[i]*) (1 Corinthians 1:24) is also affirmed in Akan thinking regarding Jesus the Nana. The *nananom*, especially the royal ones, are regarded as source(s) of *tum[i]* ("power"). Nana Yesu as both the Nyansa and *Tum* of Nyankopɔn is also the source of *nyansa* and *tum*. The Akan chief (*nana*) can go to Nana Yesu for *nyansa* and *tum* in keeping faithfully to the truth inherent in his (or her) inherited tradition.

Nana Yesu, Asɛm, and Nananom (Hebrews 1:1–4)

Seth Kissi has argued, in his exegetical study of the above block of text in the light of the Twi language, that the author's use of the adverbs πολυμερῶς and πολυτρόπως "overlap in meaning" and seeks "some emphasis which must not be glossed over."[69] Furthermore, according to Kissi, the author's choice of τοῖς (to the) rather than an expected ἡμῶν (our) equally "serves to point to something that is worth exploring." For Kissi, the two adverbs emphasize the "variety of ways through which the earlier revelation [of God] was given [to humankind]" as well as its "complex nature."[70] Accordingly, Kissi suggests a better rendering of πολυμερῶς και πολυτρόπως as *afafa ne akwan hwanyan so* or *afa ahorow ne akwan ahorow* rather than (the Akuapem Twi) *mmere horow ne su horow so*.[71] Thus *afa* and *akwan*, rendering respectively, -μέρος ("share," "part") and -τρόπος ("turn," "way") may well point to the fragmentary nature of the revelation of God prior to the Incarnation.

---

68. Gyekye translates thus "If a problem lasts for a long time, wisdom comes to it" and opines that "it is the wise person who, after grappling with a problem for a long time, succeeds in disentangling it," also noting its implication that "philosophizing is a long intellectual process" which takes time. Gyekye, *An Essay on African Philosophical Thought*, 64.

69. Kissi, "An Akan View of Jesus: Exegetical Exploration into Hebrews 1:1–4 in the Light of Insights from the Akan Mother Tongue."

70. Kissi, "An Akan View of Jesus," 5 & 95.

71. Kissi, "An Akan View of Jesus," 103,105, & 145.

Consequently, in view of a real but incomplete revelation of Nyame in the Akan tradition and the fullness of the Son's revelation,[72] Kissi concludes his study by identifying Jesus with a number of Akan historical and conceptual realities.[73] Among the other associations, Jesus is *Tweneboah Kodua Trodoo a owu gye amansan* ("the True Tweneboah Kodua who dies to save the nations") or *Egya Ahor Krɔnn a ne wu gye dɔm wɔ aman nyinaa mu afi mmusu mu* ("The Real Agya Ahor whose death has saved multitudes from all nations from their calamities"); *Yɛn adwirade ne nea oyi yɛn mmusu kɔ* ("Our purificatory sacrifice and the one who takes away our woes") and then *Amansan Nana Saman Pa a Ɔne yɛn wɔ hɔ daa* or *Nana Saman Pa a ɔte tumi mu wɔ nea ekrɔn hɔ* ("the Nation's Ancestor who is always with us" or "the Ancestor who sits in power in the exalted place").[74]

The significance of Nana Yesu as the Asɛm also reaches to *abosom* and their attendants, the *akɔmfo* (sing. *ɔkomfo*) and *asɔfo* (sing. *ɔsɔfo*) in light of the above text from Hebrews.[75] A mother-tongue reading of the John 1:1–5 and Hebrews 1:1–4 diminishes any subtle significance of the Greek words *logos* and *rhema* with the use of *asɛm* in both cases. Thus, as far as an Akan Asɛm Christology is concerned, both blocks of texts are complementary. In Hebrews, *tum asɛm* (ῥήματι τῆς δυνάμεως, "all-powerful word") is in connection with *Nyankopɔn ne Ba* (God's Son), who is the *hyerɛn* ("reflection") of his *enyimnyam* ("glory") as well as his *subea saso* ("the characteristic mark of God's actual existence").[76] The thoughts here are akin to John 1:1–3 with a noteworthy observation that while in John 1:3 "all things came into being (ἐγένετο)" through the Logos, in Hebrews 1:2 the "worlds (αἰῶνας) were made (ἐποίησεν) through" the Son.

---

72. Bujo, *African Theology in Its Social Context*, 83.

73. Kissi, "An Akan View of Jesus," 142–43.

74. Similarly Eric Adjei-Danso, in his essay on understanding the reality of Jesus Christ making use of Asante "myths, rituals, beliefs, symbols, art and language," concludes that Jesus Christ as "God-man" combines the functions of God (the Great Ancestor) and that of the Nananom so that an Asante calling him "an ancestor express(es) his multifaceted role and influence in the life of the world." Adjei-Danso, "Asante Christology: Understanding Jesus Christ in the Asante Context," x & 57.

75. John Ekem, who has notably reassessed the priestly Christology of the Epistle to the Hebrews in the light of the Akan religious tradition, argues that the *ɔkɔmfo* and the *ɔsɔfɔ* are not "identical functionaries" and that while the former is "specifically called and possessed" by the *ɔbosom* and thus able to perform the *akɔm* ('a state of being possessed by an *ɔbosom*'), the latter is a mere servant without any rigorous training who acts on the instruction of a possessed *ɔkɔmfo*. Ekem, *Priesthood in Context*, 46–47.

76. Moffatt, *A Critical and Exegetical Commentary on the Epistle to the Hebrews*, 8. Zerwick, *A Grammatical Analysis of the Greek New Testament*, 654.

The Son "upholds" (*suo / so*) all things by his "all-powerful word" (*tum asɛm*). With the backdrop of John 1:1–3, it can be inferred that the Son does this in his capacity as the Asɛm (Logos), that is the Word; for without the Logos "not one thing came into being" (*woennkwetsi no annyɛ biribiara a wɔyɛe*).[77] The significance of the Son in these introductory remarks of the Epistle points to his presence (life and work) among humans as an act of God's final *kasa* ("speech") to humanity. The Son is then in effect God's *Asɛm*.

According to the author of the Epistle, God did speak to the *egyanom* or better still *nananom* in diverse forms and ways in (*no mu*) the *nkɔmhyɛfo* or *adiyifo* (prophets) in times of old (*tsetse, tete*).[78] In Akan traditional thinking the *nkɔmhyɛfo* or *adiyifo* point to the *akɔmfo* (priests or priestesses) who do *hyɛ nkɔm* (divine or reveal an oracle) for their respective *ɔbosom* (deity) being assisted by the *ɔsɔfo* or *asɔfo* (assistants).[79] The *abosom* (deities), perceived as intermediaries, are also titled *nana* and therefore as Nana, Jesus is the true *Ɔbosom* of God, so far as the *abosom* are *Nyame mba* (children of God): Nana Yesu is the real or true *Nyame ba*.[80] Furthermore, as *Nyankopɔn*'s Son, Jesus Christ, the Asɛm and Nana, does not only become the *definitive* Asɛm surpassing the *asɛm* of the *nkɔmhyɛfo* of the *abosom* and the *nananom*, but also the *definitive* Nana to whom the *nananom*, the *abosom*, and the *akɔmfo* and cohorts are subject.

The above reflections are made without strain because Jesus is conceived in the indigenous terminology of Nana. That is, Ancestor Jesus, which many Christians try to avoid, would mean little when confronting say an *ɔkɔmfo*. However, presenting Nana Yesu (Jesus), which is implicit of his Eldership and Ancestorship, to an *ɔkɔmfo* does pose a challenge for his or her "*nana ɔbosom*."[81] Likewise an Akan chief who resolves to

---

77. Reading "καὶ χωρὶς αὐτοῦ ἐγένετο οὐδὲ ἕν. ὃ γέγονεν". Without the full stop, the reading runs "And without him not one thing came into being that has come into being. 4. In him was life."

78. Both *nkɔnhyɛfo* and *adiyifo* are conceptually synonymous but etymologically give different senses. The latter, singular *odiyini* or *odiyifo*, comprise *adi* (thing) and *yi* ("remove" or "uncover"). Christaller renders the word *adiyi* as "manifestation, revelation," so the *odiyini* basically uncovers and makes known what is hidden or unknown. The former word, *nkɔnhyɛfo*, derives from *nkɔm* ("oracle, communication, revelation or message from God or a deity") and *hyɛ* (in this case to "bring"). Christaller, *Akan Dictionary*, 85, 206, & 247.

79. Ekem, *Priesthood in Context*, 44–45. The phrase *hyɛ nkɔm* is used in Christian parlance to mean "to prophesy," *nkɔmhyɛ* being prophecy.

80. Afriyie, "*Abosom* (*Onyame mma*—children of God) and Jesus Christ (the Son of God)," 261–68, who concludes that Jesus' work in bringing humankind "right into the presence of God forever" has rendered obsolete that of the *abosom*.

81. This could be likened to the implicit senses of "word" and "reason" in the Greek word *logos*, which Logos Christology took for granted at some point. For a discussion

confess Nana Yesu rather than "Ancestor Jesus" would at once be hit with the challenge of the significance of Yesu to his *nananom* and also the implication to his or her title, *nana*.

Oseadeeyo Nana Addo Dankwa III challenged the designation of Jesus Christ as Ancestor.[82] One curious question to this effect is whether he would deny the title Nana, implicit of Elder and Ancestor, for Jesus Christ? Indeed, the mother-tongue rendering of the titular name *nana* for Akan ancestors does have both religious and political connotations perhaps akin to the Hebrew Messiah at the time of Jesus. Thus apart from his significance among the *nananom*, Nana Yesu presents a challenge for both the living elders (*nananom*), of whom the chief is *primus inter pares*, and also the *nana (tsetse) abosom* (old deities).

Conclusion

The Asɛm in Christian understanding points to that "self-evident truth or reality" that, in Danquah's thinking, the projection of the idea of *nana* aspires to. The Asɛm has been with Nyankopɔn from the beginning and is Nyankopɔn. As old as Nyankopɔn, he is the Nana of *adze nyina* "all things" because *wɔnam no do yɛɛ adze nyina* or *wɔnam no do na adze nyina bae* ("through him all things became"). A deeper understanding of Jesus as Asɛm leads to the discovery or realisation that he is Nana. In his life giving activity as the Asɛm and Nana in an Akan person, he gives the light needed for one to be a true *okaniba* ("Akan son or daughter"), pleasing to Nyankopɔn and beneficial to the community: the Nanasɛm makes *nananom* of those who receive him in faith.[83]

An Akan Asɛm Christology seems to be implicit of a Nana Christology and perhaps vice-versa. Pursuing a Nana Christology that is faithful to biblical truth leads to an affirmation of Jesus Christ as indeed that "self-evident reality" of Nyankopɔn made human for our salvation. A pursuit of an Asɛm Christology cannot be devoid of the recognition of the place of a *nana* in Akan traditional thought. Jesus as Nanasɛm, then, gives the avenue for a complementary pursuit of an Ancestor Christology in the light of (an indigenous) Logos Christology.

The influence of Danquah's thoughts on *nana* in my exploration of an Akan Ancestor Christology makes him foundational for Ancestor

---

on the challenge of *abosom* to Christianity in Ghana, see Sackey, "Recognising Other Dimensions of Epistemology," 13–30.

82. Dankwa, *Christianity and African Traditional Beliefs*, 33.

83. Quarshie, "'Jesus, Pioneer and Perfecter of Faith' (Heb. 12:2)," 33–35.

Christology akin to Philo for (Alexandrian) Logos Christology. Danquah's effort to compare the Jewish sense of Messiah with that of the Akan conception of Nana remains significant irrespective of what may be said of his method. In the understanding of Christian conversion as "turning what is there in a culture towards the direction of Jesus Christ," Danquah's effort is a *missionary* foundation that could be built upon.

Christology is a (cultural) response to Jesus Christ and whatever we say from our experience of him does not change who he *truly* is. Our right conception of him, being guided by the Holy Spirit, guarantees the desired personal and communal transformation into his image, which is the image of God. Our knowledge of him, therefore, should be germinative; we are urged to "grow [αὐξάνετε, *nnyin*] in the grace and knowledge of our Lord and Saviour Jesus Christ" (2 Peter 3:18).

Joseph Wong's observation, then, following his study on Karl Rahner's Christology, that "Christology must be the fruit of personal reflection and, above all, of personal experience of the Saviour" is apt, for indeed "in communicating the Christ symbol to others, one inevitably symbolizes one's own Christ experience."[84] Later followers of Jesus Christ can always build upon the deposit of the articulated reflections of our experience with Christ. Our proposal of a Nanasɛm discourse remains germinal; exploration in other relevant contexts would ensure its growth.

---

84. Wong, *Logos-Symbol in the Christology of Karl Rahner*, 267. Asamoah-Gyadu, "Kwame Bediako and the Eternal Christological Question," 40–41.

Conclusion

CHRISTOLOGY IS CULTURALLY DYNAMIC. The characteristics of pre-Christian concepts are hardly lost in their eventual application in Christology. The (pre-Christian) concepts of *logos* and *ancestor* examined here are certainly distinct ideas geographically and separated by some two millennia. Three themes are common to both as pre-Christian concepts, namely, *mediation, exemplarity, revelation*. Thus, they both serve well in their respective Christian usage in appropriating the person and soteriological function of Jesus Christ. A comparative treatment of the application of both concepts in Christology offer some helpful guidelines for contemporary African Christology.

Christology is the necessary by-product of the process of conversion. Hence when the process of conversion is seen in the three identifiable stages of *missionary, convert,* and *refiguration*, the growth of Christological thought is discerned. In his own articulation of the impact of the reality of Jesus Christ in his life and vocation, the Apostle Paul rightly refers to such reality as the "mystery of Christ," *Christ esumasɛmɔ* (Ephesians 3:4). This endeavor can be either a systematic written reflection (articulation) or a spontaneous oral expression (articulation) of the impact of Jesus Christ within the cultural context. In terms of a cultural response to Jesus Christ, Christology becomes a commentary, as it were, on that process of turning towards the direction of Jesus. The experience of the early disciples in their recognition of Jesus as the Messiah was a cultural response to Jesus and hence a paradigm for the view of Christology as an intricate (cultural) product of the process of conversion.

The Graeco-Roman *logos* concept developed over time being amalgamated along the way with old and contemporary ideas. Philo's exploration as a Hellenistic Jew was significant for early Christian authors whose eventual vocation as Christians was in many points akin to that of the former. Philo and the Graeco-Roman Christians had the Septuagint as their sourcebook alongside contemporary religio-philosophical ideas. The Christians, however, assessed these sources through their experience of the impact of the reality of Jesus Christ. The foundation of the New Testament documents enabled first and subsequent generations of Graeco-Roman Christian converts to reflect more deeply the significance of the reality of Jesus Christ to their own religio-cultural heritage. Jesus Christ the Logos (incarnate) was the key for both their critique and appreciation of their inherited past. The journey of Logos Christology demonstrates that a Christological model based on a pre-Christian concept or idea has its lifespan. Though such a model hardly dies out completely, its interest in subsequent generations of Christians is not linear but serial; one generation may not be enthusiastic about it, but a later generation may find it useful. Thus, the *suggestive, clarificatory* or *elucidative,* and *innovative* stages in the development of Logos Christology is more organic than mechanistic.

The idea of ancestors in Africa is operative in several societies, though the degree of influence varies. Among the Akan of Ghana, the significance of the *nananom* is invariably linked to the activities of the institution of the chief. Therefore, amid contemporary external influences and change traditional Akan societies continue to honor the *nananom* with the chief and his or her stool serving as a vital link between the people and the ancestral transcendent world. J. B. Danquah's conceptual exploration of the Akan *nana* as constituting the Akan vision of an ideal person remains helpful in any Christian missiological engagement.

Ancestor Christology is in the *refiguration* stage and as one of the authentic avenues for responding to the reality and impact of Jesus Christ, it still has the potential for further application. The efforts of the various proponents reviewed under the three stages of the process of conversion do overlap. In terms of its function in African Christianity, Ancestor Christology is an ongoing project. There is the need for more intentional context-specific exploration where the language of the context is vital. It is in the language of its context that the expressed limitations of this Christological avenue can be meaningfully addressed. To proclaim Jesus as Nana (Nana Yesu) is an invitation for a continuous engagement of how he assumes and illuminates the imagination of the *nana* idea. Proclaiming "Ancestor Jesus" to an Akan audience will not have such compelling invitation.

The agency of the translated Bible enables Christians to receive God's word in the imagination of the cultural categories. In fact, a mother-tongue reading and interpretation of the Bible invariably presents a contextual reworking of concepts assumed in the Bible. I have argued that the foundational Logos Christology in the prologue of John's Gospel can be re-imagined by the Akan Christian. From an Akan perspective, *asɛm* and *nana* can be linked to God's dealing with humanity. Jesus is the Asɛm that God has given humankind, including the Akan, as his self-revelation and our reception of and obedience to this Asɛm of or from God guarantees, in the power or strength of the Holy Spirit, a life worthy before God and beneficial to the society and thereby qualifying us into *nana*hood.

Logos-Ancestor Christology and the African Witness in World Christianity

One significant difference to note regarding Logos and Ancestor Christologies is that whereas Jesus is apparently regarded as Ancestor by "analogy," early Christian affirmation regarded him as the Logos and in his earthly sojourn as the Logos incarnate (Logos in *flesh*). My observation in this regard, then, is that by or through his death, Jesus Christ is the Ancestor not by analogy, but by his matchless obedience to the Father and the necessary reality of death as prerequisite for ancestorhood. The reality of his resurrection, however, having gone to the abode of the death, *asamando* in Akan parlance, makes Jesus Christ more than an Ancestor. In fact, he becomes the Ancestor of ancestors, both *potential* (those yet to die) and *actual* (those in *asamando*).

The re-conception of Jesus Christ within the categories of traditional world of thought is inevitable; it is only a matter of time for the individual as well as the community of believers. The New Testament image of Jesus Christ is normative for any eventual and expected cultural image of Jesus Christ. The conversion process within the Hellenistic world of thought took over Jewish images of Jesus Christ but these were reworked or remodeled eventually with others taking special significance and prominence. All the proponents of Ancestor Christology are mindful of the need to incorporate the insights of the Bible (Old and New Testament) as well as those of the early Church codified in the various creeds of the Councils. I have demonstrated a way in which present Christological endeavors in Africa can draw on developments in the New Testament and post-Palestine Graeco-Roman Christianity. In my view, the development of Logos Christology offers a helpful analogy for a reassessment of Ancestor Christology. A mother-tongue reading of the foundational text of Logos Christology in the New Testament can also inform a mother-tongue Ancestor Christology. Though what is presented in this book is explorative within the Akan worldview, the hope is that it serves as an experimental model for further exploration in other contexts where the influence ancestors remain significant at the present. One can anticipate diverse and engaging indigenous Logos Christologies, given the diversity and fecundity of African languages in theological discourse.

Ancestor Christology has a twin purpose of relevance for the Church in Africa and the wider community. Its mother-tongue exploration offers opportunity for a further deepening or rooting of the faith in and of Jesus Christ in Africa. It also becomes more relevant to the wider community in its mother-tongue exploration where the indigenous language of the respective African communities is employed. Hence proclaiming Jesus as *Nanasɛm* (the Nana and Asɛm of Onyankpɔn) reminds Akan Christians of the self-evident reality of God who became flesh for salvation as indeed the same one that embodies the strivings of the *nananom* for a full life. To the wider Akan community, the reality of the coming of God's own Nana poses a challenge to our conception of Onyankpɔn who is not seen, realizing that He is not far from us and at the same time demands our sole devotion having revealed to us His Asɛm through the *ɔbra* (life) and *adwuma* (work) or ndzeyɛ / *nneyɛe* (activity) of His Son, our Nana. This has implications for the traditional and national political setups.

The relevance of Ancestor Christology in the area of politics in Africa remains to be pursued further. What challenge does Jesus as Ancestor have for contemporary African politics, considering the role of the concept of ancestors in the political setup in the traditional setting? Proclaiming Jesus as Ancestor gives the church in Africa a viable avenue to offer critique of the political predicament of many African states. The Logos-Ancestor discourse can help preserve the value of traditional ancestral politics which can then be incorporated in both ecclesiastical and community governance. Jesus as Nana is an Asɛm (message) for all claimants of the title *nana* to live and serve before God as Jesus did.

African Christology should address the challenges of Africa's social realities. If modern African philosophy can offer "the conceptual responses to the problems and circumstances of modern African societies as well as interpretation, criticism, and clarification of concepts in African traditional thought,"[1] then there is need for a creative dialogue between modern African philosophy and African Christian thought. The Logos-Ancestor discourse can thus benefit from the insights of modern African

---

1. Gyekye, *An Essay on African Philosophical Thought*, 42.

philosophy. For Jesus Christ is at once the *Asɛm*, the One "self-evident" Reality, and the Nana, the *incarnation* of that longing of Akan traditional thought in search of full humanity.

The Logos-Ancestor (*Asɛm-Nana, Nanasɛm*) model gives the *refiguration* stage of Ancestor Christology an avenue to consciously make use of the translated Scriptures as well as indigenous terminology. The comparative view of Jesus Christ, the one Living Reality of God, as Logos (*Asɛm*) and Nana (Ancestor) also demonstrates the opened-ended nature of New Testament thought and witness: Jesus Christ is the Son of God, and Saviour of the World, Lord of both the living and the dead, the *expected* Messiah of the Jew, the *creative* Logos of the Greek, the *discovered* or *realized* Nana of the Akan. Jesus, indeed, does inhabit the world of *nana*, just as he was able to permeate the world of *logos* in Hellenistic world of thought.[2] In good faith then, African Christianity as both "the African chapter of Christian history" and "the Christian chapter of African religion,"[3] respectively, continues to remind us of our common humanity being summoned to respond to the one Reality of the God of all flesh and at the same time also proves that Christianity is very much at home on African soil.

---

2. Bediako, "The Doctrine of Christ and the Significance of Vernacular Terminology," 110–11.

3. Walls, "The Discovery of 'African Traditional Religion' and its Impact on Religious Studies," 17.

Bibliography

Abbot, Thomas K. *A Critical and Exegetical Commentary on the Epistles to the Ephesians and to the Colossians.* Edinburgh: T. & T. Clark, 1991.

Aboagye-Mensah, Robert K. "Socio-Political Thinking of Karl Barth: Trinitarian and Incarnational Christology as the Ground for His Social Action and Its Implications for Us Today." PhD diss., University of Aberdeen, 1984.

Achtemeier, Paul J., et al, *Introducing the New Testament: Its Literature and Theology.* Grand Rapids: Eerdmans, 2001.

Ackah, C. A. *Akan Ethics: A Study of the Moral Ideas and the Moral Behaviour of the Akan Tribes of Ghana.* Accra: Ghana Universities Press, 1988.

Adams, Frank K. *Odwira and the Gospel: A Study of the Asante Odwira Festival and Its Significance for Christianity in Ghana.* Oxford: Regnum, 2010.

Addo-Fening, Robert. "From Traditionalist to Christian Evangelist and Teacher: The Religious Itinerary and Legacy of Emmanuel Yaw Boakye. (1835–1914)." *Journal of African Christian Thought* 7.1 (2004) 3–13.

Adjei-Danso, Eric. "Asante Christology: Understanding Jesus Christ in the Asante Context." B.D. diss., Trinity Theological Seminary, 2007.

Afeke, B., and P. Verster. "Christianisation of Ancestor Veneration with African Traditional Religions: An Evaluation." *In die Skriflig* 38.1 (2004) 47–61.

Afriyie, Ernestina. "*Abosom.* (*Onyame mma*: Children of God) and Jesus Christ (the Son of God): An Engagement of the Intermediary Role of Abosom in Akan Religion with that of Jesus Christ in the Christian Faith." In *Seeing New Facets of the Diamond: Christianity as a Universal Faith: Essays in Honour of Kwame Bediako*, edited by Gillian M. Bediako et al., 261–68. Akropong-Akuapem: Regnum Africa, 2014.

———. "A Comparative Study of Akan and Biblical Concepts of a Human Being: A Study to Illustrate a Method of Cross-Cultural Evangelism." MTh diss., University of Natal, 2000.

———. "The Theology of the Okuapehene's Odwira: An Illustration of the Engagement of the Gospel and Culture among the Akan of Akropong-Akuapem." PhD diss., Akrofi-Christaller Institute, 2010.

Agyarko, Robert O. "God's Unique Priest (*Nyamesofopreko*): Christology in the Akan Context." PhD diss., University of the Western Cape, 2009.

Agyekum, Kofi. "The Sociolinguistic of Akan Personal Names." *Nordic Journal of African Studies* 15.2 (2006) 206–35.

Agyemang-Duah, J. "The Adae Festival." In *Asante Festivals*, 1–4. Legon: University of Ghana–Institute of African Studies, n.d.

Ahern, Emily M. "The Thai Ti Kong Festival." In *The Anthropology of Taiwanese Society*, edited by Emily M Ahern et al., 397–425. Stanford, CA: Standard University Press, 1981.

Akan Language Committee. *Akan Orthography: Spelling Rules*. Accra: Bureau of Ghana Languages, 1995.

Akrofi, Clement A. *Twi Mmbusem: Twi Proverbs with English Translations and Comments*. London: Macmillan and Co., 1958.

Akrong, Abraham A. "An Akan Christian View of Salvation from the Perspective of John Calvin's Soteriology." PhD diss., Lutheran School of Theology, 1991.

———. "Christology from an African Perspective." In *Exploring Afro-Christology*, edited by John S. Pobee, 119–30. Frankfurt am Main: Lang, 1992.

———. "Jesus with the Face of an Ancestor." *GBT (New Series)* 1.1 (2006) 20–36.

Akyeampong, H. K. *Danquah: An Immortal of Ghana*. Compiled by Danquah Funeral Committee. Accra: George Boakie, 1968.

Amaladoss, Michael, *The Asian Jesus*. Maryknoll, NY: Orbis, 2006.

Amanze, James N. "Christianity and Ancestor Veneration in Botswana." *SWC* 9.1 (2003) 43–59.

Amoah, Elizabeth, Mercy A. Oduyoye. "The Christ for African Women." In *With Passion and Compassion: Third World Women Doing Theology*, edited by Virginia Fabella et al., 35–46. Maryknoll, NY: Orbis, 1988.

Amuzu, Francis H. "The Soul in Akan, Ewe and Platonic Metaphysics." MPhil diss., University of Ghana, 2003.

Annobil, J. A. *Mbɛbusɛm Nkyerɛkyerɛemu*. 2nd ed. Cape Coast, Ghana: Methodist Book Depot, 1971.

The Apostolic Fathers, with an English Translation by Kirsopp Lake, Vol. I. The Loeb Classical Library. London: Heinemann, 1925.

Appiah-Kubi, Kofi. "Christology." In *A Reader in African Christian Theology*, edited by John Parratt, 69–79. London: SPCK, 1987.

Appiah, Joe. *The Man J. B. Danquah*. Accra: Ghana Academy of Arts and Sciences, 1974.

Appiah, Peggy, Kwame A. Appiah, Ivor Agyeman-Duah. *Bu Me Bɛ: Proverbs of the Akans*. Banbury, UK: Ayebia Clarke, 2007.

Aristotle. *De Anima with Translations, Introduction and Notes by R. D. Hicks*. Cambridge: Cambridge University Press, 1907.

———. *Ethica Nicomachea*. Translated by W. D. Ross, revised by J. O. Urmson. In *The Works of Aristotle. Translated into English*, edited by W. D. Ross. Vol. IX. Oxford: Oxford University Press, 1975.

———. *Generation of Animals with an English Translation by A. I. Peck*. London: Heinemann, 1943.

———. *Metaphysics: With an English Translation by Hugh Tredennick*. Cambridge: Harvard University Press, 1933.

———. *Politics, with English translation by H. Rackham*. Cambridge: Harvard University Press, 2005.

Armstrong, A. H. *Plotinus*. London: George Allen & Unwin, 1953.

Arthur, Cecilia. *Akanfoɔ Amammerɛ Ho Adesua 1: A Textbook on Akan Culture*. Rev. ed. Kumasi, Ghana: Paulson, 2008.

———. *Akanfo Amammerɛ Ho Adesua 2: A Textbook on Akan Culture*. Rev. ed. Kumasi, Ghana: Paulson, 2008.

Asamoah-Gyadu, J. Kwabena. "Kwame Bediako and the Eternal Christological Question." In *Seeing New Facets of the Diamond: Christianity as a Universal Faith: Essays in Honour of Kwame Bediako*, edited by Gillian M. Bediako et al., 38–55. Akropong-Akuapem: Regnum Africa, 2014.

———. "Who Do You Say That I Am? Revisiting Kwame Bediako's Responses to an Eternal Christological Question." *Kwame Bediako Memorial Lecture*. Akrofi-Christaller Institute of Theology, Mission and Culture: 2009.

Asante, Molefi Kete, Rosemary Chai. "Nkrabea and Yuan in Akan and Chinese: Cultural Intersections and Communication Implications in an African and an Asian Society." *Journal of Black Studies* 44 (2013) 119–36, DOI: 10.1177/0021934713476891.

Asmis, Elizabeth. "Myth and Philosophy in Cleanthe's Hymn to Zeus." *Greek, Roman, and Byzantine* 47 (2007) 413–29.

Asmis, Elizabeth, Shadi Bartsch, and Martha C. Nussbaum. "Seneca and His World." In Lucius Annaeus Seneca, *Natural Questions*, translated by Harry M. Hine, vii–xxvi. Chicago: The University of Chicago Press, 2010.

Aye-Addo, Charles S. *Akan Christology: An Analysis of the Christologies of John Samuel Pobee and Kwame Bediako in Conversation with the Theology of Karl Barth*. Eugene, OR: Pickwick, 2013.

Bae, Choon Sup. "Ancestor Worship and the Challenges It Poses to the Christian Mission and Ministry." PhD diss., University of Pretoria, 2007.

Bannerman, J. Yedu. Interview, 22 May 2012, Tema.

———. *Mfantse: Akan Mbɛbusɛm Nkyerɛkyerɛmu. Ghanaian Proverbs Explained and Translated into English, Vol. 1. A-K*. 2nd ed. Sɔfo J. Yedu Bannerman, 2011.

Barima, Nana Sanaa Twum. Interview, 25 February 2014, Tema.

Barker, Peter. *Peoples, Languages, and Religion in Northern Ghana: A Preliminary Report*. Ghana Evangelism Committee, 1986.

Barnard, Leslie W. "Introduction." In *Justin Martyr: The First and Second Apologies*, translated with introduction and notes by Leslie William Barnard, 1–21. New York: Paulist, 1997.

Barrera, Julio Trebolle. *The Jewish Bible and the Christian Bible: An Introduction to the History of the Bible*. Translated by Wilfred G. E. Watson. Leiden: Brill, 1998.

Barrett, C. K. *The Gospel according to St. John: An Introduction with Commentary and Notes on the Greek Text*. 2nd ed. London: SPCK, 1978.

Barrett, David B. *Schism and Renewal in Africa: An Analysis of Six Thousand Contemporary Religious Movements*. Nairobi: Oxford University Press, 1968.

Bates, W. "Justin Martyr's Logocentric Hermeneutical Transformation of Isaiah's Vision of the Nations." *JTS* 60.2 (2009) 538–55.

Beard, Mary, John North, Simon Price. *Religions of Rome: A History*. Cambridge: Cambridge University Press, 1998.

Beasley-Murray, George R. *John*. Word Biblical Commentary 36. 2nd ed. Nashville: Thomas Nelson, 1999.

Bediako, Kwame. "Biblical Christologies in the Context of African Traditional Religions." In *Sharing Jesus in the Two Thirds World*, edited by Vinay Samuel et al., 81–121. Grand Rapids: Eerdmans, 1983.

———. "Biblical Exegesis in Africa: The Significance of the Translated Scriptures." In *African Theology on the Way—Current Conversations*, edited by Diane B. Stinton, 12–20. London: SPCK, 2010.

———. *Christianity in Africa: The Renewal of a Non-Western Religion*. Edinburgh: Edinburgh University Press, 1995.

———. "Christian Tradition and the African God Revisited: A Process in the Exploration of a Theological Idiom." In *Witnessing to the Living God in Contemporary Africa: Findings and Papers of the Inaugural Meeting of Africa Theological Fraternity*, edited by David M. Gitari et al., 77–97. African Theological Fraternity. Nairobi: Uzima, 1986.

———. "Cry Jesus! Christian Theology and Presence in Modern Africa." *Vox Evangelica* XXIII (1993) 7–25.

———. "The Doctrine of Christ and the Significance of Vernacular Terminology." *International Bulletin of Missionary Research* 22.3 (1998) 110–11.

———. "Gospel and Culture: Some Insights for Our Time from the Experience of the Earliest Church." *Journal of African Christian Thought* 2.2 (1999) 8–17.

———. "Guest Editorial: Lived Christology." *Journal of African Christian Thought* 7.1 (2004) 1–2.

———. *Jesus in Africa: The Christian Gospel in African History and Experience*. Akropong, Ghana: Regnum Africa, 2000.

———. *Jesus in African Culture: A Ghanaian Perspective*. Accra: Asempa, 1990.

———. *Religion, Culture and Language: J. B Danquah Memorial Lectures* Series 37. Accra: Ghana Academy Arts Sciences, 2004.

———. "Scripture as the Hermeneutic of Culture and Tradition." *Journal of African Christian Thought* 4.1. (2001) 2–11.

———. *Theology and Identity: The Impact of Culture upon Christian Thought in the Second Century and in Modern Africa*. Oxford: Regnum, 1999.

Bentwich, Norman. *Philo-Judæus of Alexandria*. Philadelphia: Jewish Publication Society of America, 1910.

Berentsen, Jan-Martin. *Grave and Gospel*. Leiden: Brill, 1985.

Bernard, J. H. *A Critical and Exegetical Commentary on the Gospel according to St. John*. Edited by A. H. McNeile. Volume I. Edinburgh: T. & T. Clark, 1993.

Bevans, Stephen. *Models of Contextual Theology*. Rev. ed. Maryknoll, NY: Orbis, 2002.

———. "Models of Contextual Theology." *Missiology: An International Review* 8.2 (1985) 185–201.

Bierbrier, Morris L. *Historical Dictionary of Ancient Egypt*. 2nd ed. Lanham, MD: Scarecrow, 2008.

Blakely, Pamela A. R., and Thomas D. Blakely. "Ancestors, "Witchcraft", & Foregrounding the Poetic: Men's Oratory & Women's Song-Dance in Hêmbá Funerary Performance." In *Religion in Africa: Experience & Expression*, edited by Thomas D. Blakely et al., 399–442. London: Currey, 1994.

Bluck, R. S. "Logos and Forms in Plato: A Reply to Professor Cross." *Mind*, New Series, 65.260 (1956) 522–29.

Bosch, David J. *Transforming Mission: Paradigm Shifts in Theology of Mission*. Maryknoll, NY: Orbis, 1991.

Bowdwich, T. Edward. *Mission from Cape Coast Castle to Ashantee, with a Descriptive Account of that Kingdom.* New ed. London: Griffith & Farran, 1873.

Bowen, Clayton R. "The Fourth Gospel Dramatic Material." *Journal of Biblical Literature* 49.3 (1930) 292–305.

Boyarin, Daniel. "The Gospel of the Memra: Jewish Binitarianism and the Prologue to John." *The Harvard Theological Review* 94.3 (2001) 243–84.

Brown, F. et al., *The B-D-B Hebrew and Greek Lexicon*. Peabody, MA: Hendrickson, 2003.

Brown, Raymond E. *The Gospel according to John I-XII*. Anchor Bible Series Vol. 29. New York: Doubleday, 1966.

———. *The Gospel and Epistles of John: A Concise Commentary*. Collegeville, MN: Liturgical, 1988.

———. *An Introduction to New Testament Christology*. Mahwah, NJ: Paulist, 1994.

Brown, Mervyn. "Madagascar: Island of the Ancestors." *Anthropology Today* 3.1. (1987) 14–17.

Bruce, F. F. "Colossian Problems Part 2: The 'Christ Hymn' of Colossians 1:15–20." *Bibliotheca Sacra* 141 (1984) 99–111.

———. *The Spreading Flame: The Rise and Progress of Christianity from Its First Beginnings to the Conversion of the English*. Grand Rapids: Eerdmans, 1985.

Bruderer, Paul. "African Ancestor-Christologies: A Comparison and Critique." BA diss., All Nations Christian College, Easneye, May 2000.

Buck, P. Lorraine. "Justin Martyr's Apologies: Their Number, Destination, and Form." *Journal of Theological Studies* 54 (2003) 45–59.

Bujo, Bénézet. *African Theology in Its Social Context*. Translated from the German by John O'Donohue. Maryknoll, NY: Orbis, 1992.

———. *The Ethical Dimension of Community: The African Model and the Dialogue between North and South*. Translated by Cecilia Namulondo Nganda. Nairobi: Paulines, 1998.

———. *Foundations of an African Ethic: Beyond the Universal Claims of Western Morality*. Translated by Brian McNeil. Nairobi: Paulines, 2003.

Bultmann, Rudolf K. *The Gospel of John: A Commentary*. Translated by G. R. Beasley-Murray. Oxford: Blackwell, 1971.

Burkitt, F. C. *Church and Gnosis: A Study of Christian Thought and Speculation in the Second Century*. Cambridge: Cambridge University Press, 1992.

Burnet, John, ed. *Platonis Opera*. Oxford: Oxford University Press, 1903.

Burnett, David. *World of Spirits: A Christian Perspective on Traditional and Folk Religions*. Oxford: Monarch, 2002.

Burrows, Millar. "The Original Language of the Gospel of John." *Journal of Biblical Literature* 49.2 (1930) 95–139.

Busia, Kofi A. "The Ashanti." In *African Worlds: Studies in the Cosmological Ideas and Social Values of African Peoples*, edited by Daryll Forde, 190–209. Reprint of 1954 edition with New Introduction by Wendy James. Oxford: Currey, 1999.

Butterworth, G. W. *Clement of Alexandria*. London: Heinnemann, 1919.

Bywater, Ingram. *Heracliti Ephesii Reliquiae*. Oxford: Clarendon, 1877.

Cairns, Huntington. "Introduction." In *The Collected Dialogues of Plato, Including the Letters*, edited by Edith Hamilton et al. Princeton: Princeton University Press, 1961.

Chadwick, Henry. *Early Christian Thought and the Classical Tradition: Studies in Justin, Clement, and Origen*. Oxford: Oxford University Press, 1966.

Chadwick, Henry. "St. Paul and Philo of Alexandria." *The Bulletin of the John Rylands Library* 48.2 (1966) 286–307.

Chea, John C. H. "Some Observations on Parental-Children Ties in the Old Testament and Their Possible Bearing on Filial Piety." In *A.D. 2000 and Beyond: A Mission Agenda*, edited by Vinay Samuel et al., 40–55. Oxford: Regnum, 1991.

Ching, Julia. *Chinese Religions*. London: Macmillan, 1993.

Christaller, Johannes G. *Dictionary of the Asante and Fante Language called Tshi (Twi)*. 2nd ed. Basel: Basel Evangelical Missionary Society, 1933.

———. *Twi Mmebusɛm Mpensã-Ahansia Mmoaano. A Collection of Three Thousand and Six hundred Tshi Proverbs in Use among the Negroes of the Gold Coast Speaking the Asante and Fante Language*. Basel: German Evangelical Missionary Society, 1879.

Christensen, Thomas G. *An African Tree of Life*. Maryknoll, NY: Orbis, 1990.

Cicero, Marcus Tullius. *De Natura Deorum: On the Nature of the Gods*. Translated by Francis Brooks. London: Methuen, 1896.

Clarke, Clifton R. *African Christology: Jesus in Post-Missionary African Christianity*. Eugene, OR: Pickwick, 2011.

———. "Faith in Christ in Post-Missionary Africa. Christology among Akan African Indigenous Churches in Ghana." PhD diss., University of Birmingham, 2002.

Cohn, Leopold, and Paul Wenland. *Philonis Alexandrini opera quae supersunt*. Berlin: Reimer, 1896.

Cole, Jennifer, and Karen Middleton. "Rethinking Ancestors and Colonial Power in Madagascar." *Africa: Journal of the International African Institute* 71.1 (2001) 1–37.

———. "Sacrifice, Narratives and Experience in East Madagascar." *Journal of Religion in Africa* 27, Fasc. 4, Religion in Madagascar II (1997) 401–25. http://www.jstor.org/stable/1581910. Accessed 26 February 2011.

Colwell, E. C. "A Definite Rule for the Use of the Article in the Greek New Testament." *Journal of Biblical Literature* 52 (1933) 12–21.

Crentsil, Perpetual. "Death, Ancestors, and HIV/AIDS among the Akan of Ghana." Helsinki: Helsinki University Printing, 2007. PDF, http://ethesis.helsinki.fi.

Crouzel, Henri. *Origen*. Translated by A. S. Worrall. Edinburgh: T. & T. Clark, 1989.

Cross, Robert C. "Logos and Forms in Plato." *Mind*, New Series, 63.252 (1954) 433–50.

Cummings, George. "Who Do You Say That I Am? A North American Minority Answer to the Christological Question." In *Sharing Jesus in the Two Thirds World*, edited by Vinay Samuel et al., 217–36. Grand Rapids: Eerdmans, 1983.

Dah, Dorcas Ini. "A Theological Interpretation of the Birifor Practice of Funerals and Its Implications for Christian Ministry to the Birifor of Burkina Faso." MTh diss., Akrofi-Christaller Institute, 2011.

Dahl, Nils Alstrup. *Jesus the Christ: The Historical Origins of Christological Doctrine*. Edited by Donald H. Juel. Minneapolis: Fortress, 1991.

Dakubu, Mary E. Kropp. *Ga-English Dictionary, with English-Ga Index*. 2nd ed, revised and expanded. Accra: Black Mask, 2009.

Danby, Herbert. *The Mishnah: Translated from The Hebrew with Introduction and Brief Explanatory Notes*. Oxford: Oxford University Press, 1933.

Daneel, M. L. "The Christian Gospel and the Ancestor Cult." *Missionalia* 1.2 (1973) 46–73.

Daniélou, Jean. *Origen*. Translated by Walter Mitchell. London: Sheed and Ward, 1955.

———. *A History of Early Christian Doctrine before the Council of Nicaea, Volume Two: Gospel Message and Hellenistic Culture*. Translated by John A. Baker. Philadelphia: Westminster, 1980.
Dankwa III, Nana Addo. *Christianity and African Traditional Beliefs*. New York: The Power of the Word, 1990.
———. *The Institution of Chieftaincy in Ghana: The Future*. Accra: Konrad Adenauer Foundation, 2004.
Danquah, Joseph B, *The Akan Doctrine of God: A Fragment of Gold Coast Ethics and Religion*. 2nd ed. London: Cass, 1968.
———. *Ancestors, Heroes and God*. Kibi, Ghana: Boakie, 1938.
———. "Autopsy on Old Ashanti." *African Affairs* 51.203 (1952) 134–43.
———. "The Culture of Akan." *Africa: Journal of the International African Institute* 22.4 (1952) 360–66.
———. *Gold Coast Akan Laws and Customs and the Akim Abuakwa Constitution*. London: Routledge, 1928.
Darkwah, Kofi. "Antecedents of Asante Culture." *Transactions of the Historical Society of Ghana*, New Series, 3 (1999) 57–79.
Davidson, William L. *The Stoic Creed*. Edinburgh: T. & T. Clark, 1907.
de Vries, Pieter. "The Targumim as Background of the Prologue of the Gospel according to John." *The American Journal of Biblical Theology* 18.14 (2013) 1–24.
Debrunner, A. "The Words λέγω, λόγος, ῥῆμα, λαλέω in the Greek World." In *TDNT* Vol. IV, edited by Gerhard Kittel et al., 71–77. Grand Rapids: Eerdmans, 1967.
Delling, Gerhard. "Πλήρωμα." In *TDNT* Vol. VI, edited by Gerhard Kittel et al., 298–305.
Der, B. G. "God and Sacrifice in the Traditional Religions of the Kasena and Dagaba of Northern Ghana." *Journal of Religion in Africa* 11, Fasc. 3 (1980) 172–87.
Desilva, David A. "Paul and the Stoa: A Comparison." *Journal of the Evangelical Theological Society* 38.4 (1995) 549–64.
Dickson, Kwesi. *The Gospel according to Luke*. Accra: Asempa, 1988.
———. *Theology in Africa*. Maryknoll, NY: Orbis, 1984.
Diels, Hermann. *Die Fragmente der Vorsokratiker*. Berlin: Weidmannsche Buchhandlung, 1903.
Dillon, John M. *The Middle Platonists, 80 B.C to A.D 220*. Rev. ed. Ithaca, NY: Cornell University Press, 1996.
Dodd, C. H. *The Interpretation of the Fourth Gospel*. Cambridge: Cambridge University Press, 1953.
Drummond, James. *Philo Judaeus: The Jewish-Alexandrian Philosophy in Its Development and Completion*, Vols. I & II. Edinburgh: Williams and Norgate, 1888.
Dunn, James D. G. *Christology in the Making: A New Testament Inquiry into the Origins of the Doctrine of the Incarnation*. 2nd ed. Grand Rapids: Eerdmans, 1989.
Dzobo, N. K. "Values in a Changing Society: Man, Ancestors, and God." In *Person and Community: Ghanaian Philosophical Studies I*, edited by Kwasi Wiredu et al., 224–40. Washington: The Council for Research in Values and Philosophy, 1992.
Edusa-Eyison, Joseph M. Y. "Kwesi A. Dickson: The Bible and African Life and Thought in Dialogue." In *African Theology in the 21st Century: The Contribution of the Pioneers. Vol. 2.*, edited by Bénézet Bujo et al., 93–123. Nairobi: Paulines Publications Africa, 2006.

Edwards, M. J. "Clement of Alexandria and His Doctrine of the Logos." *Vigiliae Christianae* 54.2. (2000) 159–77.
———. "Justin's Logos and the Word of God." *Journal of Early Christian Studies* 3.3 (1995) 261–80.
Ekem, John D. K. *New Testament Concepts of Atonement in an African Pluralistic Setting*. Accra: SonLife, 2005.
———. *Priesthood in Context: A Study of Akan Traditional Priesthood in Dialogical Relation to the Priest-Christology of the Epistle to the Hebrews, and Its Implications for a Relevant Functional Priesthood in Selected Churches among the Akan of Ghana*. Hamburg: Verlag an der Lottbek, 1994.
———. *Priesthood in Context: A Study of Priesthood in Some Christian and Primal Communities of Ghana and Its Relevance for Mother-Tongue Biblical Interpretation*. Accra: SonLife, 2009.
Endō, Masanobu. *Creation and Christology: A Study on the Johannine Prologue in the Light of Jewish Creation Accounts*. Tübingen: Mohr Siebeck, 2002.
Ephirim-Donkor, Anthony. *African Spirituality: On Becoming Ancestors*. Trenton, NJ: Africa World, 1997.
Epstein, Isidore, ed. *The Babylonian Talmud*. 38 vols. London: Soncino, 1935–52. Online version at http://www.come-and-hear.com/talmud/index.html, accessed September 5, 2013.
Ezeh, Uchenna A. *Jesus Christ the Ancestor: An African Contextual Christology in the Light of the Major Dogmatic Christological Definitions of the Church from the Council of Nicea, 325 to Chalcedon, 451*. New York: Lang, 2003.
Ezigbo, Victor I. "Contextualizing the Christ-Event: A Christological Study of the Interpretations and Appropriations of Jesus Christ in Nigerian Christianity." PhD diss., University of Edinburgh, 2008.
———. *Re-Imagining African Christologies: Conversing with the Interpretations and Appropriations of Jesus in Contemporary African Christianity*. Eugene, OR: Pickwick, 2010.
Fah, Yong Chen. "The Spirituality of Chinese Social Obligations." *Transformation* 19.1 (2002) 34–36.
Fasholé-Luke, Edward W. "Ancestor Veneration and the Communion of Saints." In *New Testament Christianity for Africa and the World: Essays in Honour of Harry Sawyerr*, edited by Mark E. Glasswell et al., 209–21. London: SPCK, 1974.
Ferguson, John. "The Achievement of Clement of Alexandria." *Religious Studies* 12.1 (1976) 59–80.
———. *Clement of Alexandria*. New York: Twayne, 1974.
Field, M. J. *Religion and Medicine of the Gã People*. London: Oxford University Press, 1937.
Fienup-Riordan, Ann. "Eye of the Dance: Spiritual Life of the Central Yup'ik Eskimos." In *Native Religions and Cultures of North America: Anthropology of the Sacred*, edited by Lawrence E. Sullivan, 181–207. New York: Continuum, 2002.
Fine, Gail J. "Knowledge and Logos in the Theaetetus." *The Philosophical Review* 88.3 (1979) 366–97.
Finnegan, Ruth. *Oral Literature in Africa*. Cambridge: Open Book, 2012.
Fortes, Meyer. *Religion, Morality and the Person: Essays on Tallensi Religion*. Edited by Jack Goody. New York: Cambridge University Press, 1987.

———. "Some Reflections on Ancestor Worship in Africa." In *African Systems of Thought*, edited by Meyer Fortes et al., 122–42. London: Oxford University Press, 1965.

Fotland, Roar G. "Ancestor Christology in Context: Theological Perspectives of Kwame Bediako." PhD Dissertation, University of Bergen, 2005.

———. "The Christology of Kwame Bediako." *Journal of African Christian Thought* 8.1 (2005) 36–49.

Frankfort, Henri. *Ancient Egyptian Religion: An Interpretation*. Reprint, New York: Harper Torchbooks, 1961.

Freedman, H. Maurice Simon, eds. *Midrash Kabbah. Translated into English with Notes, Glossary, and Indices: Volume 1*. London: Soncino, 1961.

Freeman, Kathleen. *The Pre-Socratic Philosophers: A Companion to Diels, Fragmente der Vorsokratiker*. 2nd ed. Oxford: Blackwell, 1966.

Fuller, Reginald H. *The Foundations of New Testament Christology*. London: Lutterworth, 1965.

Gaba, Christian R. Review of Joseph Buakye Danquah, *The Akan Doctrine of God: A Fragment of Gold Coast Ethics and Religion*. 2nd ed with a new introduction by Kwesi A. Dickson." *Journal of Religion in Africa* 2, Fasc. 1 (1969).

———. *Scriptures of an African People: Ritual Utterances of the Anlo*. New York: NOK, 1973.

Gaisie, Rudolf K. "'Lord of Both the Dead and Living' (Rom. 14:9): The Continuing Significance of Ancestor Christology in the Third Stage of the African Response to Jesus Christ." *Journal of African Christian Thought* 19.1 (2016) 4–18.

Gerleman, G. דָּבָר. In *Theological Lexicon of the Old Testament Vol. 1*. Translated by Mark E. Biddle, edited by Ernst Jenni et al. Peabody, MA: Hendrickson, 1997.

Go, Byung Chan. "'Belief' and 'Logos' in the Prologue of the Gospel of John: An Analysis of Complex Parallelism". PhD diss., Stellenbosch University, 2009.

Goodenough, Erwin R. *An Introduction to Philo Judaeus*. 2nd ed. Oxford: Blackwell, 1962.

———. *The Theology of Justin Martyr*. Jena: Verlag Frommannsche Buchhandlung, 1923.

Grant, Frederick Clifton. "St. Paul and Stoicism." *The Biblical World* 45.5 (1915) 268–81.

Grant, Robert M. "The Bible of Theophilus of Antioch." *Journal of Biblical Literature* 66.2 (1947) 173–96.

———. *Gods and the One God*. Edited by Wayne A. Meeks. Philadelphia: Westminster, 1986.

———. *Irenaeus of Lyons*. The Early Fathers. Edited by Carol Harrison. London: Routledge, 1997.

———. *Jesus After the Gospels: The Christ of the Second Century*. Louisville: Westminster/John Knox, 1990.

Green, Jay P., ed. *The Interlinear Bible. One Volume Edition*. 2nd ed. Lafayette: Sovereign Grace, 1986.

Greene, Colin. *Christology in Cultural Perspective: Marking Out the Horizons*. Milton Keynes, UK: Paternoster, 2003.

Grey, Mary. "Who Do You Say That I Am? Images of Christ in Feminist Liberation Theology." In *Images of Christ: Ancient and Modern*, edited by Stanley E. Porter et al., 189–204. Sheffield, UK: Sheffield Academic Press, 1997.

Grillmeier, Aloys. *Christ in Christian Tradition: From the Apostolic Age to Chalcedon, 451, Vol. 1.* Translated by John Bowden. 2nd ed. Atlanta: John Knox, 1975.

Guthrie, William K. C. *A History of Greek Philosophy: Volume 1, The Earlier Presocratics and the Pythagoreans.* Cambridge: Cambridge University Press, 1962.

Gutiérrez, Gustavo. *A Theology of Liberation.* Rev. ed. London: SCM, 1988.

Gyekye, Kwame. *African Cultural Values: An Introduction.* Accra: Sankofa, 1996.

———. *Beyond Cultures: Perceiving a Common Humanity.* 32nd Series of J. B Danquah Memorial Lectures. Accra: Ghana Academy of Arts and Sciences, 2000.

———. *An Essay on African Philosophical Thought: The Akan Conceptual Scheme.* Rev. ed. Philadelphia: Temple University Press, 1995.

———. Interview, 30 April 2012, Dzorwulu, Accra.

———. *Tradition and Modernity: Philosophical Reflections on the African Experience.* New York: Oxford University Press 1997.

Hagan, George P. "The Ascent to the Golden Stool: Women Make the King." In *The King Returns: Enstoolment of Asantehene Otumfuo Osei Tutu II and the Eyikɛsee. Great Funeral of Otumfuo Opoku Ware II,* edited by Irene K. Odotei et al., 33–42. Legon, Ghana: University of Ghana: Institute of African Studies, 2003.

Hägg, Henny F. *Clement of Alexandria and the Beginnings of Christian Apophaticism.* Oxford: Oxford University Press, 2006.

Hahm, David E. *The Origins of Stoic Cosmology.* Columbus, OH: Ohio State University Press, 1977.

Hakim, Albert B. *Historical Introduction to Philosophy.* 5th ed. Upper Saddle River, NJ: Pearson Prentice Hall, 2006.

Harris, J. Rendel. *Fragments of Philo Judaeus.* Cambridge: Cambridge: Cambridge University Press, 1886.

———. *The Origin of the Prologue to St John's Gospel.* Cambridge: Cambridge University Press, 1917.

Hengel, Martin. *The Septuagint as Christian Scriptures: Its Prehistory and the Problem of Its Canon.* Translated by Mark E. Biddle. London: T. & T. Clark, 2004.

———. *Studies in Early Christology.* Edinburgh: T. & T. Clark, 1995.

Hennelly, Alfred T., ed. *Liberation Theology: A Documentary History.* Edited with introduction, commentary, and translation by A. T Hennelly. Maryknoll, NY: Orbis, 1990.

Heron, Alasdair. "'Logos, Image, Son': Some Models and Paradigms in Early Christology." In *Creation, Christ and Culture: Studies in Honour of T. F. Torrance,* edited by Richard W. A. McKinney, 43–62. Edinburgh: T. & T. Clark, 1976.

Hinge, Teresa M. "Jesus Christ and the Liberation of Women in Africa." In *Feminist Theology from the Third World: A Reader,* edited by Ursula King, 261–68. London: SPCK, 1994.

Hobhouse, Leonard T. *Morals in Evolution: A Study in Comparative Ethics.* New York: Holt, 1915.

Holmes, Michael W., ed., *The Apostolic Fathers.* 2nd ed. Translated by J. B. Lightfoot and J. R. Harmer. Updated ed. Grand Rapids: Baker, 1999.

Holte, Ragnar. "Logos Spermatikos: Christianity and Ancient Philosophy according to St. Justin's Apologies." Translated by Tina Pierce. *Studia Theologica* XII (1958) 109–68.

Howell, Allison M. *The Religious Itinerary of a Ghanaian People: The Kasena and the Christian Gospel.* Achimota, Ghana: Africa Christian, 2001.

Hunt, Emily J. *Christianity in the Second Century: The Case of Tatian.* London: Routledge, 2003.
Hwang, Bernard. "Ancestor Cult Today." *Missiology: An International Review* 5.3 (1977) 339–65. DOI: 10.1177/009182967700500307.
Idowu, Bolaji E. *African Traditional Religion: A Definition.* London: SCM, 1973.
———. *Olódùmaré: God in Yoruba Belief.* London: Longmans, 1962.
———. "The Predicament of the Church in Africa." In *Christianity in Tropical Africa*, edited by Christian G. Baeta, 417–36. London: Oxford University Press, 1968.
Ilo, Stanislaus Chukwudiebube. "African Christology: A Comparative Study of the Contextual Christologies of Charles Nyamiti and Bénézet Bujo and Their Implications for African Theologies." MTh diss., University of St Michael's College and University of Toronto, 2006.
Iloanusi, Obiakoizu A. *Myths of the Creation of Man and the Origin of Death in Africa.* Frankfurt am Main: Lang, 1984.
Inge, William Ralph. "Logos." In *Encyclopaedia of Religion and Ethics,* Vol. VIII, edited by James Hastings et al., 133–38. London: T. & T. Clark, 2003.
Jaeger, Werner. *The Theology of the Early Greek Philosophers.* Oxford: Oxford University Press, 1968.
Jay, Eric George. *Origen's Treatise on Prayer. Translations and Notes with an Account of the Practice and Doctrine of Prayer from New Testament Times to Origen.* London: SPCK, 1954.
Jennings, Brian K. *Leading Virtue: A Model for the Contextualisation of Christian Ethics.* Frankfurt am Main: Lang, 2009.
Jobes, Karen H., and Moisés Silva. *Invitation to the Septuagint.* Grand Rapids: Baker Academic, 2000.
Josephus. *The Works of Josephus.* New updated ed. Translated by William Whiston. Peabody, MA: Hendrickson, 1987.
Kabasélé, François. *Celebrating Jesus Christ in Africa: Liturgy and Inculturation.* Translated by Jean Smith. Maryknoll, NY: Orbis, 1998.
———. "Christ as Ancestor and Elder Brother." In *Faces of Jesus in Africa*, edited by Robert Schreiter, 116–27. New York: Orbis, 1991.
———. "Christ as Chief." In *Faces of Jesus in Africa*, edited by Robert Schreiter, 103–15. New York: Orbis, 1991.
Kahn, Charles H. *The Art and Thought of Heraclitus: An Edition of the Fragments with Translation and Commentary.* Cambridge: Cambridge University Press, 1979.
Karavites, Peter. Panayiotis. *Evil, Freedom, and the Road to Perfection in Clement of Alexandria.* Leiden: Brill, 1999.
Kärkkäinen, Veli-Matti. *Christology: A Global Introduction.* Grand Rapids: Baker Academic, 2003.
Kasper, Walter. *Jesus the Christ.* Translated by V. Green. London: Burns & Oates, 1976.
Kelly, J. N. D. *Early Christian Creeds.* 3rd ed. London: Longman, 1972.
———. *Early Christian Doctrines* 4th ed. London: Adam & Charles Black, 1968.
Kirk, G. S. *Heraclitus: The Cosmic Fragments, Edited with an Introduction and Commentary.* Cambridge: Cambridge University Press, 1962.
Kirk, G. S., J. E. Raven, and M. Schofield. *The Presocratic Philosophers: A Critical History with a Selection of Texts.* 2nd ed. Cambridge: Cambridge: Cambridge University Press, 1983.

Kirk, J. Andrew. *Liberation Theology: An Evangelical View from the Third World.* Basingstoke, UK: Marshall Morgan and Scott, 1979.

Kissi, Seth. "An Akan View of Jesus: Exegetical Exploration into Hebrews 1:1-4 in the Light of Insights from the Akan Mother Tongue." MTh diss., Trinity Theological Seminary, Legon, 2008.

Kittel, Gerhard. "Word and Speech in the New Testament." In *Theological Dictionary of the New Testament, vol. IV,* 100-136. Reprint, Grand Rapids: Eerdmans, 1976.

Kohlenberger III, John R., and James A. Swanson. *The Hebrew English Concordance to the Old Testament with the New International Version.* Grand Rapids: Zondervan, 1998.

Köstenberger, Andreas J. *John.* Baker Exegetical Commentary on the New Testament. Grand Rapids: Baker Academic, 2004.

Kramer, Werner. *Christ, Lord, Son of God.* Translated by Brian Hardy. London: SCM, 1966.

Kröger, Franz. *Ancestor Worship among the Bulsa of Northing Ghana.* Hohenschäftlarn bei München: Renner, 1982.

Kruse, Colin G. *John: An Introduction and Commentary.* Nottingham, UK: IVP, 2003.

Kuma, Afua. *Jesus of the Deep Forest: Prayers and Praises of Afua Kuma.* Translated by Jon Kirby. Accra: Asεmpa, 1980.

———. *Kwaeberentwu Ase Yesu: Ayeyi Ne Mpaebɔ.* Accra: Asεmpa, 1980.

Kuronti Odwira 2004 Brochure. Tema: Sanju Consult, 2004.

Kumuro, Naoko. "Christianity and Ancestor Worship in Japan." *SWC* 9.1 (2003) 60-68.

Küster, Volker. *The Many Faces of Jesus Christ: Intercultural Christology.* Translated by John Bowden. Maryknoll, NY: Orbis, 2001.

Kwadwo, Osei. *A Handbook on Asante Culture.* Kumasi, Ghana: O. Kwadwo Enterprise, 2002.

Laertius, Diogenes. *Lives of Eminent Philosophers with an English Translation by R. D. Hicks,* Vol. II. London: Heinemann, 1925.

Lake, Kirsopp J., E. L. Oulton, H. J. Lawlor, trans. *Eusebius, The Ecclesiastical History,* Vol. 2. Loeb Classical Library. London: Heinemann, 1932.

Lamp, Jeffrey S. "Wisdom in Col 1:15-20: Contribution and Significance." *JETS* 41.1 (1998) 45-53.

Laryea, Philip T. "Christianity as Vernacular Religion: A Study in the Theological Significance of Mother Tongue Apprehension of the Christian Faith in West Africa with Reference to the Works of Ephraim Amu. 1899-1995." PhD diss., University of KwaZulu-Natal, 2006.

———. *Ephraim Amu: Nationalist, Poet and Theologian (1899-1995).* Akropong-Akwapim, Ghana: Regnum Africa, 2012.

———. "Mother Tongue Theology: Reflections on Images of Jesus in the Poetry of Afua Kuma." *Journal African Christian Thought* 3.1 (2000) 50-60.

———. "St. Ignatius of Antioch and Afua Kuma of Kwahu: A Study in Some Images of Jesus in Second Century Christianity and Modern African Christianity." MTh diss., University of Natal, 2000.

———. *Yesu Hɔmɔwɔ Nuntsɔ: Nikasemɔ Ni Kɔɔ Bɔni Kristofoi Naa Yesu Yε Gamεi Akusumfeemɔ Kε Blema Saji Amli.* Akropong-Akuapem: Regnum Africa, 2004.

Latourette, S. Kenneth. *A History of the Expansion of Christianity, Vol. I: The First Five Centuries.* New York: Harper & Brothers, 1937.

Lifshitz, Fima. *An African Journey Through Its Art*. Bloomington, IN: AuthorHouse, 2009.

Lightfoot, R. H. *St. John's Gospel: A Commentary*. Edited by C. F. Evans. Oxford: Oxford University Press, 1956.

Lovelady, Edgar J. "The Logos Concept: A Critical Monograph on John 1:1. Abridged by the Author." *Grace Theological Journal* 4.2 (1963) 15–24.

Lyman, J. Rebecca. *Christology and Cosmology: Models of Divine Activity in Origen, Eusebius, and Athanasius*. Oxford: Clarendon, 1993.

Mackie, Scott D. "Seeing God in Philo of Alexandria: The Logos, the Powers, or the Existent One?" In *The Studia Philonica Annual: Studies in Hellenistic Judaism*, vol. 21, edited by David T. Runia et al., 25–47. 2009.

Maclagan, J. P. *Chinese Religious Ideas: A Christian Valuation*. London: SCM, 1926.

Macrae, Clare. *The Sacred Tree: Divinities and Ancestors in Encounter with Christianity in Religious Experience and History of the Early Irish and Akan people of Ghana*. Cardiff: Cardiff Academic, 2000.

Magesa, Laurenti. *African Religion: The Moral Traditions of Abundant Life*. Maryknoll, NY: Orbis, 1997.

Makwasha, Gift M. "'Not Without My Ancestors': A Christological Case Study of the Shona Ancestor Cult of Zimbabwe." DTh diss., Boston University, 2009.

Malherbe, Abraham J., and Wayne A. Meeks, eds. *The Future of Christology: Essays in Honor of Leander E. Keck*. Minneapolis: Fortress, 1993.

Markus, R. A. *Christianity in the Roman World*. London: Thames and Hudson, 1974.

Marcus, Ralph. *Philo Supplement II: Questions and Answers on Exodus*. The Loeb Classical Library. Cambridge: Harvard University Press, 1953.

Marshall, I. Howard. *The Gospel of Luke: A Commentary on the Greek Text*. Exeter, UK: Paternoster, 1978.

———. *The Origins of New Testament Christology*. Updated ed. Leicester: IVP, 1990.

———. "Titles of Jesus Christ." In *New Bible Dictionary*, 2nd ed., edited by J. D. Douglas et al., 584–93. Leicester, UK: IVP, 1982.

Martey, Emmanuel. *African Theology: Inculturation and Liberation*. Maryknoll, NY: Orbis, 1995.

Martin, Ralph P. "Pleroma." In *The International Standard Bible Encyclopedia, Vol. 3 K-P*, edited by Geoffrey W. Bromiley, 887–89. Grand Rapids: Eerdmans, 1995.

Mbiti, John S. *African Religions and Philosophy*. 2nd ed. Oxford: Heinemann Educational, 1989.

———. *Bible and Theology in African Christianity*. Nairobi: Oxford University Press, 1986.

———. *Concepts of God in Africa*. London: SPCK, 1970.

———. "Is Jesus Christ in African Religion?" In *Exploring Afro-Christology*, edited by John S. Pobee, 21–29. Frankfurt am Main: Lang, 1992.

McGuckin, John Anthony, ed. *The Westminster Handbook to Origen*. Louisville: John Knox, 2004.

McKeon, Richard, ed. *The Basic Works of Aristotle*. New York: Random House, 1941.

Meyerowitz, Eva. *The Akan of Ghana: Their Ancient Beliefs*. London: Faber & Faber, 1958.

———. *Akan Traditions of Origin*. London: Faber and Faber, 1952.

———. *The Sacred State of the Akan*. London: Faber and Faber, 1951.

Migne, Jacques P. *Patrologiae Cursus Completus*, Vols. 6–9. Paris: Migne, 1844–.

Mkhize, Nhlanhla. "Psychology: An African Perspective." In *Critical Psychology*, edited by Derek Hook, 24–52. Lansdowne: UCT, 2004.

Moffatt, James. *A Critical and Exegetical Commentary on the Epistle to the Hebrews.* Edinburgh: T. & T. Clark, 1924.

Mofokeng, Takatso A. *The Crucified among the Crossbearers: Towards a Black Christology.* Kampen: Uitgeversmaatschappij J. H. Kok, 1983.

Moloney, Raymond. "African Christology." *Theological Studies* 48 (1987) 500–515.

Moodley, Edley J. *Shembe, Ancestors, and Christ: A Christological Inquiry with Missiological Implications.* Eugene, OR: Pickwick, 2008.

Moule, C. F. D. *The Origin of Christology.* Cambridge: Cambridge University Press, 1977.

Moulton, W. F., and A. S. Geden. *A Concordance to the Greek Testament.* 5th ed., revised by H. K. Moulton. Edinburgh: T. & T. Clark, 1978.

Mounce, William D. *The Analytical Lexicon to the Greek New Testament.* Grand Rapids: Zondervan, 1993.

Mugambi, J. N. K., and Laurenti Magesa, eds. *Jesus in African Christianity: Experimentation and Diversity in African Christology.* 2nd ed. Nairobi: Acton, 1998.

Muraoka, T. *A Greek-English Lexicon of the Septuagint. Chiefly of the Pentateuch and Twelve Prophets.* Louvain: Peeters-Louvain, 2002.

Muskus, Eddy J. *The Origins and Early Development of Liberation Theology in Latin America with Particular Reference to Gustavo Gutiérrez.* Carlisle, UK: Paternoster, 2002.

Muzorewa, Gwinyai H. *The Origins and Development of African Theology.* Maryknoll, NY: Orbis, 1985.

Nasimiyu-Wasike, Anne. "Christology and an African Woman's Experience." In *Faces of Jesus in Africa*, edited by Robert Schreiter, 70–81. New York: Orbis, 1991.

Ng'ang'a, Abraham Waigi. "The Place of the Transcendent in African Life and Thought: Reading Kenyatta's 'Facing Mount Kenya' as a Contribution to African Theology." MTh diss., Akrofi-Christaller Institute, Akropong-Akuapem, 2006.

Ngewa, Samuel. "Commentary on the Gospel of John." In *Africa Bible Commentary*, edited by Tokunboh Adeyemo, 1251–96. Nairobi: WordAlive, 2008.

Niebuhr, H. Richard. *Christ and Culture.* New York, Harper & Brothers, 1951.

Niese, Benedikt. *Flavii Iosephi Opera.* Berlin: Weidmann, 1892.

Nketia, J. H. Kwabena. "Birth, Puberty and Death." In *Christianity and African Culture*, 24–38. Accra: Christian Council of the Gold Coast, 1955.

———. *The Role of Traditional Festivals in Community Life.* Legon, Ghana: University of Ghana: Institute of African Studies, n.d.

Nukunya, G. K. *Kinship and Marriage among the Anlo Ewe.* London: Athlone, 1969.

———. *Tradition and Change in Ghana: An Introduction to Sociology.* 2nd ed. Accra: Ghana Universities Press, 2003.

Nwala, T. Uzodinma. *Igbo Philosophy.* Lagos: Lantern, 1985.

Nwaogwugwu, Cletus C. *Ancestor Christology: A Christian Evaluation of the Ancestral Cult in the Traditional Religion of the Sub-Saharan Africa.* Bloomington, IN: iUniverse, 2011.

Nyamiti, Charles. "African Christologies Today." In *Faces of Jesus in Africa*, edited by Robert Schreiter, 3–23. New York: Orbis, 1991.

———. *Christ as Our Ancestor: Christology from an African Perspective*. Gweru, Zimbabwe: Mambo, 1984.

———. "Contemporary African Christologies: Assessment and Practical Suggestions." In *Paths of African Theology*, edited by Rosino Gibellini, 62–77. Maryknoll, NY: Orbis, 1994.

———. *Jesus Christ, the Ancestor of Humankind: An Essay on African Christology*. Nairobi: CUEA, 2006.

O'Collins, Gerald. *Christology: A Biblical Historical and Systematic Study of Jesus*. 2nd ed. Oxford: Oxford University Press, 2009.

Obeng, Ernest E. *Ancient Ashanti Chieftaincy*. Tema, Ghana: Ghana Publishing Corporation, 1988.

Ofosu-Appiah, L. H. *Life and Times of Joseph Boakye Danquah*. Accra: Waterville, Presbyterian Book Depot, 1974.

Onions, C. T., ed. *The Oxford Universal Dictionary on Historical Principles*. 3rd ed. Oxford: Oxford University Press, 1955.

Opoku, Kofi A. "African Traditional Religion: An Enduring Heritage." In *Religious Plurality in Africa: Essays in Honour of John S. Mbiti*, edited by Jacob K. Olupona et al., 67–82. Berlin: de Gruyter, 1993.

———. *Festivals of Ghana*. Accra: Ghana, 1970.

———. *West African Traditional Religion*. Accra: FEP International, 1978.

Origen. *Commentary on the Gospel according to John, Books 1–10*. Translated by Ronald E. Heine. Washington: Catholic University of America Press, 1989.

———. *Contra Celsum*. Translated by Henry Chadwick. Cambridge: Cambridge University Press, 1953.

———. *Homilies on Jeremiah: Homily on 1 Kings 28*. Translated by John Clark Smith. Washington, DC: Catholic University of America Press, 1998. http://www.questia.com/read/86025281.

Origenes. *Origenis Contra Celsum, libri VIII*. Edited by M. Marcovich. Leiden: Brill, 2001.

Orobator, Agbonkhianmeghe E. *Theology Brewed in an African Pot*. Maryknoll, NY: Orbis, 2008.

Osborn, E. F. *Justin Martyr*. Tübingen: Mohr, 1973.

———. *The Philosophy of Clement of Alexandria*. Cambridge: Cambridge University Press, 1957.

Ott, Martin. *African Theology in Images*. Blantyre, Malawi: Christian Literature Association in Malawi, 2000.

Oyeshile, Olatunji A. "Towards an African Concept of a Person: Person in Yoruba, Akan and Igbo Thoughts." *Orita* XXXIV.1&2 (2002) 104–14.

Pannenberg, Wolfhart. *Jesus: God and Man*. Translated from the German by Lewis L. Wilkins and Duane A. Priebe. London: SCM, 1968.

Park, Chang-Won. "Between God and Ancestors: Ancestral Practice in Korean Protestantism." *International Journal for the Study of the Christian Church* 10.4 (2010) 257–73.

Parratt, John. *Reinventing Christianity: African Theology Today*. Grand Rapids: Eerdmans, 1995.

Parrinder, Geoffrey. *West African Religion: Illustrated from the Beliefs and Practices of the Yoruba, Ewe, Akan and Kindred Peoples*. London: Epworth, 1949.

Patrick, G. T. W. *The Fragments of the Work of Heraclitus of Ephesus on Nature: Translated from the Greek Text of Bywater, with an Introduction Historical and Critical.* Baltimore, MD: Murray, 1889.

Pearson, Birger A. *Gnosticism, Judaism, and Egyptian Christianity.* Minneapolis: Fortress, 1990.

Pelikan, Jaroslav. *Jesus through the Centuries: His Place in the History of Culture.* New Heaven: Yale University Press, 1985.

Pelikan, Jaroslav, and Valerie Hotchkiss, eds. *Creeds and Confessions of Faith in the Christian Tradition: Volume I: Early, Eastern, and Medieval.* New Haven: Yale University Press, 2003.

Philo. *Questions and Answers on Genesis.* Translated from the Ancient Armenian Version of the Original Greek by Ralph Marcus. Cambridge: Harvard University Press, 1953.

Pobee, John S. "In Search of Christology in Africa: Some Considerations for Today." In *Exploring Afro-Christology*, edited by John S. Pobee, 9–20. Frankfurt am Main: Lang, 1992.

———. *Kwame Nkrumah and the Church in Ghana, 1949–1966.* Accra: Asempa, 1988.

———. *Toward an African Theology.* Nashville: Abingdon, 1979.

Polland, T. Evan. "Cosmology and the Prologue of the Fourth Gospel." *Vigiliae Christianae* 12.3 (1958) 147–53.

Prestige, G. L. *God in Patristic Thought.* 2nd ed. London: SPCK, 1952.

Procksch, O. "The Word of God in the Old Testament." In *Theological Dictionary of the New Testament*, IV, 91–100. Reprint, Grand Rapids: Eerdmans, 1976.

Puech, Aimé. *Les Apologistes grecs du deuxième siècle de notre ère.* Paris: Hachette, 1912.

Quarshie, Benhardt Y. "'Jesus, Pioneer and Perfecter of Faith' Heb. 12:2: Kwame Bediako's Hebrews-based Ancestor Christology Revisited." In *Seeing New Facets of the Diamond: Christianity as a Universal Faith: Essays in Honour of Kwame Bediako*, edited by Gillian M. Bediako et al., 21–37. Akropong-Akuapem: Regnum Africa, 2014.

Quasten, Johannes. *Patrology, Volume I: The Beginnings of Patristic Literature.* Utrecht-Antwerp: Spectrum, 1950.

Raafluab, Kurt A. "Poets, Lawgivers and the Beginnings of Political Reflections in Archaic Greece." In *The Cambridge History of Greek and Roman Political Thought*, edited by Christopher Rowe et al., 23–59. Cambridge: Cambridge University Press, 2000.

Rainbow, Paul A. "Monotheism and Christology in 1 Corinthians 8:4–6." D.Phil. diss., Oxford University, 1987.

Rattray, Robert S. *Ashanti.* Oxford: Oxford University Press, 1923.

———. *Ashanti Proverbs (The Primitive Ethics of a Savage People). Translated from the Original with Grammatical and Anthropological Notes.* Oxford: Oxford University Press, 1916.

———. *Religion and Art in Ashanti.* Oxford: Oxford University Press, 1927.

Redepenning, Ernst R. *Origenes: De Principiis.* Lipsiae: In Bibliopolio Dykiano, 1836.

Reed, David A. "How Semitic Was John? Rethinking the Hellenistic Background to John 1:1." *Anglican Theological Review* 85.4 (2003) 709–26.

Reiling, J. J. L. Swellengrebel: *A Translator's Handbook on the Gospel of Luke.* Leiden: Brill, 1971.

Rhee, Helen. *Early Christian Literature: Christ and Culture in the Second and Third Centuries.* London: Routledge, 2005.

Ridderbos, Herman. "The Structure and Scope of the Prologue to the Gospel of John." *Novem Testamentum* 8, Fasc. 2/4 (1966) 180–201.

Robinson, James M. *A New Quest of the Historical Jesus.* Naperville: Allenson, 1959.

Rogers, Rick. *Theophilus of Antioch: The Life and Thought of a Second-Century Bishop.* Lanham, MD: Lexington, 2000.

Rokéah, David. *Justin Martyr and the Jews.* Leiden: Brill, 2002.

Ross, W. D., ed. *The Works of Aristotle.* Vol. I. Oxford: Oxford University Press, 1937.

———, ed. *The Works of Aristotle.* Vol. XI. Oxford: Oxford University Press, 1946.

Rousseau, John J., and Rami Arav. *Jesus and His World: An Archaeological and Cultural Dictionary.* Minneapolis: Fortress, 1995.

Roy, Christian. *Traditional Festivals: A Multicultural Encyclopedia.* Santa Barbara: ABC-CLIO, 2005.

Rudolph, Kurt. *Gnosis: The Nature and History of Gnosticism.* New York: HarperCollins, 1987.

Runia, David T. "God the Creator as Demiurge in Philo of Alexandria." *Horizons* 3.1 (2012) 41–59.

———. "Logos." In *Dictionary of Deities and Demons in the Bible,* 2nd ed., edited by Karel van der Toorn et al., 525–31. Grand Rapids: Eerdmans, 1999.

———. "Philo, Alexandrine and Jew." In *Exegesis and Philosophy: Studies on Philo of Alexandria,* 1–18. Aldershot, UK: Variorum, 1990.

———. *Philo in Early Christian Literature: A Survey.* Assen: Van Gorcum, 1993.

———. "Philo of Alexandria and the Timaeus of Plato." Vol. I. PhD diss., Vrije Universiteit, Amsterdam, 1983.

———. "The Theme of Flight and Exile in the Allegorical Thought-World of Philo of Alexandria." In *The Studia Philonica Annual: Studies in Hellenistic Judaism,* Vol. 21, edited by David T. Runia et al., 1–24. Atlanta: SBL, 2009.

———. "'Where, Tell Me, Is the Jew . . . ?': Basil, Philo and Isidore of Pelusium." *Vigiliae Christianae* 46.2. (1992) 172–89.

Ryle, Herbert E. *Philo and Holy Scripture.* London: Macmillan, 1895.

Sackey, Brigid M. "Recognising Other Dimensions of Epistemology: Conceptualisation of *Abosom* ("Deities") in Ghanaian Experience." *Institute of African Studies: Research Review.* New Series, 16.1. (2000) 13–30.

Sanon, Anselme T. "Jesus, Master of Initiation." In *Faces of Jesus in Africa,* edited by Robert Schreiter, 85–102. New York: Orbis, 1991.

Sarpong, Peter K. "Forward." In Kofi Ron Lange and Johann Gottlieb Christaller, *Three Thousand Six Hundred Ghanaian Proverbs: From the Asante and Fante Language with English translations.* Lewiston, NY: Mellen, 2000.

———. *Dear Nana: Letters to my Ancestor.* Vol. 1. Takoradi, Ghana: Franciscan, 1998.

———. *Ghana in Retrospect: Some Aspects of Ghanaian Culture.* Tema, Ghana: Ghana Publishing, 1974.

———. *Libation.* Accra: Anansesem, 1996.

———. *The Sacral Stools of the Akan.* Tema, Ghana: Ghana Publishing, 1971.

Satyavrata, Ivan M. *God Has Not Left Himself without Witness.* Oxford: Regnum International, 2011.

Sawyerr, Harry A. *Creative Evangelism: Towards a New Christian Encounter with Africa.* London: Lutterworth, 1968.

———. *God Ancestor or Creator? Aspects of Traditional Belief in Ghana, Nigeria and Sierra Leone*. London: Longman, 1970.

———. *The Practice of Presence: Shorter Writings of Harry Sawyerr*. Edited by John Parratt; foreword by Andrew Walls. Grand Rapids: Eerdmans, 1996.

Schaff, Philip, and Henry Wace, eds. *A Select Library of Nicene and Post-Nicene Fathers of the Christian Church: Second Series Volume I. Eusebius: Church History, Life of Constantine the Great, and Oration in Praise of Constantine*. Edinburgh: T. & T. Clark, 1991.

———, eds. *A Select Library of the Nicene and Post-Nicene Fathers of the Christian Church: Second Series: Volume III Theodoret, Jerome, Gennadius, and Rufinus: Historical Writings*. Grand Rapids: Eerdmans, 1996.

Shields, Christopher. "The Logos of 'Logos': "Theaetetus" 206c–210b." *Apeiron: A Journal for Ancient Philosophy and Science* 32.4, *Recognition Remembrance & Reality: New Essays on Plato's Epistemology and Metaphysics* (1999) 107–24.

Schenck, Kenneth. *A Brief Guide to Philo*. Louisville: Westminster John Knox, 2005.

Schmidt, W. H. דָּבָר. In *Theological Dictionary of the Old Testament*, Vol. III, edited by G. Johannes Botterweck et al., translated by John T. Willis, Geoffrey W. Bromiley, David E. Green, 84–124. Grand Rapids: Eerdmans, 1978.

Schopf, J., and L. Richter. *An English-Accra or Gã Dictionary: Engliši-Gã Wiemoi: Ašišitšômo Wolo*. 2nd ed. Basel: Basel Evang. Missionary Society, 1912.

Scholer, David M. "Foreword: An Introduction to Philo Judaeus of Alexandria." In *The Works of Philo*, edited by C. D. Yonge. Peabody, MA: Hendrickson, 1993.

Schreiter, Robert, ed. *Faces of Jesus in Africa*. Maryknoll, NY: Orbis, 1991.

Schwartz, Daniel R. "Philo, His Family, and His Times." In *The Cambridge Companion to Philo*, edited by Adam Kamesar, 9–31. Cambridge: Cambridge University Press, 2009.

Scott, James Martin Clark. "Sophia and the Johannine Jesus." PhD diss., Durham University, Durham, 1990. Online: http://etheses.dur.ac.uk/6231/.

Seaman, Gary. "The Sexual Politics of Karmic Retribution." In *The Anthropology of Taiwanese Society*, edited by Emily M Ahern et al., 381–96. Standford: Standard University Press, 1981.

Sellars, John. *Stoicism*. Berkeley: University of California Press, 2006.

Septuaginta. Stuttgart: Deutsche Bibelgesellschaft, 1979.

Setiloane, Gabriel M. "I am an African." In *Primal World-Views, Christian Involvement in Dialogue with Traditional Thought Forms*, edited by J. B. Taylor, 56–59. Ibadan, Nigeria: Daystar, 1976.

Shorey, Paul. *Plato in Twelve Volumes, Vols. 5 & 6*. Translated by Paul Shorey. Cambridge: Harvard University Press, 1969.

Shutt, R. J. H. "Letter of Ariteas: A New Translation and Introduction." In *The Old Testament Psuedepigrapha*, edited by James H. Charlesworth, Vol. 2, 7–34. New York: Doubleday, 1985.

Skarsaune, Oskar. *The Proof from Prophecy: A Study in Justin Martyr's Proof-Text Tradition: Text-Type, Provenance, Theological Profile*. Leiden: Brill, 1987.

Smith, Christopher. "The Religion of Archaic Rome." In *A Companion to Roman Religion*, edited by Jörg Rüpke, 31–42. Oxford: Blackwell, 2007.

Smith, Edwin W. *African Beliefs and Christian Faith: An Introduction to Theology for African Students, Evangelists and Pastors*. London: United Society for Christian Literature, 1943.

Smith, Edwin W. "Review: The Akan Doctrine of God, a Fragment of Gold Coast Ethics and Religion by J. B. Danquah." *African Affairs*. 43.173. (1944) 186–87.
Souter, Alexander. *A Pocket Lexicon to the Greek New Testament*. Oxford: University Press, 1916.
Stählin, Otto. *Die Griechischen Christlichen Schrifsteller der ersten drei Jahrhunderte*. GCS. Leipzig: Hinrichs' sche Buchhandlung, 1906.
Stambaugh, John, and David Balch. *The Social World of the First Christians*. London: SPCK, 1986.
Stevenson, J., and W. H. C. Frend. *A New Eusebius: Documents Illustrating the History of the Church to AD 337*. London: SPCK, 1987.
Stinton, Diane B. *Jesus of Africa: Voices of Contemporary African Christology*. Maryknoll, NY: Orbis, 2004.
Studer, Basil. *Trinity and Incarnation: The Faith of the Early Church*. Translated by Matthias Westerhoff, edited by Andrew Louth. Edinburgh: T. & T. Clark, 1993.
Suk-Jay, Yim, Roger I. Janelli, Dawnhee Yim Janelli. "Korean Religion." In *The Religious Traditions of Asia*, edited by Joseph M. Kitagawa, 332–46. New York: Macmillan, 1989.
Sundkler, Bengt. *Bantu Prophets in South Africa*. 2nd ed. London: Oxford University Press, 1961.
Swain, Tony, and Garry Trompf. *The Religions of Oceania*. London: Routledge, 1995.
Swete, Henry B., ed. *The Old Testament in Greek according to the Septuagint: Vol. I Genesis: IV Kings*. 4th ed. Cambridge: Cambridge University Press, 1925.
Tappa, Louise. "The Christ-Event from the Viewpoint of African Women: A Protestant Perspective." In *With Passion and Compassion: Third World Women Doing Theology*, edited by Virginia Fabella et al., 30–34. Maryknoll, NY: Orbis, 1988.
Tasker, R. V. G. *The Gospel according to St. John: An Introduction and Commentary*. London: Tyndale, 1964.
Taylor, Alfred E. *Plato: The Man and His Work*. 6th ed. London: Methuen, 1949.
Taylor, John V. *The Primal Vision: Christian Presence amid African Religion*. London: SCM, 1963.
Tempels, Placide. *Bantu Philosophy*. English translation by Colin King. Paris: Présence Africaine, 1959.
Termini, Cristina. "Philo's Thought within the Context of Middle Judaism." Translated by Adam Kamesar. In *Cambridge Companion to Philo*, edited by Adam Kamesar, 95–123. Cambridge: Cambridge University Press, 2009.
Thackeray, H. St. J., ed. "The Letter of Aristeas." In *An Introduction to the Old Testament in Greek* by H. B. Swete. Cambridge: Cambridge University Press, 1902.
Thérèse, Souga. "The Christ-Event from the Viewpoint of African Women: A Catholic Perspective." In *With Passion and Compassion: Third World Women Doing Theology*, edited by Virginia Fabella et al., 22–29. Maryknoll, NY: Orbis, 1988.
Tollinton, R. B. *Clement of Alexandria: A Study in Christian Liberalism*, Vol. 1. London: Williams and Norgate, 1914.
Trigg, Joseph W. *Origen*. London: Routledge, 1998.
Tripolitis, Antonia. *Religions of the Hellenistic-Roman Age*. Grand Rapids: Eerdmans, 2002.
Tshehla, Maarman Samuel. "Reading John 1:1–18 in Sesotho: An Investigation of the Issues, Meanings and Interpretations Raised by Mother Tongue Exegesis." MTh diss., University of Natal, Pietermaritzburg, 2000.

Tzamalikos, Panagiōtēs. *Origen: Cosmology and Ontology of Time.* Leiden: Koninklijke Brill, 2006.

———. *Origen: Philosophy of History and Eschatology.* Leiden: Koninklijke Brill, 2007.

Udoh, Enyi Ben. *Guest Christology: An Interpretative View of the Christological Problem in Africa.* Frankfurt am Main: Lang, 1988.

Ukpong, Justin S. "Christology and Inculturation: A New Testament Perspective." In *Paths of African Theology,* edited by Rosino Gibellini, 40–61. Maryknoll, NY: Orbis, 1994.

———. "Symbols." In *Dictionary of Third World Theologies,* edited by Virginia Fabella et al., 191–92. Maryknoll, NY: Orbis, 2000.

Urban, Linwood. *A Short History of Christian Thought.* Rev. ed. Oxford: Oxford University Press, 1995.

Vähäkangas, Mika. *In Search of Foundations for African Catholicism: Charles Nyamiti's Theological Methodology.* Leiden: Brill, 1999.

Van den Hoek, Annewies. "The 'Catechetical' School of Early Christian Alexandria and Its Philonic Heritage." *The Harvard Theological Review* 90.1 (1997) 59–87.

Van der Geest, Sjaak. "Opanyin: The Ideal of Elder in the Akan Culture of Ghana." *Canadian Journal of African Studies / Revue Canadienne des Études Africaines* 32.3 (1998) 449–93.

Wachege, Patrick N. "Charles Nyamiti: Vibrant Pioneer of Inculturated African Theology." In *African Theology in the 21st Century,* edited by Bujo et al., 149–61. Nairobi: Paulines Publications Africa, 2006.

Walls, Andrew F.. "Christian Scholarship in Africa in the Twenty-first Century." *JACT* 4.2 (2001) 44–52.

———. "Converts or Proselytes? The Crisis over Conversion in the Early Church." *IBMR* 28.1 (2004) 2–6.

———. *The Cross-Cultural Process in Christian History.* Maryknoll, NY: Orbis, 2002.

———. "The Discovery of 'African Traditional Religion' and Its Impact on Religious Studies." In *Seeing New Facets of the Diamond: Christianity as a Universal Faith: Essays in Honour of Kwame Bediako,* edited by Gillian M. Bediako et al., 1–17. Akropong-Akuapem: Regnum Africa, 2014.

———. "In Quest of the Father of Mission Studies." *IBMR* 23.3 (1999) 98–105.

———. *The Missionary Movement in Christian History: Studies in the Transmission of Faith.* New York: Orbis, 1996.

———. "Old Athens and New Jerusalem: Some Signposts for Christian Scholarship in the Early History of Mission Studies." *International Bulletin of Missionary Research* 21.4. (1997) 146–53.

———. "Scholarship under the Cross: Thinking Greek and Thinking Christian." *JACT* 9.2 (2006) 16–22.

Walton, Frank E. *Development of the Logos-doctrine in Greek & Hebrew Thought.* Bristol: Wright, 1911.

Wanamaker, Charles A. "Jesus the Ancestor: Reading the Story of Jesus from an African Christian Perspective." *Scriptura* 62.3 (1997) 281–98.

Wessels, Anton. *Images of Jesus: How Jesus Is Perceived and Portrayed in Non-European Cultures.* Translated from the Dutch by John Vriend. London: SCM, 1990.

Westcott, B. F. *The Gospel according to St. John: The Authorized Version with Introduction and Notes.* Reprint, Grand Rapids: Eerdmans, 1981.

Westermann, Diedrich. *Africa and Christianity*. London: Oxford University Press, 1937.

———. *The African To-day*. London: Oxford University Press, 1934.

Wiles, Maurice F. *The Christian Fathers*. Study Edition. London: SCM, 1977.

———. *The Spiritual Gospel: The Interpretation of the Fourth Gospel in the Early Church*. Cambridge: Cambridge University Press, 1960.

Williams, A. Lukyn. *Talmudic Judaism and Christianity*. Edinburgh: Church of Scotland, 1933.

Wilson, William. "Introductory Note to Clement of Alexandria." In *ANF, Vol. 2.*, edited by Alexander Roberts and James Donaldson, revised by A. Cleveland Coxe. Grand Rapids: Eerdmans, 1989.

Wind, A. "Destination and Purpose of the Gospel of John." *Novum Testamentum* 14, Fasc. 1. (1972) 26–69.

Wolfson, Harry A. *Philo: Foundations of Religious Philosophy in Judaism, Christianity, and Islam,* Vol. I & II. 2nd ed. Cambridge: Harvard University Press, 1948.

———. *The Philosophy of the Church Fathers: Faith, Trinity, Incarnation*. Cambridge: Harvard University Press, 1970.

Wong, Joseph H. P. *Logos-Symbol in the Christology of Karl Rahner*. Roma: Libreria Ateneo Salesiano, 1984.

Yonge, C. D. *The Works of Philo*. Peabody, MA: Hendrickson, 1993.

Zerwick, Max. *A Grammatical Analysis of the Greek New Testament*. Translated by Mary Grosvenor. Roma: Editrice Pontificio Istituto Biblico, 1996.

Author Index

Ackah, C. A, 111–12, 115
Afriyie, Ernestina, 86–7, 103–4, 193
Agyarko, Robert O., 168–70
Amaladoss, Michael, 6–7
Amu, Ephraim 105–6
Appiah, Peggy, 92, 181–2
Aristotle, 14–17, 23–4, 64, 67, 121
Arthur, Cecilia, 89, 97–100, 104–5

Barnard, Leslie W., 49–50
Barrett, C. K., 30–1, 113
Bediako, K., x, xix, 1, 38–41, 48, 50–1, 72–4, 80–2, 101–2, 111, 114, 125, 136–41, 168–9, 175, 183–4, 189–90
Bernard, J. H., 2–3, 31–2, 50, 179–80, 156
Bevans, Stephen xxiii
Bujo, Bénézet, 71–2, 135, 137, 140–3, 148–9, 156, 161–2, 165–7, 190, 192
Busia, Kofi A., 87–8, 107

Celsus, 57, 61, 63, 65–6, 172
Chadwick, Henry, 27, 29, 51, 56–7, 61, 67
Christaller, Johannes G., 7, 86–90, 92, 94, 96–7, 99, 104–5, 108–10, 114–15, 120, 178, 180–3, 186, 193
Clarke, Clifton R., 170–1
Cleanthes, 15–17
Clement of Alexandria, 13, 16, 27, 38, 51–7, 67, 172

Daniélou, Jean, 38–9, 49–50, 55, 58
Dankwa III, Nana Addo, 96, 101–2, 101–4, 106–7, 153, 194
Danquah, Joseph B., 84, 87–8, 95–6, 113–26, 175–8, 181–2, 184, 187–9, 194, 197
Dickson, Kwesi A., 2, 95, 111, 115, 128, 174
Diogenes L., 13, 15–17

Edwards, M. J., 50, 54, 56
Eusebius, 43, 48, 51, 57
Ezeh, Uchenna A., xxiii, 134–5, 164–5, 170, 172
Ezigbo, Victor I., 72, 139, 164–6

Goodenough, Erwin R., 20, 25, 49–50
Grant, Robert M., 29, 35, 41, 43–4, 128, 175
Grillmeier, Aloys, 39–40, 62

AUTHOR INDEX

Gyekye, Kwame, 85, 87–8, 93, 108–10, 183, 190–1, 199

Harris, J. Rendel, 24, 35–6
Heraclitus, 13–17, 25, 66
Hobhouse Leonard T., 121–2
Holte, Ragnar, 49–51

Idowu, Bolaji E., 71, 73, 139

Josephus, 19–20
Justin Martyr, 38, 40–2, 48–51, 56, 61, 65, 67, 172, 185

Kabasélé, François, xxiv, 79, 83, 129, 160
Kasper, Walter, 4–5
Kirk, G. S., 13–14, 76
Kittel, Gerhard, 34, 37
Kuma, Afua, 80–1, 91–2
Küster, Volker, 159–62

Laryea, Philip T., 82, 92, 105–6, 174, 183
Lightfoot, R. H., 30–1, 38

Makwasha, Gift M., 85, 137, 150–2
Martey, Emmanuel, 76–8, 137
Martyr, Justin, 38, 40–1, 46–50, 56, 83, 184
Mbiti, John S., 71–2, 74–5, 81, 84, 108, 110
Meyerowitz, Eva, 85, 87–8, 93–4, 96, 102

Nketia, J. H. K., 92, 95–8, 107
Nwaogwugwu, Cletus C. xxiv
Nyamiti, Charles, 75–80, 82, 125, 135, 137, 140, 143–50, 155–68, 170, 172–3, 190

O'Collins, Gerald, 4–5, 35
Opoku, Kofi A., 87, 90, 93–9, 102–3, 108–10, 112

Origen, 17, 27, 29, 47, 51, 57–67, 69, 172
Osborn, E. F., 48–9, 51, 53

Philo of Alexandria / Judaeus, 19–29, 36–7, 44, 50, 63, 67, 69, 117, 126, 195, 197
Plato, 14–16, 20, 42, 55, 63, 67, 121
Pobee, John S., 128, 161–2

Quarshie, Benhardt Y., 136, 194
Quasten, Johannes, 38–9, 41

Rattray, Robert S., 88–9, 97, 99–100, 110, 115
Runia, David T., 17, 19–21, 23, 25–7, 67

Sarpong, Peter K., 86–7, 89–90, 95–6, 100–1, 103, 106–7, 129, 131–2
Sawyerr, Harry A., 124–5
St. Ignatius, 82, 92
Stinton, Diane B., 72–5, 78–9, 141, 152–5, 161–4
Studer, Basil, 58, 68–9

Tatian, 41–2
Tertullian, 41, 46–7
Theophilus of Antioch, 43–4
Tollinton, R. B., 52–3
Tzamalikos, Panagiōtēs, 57, 59, 61, 63, 66–7

Walls, Andrew F., x-xi, xx-xxiii, 1, 8, 10, 19, 57, 69, 71, 73, 114, 127, 173, 200
Wanamaker, Charles A., 129–31
Wessels, Anton, 7–8, 74
Westcott, B. F., 30, 186
Wolfson, Harry A., 19–28, 36–7, 44, 54–6, 63–5

Subject Index

abosom, 90-2, 100, 102, 111, 165, 192-4
Abraham, 37-8
abusua, 86, 93-4, 111, 185
academic theology, 81-2
Adae, 96-7, 99-100, 102, 104-5
Adae festival, 96-7, 104
Adam, 44, 130, 146-9
adulthood, 93, 107-8
Africa, x-xi, xx, xxiii-xxiv, xxvii, 9, 71-5, 77-9, 81, 83, 85, 128-9, 136-8, 140-1, 143-4, 152-6, 158, 161-2, 172-5, 199
African, 73-4, 78-9, 106, 112, 115, 122, 126, 130-1, 136-8, 140-4, 156, 158-9, 161, 165, 170-1
   ancestor worship, 160-1
   ancestors, 142, 164, 166
   ancestorship, 135
   Ancestral Christology, xxiii, 134, 150
   categories of thought, 71, 75
   Christian, 71, 80, 161, 163
   Christian identity, 71, 74
   Christian theology, 127
   Christianity, xx, xxii-xxiv, 72, 74-5, 78, 81, 83, 126-7, 142, 197, 200
   Christians, 75, 80, 130, 133, 174
   Christologies, xix, xxii, 71-2, 75-80, 83, 142, 146, 163-4, 166-7, 170-1, 199
   Christology of liberation, 76-7
   Churches, 79, 144, 157
   conception of ancestor, ancestorship, 128, 144, 158, 160, 174
   Culture, Cultural Values, 72, 76, 93, 109, 111, 137-41, 167
   experience of Jesus, 73, 75, 77, 79, 81, 83
   languages, 142-3, 199
   past, 71, 72, 73, 84, 124, 138
   Religions and Philosophy, 84, 108, 110
   religious past, 9, 72-4
   Spirituality, 113, 169
   Theology, 9, 71-9, 128, 137, 141-4, 148, 158-9, 163, 167, 192
   Traditional Religion (ATR), 9, 72, 75, 87, 125, 138-9, 141, 200
   traditional thought, 75, 127, 199
   Witness in World Christianity, 198
ahyɛse, 179-80, 189

SUBJECT INDEX

Akan, 84–5, 87–91, 93–6, 106–7, 109, 111–26, 133, 136–8, 153–5, 168–71, 173, 175–8, 182–5, 187–90, 192–4
  AICs, 170–1
  Ancestor Christology, 126, 175, 194
  ancestors, 86, 175, 177, 188, 194
  Asɛm Christology, 192, 194
  Christian, 92, 173, 184, 198
  Christians, 172, 175
  concept of nana, 126
  concept of Nana, 84, 175–6, 184, 188–9, 195
  ethics, 111–12, 115–16
  proverbs, 110, 114, 116, 126, 183
  society, 85, 89, 111, 113, 119, 140, 185
  thinking, 90, 109, 116, 139, 180, 191
Akwasidae, 96–7, 99, 103
akɔmfo, 192–3
Alexandria, 13, 19–21, 23, 25–9, 31, 36, 51–4, 56–7, 65, 67
analogy, 54, 65, 68, 124–5, 133, 145, 157, 159, 166, 198
Ancestor Christology, xxiii–xxiv, xxvii, 70, 76, 84, 125–7, 129, 131, 133–7, 139–41, 143, 147, 149–53, 155–7, 159–67, 169–75, 197–200
  concept, 126, 136
Ancestor Jesus, 193–4, 197
  of Humankind, 144–50, 156–60, 162–4, 167–8, 173
ancestor spirits, 168–9
  worship, 85, 106, 111–12, 153
ancestors, 2, 4, 6, 8, 10, 13–14, 16, 18, 20, 26, 68–70, 72, 74–6, 82–166, 168–200
  concept or idea of, 84
  cult of, 111, 130, 134, 139, 165
  deified, 115, 117
  first, 105, 134
  human, 132, 138
ancestorship, 130, 140, 144–50, 173–4, 193
  of Christ, 147, 164
Ancestral Christology, 125, 133–4, 144
ancestral concept, 147, 169–70

angels, 22, 45, 66, 91–2, 146–7
Apologists, 38–40, 51, 56, 59, 65
Apostolic Fathers, 38–9
asamando, 86, 89–90, 93, 99, 154, 178, 198
Asante, 85–6, 94, 97, 102–3, 132, 192
Ashanti Proverbs, 88–9, 110
Asɛm, asɛm, 173, 178–86, 188–94, 198–200
ATR *see* African Traditional Religion
Awukudae, 96–7, 99, 102–4

Bantu, 108, 113, 129–31
  Christians, 131
  concept of ancestors, 129
being, 45, 63, 90, 117, 145, 149, 153–5, 160, 165, 170, 172, 175, 179, 185, 192–3
  human, 5, 87, 130, 133–4, 146–7, 158, 168, 185
  rational, 62, 66
belief, 18, 42, 67, 75, 84, 90–1, 107–8, 112–13, 148, 165, 192
benevolent ancestors, 141, 171
Bible, xxvi, 74, 142, 170–1, 175, 180, 198
Biblical Christologies, 75, 125, 168–9
birth, 14–16, 41, 57, 90, 93, 99, 107, 110, 120, 177
black stools, 95, 98–9, 104
blood, 53, 86–7, 93, 97, 107, 116–17, 123, 126
body, 8, 30, 64, 86–7, 89, 114, 123, 153–4, 173
brother-ancestor, 143, 146, 148, 156, 158
bɛ, 92, 108–9, 181–2, 190

chief, 56, 72, 79, 83, 89, 94–102, 104, 107, 112–13, 131–2, 134, 139–40, 155, 160, 197
chief stool attendant, 98–9
chieftaincy, 79, 96, 101–4, 106–7, 112, 131, 175
Christ, ix–xi, xx, xxii–xxiii, 1–10, 27–30, 37–41, 45, 49–50, 55–64, 79, 125, 128–9, 133–5, 139, 142–4, 146–9, 153–4, 156–68, 191
  natures of, 68, 135
Christ-event, 77, 79

SUBJECT INDEX

Christian, 1, 9, 39, 42–4, 48–9, 51, 53, 62, 74, 102, 114, 125–6, 129, 137–8, 163
    conversion, 8, 50, 72, 172, 195
    faith, xxiii, 40, 57, 81, 123, 136, 173
    influence, 4, 183
    mysteries, 78, 158
    proclamation, 126, 171
    scholarship, 57, 71
    standpoint, 26, 102
    teaching, 48–9, 91, 114, 121, 144–5, 160, 176
    thought, x, 37, 142
    Tradition, 10, 39–40, 62, 80, 125
    understanding, xxi–xxii, 4, 12, 27, 43–4, 48, 59, 63, 68, 170, 176, 194
    worship, 105, 174
Christianity, ix–xi, xx–xxi, 9–10, 25, 38–9, 41–2, 48, 52, 55, 68, 72–4, 81, 113, 122, 131, 134, 182–3
    early, xix, xxii, 29, 33
    in Africa, 71, 80, 101–2, 137–8
Christians, 11, 38–9, 41–3, 48–9, 51, 57, 61, 66, 74, 92, 106, 148, 154, 164, 197–8
Christological, xxiii, xxv, 9, 69, 72–4, 79, 123, 135–6, 144
    developments, 34, 75, 134
    endeavors, 161, 172, 198
    explorations, 10, 29, 70, 83, 125, 127, 173
    images, 69, 78
    query, 161–2
    Question, 2, 128
    reflections, 71, 128–9
    themes, 77–8
    trends in Africa, 73
Christology, x, xix, xxii–xxvii, 1, 3–5, 7–11, 27–8, 33, 35, 74–8, 80–1, 83, 128–9, 132–3, 144, 156–7, 170–3, 195–6
    academic, 72
    emergent, 75
    indigenous Logos, 178, 199
    oral, 74, 80–1

church, 8, 30, 37, 39, 43–4, 71, 73, 78, 105–6, 114, 131–3, 140, 143–4, 152, 199
Church Fathers, 22, 27, 37, 44, 54–6, 65
community, 6, 82–6, 93–5, 99–101, 103–4, 111–13, 116, 118–23, 125–6, 139–41, 153, 163–4, 177–8, 185–7, 199
    akan, 94, 126, 176, 199
conceptions, 21, 25–6, 53, 55, 58, 63, 65, 131–2, 135, 140, 147, 160, 199
    pre-Christian, 26, 59, 63
concepts, 4–10, 14–15, 27, 31, 71–2, 83–5, 110–13, 124, 126–7, 129, 136–7, 141–4, 156–7, 169, 198–9
conversion, 1, 3–5, 7–12, 48, 56–7, 68, 71, 75, 83, 126–7, 129, 131, 133, 135, 196–7
    process, 8, 10, 26–7, 69, 71–2, 127, 198
correlation, 8, 97, 133
cosmological, 5, 39–40
cosmos, 15–16, 31, 67
councils, early, xxiii, 144, 159–60
creation, 17, 22–4, 28–9, 33–4, 36, 38, 40, 42, 44, 46–8, 50, 54, 56, 58, 68
creator, 20, 22, 64, 90, 124, 146, 153, 177, 189
crucifixion, 8–9
cultural concepts, pre-Christian, 159
    contexts, 3, 6–7, 10, 196
    response, 6, 11, 196
    worlds, 3–4, 8, 10, 175, 185
culture, 4, 6–11, 26, 57, 69, 76, 87, 93, 100, 107, 114, 134, 175, 183–4, 189

death, xxvi, 1–2, 8, 14, 86–90, 96, 100, 107–8, 111–12, 118–20, 130–1, 145–6, 157–8, 174, 177, 198
deities, 13, 87, 90, 100–1, 103, 111, 165, 169, 193
destiny, 1–2, 87, 118, 147
dialogue, inner, 159–60
dignity, 118–20, 122, 124, 177
disciples, 1–3, 5–6, 8, 30, 33, 56, 63

SUBJECT INDEX

discipline, 20, 52, 55
discovery, 5, 117–18, 177, 194, 200
disgrace, 86, 107, 119–20, 177
divine, 25, 54, 59–61, 64–5, 87–8, 119, 124, 134–5, 138–9, 168–9, 193
    Logos, 22, 24, 26, 52–4, 60–1, 64–6, 172
divinity, 5, 39, 60, 62, 64, 114, 117, 120, 128, 135, 149, 155, 167–9, 172–3, 177
    of Jesus Christ, 155, 172, 187
doctrine, 4, 26, 36, 40, 49, 54, 56, 63, 65, 68, 172
dogmas, 159–60

elders, 86, 91, 93, 107–10, 113, 120, 125, 133–4, 141, 155, 164, 177, 194
election, 118, 151
elements, cultural, 1, 3–4, 10, 107
enlightens, 32, 186
essence, 5, 23–4, 37, 41, 52, 62, 88, 112, 187, 190
evidence, 10, 13, 80–1, 114–15
exemplar, 67, 86, 116–18, 120, 129, 145, 169, 177–8, 187–8
exemplarity, 145–6, 196
existence, 13, 22–5, 33, 35, 43, 58, 61, 64, 75, 84, 87, 92, 116, 138, 153
experience, 1–3, 8, 13, 68, 84, 91–2, 108–10, 114, 130, 138–40, 173, 184, 195–7
    african, 70–1, 73, 138
exploration, 12, 15, 26, 38, 42, 65, 78, 83, 125, 127, 134, 173, 175–6, 185, 194–5
    mother-tongue, 150, 199

faith, x–xi, xxi, 9–10, 26, 37–8, 51–5, 57, 61, 67, 82, 136, 140, 170, 173, 187, 194, 199
family, 19, 85–6, 90, 93–4, 97, 111–14, 116, 118, 123, 126, 133–4, 150–1, 164, 177–8, 185–7
Family Ancestor, 85, 96, 137, 150–1
Father, father, 10, 24–5, 28, 32, 40–1, 43, 49, 57–63, 65, 73, 87–9, 123, 125, 132, 143–9, 180, 187–8
Father-Ancestor-Creator, 116, 118

Festivals of Ghana, 95–9, 102–3
fetishes, 90, 102, 116, 120
flesh, 3, 9, 32, 34, 37, 45–6, 53, 60, 63, 65, 69, 180, 185, 187–8, 198–200
followers, 1, 7, 15, 195
food, 99, 105–6, 164
Fourth Gospel, 3, 5, 27, 29–31, 33–4, 36–8, 40–2, 45, 50, 56, 58, 173, 176, 178, 188
functions, 22, 24–9, 62, 65, 86, 119, 128, 131–3, 153, 158, 161–2, 165, 168, 192, 197
funerals, 84, 107, 109

generation, 4, 7, 17, 43, 54, 59, 65, 68, 73, 75, 84, 173, 197
Gentile Christians, 37–8
ghosts, 88–9, 100, 169
glory, 32, 34, 36, 46, 81, 188, 192
Gnostics, 44–7
God, x, xxi, 8–10, 16–25, 31–3, 38–56, 58–69, 85–92, 113–15, 123–5, 131–5, 145–8, 168–70, 176–80, 182–5, 187–93, 198–200
    children of, 32, 187–8, 190, 193
    image of, 22–3, 54, 187, 195
    the logos of, 25, 37, 60
    Ancestor, 124, 145
God-man, 132, 135, 139, 146–7, 192
gods, 28, 44, 49, 60, 100, 111, 116, 138, 155, 165, 168–9
goodness, 116, 119–20, 122, 165
Gospel, gospel, ix–x, xxiv–xxv, xxvii, 1, 2–3, 5–6, 12, 30–7, 39, 43–4, 60–1, 77, 82, 103, 138, 156, 159, 163, 179–80, 186
    account, message, 6, 31, 39, 55, 59, 126, 160, 173
grace, 32, 34–5, 45, 61, 66, 140, 149, 187–8, 190, 195
Graeco-Roman, 10, 37, 39–42, 67
    Christian, xxvii, 67, 173, 197
    Christianity, 9, 12, 26, 48
    world, xx, 9, 30, 38–9, 67–8
grassroots, 72–3, 81–3, 152
Great Ancestor, 115–16, 123–4, 140, 192
Greek learning, 51, 57
    philosophical tradition, 20

philosophy, 19–21, 25, 41, 55
thought world, 25–6
translation, 18, 21, 67
Greeks, 10, 12–13, 18–21, 29, 31, 33, 36, 41–2, 47, 50–1, 55–7, 61, 64, 120–2, 180–1
ground, common, 67, 153, 165, 175
Guest Christology, 72, 75

head, 93, 98–9, 101, 112, 118–19, 125, 132, 151
heart, 10, 43–4, 69, 75, 121, 140, 175
Hebrew Scriptures, xxii, 18, 46, 67
Hellenistic, 10, 19–20, 26–7, 40, 42, 46, 171
  Culture, 49–50
  world of thought, 29, 198, 200
Heraclitus, 13–17, 25, 66
hero, 121, 132–3
history, 20, 37–8, 57, 67–8, 85, 94, 126, 167, 181
  Christian, x, xix–xxii, 4, 19, 71, 73, 114, 173, 200
Holy Spirit, 46–9, 53, 58, 61–2, 68, 144–5, 147–8, 195, 198
honhom, 87, 117
honor, 84, 96–7, 104, 106–7, 118, 120, 126, 197
humanity, 5, 8, 10, 22, 37, 40, 51–4, 56, 67–8, 134–5, 142, 146–7, 172–3, 181, 185
  of Jesus Christ, 77, 172
humankind, 20, 22, 35, 45, 134, 140, 144–50, 156–60, 162–4, 167–8, 173, 191, 193
humanness, 164, 173
humans, 2, 10, 14, 21–2, 31–2, 35, 48–9, 53–4, 87, 89–90, 111, 124, 160, 182, 185–8
hypostases, 62, 135

identity, 6, 33, 38–41, 48, 50–1, 73–4, 84, 86, 125–6, 130, 162, 166, 173
  question, 2–3
images, 3, 5–8, 10, 21–3, 27–9, 54, 60, 65, 68, 72, 74, 79, 169–70, 187–8, 195
  cultural, 5, 10–11, 69, 83

various, 5, 78
  of Jesus Christ, 69, 71, 171
immanent, 24, 26, 37
Incarnation, x, 4, 37, 40–1, 45–6, 50–1, 53, 55, 58, 64–5, 67–9, 135, 142, 144, 146–9, 157–8, 165, 167
inculturation, 76–8, 129, 137, 159, 162, 165
indigenous, 10, 68, 73–4, 142, 170, 175, 194
indigenous African Christian Churches, 75
indigenous African Christians, 171
initiation, 72, 79, 83, 160
Institution of Chieftaincy, 96, 101–4, 106–7, 112, 175
invitation, 18, 101, 151, 160, 197

Jesus, 1–11, 33–8, 41–5, 63–5, 69–75, 77–81, 83, 127–43, 150–5, 161–2, 164–6, 169–73, 178–81, 185–8, 191–4, 198–200
Jesus Christ, 1–4, 6–80, 82–3, 90, 92, 124–6, 128–30, 132–52, 154–73, 175–6, 178–80, 184, 186–8, 192–8, 200
  affirmation of, 137, 194
  application of, 12, 26, 32, 40
  association of, 31, 174
  designation of, 152, 194
  direction of, 62, 68, 75, 195
  the Gospel of, 77, 138
  image of, 128, 189–90, 198
  mystery of, 135, 144
  the Ancestor, 129–31
Jewish, 1, 3, 5, 8, 10, 19–20, 25, 35, 37, 187, 195
Jews, 6, 19–21, 26, 38, 51, 55, 181, 185, 200
Judaism, 20, 26, 38, 44
Justin Martyr, 38, 40–2, 48–51, 56, 61, 65, 67, 172, 185

king, 6, 18, 60, 94–5, 97–8, 100, 118, 122, 169, 181–5
knowledge, 15, 19, 21, 28, 39, 41–2, 46, 48–50, 52–3, 69, 91–2, 108–10, 114, 165, 195

knowledge of God, 92, 176
Kumawu, 102, 131

language, 4, 10, 21, 28, 37, 41, 47, 50, 53, 69, 90, 175, 178, 183–4, 197
latent, 75, 80
Latin, 10, 42, 46–7
Law, 25, 32, 34, 50, 55, 61, 67, 180
levels, 8, 36, 66, 69, 72, 80, 82–3, 118, 127, 153, 158, 163
libation, 86, 90, 99–103, 107
liberation, 76–8, 137, 152, 162
light, 5, 7, 10, 27, 31–2, 36, 41, 44, 133–4, 145, 181, 184–6, 188, 190–2, 194
limitations, 68–9, 80, 91, 113, 145, 154, 162, 166–7, 169, 182
living, 16, 22, 31, 84–6, 89–91, 93, 95–6, 101, 103, 106–7, 111–12, 119, 130–1, 136, 154–5
   chief, 95–6, 106, 155
   elders, 91, 101, 113, 194
   God, 2–3, 173
Logos, ix–xi, xxii, xxvii
   common, 16
   image of, 27, 56, 69
   right, 22, 49
   seminal, 17, 24
   term, 25, 29
   word, 18, 26, 38–9, 47, 180
   concept xxiii, 13, 24, 29, 31, 35, 59, 63, 65–7, 70, 137
   doctrine, 13, 29, 52
   endiathetos, 40, 54
   idea, 14–15, 19, 67
   intimation, 35, 50
   statement, 36–7
Logos-Ancestor, 200
   Christology, 174, 198
   discourse, 199
Logos and Ancestor Christologies, 147, 198
Logos Christology, 26–7, 28–9, 31–2, 34, 36–7, 40–4, 49, 51–2, 56, 58, 67–70, 147, 172, 175, 178, 193–5, 197–9
   application of, 48, 56, 69, 184
   journey of, 11, 197

the Logos of God, 29, 43, 45–8, 53–5, 64–6, 179
Logos Spermatikos, 49–51
Lord Jesus xx, 10, 28, 53, 171
love, 132, 147–8
LXX, 18–21, 25, 27–8, 33, 35–6, 39, 42–4, 46, 48, 50, 61, 67, 126, 171

marriage, 93–4
material, 13, 23, 43, 66, 88
matter, 16–18, 23, 64, 67, 69, 72, 74, 87, 92, 109–10, 113, 146, 176, 181–2, 184
mediator, 39, 53–4, 58, 130, 132, 135, 139–40, 145–6, 151, 160, 166
memory, 6, 84–5, 96, 113–14, 116, 125
Messiah, xx, 2–3, 5–6, 8–9, 34, 113, 116, 118–20, 123, 147, 173, 176, 195–6
   expected, 5, 126, 176–7, 185, 187–9, 200
messiahship, 8, 187
metaphysics, 162–3
Mfantse, 85–6, 93, 112, 175, 178, 180, 182, 185–6
mhondoro, 151–2
mind, 4, 15, 22–5, 43, 45, 54, 56, 58, 63, 78, 117, 156, 182
missionaries, xi, xxii–xxiii, xxvii, 27, 29, 37, 75, 78, 127, 154, 196
models, xx, xxiii, ,1, 22, 27, 63, 68, 77, 112, 138, 141, 143, 145–6, 162, 173, 197, 200
morals, 114, 117, 121
Moses, 20, 29, 32, 34, 37–8, 46, 67, 180
mother, queen, 86, 94, 99
mysteries, 20, 59, 67–8, 78, 135, 142, 144–5, 149, 158, 163, 170, 185
mystery of Christ, 135, 163, 172, 196
myths, 17, 39, 111, 139, 156, 192

names, 5, 15–18, 22, 25, 27, 32, 34, 36, 41, 43, 48–9, 93, 100, 117, 124
nana, 13, 83–7, 89, 91, 99–101, 109–13, 115–26, 128, 155, 163–4, 170–9, 181, 183–91, 193–5, 197–200
Nana Christology, 157, 194
Nyankopon, 123, 125

SUBJECT INDEX

Yesu, 125, 172, 188, 190–4, 197
nananom, 90–4, 100, 107–8, 112–13, 181, 191–4, 197, 199
   nsamanfo, 86, 89–91, 94–6, 103, 113, 155
   nsamanfoɔ, 99–100
Nanasɛm, 190, 194, 199–200
nature, 1, 4, 15–17, 21, 23–5, 28, 62–6, 86–8, 108–9, 117, 121–2, 130–1, 164–5, 167–8, 171–2
Nazareth, 3–5, 9, 33–4, 37, 69, 77, 128, 162, 178, 181
New Testament, xxvi–xxvii, 1, 9, 27, 30, 34, 36–9, 61, 78, 83, 130–1, 144, 160, 171, 176, 198–9
   Christologies, 4, 83, 167
Nicene affirmation, 168–9
nkwa, 100, 179, 181
nkɔmhyɛfo, 92, 193
noetic, 39–40
nokwar, 185–6, 188
nsɛm nyina, 183–4
nsɔrem, 104–6
Nyame, 87, 100, 115, 117, 124–5, 180, 182–4, 189, 192
Nyamesofopreko, 168–70
Nyankopɔn, 90–2, 179–81, 184, 187–9, 192, 194
nyansa, 108–9, 190–1
nyimpa, 181, 188

obedience, 9, 18, 38, 164–5, 198
Odomankoma, 117, 124, 176, 181, 184
Odwira festival, 86, 102–4
Onyame, 117, 182–4
Onyankopon, 117, 184
opanyin, 86, 113, 117–18, 120–3, 125, 177–8
Origen, x, xii, xxii–xxiii, 17, 27, 29, 47, 51, 57–67, 69, 172
origin, 5, 15, 18, 31, 33, 35–6, 56, 61, 71–2, 76, 85, 111, 116, 118, 123

palace, chief's, 97
Pantaenus, 51, 57
paradigm, 1, 25, 68–9, 120, 177, 187, 196
Paul, 9, 27–9, 37, 61, 65, 191

Pentateuch, 18, 20–1
people, 2, 4–6, 8, 10, 13, 18, 55, 58, 60, 97, 99–100, 108, 130–2, 152, 154
Perfecter, 136, 194
person, ix, xix, xxiii, 3–5, 8, 47, 68, 84, 87–9, 109–10, 118–19, 130, 132, 134–5, 146, 166, 168, 175–6
   of Christ, 4, 43, 73, 75, 144, 156, 167, 187
personage, ideal, 119–20, 184
Peter, 1, 3, 5, 8–9, 173, 195
Philo, 19–29, 36–7, 44, 50, 63, 67, 69, 117, 126, 195, 197
philosophers, 19–20, 39, 42–3, 48, 51, 114, 121, 183
philosophical, 20–1, 26, 31, 50, 67, 84, 121, 163
   speculation, 162–3
   thought, 13, 176
philosophy, xii, xxiv, 15, 17, 20, 22, 26–7, 37, 40–2, 44, 46, 48, 51–6, 60, 63, 65, 84
   modern African, 199
physical world, 90, 107
place, 87, 91, 96, 104–5, 116, 118, 122, 127, 137–8, 166–7, 177, 194
plantain, 98–9
Plato, 14–16, 20, 42, 55, 63, 67, 121
poets, 15, 42–3, 114
politics, 15, 140, 143, 151–2, 199
portrait, conceptual, 113–14, 126
power, 5, 17, 19, 21, 23, 32, 41, 47–9, 52, 64–6, 81, 138–40, 168–9, 187, 190–2
praise, 96, 105
prayers, 90, 99–101, 145–6
pre-Christian concepts, ideas, 10, 127, 135, 196–7
principles, 16, 21–2, 50, 89, 178
problem, 13, 37, 110, 144, 166, 181–2, 191, 199
Proclaiming Jesus, 126, 151–2, 172, 199
Prologue, 29–37, 40–2, 45, 176, 178–80, 185, 188–90, 198
prophecy, 48, 54
prophets, 18, 42, 44, 48, 61, 65, 91, 119, 193

proselytes, proselytism, proselytization, x, xxi
Proto-Ancestor, 132, 140–3, 162, 165
proverbs, 18–19, 28, 33–6, 43, 58, 93, 108–10, 114, 116, 120, 125, 176, 181–4, 190
  traditional, 108–9, 113, 120

qualities, 21, 64, 88, 119, 130–1

race, human, 46, 49, 65, 134, 143, 149
reason, 9, 12–16, 24, 27, 39–40, 43, 47, 49, 55–6, 60, 62, 65, 83, 95, 103
refiguration stage, 26, 56, 69, 75, 136–7, 143, 172–3, 197, 200
relation, 6, 8, 11, 14, 21–5, 27–9, 31–2, 37, 40–3, 45, 50–1, 57–8, 135, 143–4, 182–3
  sexual, 94
relationship, 40, 62, 65, 72, 74, 117, 126, 146–7, 165, 171, 184
  ancestral, 147, 171
relatives, earthly, 145
relevance, 78, 148, 155–6, 158, 163–4, 172, 176, 199
religion, 52, 84–5, 100, 107, 114–17, 122, 176, 183–4, 189
religious tradition, pre-Christian African, 71
respect, 106, 113, 129, 143, 151, 161, 165, 170, 182
responses, 3–5, 26, 39, 45, 47–8, 59, 61, 63, 65–6, 76, 79–81, 83, 91, 106, 149–50
resurrection, 1–2, 5–6, 8–9, 132, 138–9, 147, 151, 153, 162, 166, 168, 170, 174, 198
retrospect, 74, 79, 86–7, 89–90, 106–7
revelation, 4, 20, 29, 39, 53, 120, 123, 173–4, 177, 179–80, 193, 196
rhema, 18, 179, 183, 192
rituals, 95, 107, 130, 141, 145–6, 192

sacred communication, regular, 145–6, 149
Sacred State, 87, 93–4
salvation, 4, 39, 45–6, 51–3, 56, 68, 133, 141–2, 165, 194, 199

saman, 86, 88–9
Saviour Jesus Christ, 195
Scriptures, 21, 25–7, 33, 48, 53, 57, 61, 69, 72, 85, 138, 175
Septuagint, 18, 27, 33, 197
sheep, 90, 97, 99, 107, 110
shrine, 95, 103, 152
situation, 110, 143, 190–1
society, 77, 94, 102, 111–12, 122, 145, 197–8
sociocultural analysis, 162–3
Solomon, 18–19, 28–9, 35
Son, 2–3, 22, 38, 42–3, 45–7, 49, 51–4, 58–65, 67–8, 134, 144–5, 147–9, 171–3, 179–80, 187–8, 192–3, 199–200
soul, 15, 23, 43, 53, 61, 63–6, 86–8, 117, 172
  human, 64–5
source, 14, 28, 31, 33, 52, 59–60, 67–8, 84, 92, 108, 116, 131, 145–6, 181, 191
Spermatikos Logos, 40, 49–50
Stoic Cosmology, 15–16
Stoicism, Stoics, 15–17, 23–5, 29, 46, 50, 64, 66–7, 158
  early, 15, 48
stool house, 96, 98
stools, 86, 95–7, 99–100, 128, 139, 197
story, ix, xi, 8, 91, 130, 181
sub-Saharan Africa, 71–5, 84
sunsum, 86–9, 109, 117
Super-Ancestor, 136
Supreme Being, 86, 88–91, 93, 100–1, 111, 116, 118, 123–4, 128, 136, 145, 148, 151, 157, 165
  exemplar of the, 187
sore, 98, 104–6, 109
symbols, 5–6, 8, 10, 83, 95, 128, 159, 192
Synoptics, 2–3, 5

teacher, 41, 48, 51, 53–4, 65
terrorizing influence, 138, 168
Tertullian, 41, 46–7
Theaetetus, 14–15
theologians, 57, 72–3, 158, 162, 183

theology, 13, 49–50, 55, 71, 74, 78, 82, 86, 95, 103–4, 111, 114–16, 128, 137, 156
    contextual, 162
    oral, 74, 79, 81–2
    systematic, 162
    written, 74, 79, 81–2
theology of ancestors, 138
Theophilus, 43–4
thought, 12–15, 18, 25, 27, 29–30, 37, 39, 45, 50–1, 67–8, 75, 83–5, 87–9, 128, 198
    biblical, 175
    pre-Christian Graeco-Roman, 46, 56
    traditional, 26, 37, 40–1, 69, 114, 119, 127, 136, 150, 187–8, 190, 194, 200
titles, 2, 5–7, 10, 15, 41, 48, 69, 71, 78–9, 81, 128, 141–2, 145, 149, 157–9
    traditional, 79, 132, 134
Torah, 34–5, 50
tradition, 5, 20, 26, 39, 50–2, 85, 110–11, 114, 126, 142, 175
traditional
    concept, 6, 8, 124, 151, 154, 171
    Festivals, 94–8, 174
    society, 93, 95, 112, 154
traditionalists, 101–2
translation, 18, 38, 57–8, 61, 72, 79, 83, 90, 99–100, 105, 123, 142–3, 160, 178, 182
tribes, 118, 128, 130, 151
Trinity, 44, 58, 62, 68–9, 144–5, 147–8, 153, 156, 158, 163, 170
truth, 4, 13, 21, 31–2, 34, 37, 39, 44–5, 48–9, 51–2, 55, 64, 175, 188, 190–1

Unique Priest, 168–70
unity, 8, 13, 52, 58, 62, 101, 134–5
universe, 15, 17, 22, 24–5, 29, 39, 54, 56, 65

Valentinus, 45–6
veneration, 89, 104, 106–7, 147
vocation, 40, 57, 67, 99, 196–7

wellbeing, 94, 99–100, 165
West African Traditional Religion, 90, 95, 112
wiadze, 185–6
wisdom, 18–19, 23, 25, 27–9, 34–6, 39, 43–4, 47–9, 52, 54, 58–9, 63–4, 108–10, 183–4, 190–1
witness, 10, 64, 69, 74, 120, 140, 163, 182, 184–6, 200
women, 77, 86, 91, 93–4, 99, 107, 122, 147, 167, 187
words, 12–15, 18, 31, 33–5, 37–40, 47–8, 50–1, 53–6, 58, 103–5, 141–2, 177, 179–81, 185–6, 188–91
    all-powerful, 192–3
    spoken, 190–1
worship, 75, 90, 103–7, 154, 170
worshippers, idol, 101–2
Written Christology, 71, 74, 79–81
wɔ hɔ, 178–80, 184, 189
wɔnam, 179–81, 185–6, 189, 194

yɛ, 7, 180, 183
Yesu, xxv–xxvi

Zeus, 16–17, 24, 66

www.ingramcontent.com/pod-product-compliance
Lightning Source LLC
Chambersburg PA
CBHW050847230426
43667CB00012B/2186